An Advocate Persuades

An Advocate Persuades

Joan M. Rocklin
Robert B. Rocklin
Christine Coughlin
Sandy Patrick

CAROLINA ACADEMIC PRESS
Durham, North Carolina

Library of Congress Cataloging-in-Publication Data

Malmud, Joan, author.
 An advocate persuades / Joan Malmud Rocklin, Robert B. Rocklin,
Christine Coughlin, and Sandy Patrick.
    pages cm
 Includes bibliographical references and index.
 ISBN 978-1-61163-150-0 (alk. paper)
1. Trial practice—United States. 2. Communication in law—
United States. 3. Forensic oratory. 4. Persuasion (Psychology)
I. Rocklin, Robert B. II. Coughlin, Christine Nero, author.
III. Patrick, Sandy, author. IV. Title.

KF8915.M338 2015
347.73'5—dc23   2015034438

CAROLINA ACADEMIC PRESS
700 Kent Street
Durham, NC 27701
Telephone (919) 489-7486
Fax (919) 493-5668
www.cap-press.com

2022 Printing
Printed in the United States of America

Dedication

To our son, Sam, who we welcomed to our family as we wrote this book, and to Sol Rocklin, to whom we said goodbye.
RBR & JMR

To my family, and especially my mother and father, for their unconditional love and unfailing support.
CNC

To my mom, Linda Copous, who taught me to love books, and to my lifelong mentor, Amy Blake Hearn, who inspired me to write one.
SCP

Contents

Acknowledgments

This book would not exist without all those who read *A Lawyer Writes* and encouraged us to write a second book, one focused on the advocate. So, we must begin by thanking every professor who has adopted *A Lawyer Writes* and encouraged us to write again. The three of us who wrote *A Lawyer Writes*, want to welcome Bob Rocklin, who joined us for this second journey and contributed his experience as an advocate and writer and his ever-present sense of humor to the task.

We depended on many others as we wrote. Our legal writing colleagues read initial drafts and provided us with invaluable feedback. Particular thanks go to Susan Bay (Marquette), Liz Frost (Oregon), Alison Julien (Marquette), Megan McAlpin (Oregon), Judith Miller (Lewis & Clark), and Suzanne Rowe (Oregon), for their willingness to contribute their time and energy to improve the quality, scope, and organization of this book.

Other colleagues provided us with thoughtful comments and enduring support. A hearty thank you goes to Lewis & Clark colleagues Steve Johansen, Daryl Wilson, Toni Berres-Paul, Bill Chin, Anne Villella, Judith Miller, Aliza Kaplan, and Hadley Van Vactor Kroll; to Wake Forest Colleagues Jarrod Atchison, Maureen Eggert, Tracey Coan, Miki Felsenburg, Steve Garland, Barb Lentz, Hal Lloyd, Catherine Irwin-Smiler, Sally Irvin, Elizabeth Johnson, Chris Knott, Ruth Morton, Abigail Perdue, and Vanessa Zboreak; and to our friend, colleague, and expert legal writer, Lora Keenan.

The University of Oregon School of Law, Lewis & Clark School of Law, and Wake Forest School of Law also provided financial support for this work through summer research and writing grants. We also thank the Deans and Associate Deans who encourage our scholarship.

The examples within the book play a critical role in helping students see how to create an effective a work product. We thank our colleagues— practicing lawyers and legal writing professors—who provided us with materials and examples: Laura Anderson, Luellen Curry (Wake Forest), Sue Grebeldinger (Wake Forest) Laura Graham (Wake Forest), John Korzen (Wake Forest), Leslie Oster (formerly, Northwestern), Terri Pollman (UNLV), Linda Rogers (Wake Forest), Jordan Silk, and Anne Villella (Lewis & Clark).

Research assistants helped us develop material and review drafts. Kamay LaFalaise, Christine Meier, Stephen Pritchard, and Ashley Sadler researched and prepared materials that assisted in ideas that developed into Chapter 1, *The Nature of Persuasion*. Rachel Tricket and Michael Goetz conducted the research that became Chapter 2, *The Ethical, Professional Advocate*. Jaime Garcia, David Giffin, and Shirley Smircic researched, developed materials, and reviewed drafts that became Chapter 3, *The Litigation Process*, and Chapter 13, *Editing and Polishing Your Persuasive Brief*.

Other students who read early drafts also provided valuable feedback. Noah Gordon, Corbett Hodson, Garrett Leatham, Kathryn Napier, and Shirley Smircic provided insightful ideas and candid suggestions as we revised each chapter. Lauren Boyd, Beth Ford, Corbrett Hodson, and David Mintz edited later drafts. We hope we have not introduced too many typographical errors since their review.

Our work, without question, draws upon the research and scholarship of respected professors and authors in our field. Again we find ourselves standing on the shoulders of giants. Michael Smith, Ruth Anne Robbins, Brian Foley, Kathy Stanchi, Ellie Margolis, Mary Beth Beazley, Linda Edwards, Ken Chestek, and Steve Johansen are but a few of the people whose words and works influenced this text. We continue to marvel at the depth and breadth of ideas offered by members of our national legal writing community. Undoubtedly, many of those ideas contributed to this book in some way. Although we have attempted to acknowledge everyone whose work contributed to this book, if we have missed someone, please forgive our unintentional error.

Several judges have substantially contributed to our understanding of persuasive writing and oral argument. Among others, we would like to acknowledge Senior Oregon Court of Appeals Judge David Schuman, Senior Oregon Supreme Court Justice Virginia Linder, Oregon Supreme Court Justice Jack Landau, and Federal Magistrate Judge John Acosta.

Once again, great thanks go to our families who sacrificed their time for this project, either by reading chapters or by carving out time for us to write and edit. In particular, Tom Malmud and Rick Coughlin read drafts and, drawing upon their experience as lawyers and readers, helped us improve our work. Others in our families adjusted their schedules, postponed events, stayed with babysitters, or just made their own suppers so that we could have more time to write, edit, or have a conference call.

Finally, we would like to thank Carolina Academic Press and the wonderful people who work there. The folks at CAP are truly our publishing family—they guided us, encouraged us, and helped us maneuver every bumpy road. Special thanks must go to Linda Lacy, our editor, and Tim Colton, the most patient typesetting expert around, for all that they did in getting this book to press. We could not have done this work without you.

Introduction

Lawyers, in representing their clients, often ask a court to act. A lawyer might ask the court to set bail, exclude certain evidence at trial, order that one party compensate another party, or review a legal decision from a lower court. When asking the court to do something, the underlying question is this: How do you persuade a court to act in a way that benefits your client?

This book answers that question. It explains how to marshal law and facts in the way that will most likely persuade a court that the outcome you seek is justified. In other words, it teaches you how to advocate for your client, in writing and orally.

Before reading on, always remember this: Persuasive writing is not so very different from objective writing. Objective writing seeks to persuade a colleague that your legal analysis is correct. To achieve that end, your arguments must be well organized, make a clear point, and be supported by the law and facts. In addition, your colleague will be more receptive to your arguments if your arguments are presented in a polished, professional-looking document. So, too, with persuasive writing. When writing to a court, your arguments must also be well organized, make a clear point, and be supported by the law and facts. Moreover, a judge, like any other lawyer, will be more receptive to your arguments if they are polished and comply with the court's rules. Thus, when writing as an advocate, you will rely on all the skills you learned when writing objectively.

Accordingly, this book builds on your existing ability to objectively analyze a client's legal question. Here, you will learn about the subtle shift from objective analysis to persuasive argument. For example, persuasive writing usually takes the form of a brief or motion, rather than an objective memorandum of law. The briefs and motions are also directed at a different audience—judges and their law clerks. Writing for this different audience will require you to present both facts and law in a slightly different way, highlighting your strong points and explaining why weaknesses, ultimately, do not undermine your argument.

To help you make the shift from objective analysis to persuasive argument, this book begins by providing some background. In the initial chapters, this book explains what makes an argument persuasive, describes the ethical and professional responsibilities of an advocate, provides an overview of the litigation process, and introduces you to trial motions and appellate briefs.

The book then walks you through the steps necessary to build a trial motion or appellate brief and to expertly revise and polish your work. The last chapter explains how to prepare for and present oral arguments before trial and appellate courts.

Finally, the appendices provide advice if you are competing in a moot court competition and additional examples of trial motions and appellate briefs. Through these chapters, *An Advocate Persuades* provides a step-by-step guide to producing arguments that can persuade a court to act in your client's favor.

An Advocate Persuades

Chapter 1

The Nature of Persuasion

Persuasion has been defined in various ways, but for our purposes, to persuade is to prevail on a person or persons to do something or to believe something.[1] For example, a lawyer may persuade a judge to issue a discovery order—that is, to prevail on the judge to do something. Similarly, as part of a brief, a lawyer might persuade an appellate court that the law should be interpreted or applied in a certain way. A lawyer might, for example, argue that the First Amendment does not prohibit states from restricting judges' ability to solicit campaign funds. The lawyer might then argue that the appellate court should affirm the lower court's ruling. In that case, the lawyer has convinced the judges to believe something and then argued that a course of action should follow from that belief. Oral persuasion, too, aims to prevail on the court to believe something or to do something.

To persuade a judge or a panel of judges, the advocate must transfer the view of the universe in the advocate's head into the head of the judge or judges before whom the advocate is appearing. Only then—when the court perceives the universe as the advocate does—will the court be moved to act in the advocate's favor.

I. Principles of Persuasion

To bring the court around to your view of the universe, your argument must take into account the three parts of persuasion: the source of

---

1. *See, e.g.*, Ken Kister, *The American Heritage Dictionary of the English Language* 1352 (Anne H. Soukhanov ed., 3d ed. 1992) (defining "persuade" as the ability to induce someone "to undertake a course of action or embrace a point of view by means of argument, reasoning, or entreaty").

the message, the content of the message, and the audience that receives the message. By understanding those three components of persuasion, and by putting each to use, you can determine how best to persuade a court. This chapter explains how the source of a message, the content of a message, and the audience hearing the message each play a part in whether a message—such as your legal argument—will be persuasive.

Source, content, and audience are not, however, the only ways to think about persuasion. The field of classical rhetoric recognizes three modes of persuasion: *ethos*, *logos*, and *pathos*. *Logos* is the appeal to the logic and reasoning of the listener. *Ethos* is an appeal based on the credibility and trustworthiness of the material and the author. *Pathos* is an appeal to the emotion or passion of the listener. To effectively persuade, you will use all three principles in varying degrees depending upon your audience and the purpose of the communication.

This chapter explains the relationship between the ideas of source, content, and audience on the one hand and *ethos*, *logos*, and *pathos* on the other. It concludes by examining how those different modes of persuasion can be used in combination to persuade judges.

What Is Classical Rhetoric?

Originating in Greece around 450 B.C., classical rhetoric involved the comprehensive and systematic study of the art of persuading through written and verbal expression. In fact, Aristotle—one of the first and best known of the classical rhetoricians—defined rhetoric as the power "of discovering in the particular case what are the available means of persuasion."

Michael R. Smith, *Advanced Legal Writing: Theories and Strategies in Persuasive Writing* 11 (3d ed. 2012) (footnotes omitted).

A. Source and *Ethos*

As mentioned above, the source of a message plays an important role in persuasion. In persuasive legal writing and oral argument, *you* are the source of the message. Thus, you must ask yourself, what about you will enhance, or detract from, the persuasive force of your message? The short answer is this: your credibility.

Credibility is the "quality, capability, or power to elicit belief."[2] That is to say, whether the source of a message persuades depends on whether

---

2. Kister, *supra* note 1, at 438.

that source is credible to the audience. You enhance your credibility as a source by using the persuasive method of *ethos* from classical rhetoric.

A number of factors influence the audience's perception of the source's credibility. In some instances, you may be able to immediately influence your audience's perception of your credibility, perhaps based on the professional look of your work or by your status as a lawyer in the community. In other instances, you must wait and allow the acquisition of time and experience to develop your credibility before your audience. Whether or not you can take immediate action to increase your credibility, you should be aware of all the factors that will affect it.

The first factor that influences the audience's perception of the source is the source's status or position. Imagine, for example, that you are a judge. You read a brief stating that no court anywhere in the country has held that distinctions based on sexual orientation are subject to strict scrutiny for purposes of the Equal Protection Clause of the Fourteenth Amendment to the United States Constitution. On the cover of the brief, you note the name of the attorney who wrote the brief, and you note the attorney's bar number. The bar number shows that he is newly admitted to the bar. You then turn to an opposing brief stating that a number of intermediate state appellate courts have held the opposite—that sexual orientation classifications are subject to strict scrutiny. That brief, you observe, was written by a noted constitutional scholar.

Without doing any research, which source are you likely to find more credible? The constitutional scholar, you might agree, will have greater initial credibility and his brief will, at the outset, be more persuasive. Has the constitutional scholar done anything to enhance his credibility by what he wrote? No—he is highly credible simply because of his status.

Although you may not be able to change your status or position overnight, you can do other things as you interact with the court that will enhance your credibility. In classical rhetoric, the three components of *ethos* are character, intelligence, and good will. By demonstrating each of those three components, a source uses *ethos* to create credibility.[3]

For example, you can employ *ethos* by demonstrating your good character. As an advocate, you establish your good character when you are consistently honest, candid, and trustworthy in all professional interactions. You must always explain the law accurately, which requires you to acknowledge any weaknesses in the facts or law that may support the other party's argument. You should also pay attention to details. Submit documents that are grammatically correct, are properly cited, and conform to

---

3. Michael R. Smith, *Advanced Legal Writing: Theories and Strategies in Persuasive Writing* 127 (3d ed. 2013). Smith's book gives an excellent in-depth discussion of these three components with examples, and this chapter draws heavily from his excellent work.

Ethos—**Establishing Credibility**

Amicus curiae (friend of the court) briefs in the United States Supreme Court must include a statement of the *amicus*'s interest in the case. In that section, most *amici* use *ethos* to establish their credibility. Consider, for example, this excerpt from a brief filed by the American Bar Association (ABA). In it, the ABA uses the breadth of its membership to establish its credibility:

> The ABA is the leading association of legal professionals and one of the largest voluntary professional membership organizations in the United States. Its membership comprises nearly 400,000 attorneys in all fifty states, the District of Columbia, and the U.S. territories, and includes attorneys in private firms, corporations, non-profit organizations, and government agencies. Membership also includes judges, legislators, law professors, law students, and non-lawyer associates in related fields.
> Since its founding in 1878, . . .

Brief of Amicus Curiae American Bar Association In Support of Petitioners in *Obergefell v. Hodges* (No. 14-556).

> As a judge, aren't you likely to say to yourself, "Gee, these folks must know what they're talking about"?

court rules. Those details establish your reliability in small things and will lead the court to assume that you are also reliable in the larger issues of explaining the law and why that law supports the outcome you seek.

Portraying good character is vital for an audience to accept your argument:

> If a reader believes that a writer is, to use Aristotle's word, a rascal, that is, if a reader believes that a writer is not above lying, cheating, deceiving, or misleading, then the reader will view the writer's arguments with skepticism and doubt. Conversely, if a reader believes that a writer possesses good character—or at least if the reader has no reason to question the writer's character—then the reader will be more receptive to the writer's arguments and assertions.[4]

Thus, to persuade, begin by establishing and maintaining your good character.

In addition to developing a reputation as a trustworthy lawyer, you can also influence the court's perception of your credibility by demonstrating your intelligence. You can demonstrate your intelligence to the court by showing a comprehensive knowledge of the governing law and

---

4. *Id.*

The Pitfalls of Being Perceived as a "Rascal"

An advocate's inaccurate statements in a brief can cause judges to become skeptical of the source of the message:

JUSTICE SOTOMAYOR: I—I have a real problem with whatever you're reading, because I'm going to have to go back to that article. I am substantially disturbed that in your brief you made factual statements that were not supported by the cited . . . sources and in fact directly contradicted.

I'm going to give you just three small examples among many I found. So nothing you say or read to me am I going to believe, frankly, until I see . . . with my own eyes the context, okay?

Oral Argument in *Gross v. Glossip*, 135 S. Ct. 2726 (2015).

---

the facts of your case.[5] Such comprehensive knowledge will lead the court to believe you and to have confidence in your work product.

Finally, you can establish your credibility by showing "good will" toward others.[6] Attorneys show good will toward others in how they refer to parties, opposing counsel, the judges, or the jury. A respectful tone toward all players when writing or speaking to a court establishes your good will toward others involved in the litigation. A condescending, insensitive, or overly passionate tone can negate good will and leave the judge less favorably disposed toward you and your arguments.

To maximize your credibility through the use of *ethos*, you will want to ask yourself the following questions:

- Am I consistently professional, honest, and ethical in all my professional dealings?
- Do the arguments and authorities I assert accurately present the law and facts, while still representing the interests of my client?
- Does this document or oral argument reflect my competence and professionalism as a lawyer?
- Is the argument that I am presenting respectful of all parties involved in the litigation?

B. Content and *Logos*

Not surprisingly, *what* the source says to the audience strongly influences whether the audience will be persuaded. The content of the mes-

---

5. *Id.* at 155.
6. *Id.* at 144.

sage obviously matters. In written advocacy before a court, the content of the message is delivered through a brief, a motion, or a memorandum in support of a motion. In oral advocacy, the oral argument delivers the content. No matter the vehicle, the content of your message should be crafted to persuade.

In crafting your message, you may try this approach: (1) Decide where you want the court to go, that is, what result you seek; (2) give the court a reason to want to go there; and (3) provide the court with a valid means of getting there.[7] For example, when arguing in favor of a motion to dismiss an indictment, you first must know the relief you seek (dismissal of the indictment). You must then make the court *want* to dismiss the indictment. Finally—using the law and the facts—you must give the court a legally valid basis to grant the relief you seek.

To be persuasive, that content—the result you want, the desire to get there, and the means to go there—must be structured logically. The court must be able to see the relationship between the result you seek and the law and facts that support that result—and the court must want to reach the result you seek because it believes that result is the correct one.[8]

This idea brings us to the idea of *logos*. *Logos* is an appeal to logic. And logic, it has been said, is "the lifeblood of American law."[9] At its core, *logos* provides the substance of your legal argument in a clear, organized structure. In a sense, *logos* is the message's content, exclusive of the audience or the source.[10] Thus, regardless of the source and her credibility, regardless of the audience, a message must always be rationally and logically presented to be persuasive.

As a lawyer, you will invoke *logos*—that is, you will appeal to the court's logic—if you use an expected organizational structure. You likely already know the particular structures that lawyers use to present their arguments. Lawyers begin an argument by stating the issue the argument addresses or the conclusion the argument will reach. Lawyers then explain the relevant law, apply that law to the facts of the client's case, and

---

7. Bradley G. Clary, Sharon Reich Paulsen, & Michael J. Vanselow, *Advocacy on Appeal* 4 (3d ed. 2008); *see also* Bradley G. Clary, *Primer on the Analysis and Presentation of Legal Argument* 45 (1992) ("You have to know where you are going before you can persuade someone else to go there with you.").

8. Making the court want to reach a certain result includes appealing to the court's emotions through the use of *pathos*, discussed below.

9. Ruggero Aldisert, Stephen Clowney, & Jeremy D. Peterson, *Logic for Law Students: How to Think Like a Lawyer*, 69 U. Pitt. L. Rev. 1, 1 (2007). This article is both informative and witty—a great read for law students and attorneys.

10. Carole C. Berry, *Effective Appellate Advocacy: Brief Writing and Oral Argument* 53 (4th ed. 2009).

conclude. "IRAC," "CREAC," "CRRPAP," and other organizational structures you may have learned are the mechanisms by which attorneys create rational, organized argument—using *logos* to persuade. Because these structures play such an important role in persuading, Chapter 7, *Organizing Persuasive Arguments*, is devoted to reminding you of the logical structures attorneys use in their written work, and it provides examples so that you can see how logical, organized structures can be used for persuasive effect.

In addition to structuring your arguments in a logical way, you can also enhance the persuasiveness of your message by emphasizing those aspects of your argument that are strongest and explaining why any weaknesses ultimately should not dissuade the court from reaching the result you seek. Chapters 8 and 9, *Developing Persuasive Arguments* and *Refining Persuasive Arguments*, explain how to craft such a message. Chapter 6, *Themes for Persuasive Arguments*, addresses how to use themes to tie the content of your message together.

Thus, when assessing the persuasiveness of your message content, ask yourself the following questions:

- Did I organize each argument in a logical manner?
- Is each argument rational and logical?
- Is each argument supported by relevant law and facts?
- Did I eliminate extraneous arguments and include only those arguments that are strong and directly relevant for the judge to decide the case?
- Did I clearly set out and deal with any weaknesses in my client's facts or relevant law?

C. Audience and *Pathos*

The final consideration in any attempt to persuade is the audience. Who is your target audience? What use will that person or those people make of your argument? What kinds of messages might the audience be predisposed to accept? How should you craft your argument in light of your responses to those questions? To be sure, many messages are directed at diverse audiences with different goals. Most advertising, for example, is directed at a diverse audience whose members will make different uses of the message. So, while you might pay attention to that slick car commercial because you are in the market for a car, your classmate may pay attention because he wants to know what band is on the soundtrack. Advertisers have to consider a diverse audience with myriad interests when they craft their persuasive messages.

Your job as a legal advocate is, in a sense, easier. Your goal is to persuade a judge or a panel of judges; that's a fairly narrow audience. That audience will use the information you convey for only one purpose: to decide. Knowing that you have a judge audience whose goal is to decide a legal question will help you craft a more persuasive document or oral argument. At bottom, your message should be aimed at helping that audience do its job: issue a decision.

Moreover, because judges have the same goal, they share several predispositions. One predisposition that all judges are likely to share is the predisposition, discussed above, for a logically structured argument. Judges are educated, intelligent, law-trained decision makers. They have gone through the same educational system as the advocates and will thus be predisposed to "think like a lawyer." Use of *logos*—logical argument— will resonate with them.

Another predisposition that judges are likely to share is for an advocate to get to his or her point quickly. Judges are busy people. Federal appellate court judges read approximately 13,000 pages of briefs each year—and that staggering number does not include the pages of records, trial transcripts, and background materials for each case.[11] Because your reader is busy, write efficiently. Tell the court what decision you seek and provide the necessary law and facts to support that decision. Include only the most important arguments rather than presenting every possible argument. Do not include extraneous information, incorrect information, or incomplete information—all of which will slow the court down and make your argument less persuasive.

Other preferences are likely to be more specific to the court in which you are appearing or the particular judge who will be hearing the case. As an advocate, you should learn as much about your audience as possible. Although you know that your audience is law-trained, intelligent, and tasked with making a decision, there is more you can learn about the court. Is this a court that handles only Social Security matters, or is it a court that handles everything from dog bite disputes to intellectual property issues? Put differently, knowing whether your audience is composed of specialists or generalists may help you decide the depth or breadth of the content you provide. For example, if you are arguing to a specialized court or to a particular judge who you know has experience in the area, you may be able to omit background information about the law that governs the case. Conversely, if you are appearing before a generalist or a panel of generalists, you will need to begin your complex corporate income tax argument with some fundamental tax concepts.

On a more individual level, think about whether anything about the particular judge or judges before whom you are appearing will make that judge or panel of judges more or less receptive to your legal argument. If, for example, the judge before whom you are appearing has rejected

---

11. Mark P. Painter, *Appellate Practice—Including Legal Writing from a Judge's Perspective* 2 (May 1, 2000), http://www.plainlanguage.gov/examples/legal (last visited June 26, 2015).

your position in the past based on a certain argument, you should consider a different argument. If you are presenting a statutory construction argument, evaluate whether the judge will be more likely to rely on legislative history to interpret the statute or simply to stick with the plain language.

Personal characteristics of the judge who will be hearing your case may also be relevant to how you go about persuading. Is the judge before whom you are appearing particularly conservative or liberal politically, "tough on crime" or pro-defendant, sympathetic to corporate interests or sympathetic to interests of the individual person or community? Has the judge had life experiences that are relevant to this case? Knowing that kind of information, like more general information about the court and about the court's legal preferences, will increase your ability to persuade.

Finally, remember that judges are human. That fact brings us to the third classical rhetorical device, *pathos*. *Pathos* involves persuading by appealing to the audience's emotions. Although subtle, *pathos* exerts its influence by appealing to your legal reader's emotion.

> The effective use of emotion involves creating a response in the audience that makes the audience want to do things your way. It means the audience not only believes at an intellectual level that you are right, but feels it at a gut level and wants to do something about it.[12]

Pathos is a powerful mode of persuasion because most people, especially legally-trained people who are taught to focus on *logos*, underestimate it. Watch, for example, any political or product advertisement. Which emotion was the advertisement designed to evoke? The political advertisement was probably designed to produce fear if the opposing party is elected and a sense of well-being based on the election of the proposed candidate. The product advertisement probably focused on happiness, love, and success based on the preferred product choice. All of these emotional appeals can be powerful and sometimes unconscious influences on your decision-making process.

With respect to your legal argument, you can use *pathos* to create a "commanding narrative"[13] that can move a judge in a variety of ways. You can use emotion to help the judge understand what motivated the parties to act or react in a particular way; emotion can help the judge understand why the outcome you seek is just or fair; and it can help the judge sympathize with your client's position.

---

12. Louis J. Sirico, Jr., & Nancy L. Schultz, *Persuasive Legal Writing* 12 (4th ed. 2015).

13. *See* Steven D. Stark, *Writing to Win: The Legal Writer* 110 (2d ed. 2012).

> **The Use of *Pathos* in a Judicial Opinion**
>
> In *DeShaney v. Winnebago County Department of Social Services,* the Court held that a state agency that failed to adequately investigate reports of child abuse could not be held liable under the Due Process Clause for resulting injuries to the child, Joshua DeShaney. In his dissent, Justice Blackman employed *pathos* to make his point:
>
> > Poor Joshua! Victim of repeated attacks by an irresponsible, bullying, cowardly, and intemperate father, and abandoned by respondents who placed him in a dangerous predicament and who knew or learned what was going on, and yet did essentially nothing except, as the Court revealingly observes, . . . "dutifully recorded these incidents in [their] files." It is a sad commentary upon American life, and constitutional principles — so full of late of patriotic fervor and proud proclamations about "liberty and justice for all" — that this child, Joshua DeShaney, now is assigned to live out the remainder of his life profoundly retarded.
>
> 489 U.S. 189, 213 (1989) (Blackmun, J., dissenting).

Although most judges are trained to check their emotions — law is, after all, a *logos*-based discipline — judges are still human. They too feel anger, fear of loss, guilt, sadness, and happiness. Importantly, they want to do the right thing. Subtly invoking emotions can powerfully influence rational judgment and a judge's decision. Reminding the court, for example, that your seemingly unsympathetic client is not just a criminal "defendant," but is also a human with typical human frailties invokes *pathos*. As mentioned above, your message's content should, among other things, make a judge *want* to reach the conclusion you seek. *Pathos* is the means to do that.

Emotional appeals can be tricky, however, and should be done in an understated manner. The best way to make an emotional appeal without sounding emotional is to allow the facts to speak for themselves and to provide little to no commentary. For example, when Chief Justice John Roberts (then, attorney John Roberts) wanted to show the vital role a mine played in a remote Alaskan community, he did not say, "The Red Dog Mine is vital to the economy." Rather, he said this:

> Operating 365 days a year, 24 hours a day, the Red Dog Mine is the largest private employer in the Northwest Arctic Borough, an area roughly the size of the State of Indiana with a population of about 7,000. The vast majority of the area's residents are Inupiat Eskimos whose ancestors have inhabited the region for thousands of years. The region offers only limited year-round employment opportunities, particularly in the private sector . . . .

> Prior to the mine's opening, the average wage in the borough was well below the state average; a year after its opening, the borough's average exceeded that of the State.[14]

In other words, Justice Roberts allowed the facts to speak for themselves so that the Justices who read his brief could feel the importance of the mine to the community. Without making any overtly emotional appeal, his phrasing creates a commanding narrative that helps the legal reader connect to that litigant's side of the story.

As you consider your audience, ask yourself the following questions:

- Did I structure my arguments in a way that makes the judge feel good about ruling in my client's favor?
- Did I create and explain rules, and acknowledge unfavorable rules, from my client's perspective in a manner that advances my client's argument?
- Have I effectively addressed any weaknesses in my client's facts or authority?
- Have I made my client come across as likable?
- Does my brief or document (or my oral argument) evoke the intended emotion from my audience?

II. Using the Principles Together

When writing to a court and in oral argument, you will use all of the above principles in varying degrees depending on your audience and the purpose of the legal document or argument. *Logos*—the structure of your message—is the most basic mode of persuasion attorneys use, but *logos* is intertwined with other aspects of persuasion: the substantive content of your message; your credibility as the source of the message; and the judge's predisposition to agreeing with your message. Understanding these different aspects of persuasion and how you will use them in your arguments will enhance the persuasiveness of your document or oral argument.

Different sections of your document may rely more heavily on one mode of persuasion than another. For example, you are more likely to employ *pathos* in your statement of facts (see Chapter 12, *Statement of Facts and of the Case*), where *how* you present the facts can have a significant impact on how the court feels about your client. Your argument section likely will be more *logos*-intensive, but you should nonetheless consider how *pathos* may play into your argument. Finally, *ethos* should perme-

---

14. From Brief for Petitioner, *Alaska, Dept. of Envtl. Conservation v. U.S. E.P.A*, 540 U.S. 461 (2004), available at 2003 WL 2010655 (citations omitted); *see also* Ross Guberman, *Five Ways to Write Like John Roberts*, http://www.legalwritingpro.com/articles/john-roberts.pdf (last visited October 9, 2015).

ate every part of every document you prepare, from the cover to the last page; you always want the court to perceive you as a reliable, believable, and credible source.

Different types of cases and the court in which you are appearing also will affect how you use the rhetorical devices introduced above and how considerations of source, content, and audience play out. For example, there may be less room for the use of *pathos* in a technical statutory construction problem before a supreme court. But skillful use of *pathos* is indispensable if you represent a parent in a termination of parental rights case, a defendant in a criminal case, or an injured plaintiff in a tort case—especially when you are addressing a trial court.

Consciously considering how the audience will perceive you, the message you want to convey, and the needs of your audience is vital to producing a persuasive document or oral argument. Similarly, crafting your message by creating just the right mix of *ethos*, *logos*, and *pathos* will allow you to transfer your view of the case and your desired outcome into the head of the judge to whom you are presenting your argument.

As you read the rest of this book, keep in mind considerations of source, message content, and audience. Think about how the rhetorical devices of *ethos*, *logos*, and *pathos* can be used together to persuade your judge audience. Finally, always be mindful of the purpose of your argument: to make the court want to rule in your client's favor and to give the court everything it needs to do so.

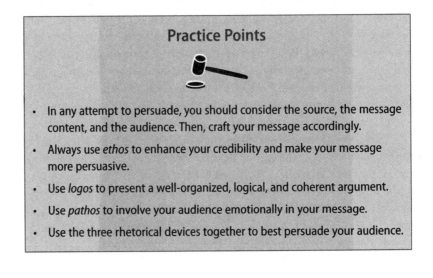

Practice Points

- In any attempt to persuade, you should consider the source, the message content, and the audience. Then, craft your message accordingly.
- Always use *ethos* to enhance your credibility and make your message more persuasive.
- Use *logos* to present a well-organized, logical, and coherent argument.
- Use *pathos* to involve your audience emotionally in your message.
- Use the three rhetorical devices together to best persuade your audience.

Chapter 2

The Ethical, Professional Advocate

I. Why Act Ethically and Professionally?
II. Some Guiding Principles
    A. A "Zealous Advocate" Is Not a "Zealot"
    B. "It Is What It Is"
    C. "Winning" Is a Relative Term
III. Specific Rules an Advocate Should Know

The majority of this book focuses on *how* to present arguments to a court; this chapter, by contrast, focuses on *who* you present to the court. In other words, this chapter focuses on you—the source of the message. Every interaction you have as an attorney, whether that interaction is with the court, opposing counsel, or a client, gives you the opportunity to demonstrate—and others the opportunity to observe—what kind of lawyer you have chosen to be. Have you chosen to be fair? Truthful? Respectful? Aggressive? Evasive? Sloppy? Your goal should be to always act as—and to be perceived as—an ethical, professional, and credible lawyer.

In an adversarial setting, it is easy to get caught up in the fight and to become lax about acting ethically and professionally. This chapter serves as a gentle reminder not to leave your ethics and professionalism at the door when you transition to situations that require persuasive, rather than objective, writing.

I. Why Act Ethically and Professionally?

As you learned in the last chapter, *The Nature of Persuasion*, one reason to act ethically and professionally is because your credibility as an advocate affects the persuasiveness of your argument. A court will be more receptive to your argument if it perceives you, the source of that message, as credible. For example, if you tell the court, "Your Honor, the evidence will show that the police officers continued to question my client even after my client unequivocally invoked her right to counsel," the court

---

"Ethics" and "Professionalism"

The two terms we use throughout this chapter are broad. "Ethics" at its broadest means "[a] set of principles of right conduct." *The American Heritage Dictionary of the English Language* 630 (3d ed. 1992). "Professionalism" often refers to the standards of people practicing an occupation when that occupation requires significant training and study. *See id.* at 1446 (defining "professionalism" and "professional").

Those terms can be narrowed to "professional ethics," "legal ethics," or "rules of professional conduct." Generally, those more narrow terms refer to required standards that govern a lawyer's conduct. An attorney who fails to follow those governing standards risks a disciplinary action or disbarment.

This chapter uses the broader terms—ethics and professionalism—to encourage you to think broadly about the set of principles or standards you will adhere to in your practice.

---

must be able to assume that you have diligently investigated the facts and that you are representing those facts accurately. Although you might prevail the first, or even the second, time that you inaccurately represent the facts or the law to the court, your luck will eventually run out. When it does, you will have tarnished your credibility. Moreover, in the extreme case, it will become impossible to persuade a court of anything because you will have been suspended from practice or disbarred for unethical conduct. Thus, if your goal is to persuade courts on behalf of your clients, become an unfailingly credible resource for the court.

You should, however, keep in mind one other important reason for acting ethically and professionally: It is the right thing to do. Members of the public who seek out an attorney are vulnerable. They have an important matter they are unable to resolve. To resolve that matter, they need to enter the legal system—a system whose procedures can seem confusing and inaccessible. Ethical and professional rules protect those members of the public and the integrity of the court system. The rules ensure fairness amongst the parties before the court. Acting in an ethical and professional way—even when doing so is not required by a rule—protects us and our profession. We must face ourselves in the mirror every day, and we must interact with other lawyers nearly every day. Those everyday interactions are more satisfying and vastly easier when we act ethically and professionally.

II. Some Guiding Principles

Although specific rules govern the conduct of an advocate, a few general principles will make those specific rules much easier to follow. Here, we present a few general principles before we turn to the specific rules that govern a lawyer's conduct.

A. A "Zealous Advocate" Is Not a "Zealot"

First, understand what it means to be a "zealous" advocate. You will hear the word "zealous" bandied about a lot in the context of representing clients. Lawyers sometimes use the obligation to represent clients zealously as a justification for unethical, unprofessional, aggressive, or inappropriate behavior. Those lawyers, however, misunderstand the term.

The concept of "zeal" as a professional ethic was first introduced in 1908 when the Canons of Professional Ethics explained that a lawyer owes his client "warm zeal in the maintenance and defense of [the client's] rights."[1] But even then, the Canons took care to remind lawyers that "[t]he office of attorney does not permit, much less does it demand … violation of law or any manner of fraud or chicane. He must obey his own conscience and not that of his client."[2] By 1980, the professional code emphasized that being a zealous advocate does not change a lawyer's duty to "treat with consideration all persons involved in the legal process and to avoid the infliction of needless harm."[3]

Nevertheless, concerns arose that attorneys misunderstood what it means to "represent a client zealously." Thus, in the most recent revision, the concept of "zeal" has been replaced by the requirements of diligence and promptness.[4] The commentary to today's rules discusses the idea of "zeal in advocacy." That commentary explains that, "[a] lawyer is not bound … to press for every advantage that might be realized for a client" and "the lawyer's duty to act with reasonable diligence does not require the use of offensive tactics or preclude the treating of all persons in the legal process with courtesy and respect."[5] As one court put it, "[t]o be vigorous … does not mean to be disruptively argumentative; to be aggressive is not a license to ignore the rules of evidence and decorum; and to be zealous is not to be uncivil."[6]

Thus, "zeal" does not mean you should become a "zealot."[7] The first term means "enthusiastic diligence"; the second means "fanatic." Do not

---

1. ABA Canons of Prof'l Ethics Canon 15 (1908).

2. *Id.*

3. Model Code of Prof'l Responsibility EC 7-10 (1980).

4. Annotated Rules of Prof'l Conduct 43 (1992) ("Rule 1.3 substitutes reasonable diligence and promptness for zeal; the comment [explaining Rule 1.3 does], however, … requir[e] zeal in advocacy upon the client's behalf.").

5. Annotated Model Rules of Prof'l Conduct R. 1.3 cmt. (2007).

6. *In re Williams*, 414 N.W.2d 394, 397 (Minn. 1987).

7. *See* G.C. Hazard, Jr., & W.W. Holdes, *The Law of Lawyering* 70 (2d ed. 1990); *see also* Michael D. Murray & Christy H. DeSanctis, *Advanced Legal Writing and Oral Advocacy: Trials, Appeals, and Moot Courts* 3 (2009) (commenting that attorneys misunderstood the term "zeal" to mean "fanatically" or "cravenly").

> **Who's in Charge Here?**
>
> As you can see from the discussion about the word "zealous," the rules governing professional conduct have changed over time. Those changes can sometimes be confusing, in particular, because those changes involve a variety of "rules," "codes," and "canons." In an effort to help you sort through the different "rules," "codes," and "canons," here is a brief explanation of the rules governing the professional conduct of lawyers.
>
> To begin, individual states adopt the rules that govern the conduct of lawyers practicing within that state. Thus, every state has its own unique set of rules governing the professional conduct of its practicing lawyers.
>
> The American Bar Association (ABA) has, however, exerted enormous influence on the rules that each state has adopted. Since 1908, the ABA has published a set of model rules of professional conduct. As "model" rules, the ABA's rules are merely a recommended set of rules and have no binding authority. However, because most states have, to one degree or another, adopted the ABA's model rules, the ABA's rules provide a fairly good gauge for the rules that states have adopted. Over time, the ABA's model rules have changed. So that the change in names does not confuse you, here's a short history of the model rules of professional conduct.
>
> **1908** ABA adopts the Canons of Professional Ethics.
>
> **1969** ABA adopts the Model Code of Professional Conduct.
>
> **1983** ABA adopts the Model Rules of Professional Conduct.
>
> Each new set of rules replaced the preceding set of rules. Thus, today, the ABA's recommended rules are the Model Rules of Professional Conduct. However, as mentioned above, each state is free to adopt the ABA's revisions or not.

confuse the two. Although others will cry "zealous advocacy" to justify boorish behavior, you know better.

B. "It Is What It Is"

Next, practice saying, "It is what it is." In your life as a lawyer, you will undoubtedly encounter facts that are inconvenient and law that is unfavorable. When you encounter an inconvenient fact or unfavorable law, you should say to yourself, "It is what it is." Face the facts. Acknowledge the law. And then explain why, despite the one or the other, your client should still prevail. If the particular facts or relevant law preclude you from arguing that your client still wins, then you must admit that conclusion. Talk to your client about the available options and, if necessary, settle or withdraw your complaint or appeal.

The alternative—ignoring inconvenient facts or unfavorable law— will ultimately do more harm than good. For example, if you avoid the undesirable facts or law, you will lose the opportunity to present them in the light that will best serve your client. Worse, if the problematic facts or law prevent you from arguing that your client should still prevail, then you will have pursued a frivolous argument, wasting your client's money and exposing yourself to sanctions. Either way, when those bad facts or contrary law come to light—and they will—your credibility will be tarnished and possibly damaged beyond repair. Thus, although skirting some facts or a part of the law may seem like a good idea in the short term, the damage to you and to your client is simply not worth it. Instead, accept "it is what it is," and take the opportunity to couch the problematic facts and law in a way that minimizes their impact.

C. "Winning" Is a Relative Term

Finally, as an advocate, you should think carefully about what it means to "win." In adversarial settings, people talk a lot about winning and losing. Trials often are conceived as battles or, if really long and drawn-out, as wars. On appeal, people win or lose, as if appeals are sporting events in which one team is a winner and the other a loser. Lawyers refer to counsel representing other parties as their opponents, and they often revel in beating them.

Although that kind of shorthand for adversarial proceedings is common and sometimes useful, try to view proceedings as something other than a to-the-death battle. Doing so helps to avoid some of the ethical and professional pitfalls that befall those who become too caught up in the battle. Avoid seeing adversarial settings as wars in which all opponents are to be mercilessly crushed, and you may also avoid the temptations to take unethical or unprofessional shortcuts.

What does it mean to win? Winning in an adversarial setting may be defined as achieving the best possible outcome for your client in light of the existing facts and law and consistent with acting professionally and ethically.

An example involving an inmate's appeal and an assistant attorney general will illustrate the point. Along the way, you will also see how an attorney can accept that "it is what it is" and still act as a zealous advocate. In that case, an inmate brought a tort action against the prison. The inmate lost and—acting *pro se*—appealed the decision arguing that the trial court judge had erroneously granted summary judgment in favor of the state. An assistant attorney general was assigned to the case to represent the state government. Upon reviewing the facts and the law, the assistant attorney general determined that the inmate was correct: The trial court had, in fact, erroneously granted judgment in favor of the state. Although a non-frivolous argument could have been made that the appellate court should uphold the trial court's judgment, it had little chance of succeeding. Worse, if the appellate court rejected the inmate's argument, there was a chance that the appellate court would announce a rule that would be detrimental to the state in the many other tort actions filed by prison inmates.

The assistant attorney general decided that the best outcome would be achieved by conceding that the trial court had erred but suggesting a rule that would benefit the state in the long run.[8] The court adopted the state's proposed rule. Although the appellate court held in favor of the inmate, the state "won" the appeal in the sense that it achieved the best possible outcome given the facts and the law.

Winning is not always about winning the case. If you carefully and objectively assess the facts and law, and make the best of what you have, you are less likely to push the boundaries of professionalism to achieve an illusory victory.

III. Specific Rules an Advocate Should Know

Although the general principles above will point you in the right direction most of the time, you can also turn to the rules of professional conduct. Each state's bar adopts rules of professional conduct that apply to members of that bar, which you can find by going to your state bar's website.[9] In most states, though, the rules of professional conduct generally follow the American Bar Association's Model Rules of Professional Conduct. Based on those model rules, here are some guidelines about how to conduct yourself as an ethical, professional advocate.

RULE	DO	DON'T
1.1	**Be competent**, which includes • Investigating the law and facts sufficiently to determine whether your client has grounds for a claim. • Submitting briefs that are organized, thoroughly researched, and supported by legal authority.	**Demonstrate incompetence by** • Failing to educate yourself about claims or arguments that your client might assert or about facts that might support those claims or arguments. • Submitting briefs that are so disorganized or unsupported by legal authority that the court is "called upon to supply the legal research and organization to flesh out a party's arguments." *Smith v. Eaton*, 910 F.2d 1469, 1471 (7th Cir. 1990)

---

8. *See Canell v. Oregon*, 58 P.3d 847 (Or. Ct. App. 2002) (adopting state's proposed rule).

9. You can find a link to the various states' rules on the American Bar Association's website: http://www.americanbar.org/groups/professional_responsibility/resources/links_of_interest.html#States.

RULE	DO	DON'T
1.3	**Be diligent**. "Diligence" is an earnest, persistent effort to accomplish the task at hand, in this case, representing your client.	Allow an ever-expanding workload (or other personal events in your life) to cause you to **neglect** a client's case.
1.3	**Be prompt** in communicating with your client and attending to your client's matter.	**Procrastinate** such that you needlessly raise your client's anxiety; undermine your client's confidence in you; or, worst of all, adversely affect your client's legal position.
1.4	**Communicate regularly with your client**, both to consult about the means of achieving your client's objectives and to keep the client informed about the status of the case.	Avoid returning phone calls, letters, or e-mails.
1.6	**Maintain confidences**. Except under limited circumstances designated in the model rules or under the law, you cannot reveal any information relating to the representation of your client.	Gossip, tell tales, or post information about your clients, especially in a manner that would allow someone to identify your client.
3.1	**Assert an argument only if it can be supported by both the law and facts.** If winning your argument would require the court to overturn existing case law or a statute, your argument must recognize that.	**Assert a frivolous argument.** A lawyer makes a frivolous argument when it is wholly unsupported by either the law or the facts of the case. Although an attorney can argue that the law should be extended to new areas or that a previous decision should be overruled, such an argument should acknowledge that it is attempting to extend or overrule current law.
3.3	**Acknowledge contrary authority from the governing jurisdiction.** Doing so is not only ethical, but is good advocacy.	**Ignore contrary authority in the governing jurisdiction**. If you find yourself thinking, "maybe the court and opposing counsel won't find this case," you're asking for trouble.
3.3	**Correct a false statement of law or fact.** You may, at some time, inadvertently state the law or a fact incorrectly, or the law may change while your client's case is being considered. In either situation, you must alert the court.	**Knowingly make a false statement of law or fact** to the court. Never stretch your reading of the law or the facts such that you are misrepresenting one or the other.
3.4	**Follow court rules.**	Fail to research and, thereby, fail to become familiar with a court's rules.
3.4	**Be fair to the opposing party and counsel.**	**Be unreasonable by** • Making frivolous discovery requests. • Failing to respond to, or delaying a response to, a reasonable discovery request. • Raising a fact or issue at trial when you believe that the fact or issue is irrelevant or inadmissible.

RULE	DO	DON'T
3.5	**Avoid improper communications** with the court, counsel, or others.	**Communicate ex parte** with the judge or jury, unless permitted or required to do so by law. "Ex parte" means the communication occurs without the other party (or counsel for the other party) being present.

If the above basic principles and specific guidelines prove insufficient, and you find yourself confronting a decision about which you are uncertain, imagine that whatever you are about to do will end up on the front page of the *New York Times*. Or, imagine that your decision "goes viral." In other words, imagine that anyone with an Internet connection—that is, everyone—knows about the decision you just made. Do you still feel comfortable? If you have to spend much time and effort deciding whether a proposed course of action is ethical or professionally appropriate, you probably shouldn't do it.

Finally, remember that being a decent person will go a long way toward being an ethical lawyer. As one professor of legal ethics explained, "Being an ethical lawyer is not much different from being an ethical doctor or mail carrier or gas station attendant. You should treat others as you want them to treat you. Be honest and fair. Show respect and compassion. Keep your promises."[10] A good lawyer can competently and vigorously represent her client and, at the same time, be a decent person.

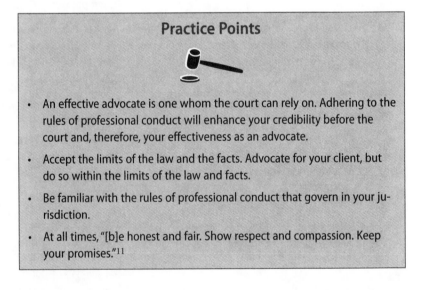

Practice Points

- An effective advocate is one whom the court can rely on. Adhering to the rules of professional conduct will enhance your credibility before the court and, therefore, your effectiveness as an advocate.

- Accept the limits of the law and the facts. Advocate for your client, but do so within the limits of the law and facts.

- Be familiar with the rules of professional conduct that govern in your jurisdiction.

- At all times, "[b]e honest and fair. Show respect and compassion. Keep your promises."[11]

---

10. Patrick J. Schiltz, *On Being a Happy, Healthy, and Ethical Member of an Unhappy, Unhealthy, and Unethical Profession*, 52 Vand. L. Rev. 871, 909 (1999).

11. *Id.*

Chapter 3

A Litigation Overview

Before you draft documents for your client, you must understand the litigation that has generated the need for your document. Lawyers submit different documents depending on whether litigation is "civil" or "criminal" litigation. Lawyers also submit different documents depending on whether litigation has just begun or is nearing its conclusion. These variables—whether a case is a civil case or a criminal case and whether the motion or brief is submitted earlier or later in the litigation—affect which facts are available, what law applies, and the arguments you may make. Thus, you must be aware of the litigation process and where your case is located within that process before you draft.

To that end, this chapter briefly describes the difference between civil and criminal litigation and then explains the different documents that are produced along each of those litigation tracks. As you read, you should note the different purposes for the different documents. Some documents present persuasive arguments and ask the court to take action or to refrain from taking an action. Those documents are usually called a "motion" or "brief." A motion is often accompanied by a "memorandum of law," which explains the arguments in detail.

Other documents merely inform. For example, "pleadings," such as a complaint or an answer, inform the court and opposing party of alle-

> **Oral vs. Written Motions**
>
> Not all motions are in writing. During a hearing or trial, motions are usually made orally and ruled upon by the judge. Other motions, especially those before and after a trial, are usually in writing. This book focuses on written motions.

23

gations, denials, or defenses in a lawsuit, but make no arguments about those allegations, denials, or defenses. Similarly, lawyers will notify opposing counsel of depositions they intend to take, documents the other side must produce, and witnesses they plan to call at trial.

In providing an overview of the civil and criminal litigation processes, this chapter describes both kinds of documents—those that seek to persuade and those that inform. In that way, you can see the different roles that different documents play. After this overview, however, this book focuses more specifically on how to develop those documents that will persuade a court to take action on your client's behalf.

I. Civil vs. Criminal Litigation

Table 3-A sets out some of the more significant differences between a civil case and a criminal case.

Table 3-A · Differences between a civil case and a criminal case

	Civil Litigation	Criminal Prosecution
Definition	Civil litigation addresses disputes between two or more parties, whether those parties are individuals, organizations, or a government.	Criminal litigation addresses crimes against society. Criminal litigation is often called criminal "prosecution" because the government prosecutes an individual or other entity for alleged crimes.
Case filed by	A private party or the government	The government
Burden of proof	The plaintiff has the burden of proof. The plaintiff must prove each claim by a preponderance of the evidence.	The burden of proof is on the government. The government must prove its case beyond a reasonable doubt.
Examples	Landlord/tenant disputes, divorce proceedings, personal injuries, and medical malpractice	Theft, assault, robbery, trafficking in controlled substances, and murder
Redress	The plaintiff seeks monetary damages or an injunction. An injunction requires a person to act or refrain from acting.	The prosecutor seeks jail time, probation, fines, or in exceptional cases and in some states, a death sentence
Appeal	The losing party appeals	Usually only the defendant appeals
Effect of judgment	Liability	Guilt

Civil and criminal cases are governed by different rules of procedure, which permit different kinds of motions and appeals.[1] The rules of civil and criminal procedure differ from jurisdiction to jurisdiction. Moreover, local custom may affect how a particular procedural step is performed. For those reasons, cases within different jurisdictions will always look a little bit different. Nevertheless, regardless of whether a case is a civil or criminal case and no matter the jurisdiction, the litigation will have four distinct stages: pre-trial, trial, post-trial, and appeals.

The two sections that follow provide a tabular overview of a civil matter and, then, a criminal matter. The tables are by no means exhaustive. The tables do, however, describe the major stages of litigation and the motions or briefs that are produced along the way. To give you a sense of the pace of litigation, the tables provide the time frames within which documents must be filed. The time frames are from the federal rules of civil, criminal, and appellate procedure. State procedural rules will govern the time frames in state court, and those rules may result in slightly different time frames.

As you read, remember that, although you may be permitted to file a motion or brief at a particular stage, whether you actually file a particular motion or brief always depends on the facts and law available to you.

II. Civil Litigation

Every civil case begins with a dispute between two or more parties. For example, one neighbor builds an addition to his house that blocks the view that another neighbor had previously enjoyed; a business owner receives a delivery of goods that do not look or perform as expected; a bicyclist runs into you while you're on your skateboard. Although the kinds of disputes are limitless, the general process of litigation is the same.

A. Pre-Trial

As an attorney, you begin by listening to the client's problem and investigating the relevant facts and law. After your preliminary investigation, you will likely contact the other party or that party's attorney. You may send a "demand letter" that asks the other party to stop certain conduct or pay damages. If a dispute cannot be settled informally, then one of the parties may decide to initiate a claim in court. The typical pre-trial path is set forth in Table 3-B.

---

1. Specialized courts—such as tax courts, bankruptcy courts, or specialized business courts—have their own, somewhat different, procedural steps; however, because the majority of cases follow either the civil or criminal procedural tracks, this chapter focuses on those two paths.

Table 3-B · Typical civil pre-trial stages

Pre-trial stage	Explanation
Complaint	The first formal step in civil litigation is to file a complaint. A complaint notifies the opposing party that some individual (or entity) has initiated a legal action in court. The complaint outlines the plaintiff's legal claims and the factual basis for those claims.
Motion to dismiss	After the complaint is filed, the defendant's attorney has an initial opportunity to ask the court to take action to dismiss all or part of the complaint. A defendant can ask the court to dismiss a complaint for a variety of reasons. Some common reasons for asking the court to dismiss the complaint are because the complaint fails to state a claim upon which relief can be granted, the court lacks jurisdiction, the complaint was not properly served on the defendant, or because the plaintiff waited too long to initiate the litigation (i.e., "the statute of limitations" has run). If the judge grants the motion to dismiss, the dismissal may be granted "with prejudice" or "without prejudice." If the motion is granted with prejudice the case is dismissed, the litigation in the trial court ends, and the plaintiff's only recourse is to appeal. If the motion is granted without prejudice, the plaintiff can still amend and re-file the complaint to continue the litigation.
Answer	If the case is not dismissed, the defendant must file an answer to the plaintiff's complaint. In the answer, the defendant must admit or deny each of the allegations in the complaint. Failure to do so results in the defendant admitting to the complaint's allegations. In the answer, the defendant can set out affirmative defenses and counterclaims. An affirmative defense asserts claims that, if true, will defeat one or more plaintiff's claims. An example of an affirmative defense might be a claim that the statute of limitations has run. A counter-claim is a claim brought by the defendant that, if later proved true, would entitle defendant to some relief.
Reply	If the defendant's answer included counter-claims, the plaintiff may be able to file a "reply," similar to the defendant's answer. In a reply, the plaintiff admits or denies the allegations that support the counter-claim.
Discovery	After the lawsuit is filed, a great deal of activity occurs in the form of discovery. Discovery provides relevant information to both parties in terms of facts, expected testimony, and exhibits. Common types of discovery include: (1) interrogatories, which are a list of questions that one party is asking the other party to answer; (2) requests to produce documents; (3) requests that the opposing party admit to certain facts; and (4) depositions, during which an attorney questions a witness who is under oath. The majority of discovery is handled without judicial involvement. Sometimes, however, if the parties cannot agree, one party will file a motion asking the court to take action related to the discovery process. Typical discovery-related motions include a motion to compel discovery, a motion for a protective order to prevent discovery, or a motion to limit discovery. A court may also order parties to engage in a mediated settlement conference. Mediation is an informal settlement conference led by a trained mediator who seeks to find a resolution to the case that is acceptable to all parties.

Chart continues on the next page

Table 3-B · Typical civil pre-trial stages, *continued*

Pre-trial stage	Explanation
Motion for summary judgment	A motion for summary judgment asks the court to dismiss the case based on the known facts. In a motion for summary judgment, the moving party argues that, based on the undisputed facts, that party is entitled to judgment as a matter of law. The well-known standard is that a party is entitled to summary judgment if "there is no genuine dispute as to any material fact and the movant is entitled to judgment as a matter of law." Fed. R. Civ. P. 56(a). If the court grants summary judgment in either party's favor, judgment is entered in the prevailing party's favor and litigation at the trial level ends. The case will continue only if the losing party appeals.
Motion in limine	Motions in limine are requests that certain materials be excluded from the trial or be deemed admissible. Usually, a party will request that material be excluded from the trial because the material was improperly obtained, would be overly prejudicial, or irrelevant to the proceedings.
Pre-trial order	Before trial begins, the parties will draft a proposed pre-trial order outlining the case as it will be presented at trial. If the proposed order is acceptable to the judge, the judge signs the pre-trial order and it governs the events at trial. The pre-trial order addresses the issues that remain in dispute, the witnesses that will appear at trial, and the need for further decisions by the court.

B. Trial

Most civil cases settle before the trial begins. In fact, in most jurisdictions, and depending on the type of case, less than five percent of all complaints filed proceed to trial.[2] Those cases that proceed to trial usually unfold as shown in Table 3-C.

Table 3-C · Typical stages of a civil trial

Stage	Explanation
Jury selection	In a civil case, a plaintiff or defendant must request a jury for the case to be heard by a jury. If a party does not request a jury trial, the case will be heard and decided by a judge. See Fed. R. Civ. P. 38, 39. When a case is to be heard by a jury, the trial begins by selecting the jury from a pool of potential jurors. This process is called "voir dire." During voir dire, attorneys or the judge, depending on the court's procedures, will talk with potential jurors about any pre-existing beliefs or experiences that may affect the juror's perception of the case. A juror can be dismissed "for cause" when the voir dire establishes that the juror cannot be impartial or will be unable to attend the trial. An attorney can also use one of several "peremptory" challenges or strikes to exclude a person from the panel without providing a reason for the exclusion.

Chart continues on the next page

2. *See, e.g.*, U.S. Dept. of Justice, Civil Justice Survey of State Courts, 2005, at 1 (Oct. 2008) (available at http://www.bjs.gov/content/pub/pdf/cbjtsc05.pdf).

Table 3-C · Typical stages of a civil trial, *continued*

Stage	Explanation
Opening statement	The plaintiff's lawyer opens the trial by making an "opening statement." In the opening statement, counsel describes what will be proved during the trial. The defendant's attorney then follows with an opening statement describing, from the defendant's perspective, what the trial will show.
Plaintiff's case-in-chief	Because the plaintiff has the burden of proof, the plaintiff's case is presented first. Plaintiff's counsel provides evidence witness-by-witness. Each witness's testimony is recorded. Witnesses also can identify and present documentary or other physical evidence, which is then entered into the record. After plaintiff's attorney examines each witness, defendant's attorney has the opportunity to cross-examine that witness.
Motion for judgment as a matter of law	After plaintiff's case-in-chief, the defendant will often move that the case be dismissed because the evidence presented was insufficient to prove the plaintiff's case. Such a motion is usually made orally and is often ruled upon quickly. In federal courts, such a motion is called a "motion for judgment as a matter of law." However, in state courts, the same motion is often called a "motion for directed verdict" in jury trials, or a "motion to dismiss" in bench trials.
Defendant's case-in-chief	Next, the defendant puts on his case-in-chief by producing witnesses and evidence to respond to the plaintiff's case and to establish any affirmative defenses or counterclaims. Like the process in the plaintiff's case-in-chief, each witness is questioned by the defense attorney and may be cross-examined by plaintiff's counsel.
Rebuttal and sur-rebuttal	At the end of the defendant's evidence, the plaintiff may put on rebuttal witnesses or evidence to refute the evidence presented by the defendant. The defendant then has the opportunity for a sur-rebuttal, essentially a rebuttal to the rebuttal.
Motion for judgment as a matter of law	After defendant's case has been presented, the plaintiff has the opportunity to move for judgment on the ground that plaintiff's case has been proved and the defendant has failed to undermine that case or prove a defense. This motion must be made before the case goes to the jury.
Closing arguments	During closing arguments, also called summation, each attorney recaps the evidence and organizes it for the jury, explaining why the evidence supports a verdict favorable to that attorney's client. Counsel's closing argument must be consistent with the jury instructions that the court will give (see below). Usually, the plaintiff's counsel will present closing argument first, and the defendant will follow. The plaintiff may follow with a short rebuttal.
Jury instructions	After closing arguments, and if the case is being heard by a jury, the judge will instruct the jury regarding the law that the jury will follow to reach a decision. The instructions that will be read to the jury are often the subject of argument, and counsel may have previously submitted arguments to the court about the precise language that should be read to the jury.

Chart continues on the next page

Table 3-C • Typical stages of a civil trial, *continued*

Stage	Explanation
Verdict	After instructions are read, the jury will deliberate and return a verdict. A jury may return a "general" or "special" verdict. A general verdict simply states which side wins. A special verdict lists the jury's findings with respect to each factual issue or with respect to selected issues. In a bench trial, instead of a verdict, the judge will prepare an order with findings of fact and conclusions of law. Usually, attorneys from each side will submit proposed findings of fact and conclusions of law, and the judge will draft a final order based on those submissions.
Entry of judgment	To conclude a trial, the court must enter a judgment into the court's records. The judgment is a document that is separate from either the jury's verdict or the judge's findings of fact and conclusions of law.

C. Post-Trial

After the trial, verdict, and entry of judgment, the losing party may seek relief from the decision by filing one of the motions described in Table 3-D.

Table 3-D • Typical civil post-trial motions

Type of Motion	Explanation
Motion for judgment as a matter of law	Within 28 days after a judgment has been entered, a party can move for a judgment as a matter of law. Such a motion is permitted only if the party has also made a motion for a judgment as a matter of law at the close of all of the evidence. Fed. R. Civ. P. 50(b).
Motion for a new trial	Within 28 days after a judgment has been entered, a party may move for a new trial. Fed. R. Civ. P. 59.
Motion to alter or amend judgment	If an attorney believes that the court's judgment needs to be corrected in some way, the attorney can, within 28 days of the entry of judgment, file a motion explaining why that correction is warranted. Fed. R. Civ. P. 59(e).
Motion to set aside judgment	A motion to set aside the judgment asks the court to relieve a party from a final judgment on the ground that it would be unjust or unnecessary for the court to carry out its judgment. A party might argue that fraud, mistake, or newly discovered evidence would make it unjust for the court to exercise its authority. Fed. R. Civ. P. 60(b).
Motion for attorneys' fees	While parties typically pay their own litigation costs, sometimes the winning party may move to recoup attorneys' fees. Attorneys' fees can be awarded by statute, contract, or as a matter of public policy, depending upon the jurisdiction.

D. Appeals

After judgment is entered at the trial level, the losing party has the opportunity to appeal. The appellate process is described briefly in Table 3-E.[3] Chapter 5, *Appellate Practice*, describes the world of appeals in more detail.

Table 3-E • Appellate process

Terminology	Explanation
Appeal as of right	After a final judgment is entered, the losing party is generally entitled "as of right" to have an intermediate appellate court review the decision of the lower court. In an appeal as of right, the intermediate court cannot refuse to hear the case.
Notice of appeal	A notice of appeal must be filed within 30 days of entry of judgment. Fed. R. App. P. 4(a)(1)(A). As its name suggests, a notice of appeal notifies the parties and the courts of the party's intention to appeal.
Forwarding the record	After filing a notice of appeal, the party appealing the decision must order from the court reporter a copy of those portions of the trial transcript that will be relevant to the appeal. That record will then be forwarded to the appellate court. Fed. R. App. P. 10(b), 11(b).
Submission of briefs	The party filing the appeal must file his opening brief within 40 days after the record is filed. The party responding to the appeal has an additional 30 days to file its brief in response. The party appealing then has another 14 days to file a reply brief. Fed. R. App. P. 31.
Oral argument	In many cases, the appellate court allows the attorneys to present oral arguments related to the issues on appeal. During the arguments, the judges may interrupt and ask questions about various points of law or fact.
Opinion	A court issues an opinion to announce its decision in the case and to explain its reasoning regarding the legal issues raised on appeal. When an opinion is published, it both resolves that particular controversy and gives guidance to other potential litigants who have similar issues.

Chart continues on the next page

---

3. Table 3-E assumes an intermediate appellate court. Although most jurisdictions in the United States have an intermediate appellate court, the following states either lack an intermediate court or have an atypical structure for their intermediate courts: Delaware, Maine, Montana, New Hampshire, Rhode Island, North Dakota, South Dakota, Vermont, West Virginia, and Wyoming.

Table 3-E • Appellate process, *continued*

Terminology	Explanation
Disposition	A "disposition" is the appellate court's final determination of the matter. Typical dispositions are listed below. Sometimes an appellate court will have different dispositions for the different legal issues raised on appeal, or will combine dispositions, for example, by reversing and remanding the decision of the lower court.
Affirm	The appellate court agrees with the trial court's decision.
Reverse	The appellate court disagrees with the trial court's decision and overturns it.
Remand	The appellate court sends the case back to the trial court with instructions for further action.
Vacate	The appellate court makes the trial court's decision legally void.
Writ of certiorari	To have a decision heard by the highest appellate court, the parties must, in most cases, file a petition for a writ of certiorari to provide reasons why the court should exercise its discretion and review the case.

III. Criminal Litigation

Whereas a civil case begins with a dispute between two private parties, a criminal case begins when the government suspects an individual or organization has engaged or is about to engage in some criminal activity. A police officer may actually see a crime take place, or the police may learn about possible criminal activity. Two steps then follow: an investigation and an arrest. Depending on the circumstances, the investigation may precede the arrest; however, under some circumstances, a person is first arrested and then police investigate the alleged crime to support the prosecution of the arrestee.

During an investigation, officers may question witnesses, ask a witness to identify the suspect in a line-up, or obtain a search warrant to search a particular location for evidence. Prosecutors may also be involved in an investigation by, for example, issuing a subpoena for documents.

An officer will arrest a suspect when the officer or a prosecutor believes the evidence provides "probable cause" to believe that the suspect has committed a crime.[4]

A. Pre-Trial

After the arrest, the state begins its formal prosecution. Table 3-F describes the typical pre-trial proceedings in a criminal case.

---

4. The tables below draw heavily from the work of Wayne R. LaFave, Jerold H. Israel, Nancy J. King & Olin S. Kerr, *Criminal Procedure* (5th ed. 2009), and from

Table 3-F · Typical criminal pre-trial stages

Stage	Explanation
Complaint	After the defendant is arrested, the prosecutor reviews the case to decide whether to file charges and, if so, what charges to file. If the prosecutor decides to prosecute the case, he will prepare a complaint. The complaint describes the crime allegedly committed and the basic facts that, if proved, would establish the crime. The complaint must be filed with the court within 24 to 48 hours after the arrest. Once the complaint is filed, the arrestee becomes a criminal defendant.
Initial appearance	After the complaint is filed, the defendant is brought before a judge for an initial appearance. This appearance must also occur within 24 to 48 hours after the defendant is arrested. During the initial appearance, the defendant is formally notified of the charges contained in the complaint. If the suspect was arrested without an arrest warrant, the court will also determine whether the officer had probable cause to arrest the suspect. If the officer did not have probable cause to arrest the defendant, the complaint is dismissed. If probable cause did exist, the judge will determine whether the defendant will continue to be held in custody. The judge may temporarily release the defendant based on the defendant's promise to return for future proceedings—that is, released "on her own recognizance." Alternatively, the judge may set bail or other conditions of release, such as a curfew, travel restrictions, or wearing a monitoring device, or the defendant may be held in jail until the next proceeding.
Information or indictment	The next step in the criminal process takes place within two or three weeks after the initial appearance; however, this step differs depending on whether the jurisdiction is an "information jurisdiction" or an "indictment jurisdiction." The majority of jurisdictions are information jurisdictions. In an information jurisdiction, the next step in a criminal case is a "preliminary hearing." The purpose of this preliminary hearing is to review whether probable cause exists to proceed with the case. If a judge determines that probable cause supports each of the allegations in the complaint, the prosecutor files the "information" with the trial court that states the charges against the defendant and the essential facts establishing those charges. A minority of jurisdictions are indictment jurisdictions. In an indictment jurisdiction the grand jury determines whether sufficient probable cause exists for the case to continue. When the grand jury hears the evidence, the grand jury will hear only from the prosecutor. Neither the defendant nor defendant's counsel will be present. If the grand jury determines sufficient evidence exists, the grand jury (through the prosecutor) will issue an indictment, which sets forth the charges against the defendant and the related facts. Each charge and the related facts are listed as one "count." At this point, the information or the indictment replaces the complaint as the official "charging" or "accusatory" instrument in the case.

Chart continues on the next page

Harry I. Subin, Chester L Mirsky & Ian S. Weinstein, *Federal Criminal Practice: Prosecution and Defense* (1992).

Table 3-F · **Typical criminal pre-trial stages**, *continued*

Stage	Explanation
Arraignment	After an information or indictment is filed, the defendant is arraigned. At an arraignment, the defendant is informed of the charges against her. The defendant can plead "guilty," "not guilty," or if permitted in the jurisdiction, "*nolo contendere*," which means "no contest." The judge then sets a date for trial or for sentencing, depending on the plea.
Motions to dismiss	Like the defendant in a civil case, the criminal defendant may move to dismiss the case. A criminal defendant may move to dismiss a case because the information or indictment fails to allege an essential element; because critical evidence should be suppressed, Fed. R. Crim. P. 8, 14; because the prosecution is constitutionally barred, for example, because of double jeopardy or violation of speedy trial requirements, *id.*; or because of some other affirmative defenses such as self-defense, insanity, or a statute of limitations.
Discovery	The discovery rules in most jurisdictions require more disclosure by the government than by the defense. In those jurisdictions that require the government to disclose certain information, the government usually must disclose defendant's oral statements; defendant's written or recorded statements; defendant's prior record; documents and objects that the government plans to rely on at trial or that would be material to a defense; reports of examinations or tests that would be material to the defense; and any summary of expert testimony the government intends to introduce. Fed. R. Crim. P. 16(a). The defendant, however, need only disclose documents, objects, reports, and expert testimony that the defendant intends to use at trial. Fed. R. Crim. P. 16(b). In some states, however, the government is not required to disclose any documents. Rather, the defense must show why requested materials should be made available.
Motions to suppress	Motions to suppress are requests that certain materials be excluded from the trial. If a motion to suppress is granted, counsel and witnesses are prohibited from referring to that material during the trial.

B. Trial

The time span from arrest to the start of a felony trial usually falls within five to eight months.[5] However, just as most civil cases settle before making it to court, most criminal cases end in settlement—that is, a plea agreement. "Most defendants—more than 90%—plead guilty

---

5. LaFave, *supra* note 4, at 15.

rather than go to trial."[6] If a criminal case does go to trial, that case will most likely conclude in two to three days[7] and result in a conviction.[8] The stages of that trial are described in Table 3-G.

Table 3-G · Typical stages of a criminal trial

Stage	Explanation
Jury selection	A defendant facing more than six months of incarceration always has a right to a jury trial; however, a criminal defendant may waive that right and have the case tried by a judge instead of a jury. Fed. R. Crim. P. 23(a). When a criminal case is to be heard by a jury, the trial begins (as it does in a civil case) by selecting the jury from a pool of potential jurors. This process is called "voir dire." During voir dire, the judge or the attorneys talk with potential jurors about any pre-existing beliefs or experiences that may affect the juror's perception of the case. A juror can be dismissed "for cause" when the voir dire establishes the juror cannot be impartial or will be unable to attend the trial. There is no limit to the number of jurors who can be dismissed for cause. An attorney can also use one of a limited number of "peremptory" challenges or strikes to exclude a person from the panel without providing a reason for the exclusion.
Opening statement	The prosecutor opens the trial by making an opening statement. In the opening statement, the prosecutor will identify the charges being brought against the defendant and describe the evidence the government will introduce to prove the charges. The defendant's attorney may present an opening statement or not. In addition, the defense is often given the choice as to whether to follow the prosecutor's opening statement with its own or whether to wait until the beginning of its case.
Government's case-in-chief	Like the plaintiff in a civil action, the government has the burden of proof so the government's case is presented first. The prosecutor presents evidence witness-by-witness. Each witness's testimony is recorded. Witnesses also can identify and present documentary or other physical evidence, which is then entered into the record. Each witness is examined by the prosecutor and, usually, cross-examined by the defendant's attorney. The government may then conduct a redirect examination of the same witness. The government may never call the defendant to the witness stand in its case-in-chief.

Chart continues on the next page

---

6. *How the Federal Courts Work: Criminal Cases*, U.S. Courts, http://www.uscourts.gov/FederalCourts/UnderstandingtheFederalCourts/HowCourtsWork/CriminalCases.aspx; *see also* LaFave, *supra* note 4, at 15 ("The ratio of guilty pleas to trials quite often will be 12 to 1 or higher.").

7. LaFave, *supra* note 4, at 16.

8. There are approximately three convictions for every one acquittal. *Id.*

Table 3-G · Typical stages of a criminal trial, *continued*

Stage	Explanation
Motion for judgment of acquittal	After the government's case-in-chief, the defendant will often move for the case to be dismissed because the evidence presented was insufficient to prove the government's case beyond a reasonable doubt. Such a motion is usually made orally and is often ruled upon quickly.
Defendant's case-in-chief	In a criminal trial, a defendant need not present any evidence on the theory that the government has failed to meet its burden of proof. If a defendant chooses to present a case-in-chief, the defendant will also produce witnesses and evidence to establish an alternative narrative or present an affirmative defense. The defense attorney will examine each witness. The government will have the opportunity to cross-examine the witness. Then, finally, the defense attorney may choose to conduct a redirect examination.
Rebuttal	If the defendant has presented evidence, the government may put on rebuttal witnesses or evidence to refute the evidence presented by the defendant.
Closing arguments	During closing arguments, the attorneys recap their version of events and organize the evidence for the jury, explaining why the evidence supports a particular verdict. The arguments must be consistent with the jury instructions that the court gives (see below). The government will present its closing argument first, and the defendant will follow. The government may follow with a short rebuttal.
Jury instructions	The judge will instruct the jury regarding the law that the jury will follow to reach a decision. Usually, instructions are given after closing arguments. The instructions that will be read to the jury are often the subject of argument, and counsel may have previously submitted to the court the precise language that should be read to the jury.
Verdict	After instructions are read, the jury will deliberate and return a verdict. A jury may return a "general" or "special" verdict. A general verdict simply states which side wins. A special verdict lists the jury's findings with respect to selected issues. In federal courts, and in every state except Louisiana and Oregon, a jury verdict in a criminal case must be unanimous.

C. Post-Trial

If a jury finds a defendant guilty, that verdict is often followed by post-trial motions. If, after those motions, the guilty verdict stands, the court will sentence the defendant and enter judgment.

1. Motions

Common post-trial motions in a criminal case include those set forth in Table 3-H.

Table 3-H · Common post-trial motions in criminal cases

Post-verdict proceeding	Explanation
Motion for judgment of acquittal	A defendant may move for a judgment of acquittal (or renew such a motion) within 14 days after a guilty verdict or after the jury has been discharged. Fed. R. Crim. P. 29.
Motion to stay sentence	A defendant may ask the court to stay a sentence while the defendant appeals the judgment. Fed. R. Crim. P. 38.
Motion for a new trial	A motion for a new trial is usually filed when new evidence is discovered that may exonerate the client, or the attorney has discovered some procedural error or misconduct that casts doubt on the verdict. Fed. R. Crim. P. 33. In some states, before filing an appeal, the party that lost must make a motion for a new trial.

2. Sentencing

After a guilty plea, a plea of no contest, or a guilty verdict has been entered, the defendant will be sentenced. Sentencing procedures vary at the state and federal levels. However, in most states and at the federal level, the judge determines the sentence for a convicted defendant.[9]

Before sentencing the defendant, judges will often consider facts that did not or were not allowed to come to light at trial, such as a defendant's prior criminal record, family relationships, health, and work record.[10]

Some states and the federal courts have sentencing guidelines that guide judges when they impose a sentence. The guidelines are intended to help judges impose proportionate sentences and to foster uniform sentencing.[11]

---

9. *See* LaFave, *supra* note 4, at 16. The major exception is death penalty cases. In death penalty cases, a jury determines whether to give the death penalty sentence to a convicted defendant.

10. So that a judge can determine an appropriate sentence, a probation officer usually submits a presentencing report that includes biographical information about the defendant, major information about his or her living situation, and relevant legal information about the crimes he or she is accused of committing. After addressing any objections, the report is then submitted to the court for consideration as a part of the sentencing. *See* Fed. R. Crim. P. 32(e)-(f); Fed. R. Crim. P. 32(d); *see also* LaFave, *supra* note 15, at 16 (describing the role of a presentence report and the parties' ability to present additional information or challenge information in a report).

11. LaFave, *supra* note 4, at 16.

In jurisdictions where the sentencing judge's discretion is limited by sentencing guidelines, a judge is also usually required to make findings of fact regarding those factors that led to the sentence.[12]

3. Entry of judgment

Finally, the court must enter judgment. The judgment must state the plea or jury verdict and, if the defendant is found guilty, the final sentence imposed.[13] Once the judgment has been entered, the trial concludes.

D. Appeals and Other Post-Conviction Remedies

In criminal cases, usually only the defendant has a right to appeal.[14] The government's ability to appeal is limited by double-jeopardy, the constitutional prohibition against a defendant being tried twice for the same crime. When a defendant does appeal, the conviction will usually be affirmed. Convictions are affirmed 90 to 95 percent of the time.[15]

Criminal appeals generally proceed in the same way that civil appeals proceed. That is, the defendant appeals to an appellate court and asks the appellate court to review the record below for some error. Because a criminal appeal generally follows the same process as a civil appeal, you can review Table 3-E, Appellate Process, for an overview of the criminal appellate process. The one difference between a criminal appeal and a civil appeal is that, in a criminal appeal, the defendant must file a notice of appeal within 14 days of entry of judgment.[16] By contrast, the civil appellant has 30 days to file a notice of appeal.[17]

In addition to filing a traditional appeal, sometimes called a "direct appeal," defendants can challenge the legality of their conviction or sentence in ways that are unavailable to the civil litigant. Defendants convicted in state courts can seek review of their conviction or sentence under that state's post-conviction review proceedings. If that fails, the defendant may then file a petition for a writ of habeas corpus in federal court. Defendants convicted in a federal court can seek review of their conviction by filing a petition for a writ of habeas corpus in federal court.

---

12. *See id.*

13. Fed. R. Crim. P. 32(k). In the case of a bench trial, the judgment will state the court's finding of facts and its adjudication. *Id.*

14. *Id.* Some states do allow the state to appeal in limited circumstances, most frequently to clarify aspects of the law. Because of double jeopardy (the federal constitutional prohibition against being tried twice for the same crime), if the state can appeal, it usually must appeal before the trial and not after the verdict.

15. LaFave, *supra* note 4, at 17.

16. Fed. R. App. P. 4(b)(1)(A).

17. Fed. R. App. P. 4(a)(1)(A).

These procedures are called "collateral remedies." "Collateral" means "[b]y the side" or "[n]ot lineal,"[18] and these attacks on the conviction are all by means other than direct appeals. These processes are briefly explained in Table 3-I.

Table 3-I · Additional post-conviction (collateral) remedies

Terminology	Explanation
State post-conviction review	A defendant convicted in state court may challenge his conviction or sentence (or both) in state court on the ground that it violates the state or federal constitutions. How a defendant seeks post-conviction review in state court varies from state to state. In some states, the defendant files a motion or application in the court in which he was convicted. In other states, the defendant files a separate petition for post-conviction review, initiating a new civil action. If a defendant loses a post-conviction review at the trial level, the defendant may then appeal the trial court's decision through the normal appeals process.
Federal writ of habeas corpus	A defendant convicted in federal court who has exhausted his appeals has a collateral remedy in federal court. The defendant can file a petition for a writ of habeas corpus in a federal district court, asserting that his conviction or sentence violates the United States Constitution. 22 U.S.C. §§ 2241-2255 (2012). Again, if a defendant loses at the district court level, the defendant may appeal the decision through the normal appeals process. In addition, a state court defendant who has exhausted all his state court remedies can then file a petition for a writ of habeas corpus in federal court. In essence, state-court defendants get two chances (in addition to direct appeal) to challenge their convictions and sentences; federal court defendants get only one.

Now that you have an overview of the litigation process, you can turn to your client's case and consider the document that needs to be drafted. The next two chapters, Chapter 4, *Motion Practice*, and Chapter 5, *Appellate Practice*, explain the documents that lawyers use to persuade a court to act—the motion and the appellate brief.

---

18. Black's Law Dictionary 317-18 (10th ed. 2014).

Chapter 4

Motion Practice

I. A Trial Motion and Its Parts
   A. The Motion
   B. The Supporting Memorandum of Law
   C. Factual Support

II. The Rules that Govern Trial Motions
   A. Procedural Rules
   B. Local Rules
   C. Standing Orders
   D. Finding the Rules
   E. Following the Rules
   F. Unwritten Rules

III. After the Motion Is Drafted
   A. Service and Its Proof
   B. Filing with the Court
   C. The Opposing Party's Response
      1. Statement of non-opposition
      2. Consent order
      3. Memorandum of law in opposition
   D. The Moving Party's Reply Memorandum

The last chapters have provided background information about the nature of persuasion, the ethics and professional responsibilities of a litigator, and the litigation process. The purpose of this chapter is, first, to introduce the trial motion. Whenever you begin a writing project, you should have a clear idea of what you will be producing. Thus, this chapter begins by showing you a typical motion and its parts. It also explains the rules that will govern your motion so that you can determine what a motion in your jurisdiction should look like. In addition, this chapter provides you with background about what happens after a motion is drafted, that is, how it is served, how it is filed, and how it is responded to. Although this book focuses on developing the written product, understanding what happens to that written product after it is written often provides useful context for the writing project. This chapter provides that background.

I. A Trial Motion and Its Parts

To begin, we must clarify what lawyers mean when they use the word "motion." Lawyers use the word "motion" in two very different ways. Technically, the word "motion" refers to a short document (often, only one to two pages) in which the lawyer requests the court to take some action. The one or two page document that makes the request is the motion, and it provides little explanation for why the court should act.

Lawyers also use the word "motion" in a more colloquial way. In this more colloquial usage, the word "motion" refers to not just the request, but all the documents that are submitted along with the request. Those additional documents include, most typically, a supporting memorandum of law and supporting evidence.[1]

Because lawyers use the word "motion" in two different ways — to refer to the motion itself and to refer to the motion and all the accompanying documents — be attentive to the word "motion." If you are ever uncertain about the way in which the lawyer is using the word, just ask.

A. The Motion

As explained above, a motion is a request that a court act. The request can be anything that the court has in its power to order. For example, a motion can request the mundane, such as an order to reschedule a hearing or an order to permit additional pages. Other motions go to the heart of a dispute. For example, a motion can request that a complaint be dismissed, that certain evidence be suppressed, or that a jury's decision be overruled.

Most motions are written. Sometimes, however, events during a trial may prompt a lawyer to make a motion orally. This chapter addresses written motions only.

Written motions have typical parts: (1) a caption, (2) a statement of the relief the party seeks, (3) a brief statement of the grounds for that request, and (4) the attorney's signature. Examples 4-A and 4-B show two different motions and their constituent parts.

"Motion" is not a verb

A party *never* "motions" for summary judgment. A party "moves" for summary judgment. Similarly, a party does not "motion" the court to dismiss plaintiff's complaint; a party "moves" the court to dismiss the complaint.

---

1. When a lawyer files a motion with a court, the motion may also include a notice of motion, a draft order, and proof of service. To keep things simple, we have focused on the primary parts of an ordinary motion: the motion, the supporting memorandum of law, and supporting evidence.

Example 4-A • A motion to suppress

IN THE CIRCUIT COURT OF THE STATE OF OREGON
FOR LANE COUNTY

THE STATE OF OREGON,   )
)   Case No. 21-15-18156
              Plaintiff,   )
)   DEFENDANT'S MOTION TO   ⎤ Caption
vs.   )   SUPPRESS EVIDENCE
)
TRAVIS Z. TREATSKY,   )
)
              Defendant.   )
_____)

The defendant, through his attorney, Jordan R. Silk, moves this Court for the following orders:

> This paragraph is a typical lead-in to a motion's actual request.

1. An order suppressing any and all evidence of the field sobriety tests performed by the defendant on May 21, 2015, and

> The statement of the relief defendant seeks.

2. An order suppressing all evidence of the breath test performed by the defendant on May 22, 2015.

This motion is based on the attached memorandum of law and is, in the opinion of counsel, well-founded in law and not made or filed for the purpose of delay.

> The motion cross-references the memorandum of law, which explains the grounds for relief. That memorandum is provided at Example 4-C.

DATED this _____ day of November, 2015.

> The lawyer's signature

_____
Jordan R. Silk
OSB # 105031
Lane County Public Defender's Office
555 Willamette Street
Eugene, OR 97401
Appearing for Defendant

Example 4-B · A motion to dismiss

**United States District Court
For the District of Utah**

KATELYN MASON and	:	Civil Action No. 14 CV 921
JENNIFER WELCH, individually	:	
and on behalf of those	:	
similarly situated,	:	DEFENDANT'S MOTION TO
	:	DISMISS PLAINTIFF
	:	WELCH'S COMPLAINT
Plaintiffs,	:	
	:	
v.	:	
	:	
CENTRAL STATE UNIVERSITY	:	
OF UTAH,	:	
	:	
Defendant.	:	MAY 5, 2015

The first paragraph of the motion states both the relief it seeks (dismissal of portions of the complaint) and the grounds for that relief (Rule 12(b)(6)).

Pursuant to Federal Rule of Civil Procedure 12(b)(6), defendant Central State University of Utah hereby moves to dismiss that portion of the Complaint that relates to plaintiff Jennifer Welch because plaintiff Welch lacks standing.

The next paragraph briefly elaborates on the grounds, but cross-references a memorandum of law for further explanation.

Specifically, all claims asserted by plaintiff Welch must be dismissed because plaintiff Welch, by her own allegations, did not suffer any present or past injury, and she cannot establish future injury because she is graduating this year. For these reasons, and as explained more fully in the attached memorandum of law, she lacks standing to bring her Title IX claim.

Therefore, defendant Central State University of Utah respectfully requests that this Court grant its Motion to Dismiss Plaintiff Welch's Complaint.

Hepworth & Peterson LLP

The lawyer's signature

By: _____
Justin Hepworth, Esq.
jhepworth@wiggin.com
Federal Bar No. ut01386
350 Lake Street
Provo, UT 84601
Phone: (203) 363-7512
Fax: (203) 262-7676
Attorney for Defendant

B. The Supporting Memorandum of Law

Motions are often, but not always, accompanied by a supporting memorandum of law. The supporting memorandum of law explains why the motion should be granted. It explains the relevant law and applies that law to the facts of the case.[2]

Different jurisdictions have different names for the supporting memorandum of law. It may be called a "memorandum of law" in support of the motion, or it may be called a "brief," "a memorandum of points and authorities," or something else entirely. Whatever the name, the supporting memorandum of law is where the court will find all your persuasive arguments.

Although many motions are accompanied by a supporting memorandum, other motions are not. Some requests to a court are so straightforward that no accompanying memorandum is necessary. For example, a motion asking the court to reschedule a hearing would likely not need to be supported by a memorandum because the motion itself would simply explain the conflict and request the change. There would be no need to provide the court with a legal analysis justifying the scheduling change. Other requests are less straightforward and require further explanation. For example, a motion that asks the court to dismiss a case or suppress evidence needs an explanatory memorandum to explain why the requested relief should be granted.

When a memorandum of law accompanies a motion, the memorandum usually has these parts: (1) a caption, (2) an introduction or preliminary statement, (3) the statement of facts, (4) the argument, (5) the conclusion, and (6) the lawyer's signature. Example 4-C provides an example of a full memorandum of law and identifies each of those parts.

---

2. In some jurisdictions, the legal argument explaining why the motion should be granted is presented in the same document as the motion. For simplicity, this book assumes that the request asking the court to act is one document called a "motion" and the legal argument supporting that request is in a separate document called a "memorandum of law."

Example 4-C · A memorandum of law in support of a motion to suppress

IN THE CIRCUIT COURT OF THE STATE OF OREGON
FOR LANE COUNTY

The caption identifies the court to which the motion is submitted, the parties to the litigation, the docket number, and the title of the document.

THE STATE OF OREGON,	)	
	)	Case No. 21-16-18156
Plaintiff,	)	
	)	
vs.	)	MEMORANDUM OF LAW IN
	)	SUPPORT OF DEFENDANT'S
TRAVIS Z. TREATSKY,	)	MOTION
	)	
Defendant.	)	
_____	)	

INTRODUCTION

The introduction to a supporting memorandum provides context for the arguments that follow by explaining the nature of the case and its procedural history. It may also provide a short summary of the arguments that follow.

On May 21-22, 2015, the state violated Article I, Section 9 of the Oregon Constitution when Trooper Evan Sether administered field sobriety tests and then a breath test to defendant Travis Treatsky. Trooper Evan Sether did not obtain warrants to administer those tests. With respect to the field sobriety test, Trooper Sether lacked probable cause to administer the test, and Mr. Treatsky did not voluntarily consent to field sobriety tests. Because the state obtained evidence from the tests in violation of Article I, Section 9 of the Oregon Constitution, all evidence resulting from the field sobriety tests — including results from the breath test — should be suppressed.

FACTUAL BACKGROUND

The statement of facts explains all the facts relevant to the motion and the arguments supporting the motion.

On the evening of May 21, 2015, Mr. Travis Treatsky was driving westbound on Highway 126 after a long day of travel and visiting with family. Earlier that day, Mr. Treatsky had driven from northern California where he attends the College of the Siskiyous to his home in Springfield, Oregon. After the long drive home, Mr. Treatsky visited with his mother and sister, and then drove to visit his stepfather. (Aff. Jordan Silk ¶ 3, Nov. 11, 2015.) Returning home from his stepfather's house, Trooper Sether stopped Mr. Treatsky because the lens on one of Mr. Treatsky's taillights was broken. Trooper Sether observed Mr. Treatsky's fatigued demeanor and concluded that Mr. Treatsky was under the influence of an intoxicant. (Police Rep. of Trooper Sether 1-2, May 22, 2015.)

Trooper Sether asked Mr. Treatsky to perform two separate field sobriety tests. Trooper Sether read to Mr. Treatsky his rights with respect to taking a field sobriety test, and Trooper Sether explained the consequences if Mr. Treatsky failed to take the field sobriety. Those consequences included immediate seizure and then a likely suspension of his driver's license.

Mr. Treatsky then took the field sobriety tests. According to Trooper Sether, Mr. Treatsky failed both field sobriety tests. (Police Rep. Sether 2.)

Trooper Sether then placed Mr. Treatsky under arrest, took him to the police station, and administered a breath test yielding a result of 0.08% BAC. (Police Rep. Sether 2).

ARGUMENT

The evidence in this case was illegally seized and must, therefore, be suppressed. Article I, Section 9 protects individuals from unreasonable searches and seizures by the state. Under that section, when the state searches an individual without a warrant, such "searches and seizures are *per se* unreasonable unless the state proves an exception to the warrant requirement." *State v. Bridewell*, 759 P.2d 1054, 1057 (Or. 1988). To show an exception to the warrant requirement, the state generally must show either that probable cause and exigent circumstances justified the search or that the individual voluntarily consented to the search. *See id.*; *State v. Nagel*, 880 P.2d 451, 456 (Or. 1994). In this case, Trooper Sether did not obtain a warrant to administer any of the tests. Thus, for each test, the state must show either that probable cause and exigent circumstances justified the search or that the defendant consented to the search. The State cannot meet that test. Thus, the field sobriety tests and the evidence from them were unlawfully seized, and that evidence must be suppressed.

The argument section is the heart of the supporting memorandum. It explains all the reasons the court should order the relief you seek.

A. Trooper Sether administered field sobriety tests in violation of Article I, Section 9 of the Oregon Constitution.

Because the field sobriety tests were administered in violation of Article 1, Section 9 of the Oregon Constitution, evidence from those tests should be suppressed.

1. Trooper Sether lacked probable cause to administer field sobriety tests.

First, Trooper Sether lacked probable cause to administer the two field sobriety tests. A field sobriety test is a search and seizure within the scope of Article I, Section 9. *Nagel*, 880 P.2d at 456. To lawfully administer such a test without a warrant, the officer must have probable cause to believe that the person is under the influence of an intoxicant. *Id.*; *State v. Stroup*, 935 P.2d 438, 440 (Or. App. 1997). An officer has probable cause when the "officer subjectively believes that a crime has been committed and evidence of the crime can be procured by the seizure of the person or the thing"; however, "the officer's belief must be objectively reasonable under the circumstances." *Stroup*, 935 P.2d at 456 (citing *State v. Owens*, 729 P.2d 524, 529 (Or. 1986)). In *Stroup*, the court held the officer did not have probable cause to administer field sobriety tests because the only evidence was "a slight odor of alcohol, bloodshot eyes, and an admission of drinking alcoholic beverages." *Id.* at 441-42. In ruling that the officer lacked probable cause to administer the field sobriety test, the court emphasized that the defendant was initially stopped for an equipment violation, not for unsafe driving. *Id.* at 440.

The defendant's attorney uses an analogical argument to support his argument that the officer lacked probable cause to support the administration of a field sobriety test.

Here, Trooper Sether had even less evidence supporting probable cause than did the officer in *Stroup*. In *Stroup,* the officer pointed to an alcoholic odor and bloodshot eyes to establish probable cause. Trooper Sether's only evidence was the defendant's general weariness. (Sether's Report, p 1). And, in both cases, the defendants were stopped for an equipment violation, not for unsafe driving. Thus, Trooper Sether believed he had probable cause based on far less evidence than was present in *Stroup*, where the Court of Appeals found no probable cause to administer field sobriety tests. Accordingly, Trooper Sether's belief was not objectively reasonable, and absent consent from Mr. Treatsky, the State obtained Mr. Treatsky's field sobriety tests in violation of Article I, Section 9 of the Oregon Constitution.

2. Mr. Treatsky did not voluntarily consent to perform field sobriety tests.

In addition to not having probable cause to administer the field sobriety tests, Trooper Sether also never obtained Mr. Treatsky's voluntary consent. In determining the voluntariness of consent to a warrantless search "the test is whether, under the totality of the circumstances, the defendant's consent was an act of free will *or, instead, resulted from police coercion, either express or implied.*" *State v. Hall*, 115 P.3d 908, 918 (Or. 2005) (emphasis added).

Police coercion includes informing a person of economic harm and loss of privileges that will result if the person refuses a request to take a test. In *State v. Machuca*, a police officer suspected the defendant of drunk driving and requested the defendant take a blood test. 218 P.3d 145, 147 (Or. App. 2009), *overruled on other grounds*, 227 P.3d 729 (Or. 2010). Before the defendant gave his consent, the police officer read to the defendant the "rights and consequences" of refusing consent. *Id.* The consequences included seizing defendant's driver's license and likely suspension of the defendant's right to drive. *Id.* The defendant then consented to the blood test. *Id.*; Or. Rev. Stat. §813.130(2). Before trial, the defendant moved to suppress the evidence from his blood test. *Machuca*, 218 P.3d at 148. Upon review, the Oregon Court of Appeals held that consent to the blood test was not effective because the consent was obtained "through a threat of economic harm and loss of privileges." *Id.* at 150. Such consent, the court held, "is coerced by the fear of adverse consequences and is ineffective to excuse the requirement to obtain a search warrant." *Id.*

The defendant's attorney uses another analogical argument, this time to support his argument that the defendant did not consent to field sobriety tests.

Here, too, Mr. Treatsky's consent was not voluntary. Just like the officer in *Machuca*, the officer in this case read to the defendant the "rights and consequences" of refusing consent. In this case, as in the *Machuca* case, those rights and consequences included the seizure of his driver's license and the likely suspension of his right to drive. Thus, Mr. Treatsky's consent, like the defendant's consent in *Machuca*, was "coerced by the fear of adverse consequences and is ineffective to excuse the requirement to obtain a search warrant."

Because Trooper Sether lacked probable cause to administer field sobriety tests and Mr. Treatsky did not voluntarily consent to the tests, evidence of the tests should be suppressed.

B. If the Court concludes Trooper Sether lacked probable cause, all evidence obtained as a result of the illegal search must be suppressed.

The results of the breath test must also be suppressed. Oregon employs an exclusionary rule that prevents the state from offering evidence obtained as a result of illegal police conduct. *Hall*, 115 P.3d at 920. "[T]he critical inquiry is whether the state obtained the evidence sought to be suppressed as a result of a violation of the defendant's rights under Article I, section 9." *Id.* If so, evidence from the illegal search and seizure must be suppressed. *See id.*

Here, the illegal search produced evidence that resulted in unconstitutionally obtained evidence. Had Trooper Sether not administered illegal field sobriety tests, he would not have arrested Mr. Treatsky and taken him to the police station, and the breath test would not have taken place. Because Trooper Sether lacked probable cause and voluntary consent to perform field sobriety tests, the breath test and its results were obtained in violation of Article I, Section 9. The Court should therefore suppress all evidence that was obtained as a result of any search conducted in violation of Article I, Section 9.

CONCLUSION

Because evidence of Mr. Treatsky's performance of field sobriety tests and from the breath test were obtained in violation of Article I, Section 9 of the Oregon Constitution, this Court should suppress all such evidence.

The conclusion is a short statement of the relief you seek.

DATED this _____ day of November, 2015.

_____
Jordan R. Silk
OSB # 105031
Appearing for Defendant

The lawyer's signature

CERTIFICATE OF SERVICE

I, Jordan R. Silk, hereby certify that on this _____ day of November, 2015, I had served a true and correct copy of the foregoing Memorandum of Law in Support of Defendant's Motion upon Aileen Santoyo, # 127355, Assistant District Attorney, at the following address

ADA Aileen Santoyo
Lane County District Attorney's Office
125 East 8th Avenue
Eugene, Oregon 97401

Jordan B. Silk
OSB # 105031
Attorney for Travis B. Treatsky

C. Factual Support

Sometimes an argument in the memorandum of law needs to be supported by evidence. For example, if the court must interpret a contract, you will need to attach a copy of the contract to the supporting memorandum. If the court is considering a motion for summary judgment, you may need to attach excerpts from depositions to prove that no material issues of fact exist. Sometimes a party or the lawyer submitting the motion will submit an affidavit as evidence of the facts provided to the court. An affidavit is a sworn statement and, in that way, is treated the same as testimony presented in court.

If you are submitting your motion in hard copy, you will likely staple the supporting evidence to the memorandum of law. You may be able to include a tabbed divider or label it as an appendix to make it easier for the court to find. If you are submitting your document electronically, you should look for instructions about whether the supporting evidence and the memorandum should be combined and uploaded as a single document or whether they should be uploaded separately. Always consult the procedural or local court rules to determine the court's particular requirements regarding how to file supporting documents.

II. The Rules That Govern Trial Motions

Above, we have described what a typical motion looks like in a typical jurisdiction. The truth is that motions (and their supporting documents) vary from jurisdiction to jurisdiction. Some local rules require that a separate memorandum of law be submitted with every motion.[3] If that is the rule, then submit a motion that is separate from the memorandum of law. By contrast, in some jurisdictions a separate memorandum of law is not required; rather, the custom or the rule is to combine the motion and supporting memorandum into one document.

Thus, before drafting a motion familiarize yourself with all the rules and customs that govern the motion you are planning to submit. You will usually look for three different kinds of rules: the jurisdiction's procedural rules, "local" court rules, and "standing orders" of the judge before whom you will be appearing.

A. Procedural Rules

The first set of rules to become familiar with are the jurisdiction's procedural rules that govern trial practice. The federal courts and all state courts have their own rules of procedure. Those rules—the rules of civil procedure and the rules of criminal procedure—govern practices in those jurisdictions.

The procedural rules at the federal and state level provide only the most general guidance with respect to motion drafting. For example, the Federal Rules of Civil and Criminal Procedure require that motions be in writing, unless made during trial; state the grounds for seeking an order; and state the specific relief or order sought.[4]

For a limited number of motions, however, the jurisdiction's procedural rules will provide more detailed guidance. For example, the Federal Rules of Civil Procedure require that, when filing a motion for summary judgment, the motion must prove that no fact is in dispute "by citing to particular parts of the record," such as depositions, answers to interrogatories, affidavits, or other materials in the record.[5] Similarly, if a party seeks an order protecting it from discovery, a motion filed in federal court must also include a statement that the parties attempted, in good faith to resolve the dispute.[6]

---

3. For example, the trial court rules in Oregon state that a motion to suppress evidence in a criminal case must be accompanied by "the moving party's brief, which must sufficiently apprise the court and the adverse party of the arguments and authorities relied upon." Unif. Tr. Ct. R. 4.060(1)(b).

4. Fed. R. Civ. P. 7(b) (requiring that the grounds for the order be stated "with particularity").

5. Fed. R. Civ. P. 56(c)(1).

6. Fed. R. Civ. P. 26(c).

Thus, although the jurisdiction's rules may not ultimately provide significant guidance for the particular motion you are writing, you should always start your research there, just in case they do.

B. Local Rules

Next, you will want to become familiar with the court's local rules. For management purposes, federal and state trial court systems are further divided. For example, the federal trial court system is divided into ninety-four districts, and state trial courts are often divided by county. Each subdivision usually has its own set of rules. These rules are often called "local rules."

Local rules are rules adopted by courts and apply regardless of the particular judge hearing the case.[7] These local rules tend to provide more specific guidance than the procedural rules. Local rules will often dictate details about the content and format of a motion and its accompanying memorandum of law, including the sections that must be included in a memorandum of law, page limits, margin sizes, fonts, and whether a cover sheet must be attached.[8]

C. Standing Orders

In addition to the local rules that are adopted court-wide, individual judges may issue standing orders—ongoing orders that apply to all lawyers who appear before that particular judge. Standing orders can include the same kinds of information that local rules include. In the case of a standing order, however, the rule applies only to those cases before a particular judge. Not all judges have standing orders, and at the time you are submitting a motion, your case may not have been assigned to a particular judge. Thus, a set of standing orders may not govern your motion. If, however, your case has been assigned to a particular judge, you should determine whether that judge has any standing orders relevant to your case.

---

7. The Federal Rules of Civil Procedure explain that, in federal courts, "a district court, acting by a majority of its district judges, may adopt and amend rules governing its practice. A local rule must be consistent with—but not duplicate—federal statutes and rules . . . ." Fed. R. Civ. P. 83.

8. Local rules also often provide a wealth of practical information helpful to an attorney, including the hours that a court is open, where documents are received, how cases are assigned, when motions will be heard, what methods of delivery constitute service, appropriate attire for court, whether cell phones and other electronic devices will be permitted, who must provide playback equipment if a video or other recording is entered into evidence, and much more.

D. Finding the Rules

All of the rules mentioned above are usually available on the website of the court to which you will be submitting your motion. So, go to the court's website first to determine the relevant rules. If you cannot find the rules on the court's website, you can check with the Clerk of Court to determine how to get a copy of the local rules. If your case has been assigned to a particular judge, you can also ask the Clerk of Court if the judge has any standing orders, or you can call the judge's chambers to determine whether the judge has issued any standing orders.

All of these rules—and especially the local rules and standing orders—are subject to change. Whenever submitting a motion, always check to make sure you are relying on the most up-to-date set of rules.

You might want to take a minute right now to find your local court's website to see what they look like. For example, if you searched the Internet for "local rules Southern District of New York," your search will lead you to the home page for the United States District Court for the Southern District of New York, shown in Figure 4-D. To find an example of a standing order, as in Example 4-E, you might search the Internet for "judge standing order."

Figure 4-D · Local rules

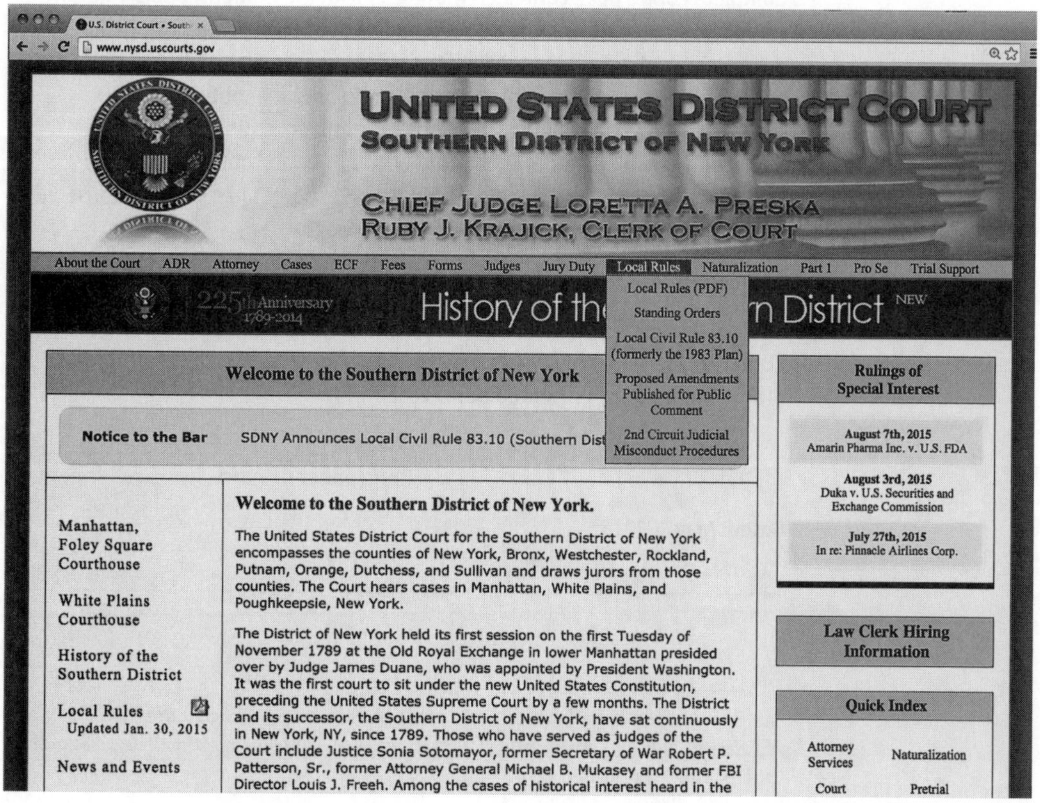

Example 4-E · A standing order[9]

Motion Practice Standing Order
Courtroom 303
Judge Christopher C. Starck

Motion practice

All motions shall be set on Tuesday or Wednesday morning. Uncontested or agreed motions shall be set at 9:00 a.m. Contested motions shall be set at 9:15 a.m.

All motions for default judgment shall be set at 9:15 a.m. with copies of the proof of service attached to the motion.

Prior to noticing a motion for hearing, counsel must contact the courtroom clerk and have the matter placed on the call for the desired date. No motions may be noticed for hearing unless counsel personally contacts the courtroom clerk prior to sending out the notice of motion. Failure to follow this rule will cause the Court to strike the motion from the call.

Contested motions shall not be placed on the call for hearing during the first week of the Court's jury trial call, other than by approval of the Court or due to emergency circumstances. Agreed and routine motions are allowed during the first week of the Court's jury trial call.

Complete copies of all contested motions, including motions, briefs, relevant pleadings, and exhibits must be delivered to the Court at least 7 days before the hearing date. Failure to deliver the motion packet in advance of the hearing date may cause the Court to refuse to hear the motion when presented. Multiple copies of the same pleading or motion should not be tendered to the Court. The parties are encouraged to confer and to send a single packet of the motions and exhibits to the Court in an effort to conserve natural resources.

At times, the Court may require electronic copies of the motions and briefs. Counsel shall produce electronic copies of pleading when requested by the Court.

Court reporters are not provided by the Court for oral arguments at motions, other than motions presented during trial.

Entered:_____
Christopher C. Starck

Dated: May 1, 2015

---

9. Nineteenth Judicial Circuit Court of Lake Cnty. Ill., *Standing Orders of the Nineteenth Judicial Circuit*, http://19thcircuitcourt.state.il.us/resources/Pages/Standing Orders.aspx (last visited Feb. 1, 2015).

E. Following the Rules

Following all the relevant rules is important. In some instances, failing to follow the rules could result in your motion being rejected. If you are filing on a deadline, you may not have time to resubmit. On that basis alone, you could have your motion denied and possibly even lose the case.

While other consequences are less dire, you should still scrupulously follow the rules. First, following the rules will make your arguments easier to absorb. Judges are very busy, and they read many motions and their accompanying legal arguments. They expect the motion and the accompanying argument to look a certain way, to have the sections in a certain order, and to contain all the information required by the rules. To the extent that a motion or memorandum of law does not do those things, the judge has to work harder to follow it and will have less mental energy to devote to the legal argument.

Carefully following the rules also enhances your credibility—that is, your *ethos*—with the court. Following the rules shows the court that you know how to, and make the effort to, find and follow rules. A judge will assume that someone who can find and follow the rules of practice can also find and follow the substantive law. By contrast, if a judge sees that you cannot find and follow the rules of practice, the judge may begin to wonder whether you can find and follow the substantive law. You want the judge to read your motion and memorandum of law with complete confidence that what follows was written by a smart, careful, trustworthy lawyer. Thus, find and follow all relevant rules of practice.

F. Unwritten Rules

In addition to all the formal rules that you must follow, it is worth your while to find out about local customs. Often local jurisdictions have common ways of presenting a motion. Sometimes particular judges have preferences about how information is presented. So, ask around. Ask a trusted colleague for a sample motion or memorandum of law. If you know which judge has been assigned to hear your motion, ask if that judge has preferences about how information is presented. Although you are not bound by these customs or preferences, you and your client will be well-served if you know of them in advance.

III. After the Motion Is Drafted

After you have drafted the motion and gathered any supporting documents, you will serve a copy of those documents on opposing counsel and provide a copy to the court.

A. Service and Its Proof

Each jurisdiction's rules of civil and criminal procedure provide detailed instructions about how to properly serve opposing counsel. The purpose of this book is not to provide those detailed rules, but to give you a picture of that process and of any documents you might have to draft. Thus, we skip over the exact ways in which you will serve opposing counsel and address the document you will have to draft to prove you have served opposing counsel.

"Proof of service" is a document that shows you have served opposing counsel the same documents that you have filed with the court. Failure to provide such proof can be grounds for dismissing the motion. That proof is usually provided in a sworn statement by the person who served the opposing party, as in Example 4-F. That statement is then appended to the documents provided to the court.

Example 4-F • Proof of service when opposing party served by mail

CIVIL COURT OF THE CITY OF NEW YORK   Index No. 15-SC-52975
COUNTY OF NEW YORK: PART 28

Randall Runco,
                Plaintiff,   AFFIDAVIT OF SERVICE
                                                    BY MAIL

-against-

HammerTime Construction, Inc.,
                Defendant.

Glenna Gilbert, being duly sworn, states as follows:

I am over 18 years of age and not a party to this action.

On September 16, 2015, I served Plaintiff's Motion to Compel Evidence on HammerTime Construction, Inc., the defendant in this proceeding. I enclosed a true copy of the attached papers in a properly sealed postpaid envelope. I deposited that sealed envelope in an official depository of the United States Postal Services within the State of New York. The envelope was addressed to HammerTime Construction, Inc., the defendant, at 5555 Broadway, New York, NY, 10036.

                                       Signature:_____

Sworn to me this ___ day of _____ 20__

_____
Notary Public or Court Employee

Alternatively, and as discussed further below, most courts now accept (or even require) electronic filing. If papers are filed electronically, proof of service might be provided as in Example 4-G.

Example 4-G · Proof of service when filing electronically

CERTIFICATE OF SERVICE

I certify that on May 5, 2015, the above defendant's Motion to Dismiss Plaintiff Overdevest's Complaint was filed electronically, and notice of this filing will be sent by e-mail to all parties by operation of the Court's electronic filing system or by mail to anyone unable to accept electronic filing as indicated on the Notice of Electronic Filing.

_____

Jonathan Bardavid, Esq.

B. Filing with the Court

You will then file your notice of motion, motion, memorandum of law in support of the motion, supporting documents (if any), draft order (if any), and proof of service with the court. Again, you should first consult the local rules to determine how to file with the court.

Traditionally, to file your documents with the court, you or someone you work with goes to the courthouse. Once at the courthouse, you go to the clerk of court and submit two or three copies of your motion and all accompanying documents. The clerk of court examines the motion and the accompanying documents to ensure compliance with the court rules. Once approved, you pay a filing fee. Then, the clerk of court stamps the documents as filed. The stamp shows the date on which the documents were filed. One stamped copy is returned to you so that you have proof that your motion was properly filed.

More recently, many courts have adopted electronic filing systems. In some courts, parties are permitted, but not required, to file electronically. In other court systems, parties must file electronically. In such electronic filing systems, counsel can submit documents to the court electronically. Often, counsel can also serve opposing counsel electronically. Courts with electronic filing systems have detailed explanations about how to use the electronic filing systems on their websites, as in Figure 4-H on the next page.

Figure 4-H • An electronic filing system

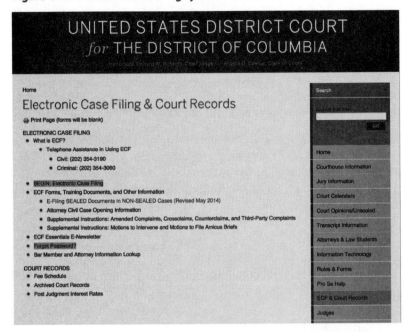

C. The Opposing Party's Response

In some instances, you may be the one who drafts, serves, and files a motion and its accompanying documents. In other cases, you will represent the party who is being served. If you represent the party being served, you will have to respond to the motion. You can do so in one of several ways.[10]

1. Statement of non-opposition

If you do not oppose the motion, you can notify opposing counsel of your lack of opposition. At the hearing, opposing counsel can inform the judge of the lack of opposition, and you will not need to attend the hearing. A good practice, however, is to submit a statement of non-opposition. Doing so creates a record of your position and ensures that your position is not misrepresented.

You are most likely to take this route when the matter is a ministerial one, as in Example 4-I.

---

10. The discussion of opposing party's possible responses was drawn from Thomas A. Mauet, *Pretrial* 336 (7th ed. 2008).

Example 4-I • A statement of non-opposition[11]

SUPERIOR COURT OF THE STATE OF CALIFORNIA
FOR THE COUNTY OF INYO

CITY OF LOS ANGELES DEPARTMENT OF WATER AND POWER, Plaintiff, vs. GREAT BASIN UNIFIED AIR POLLUTION CONTROL DISTRICT, Defendant.	Case No. SJCVPT-15-41092 Assigned for all purposes to the Honorable Dean T. Stout **PLAINTIFF CITY OF LOS ANGELES DEPARTMENT OF WATER AND POWER'S NOTICE OF NON-OPPOSITION TO DEFENDANT GREAT BASIN UNIFIED AIR POLLUTION CONTROL DISTRICT'S MOTION FOR MANDATORY TRANSFER OF VENUE** Date: July 10, 2015 Time: 1:00 P.M.

TO ALL PARTIES AND THEIR ATTORNEYS OF RECORD HEREIN:

PLEASE TAKE NOTICE THAT Plaintiff City of Los Angeles Department of Water and Power has received and reviewed Defendant Great Basin Unified Air Pollution Control District's Notice of Motion and Motion for Mandatory Transfer of Venue and does not oppose the motion. In fact, the Department of Water and Power supports the motion and joins in the request to transfer this action to the Kern County Superior Court pursuant to Code of Civil Procedure § 394(a).

Dated: June 23, 2015   MANATT, PHELPS & PHILLIPS, LLP
                                 Mark D. Johnson

                                 By:_____
                                 Mark D. Johnson
                                 Attorney for the City of Los Angeles
                                 Department of Water and Power

---

2. Consent order

Another possibility is to consult with counsel to determine whether the parties might be able to craft a consent order. This approach, common in state courts but not in federal courts, allows the parties to negotiate a proposed order and then submit it to the court for its approval. Although

---

11. Example drawn from a motion of non-opposition filed in *City of Los Angeles Department of Water & Power v. Great Basin Unified Air Pollution District*, No. SICVPT-06-41092 (Cal. Sup. Ct. June 26, 2006).

a judge is not required to grant an order simply because the parties agree on it, a judge usually will.

3. Memorandum of law in opposition

Finally, you might oppose the motion. When you oppose a motion, you ordinarily do not submit a motion in opposition. Instead, you submit a memorandum of law in opposition to the motion. That memorandum of law explains why the motion should not be granted. A memorandum of law in opposition to a motion has all the same parts as the moving party's memorandum of law in support of the motion.

D. The Moving Party's Reply Memorandum

If the rules permit, the moving party may file a final reply. A reply memorandum, when it is allowed, may have all the same parts as an opening memorandum of law; often, however, it does not. A reply memorandum responds to new issues raised in the opposing memorandum of law; it should not repeat arguments already presented in the opening memorandum of law. Because the reply memorandum addresses only those issues not already addressed in the opening memorandum, the reply is often limited to a short argument section and a conclusion.

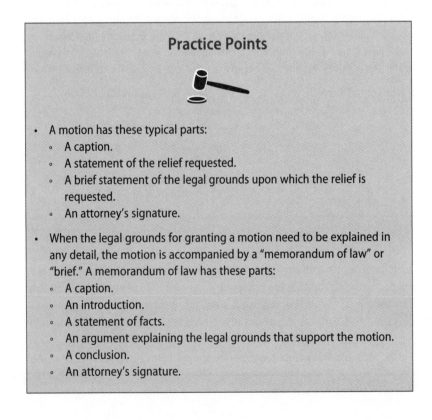

Practice Points

- A motion has these typical parts:
  - A caption.
  - A statement of the relief requested.
  - A brief statement of the legal grounds upon which the relief is requested.
  - An attorney's signature.

- When the legal grounds for granting a motion need to be explained in any detail, the motion is accompanied by a "memorandum of law" or "brief." A memorandum of law has these parts:
  - A caption.
  - An introduction.
  - A statement of facts.
  - An argument explaining the legal grounds that support the motion.
  - A conclusion.
  - An attorney's signature.

- Before drafting your own motion
  - Review the governing procedural rules.
  - Review the local rules.
  - If a particular judge will be hearing your motion, determine whether that judge has standing orders or preferences that will affect the motion.

- After drafting your motion, make sure it is properly filed with the court and served on opposing counsel.

- If you are served with a motion, carefully consider whether you, in fact, oppose the motion.
  - If you do oppose the motion, you must submit a reply.
  - If, however, you do not oppose the motion, you can submit a statement of non-opposition.
  - If you can work out a settlement with opposing counsel, you can submit a motion asking the judge to approve a consent order.

Chapter 5

Appellate Practice

This chapter introduces you to the world of appeals. An appeal, as you likely know, is the way in which a lawyer asks an appellate court to review the decisions of a lower court.

The chapter begins by introducing you to the appellate brief. As we explained with respect to trial motions, before you begin any writing project, you should have a clear idea of how the end product should look. This chapter will help you envision that end product.

In addition, to write an effective appellate brief, you will need to know more about your audience and the rules that govern your appeal. The chapter thus describes the appellate process—from the initial decision to appeal to requesting review from the highest appellate court. That discussion is followed by a whirlwind tour of some uniquely appellate concepts that play into appellate brief writing.

I. Appellate Briefs

After a trial, a party dissatisfied with the results can ask an appellate court to review the trial court's legal decisions. That party would file an appeal. In that party's appellate brief, the party would explain the error the lower court made and why one or more errors should result in the lower court's decision being reversed. Although the components and their order vary by jurisdiction, the typical appellate brief includes the following components:

- Cover
- Table of contents
- Table of authorities
- Statement of jurisdiction
- Statement of the issues (or questions) presented
- Statement of the case
- Summary of the argument
- Argument
- Conclusion and relief sought
- Lawyer's signature

Each of those parts is identified in Example 5-A.[1]

---

1. Example 5-A shows a typical appellate brief. Although this brief was filed with the Oregon courts, the format has been changed to show what a typical brief looks like. This example does not follow the format required by Oregon's local rules governing appellate briefs.

Example 5-A • An appellate brief

IN THE COURT OF APPEALS OF THE STATE OF OREGON

STATE OF OREGON	Malheur County Circuit Court No. 04065087C
Plaintiff-Respondent,	
v.	
RUBEN E. RODRIGUEZ,	CA A126339
Defendant-Appellant.	

RESPONDENT'S BRIEF

_____

Appeal from the Judgment of the Circuit Court
For Malheur County
Honorable PATRICIA A. SULLIVAN, Judge

The cover identifies the parties, their lawyers, the court from which the case is being appealed, the court in which the appeal is being heard, and the docket numbers for the trial and the appellate cases.

LELAND R. BERGER #83020
Attorney at Law
3527 NE 15th Ave. #103
Portland, OR 97212
Telephone: (503) 287-4688

ANTHONY L. JOHNSON #05070
Attorney at Law
8425 SE 19th Avenue
Portland, Oregon 97202
Telephone: (503) 238-2781

Attorneys for Defendant-Appellant

HARDY MYERS #64077
Attorney General
MARY H. WILLIAMS #91124
Solicitor General

LAURA S. ANDERSON #88150
Assistant Attorney General
1162 Court St. NE
Salem, Oregon 97301-4096
Telephone: (503) 378-4402

Attorneys for Plaintiff-Respondent

TABLE OF CONTENTS

The table of contents provides
an overview of the argument to
come. It also tells the judge
where to find the different parts
of the argument within the brief.

TABLE OF AUTHORITIES

Cases Cited

Statutory Provisions

Other Authorities

RESPONDENT'S BRIEF

JURISDICTION

This court has jurisdiction pursuant to Oregon Revised Statute § 138.050.

This statement of jurisdiction establishes that the court has jurisdiction to hear this case.

QUESTION PRESENTED

Should the language of *former* Oregon Revised Statute § 809.235(1)(b), providing that a person's driver's license shall be permanently revoked if the person is convicted of a misdemeanor DUI "for a third time," be construed to preclude revoking a person's driver's license after a fourth, fifth, or other succeeding misdemeanor DUI?

The question presented states the legal question that needs to be resolved on appeal.

STATEMENT OF THE CASE

Defendant has been convicted of driving under the influence (DUI) on four separate occasions. In Oregon, he was convicted of a DUI in 1976 and 1980. While in California in 1989, he was also convicted of a DUI. Finally, last year, defendant pleaded guilty and was then convicted of a DUI when he drove with a blood alcohol content of .27 percent. At sentencing, the trial court permanently revoked defendant's driving privileges. Defendant now appeals that sentence.

The statement of the case states the facts relevant to the appeal. In some jurisdictions, this section is called the statement of facts. Other jurisdictions require both a statement of facts and a statement of the case.

SUMMARY OF ARGUMENT

After defendant pleaded guilty to a misdemeanor DUI, the trial court permanently revoked his driver's license pursuant to *former* Oregon Revised Statute § 809.235(1)(b) (amended 2005) because defendant had been previously convicted of a DUI at least two times. *Former* Oregon Revised Statute § 809.235(1)(b) requires a court to permanently revoke a person's driver's license if the person "is convicted of misdemeanor [DUI] . . . *for a third time.*"

The summary of the argument, not surprisingly, gives a summary of the argument to come. Judges will return to this section if they need a quick overview of the argument.

On appeal, defendant argues that the trial court was not permitted to permanently revoke his license because he had three previous DUI convictions, and the statute allowed permanent revocation only upon a third conviction, not upon a fourth. This court should affirm the permanent revocation.

First, revocation was mandatory under *former* Oregon Revised Statute § 809.235(1)(b). That statute is ambiguous because it can plausibly be read to mean that permanent revocation is mandatory in cases where either (1) a person had *only* two prior convictions for DUI, or, as the state argues, (2) a person had *at least* two prior convictions for DUI.

Because the statute is ambiguous, this court should look to the legislative history of *former* Oregon Revised Statute § 809.235(1)(b) to discern the legislature's intent. That history shows that the legislature recognized that repeat drunk drivers pose a significant danger to the public, and revocation of driving privileges is one means for protecting the public from habitual drunk drivers. Given the legislature's intention to protect the public and sanction repeat DUI offenders, construing the statute as defendant proposes, to revoke third-time offenders, but not revoke fourth-, fifth-, or more-time offenders, would be contrary to the legislature's intent as evidenced by the legislative history.

ARGUMENT

The argument explains why the
desired outcome is supported
by the law and facts.

I. The trial court's permanent revocation of the defendant's driver's license was proper.

This argument provides an
example of a statutory
construction analysis.

At sentencing, the trial court correctly revoked defendant's driving privileges pursuant to *former* Oregon Revised Statute § 809.235(1)(b).[1] That statute provided as follows:

> The court shall order that a person's driving privileges be permanently revoked if the person is convicted of felony driving while under the influence of intoxicants under Oregon Revised Statute § 813.010 or *if the person is convicted of misdemeanor driving while under the influence of intoxicants under Oregon Revised Statute § 813.010 for a third time.*

Or. Rev. Stat. § 809.235(1)(b) (amended 2005) (emphasis added).

A. Oregon's method of statutory construction

A trial court's construction of a statute is reviewed for errors of law. *State v. Thompson*, 971 P.2d 879, 885 (Or. 1999); *Chaffee v. Shaffer Trucking, Inc.*, 948 P.2d 760, 761 (Or. Ct. App. 1997). That construction is governed by Oregon statutes pertaining to statutory construction, Or. Rev. Stat. §§ 174.010-.090, and the methodology set out in *Portland General Electric Co. v. Bureau of Labor & Industries*, 859 P.2d 1143, 1145-47 (Or. 1993).

The aim of statutory construction — both under Oregon statute and case law — is to discern what the legislature intended when it enacted the particular statute: "In the construction of a statute, a court shall pursue the intention of the legislature if possible." Or. Rev. Stat. § 174.020(1)(a); *Portland Gen. Elec. Co.*, 859 P.2d at 1146-47.

To ascertain the legislature's intent, the text and context of the relevant statutes must be analyzed first because the text and context together represent the best evidence of the legislature's intent. *Portland Gen. Elec. Co.*, 859 P.2d at 1145-46. In examining the text of a statute, the construing court generally assumes that the legislature intended the words of the statute to carry their ordinary meanings unless the phrasing of the statute suggests that the legislature intended different meanings to apply. *Id.* at 1146; *see also State v. Ausmus*, 85 P.3d 864, 869 (Or. 2003) (stating that a court usually "gives words of

---

1. Oregon Revised Statute § 809.235(1)(b) (amended 2005) was amended by Oregon Laws 2005, chapter 436, section 1, and now reads as follows:

> (b) The court shall order that a person's driving privileges be permanently revoked if the person is convicted of felony driving while under the influence of intoxicants in violation of Oregon Revised Statute § 813.010 or if the person is convicted of misdemeanor driving while under the influence of intoxicants in violation of Oregon Revised Statute § 813.010 or its statutory counterpart in any other jurisdiction for a third or subsequent time.

common usage their plain, natural and ordinary meaning"); *State v. Stamper,* 106 P.3d 172, 174 (Or. Ct. App. 2005) (phrasing of statute may indicate legislature intended different meaning to apply).

The text, however, should not be considered in isolation, but in its context. *Vsetecka v. Safeway Stores, Inc.,* 98 P.3d 1116, 1119 (Or. 2004). The context of a statute includes other parts of the same statute, along with other related statutes, prior versions of the statute, prior judicial interpretations of the relevant statutory language, and pre-existing common law. *See In re Marriage of Denton,* 951 P.2d 693, 697 (Or. 1998); *Krieger v. Just,* 876 P.2d 754, 758 (Or. 1994); *Portland Gen. Elec. Co.,* 859 P.2d at 1146; *Stephens v. Bohlman,* 838 P.2d 600, 603 n.6 (Or. 1992). At this first step in the analysis, rules of construction, both statutory and judicial, may be applied to assist in discerning the meaning of the language at issue. *Portland Gen. Elec. Co.,* 859 P.2d at 1146.

If, after examining the text in context, the court concludes that the statute is ambiguous, that is, capable of multiple constructions that are not "wholly implausible," the court may resort to legislative history and, if necessary, other aids to assist in its construction. *Owens v. Motor Vehicle Div.,* 875 P.2d 463, 468 (Or. 1994) (explaining that resort to legislative history is necessary unless alternative interpretations are "wholly implausible").

If the intent of the legislature still remains unclear even after considering the text, context, and legislative history, then this court may resort to general maxims of statutory construction to resolve the remaining uncertainty. *Portland Gen. Elec. Co.,* 859 P.2d at 1146. Among these general maxims is the principle that the court will not adopt a statutory meaning that is inconsistent with the apparent policy of the legislation as a whole and that leads to an incongruous result. *See State v. Vasquez-Rubio,* 917 P.2d 494, 497 (Or. 1996) (explaining that absurd-result maxim best suited for helping court determine which of a number of plausible meanings legislature intended).

B. Oregon Revised Statute § 809.235(1)(b) is ambiguous because the phrase "for a third time" is capable of multiple constructions that are "not wholly implausible."

The subject phrase, "for a third time," is ambiguous because it has more than one plausible meaning. It could mean, as defendant argues, that (1) a person had *only* two prior convictions for DUI, or, as the state argues, that (2) a defendant had *at least* two prior convictions for DUI, and the present conviction for which revocation is mandatory constitutes the "third." The latter construction is plausible for several reasons.

First, the legislature created an indefinite reference. The indefinite article "a" is an indefinite determiner with an indefinite reference. *See* Sidney Greenbaum, *Oxford English Grammar* 165 (1996) ("The definite article is used when the speaker (or writer) assumes that the hearer (or reader) can identify the reference of a noun phrase[.] . . . The indefinite article is used when that assumption cannot be made[.]"); *see also* Ronald Carter & Michael McCarthy, *Cambridge Grammar of English* 907 (2006) ("Indefinite article refers to the determiner *a/an* that is used to express an indefinite meaning."). It is "used as a function word before . . . mass nouns when the individual in question is undetermined, unidentified, or unspecified . . . ." *Webster's Third New Int'l Dictionary* 1 (unabridged ed. 1993); *see also Galfano v. KTVL-TV,* 102 P.3d 766, 772 (Or. Ct. App. 2004) (relying on *Webster's* definition of the article "a" in ruling that the phrase *"a* judgment pursuant to Rule 67" in ORCP 68 C(5)(b) authorizes a trial court to render a supplemental judgment after *any* ORCP 67 judgment has been entered). *Compare Anderson v. Jensen Racing, Inc.,* 931 P.2d 763, 767 (Or. 1997) (explaining that the definite article "the" functions as an adjective that denotes a particular, specified thing).

The indefinite article "a" used with the ordinal determiner "third" suggests that the legislature intended an indefinite third. The word "third" is an ordinal number; ordinals refer to positions in a sequence. *See* Greenbaum, *supra*, 199. Thus, the combination of the indefinite "a" with the ordinal "third," creates an indefinite third. Because the statute refers to an indefinite third position in a sequence, the ordinary meaning of the statutory text mandates license revocation upon any conviction, following two prior convictions.

Reading the text of *former* Oregon Revised Statute § 809.235(1)(b) in its context also leads to the conclusion that the statute mandates revocation of a person's driver's license upon any conviction after two prior convictions. The stated policies of the legislature are context within which the text of each statute should be read. *State v. McBroom*, 39 P.3d 226, 228 n.2 (Or. Ct. App. 2002) (explaining that statutory statement of general policy in vehicle code is context for interpretation of specific provision pertaining to offense of failure to drive within a lane). With respect to Oregon's vehicle code, the legislature's stated polices are to protect the public, Or. Rev. Stat. § 801.020(11)(a), to "deny the privilege of operating motor vehicles on the public highways to persons who by their conduct and record have demonstrated their indifference for the safety and welfare of others," Or. Rev. Stat. § 801.020(11)(b), and to "discourage repetition of criminal acts," Or. Rev. Stat. § 801.020(11)(c). Thus, understanding *former* Oregon Revised Statute § 809.235(1)(b) to require the revocation of a driver's license upon any conviction, following two prior convictions, is also consistent with the statute's context.

The alternate construction advanced by defendant is not consistent with the statutory context. If defendant's argument prevails, a person with a *greater* number of DUI convictions (i.e., more than three convictions) prior to the enactment of the statute would lose his or her license for a substantially *lesser* period of time than a person who has been convicted of only two DUIs before the effective date of the statute. *See* Or. Rev. Stat. §§ 809.400(1), .428(2). Not only is such a construction patently inequitable, such an eventuality would be contrary to the stated policies of the legislature to protect the public and to deny driving privileges in relation to driving offenses.

Moreover, the fact that the legislature has in other instances used the phrase "at least three times," does not mean the absence of that language here requires the court to adopt the defendant's interpretation. Previously, this court has explained that, when the legislature uses a particular phrase in one statute but not another, it permits an inference that the omission was intentional, but this court "c[ould] not say that the text speaks conclusively in that regard." *State v. Robison*, 120 P.3d 1285, 1287 (Or. App. 2005). Thus, the absence of the "at

4

least three time language" merely creates an ambiguity, which allows this court to consider the statute's legislative history when interpreting the statute.

C. The legislative history demonstrates that the legislature intended to mandate license revocation any time after two prior convictions.

The legislative history for House Bill 2885, which eventually became Oregon Revised Statute § 809.235, reflects an intent that sanctions for DUI increase as the number of DUI convictions increases.

For example, Representative Barker, a chief sponsor of the bill, testified before the House Judiciary Committee in support of the bill. He expressed frustration with current law, which allowed courts to revoke driving privileges only upon a fourth conviction. He wanted revocation to occur sooner:

> I introduced this bill, brought this bill forward, that would revoke driving privileges after a third conviction of driving under the influence. At the present time, it's four convictions. And * * * to keep it really brief the only objections I've heard about this so far at town halls and so on in meetings with citizens in my district is they can't imagine why we're waiting for the third time, why it isn't done sooner.

House Judiciary Committee, April 3, 2003, Tape 123 Side A at 50, Internet RealOne Player at 1:51:52.

When Representative Barker carried the bill on the House floor, he explained waiting until a fourth DUI conviction to revoke a driver's license was "unacceptably tolerant towards reckless behavior":

> HB 2885 comes to you from your Judiciary Committee where it passed with a unanimous vote. Currently someone convicted of driving under the influence of intoxicants does not permanently lose their driving privileges until after their fourth conviction. This means that after the initial DUI arrest which often results in a diversion program someone has to be convicted four more times to lose their privileges. As an Oregonian and the father of two daughters I find this to be unacceptably tolerant towards such reckless behavior. As a retired police lieutenant I could tell you that someone who gets convicted of drunk driving four times has a substance abuse problem[,] and colleagues[,] they need to be off the road.

> This bill revokes rather than suspends the driver's license of a person convicted for the third DUI. This revocation can be appealed after ten years. I don't feel it's necessary to give you a long speech about the dangers of driving while intoxicated. Most of us know someone who's been victimized by an intoxicated driver.

House Floor Debate on HB 2885, April 10, 2003, Tape 49 Side A at 314 to 356, Internet RealOne Player at 3 6:27 to 3 9:56.

5

On the Senate floor, prior to passage of the bill, other senators expressed their frustration with drivers who, despite prior convictions and other sanctions, continued to drink and drive:

> Senator Stan: HB 2885 is a DUI bill that changes the penalty for conviction for DUI from suspension to revocation of a driver's license after three convictions. We understand on the first conviction an individual may go through a diversion program and have the conviction removed so it's very likely a person convicted of three DUI has also offended one other time. It's very clear that people who continue to offend in this way have a very serious addiction problem and we believe that it's important to revoke their privilege to drive and so members I urge your support of HB 2885.

> Senator Dukes: This is a good bill because it makes a very small incremental improvement. But I stand today in utter frustration, if you listen to the carrier when to get around to a Class A misdemeanor— which by the way folks we're not even prosecuting at the moment because we don't have enough court time to do all of that. We're going to do that after the fifth DUI, We're going to finally—it's just the penalty really small for turning someone lethal loose on the roads in Oregon. And I think that one of the failures that the legislature has made over the years is an inability to be able to deal with that. I mean after you've gone out and driven and then convicted, and driven and then convicted, and driven and then convicted—we're going to give you a Class A misdemeanor. And then if you go drive and get convicted again we'll finally get to a felony. And we'll get serious about it maybe and I just think in that process we have given people far too many opportunities to kill and maim people. And that is a mistake. However, as I said this bill is an improvement, but at this rate we're going to have a lot more deaths from drunk drivers that we could have stopped if we would simply have the guts to strengthen these laws.

> Senator Minnis: Mr. President I just wanted to stand and say that I agree one hundred percent with the senator from Astoria [Senator Dukes]. There were over 25,000 DUI arrests in Oregon in 2001. That is simply not acceptable. Thank you.

Senate Floor Debate on H.B. 2285, May 21, 2003, Tape 165 Side B at 16 to 74, Internet RealOne Player at 59:18 to 1:00:52.

Nowhere does the legislative history suggest that the legislature was enacting a bill that would allow revocation of driving privileges at the third conviction but not upon a fourth. Such an interpretation would lead to the incongruous result that a person with a greater number of DUI convictions would be subject to a lesser penalty.

Accordingly, this court should construe *former* Oregon Revised Statute §809.235(1)(b) to mandate permanent driver's license revocation in cases in which a person is convicted of a misdemeanor DUI and has previously been convicted at *least twice* for DUI.

In this case, Mr. Rodriguez had three times been convicted for DUI when, on September 13, 2004, he pleaded guilty to a fourth misdemeanor charge of driving under the influence of intoxicants. Because he had been convicted for DUI at least twice before, pursuant to *former* Oregon Revised Statute §809.235(1)(b), the court properly imposed a permanent revocation of Mr. Rodriguez's driving privileges.

CONCLUSION

The trial court's judgment wherein defendant's driver's license is permanently revoked should be affirmed.

Final conclusions to a brief are often short and formulaic, such as this one. The final conclusion will always ask for the relief sought.

Respectfully submitted,

_____
LAURA S. ANDERSON
Senior Assistant Attorney General

The lawyer's signature

Attorneys for Plaintiff-Respondent
State of Oregon

The party who files the appeal is called the appellant (or petitioner). The party responding to the appeal is called the respondent. After an appellant files an opening brief, the party who won below can file a brief explaining why the trial court's decision was in fact correct and should be upheld. As a general matter, a respondent's brief includes all the same parts as an appellant's brief. Many courts, however, allow a respondent to accept parts of the appellant's brief and not repeat those parts in the respondent's brief. The federal rules, for example, state that, unless the respondent is dissatisfied with the appellant's statement, a respondent's answering brief need not include the jurisdictional statement, the statement of the issues, the statement of the case, or the statement of the standard of review.[3] Whether to accept any of appellant's statements is a strategic decision that Chapter 11, *Constructing an Appellate Brief*, discusses at more length. For now, you should know that respondent's brief usually includes all the same parts as the appellant's opening brief, but the respondent has the option of omitting a section and accepting one or more of the appellant's statements.

Finally, in some instances, the appellant or petitioner can file a response to the respondent's brief. Reply briefs are not always allowed as a matter of right.[4] If a reply brief is permitted and the respondent decides to file one, then the reply brief will look very much like the opening or responding brief. However, you will include only those parts of the brief that are necessary to respond to the opposing arguments. Usually, after a cover, table of contents, and table of authorities, the reply brief jumps straight into the argument.

Appellee vs. Respondent

"Appellee" and "respondent" refer to the same party: the party who is responding to the appeal.

The Federal Rules of Appellate Procedure use the word "appellee." "Respondent," however, is the more intuitively meaningful word. When using the word "respondent," the reader does not have to sort out the difference between "appellant" and "appellee," two very similar sounding words. For these reasons, this chapter uses the word "respondent" throughout.

---

3. Fed. R. App. P. 28(b).

4. For example, under the Oregon Rules of Appellate Procedure, the appellant in a criminal case is not allowed to file a reply brief without leave of court. Or. R. App. P. 5.70(3). Other jurisdictions may have similar rules.

II. The Rules that Govern Appeals

The above section describes how an appellate brief typically looks. Appellate briefs do, however, vary from jurisdiction to jurisdiction. To determine what your brief should include, you will have to consult the rules that govern appeals in your jurisdiction. These same rules will also provide other important information such as the time frame in which you must file your brief.

Keep in mind that some jurisdictions have more than one set of rules governing their appeals. For example, appeals in the federal courts of appeal are governed first by the Federal Rules of Appellate Procedure. Then, the various federal circuit courts have their own local rules that supplement the Federal Rules of Appellate Procedure. Similarly, in state courts, the state's highest court usually adopts a set of rules that govern its proceedings, while the intermediate appellate court adopts different rules for its proceedings.

Two resources can help you find and understand the governing appellate rules. First, most courts have valuable information on their websites. In addition to appellate rules of procedure, you will often find sample documents and how-to advice on courts' websites. Second, a number of good treatises on appellate practice are available, some of which address practice in certain courts (such as the United States Supreme Court or the Ninth Circuit Court of Appeals) and others that are more general. A law librarian will be able to direct you to the most suitable treatise. The bottom line for your practice: Long before you even think about writing a brief, make sure you have consulted the rules that govern the appeal.

III. The Court and Its Players: Judges, Law Clerks, and Staff Attorneys

Understanding the institution that you are addressing and the players in the appellate process will help you craft your brief to be more persuasive. A concise overview follows.

Of course, appellate courts have judges or justices. Normally, courts have an odd number of judges; however, if there are vacancies or recusals, your appeal may be heard by an even number of judges. Courts may sit in panels (usually of three judges), or the entire court may sit together (en banc).

In addition to the judges or justices, most appellate courts have two other categories of lawyers who may be involved in your appeal: law clerks and staff attorneys. Although the terminology and functions vary from court to court, law clerks are often recent law school graduates who work

> ### Be Precise!
> ### Know Your Judges from Your Justices
>
> In most jurisdictions, a judge who is appointed or elected to the highest appellate court is called a "justice." A judge who sits on an intermediate appellate court is called a "judge." Exceptions do exist. In California, for example, the Court of Appeal jurists are called justices. Be sure to know the correct title for the person who will be deciding your case. It can only help.

for an individual judge for one to two years.[5] Staff attorneys are permanent lawyer-employees who may work for the court as a whole or for individual judges. Some staff attorneys have many years of experience and may have expertise in a given area of law. In most appellate courts, law clerks and staff attorneys assist the judges by conducting legal research, preparing bench memoranda (a memorandum that summarizes a case for a judge, usually prepared before oral arguments), preparing initial drafts of opinions, and editing and finalizing opinions.

When drafting an appellate brief, keep those various audiences in mind. Specifically, keep in mind that, in most cases, the judges and most of the legal staff working with the judges are generalists. That is, they are educated attorneys, but they are likely not experts in the subject matter central to your client's case. You should always assume that you know your case better than the appellate judges who will hear your appeal. Thus, in most instances, to persuade the court of your client's desired outcome, you must first educate the court about the facts of your case and the underlying law that applies to the case.

IV. The Appellate Process

Before you begin writing an appellate brief, you should also understand the overall process by which an appeal is filed, argued, and decided. This part of the chapter provides that overview.

A. The Decision to Appeal

A lower tribunal—a trial court, administrative agency, or other tribunal—has just disposed of a matter in a way that is contrary to your client's position. Do you appeal the decision?

---

5. Increasingly, judges are hiring permanent law clerks. When a law clerk is hired on a permanent basis, the most significant difference between a "law clerk" and a "staff attorney" is the title. Otherwise, both are experienced lawyers assisting a judge or group of judges with research, drafting opinions, and preparing for oral arguments.

1. Whether to appeal

Lawyers should put a lot of thought in deciding whether to appeal. The first question in deciding whether to file an appeal is whether the tribunal's ruling is appealable. As a general matter, a losing party has no inherent right to appeal; rather, the right to appeal typically is conferred by statute. Usually, statutes permit litigants to appeal decisions that end the litigation but not those decisions that occur during the litigation process. For example, you may appeal after a decision granting a motion to dismiss or for summary judgment if the decision ends the litigation by disposing of all the claims before the court. By contrast, you typically may not appeal a decision denying summary judgment because that decision does not end the litigation but rather permits the case to proceed to trial.

Some exceptions do exist. Statutes permit some "interlocutory" appeals—that is, appeals before the litigation is concluded—if continuing the litigation would be particularly prejudicial to a party. For example, many jurisdictions permit a litigant to appeal a decision when a court concludes that a defendant does not have immunity from suit or when the court concludes that it has personal jurisdiction over the defendant, despite the defendant's arguments to the contrary. In both cases, proceeding to the trial would effectively deny the defendant the right to be protected from trial, and that right could not be re-gained after trial. Thus, when an interlocutory appeal is taken, the appellate court will review the specific issue permitted by the interlocutory appeal, and after the appellate court's decision, the case will either be dismissed or returned to the trial court to continue with the litigation.

Assuming that you have an appealable decision in hand, you must still decide whether you should appeal. In reaching that decision, consider whether an appeal will be worthwhile to your client:

- What is the projected cost of the appeal?
- What is the likelihood of obtaining a better outcome on appeal?
- How will the delay inherent in pursuing the appeal affect your client?
- Is another route—such as seeking a settlement or asking the trial court or other tribunal to modify its ruling—a better approach?

In short, before filing an appeal, you must carefully consider whether an appeal is the best way to serve your client's needs. Producing a persuasive brief in an otherwise ill-advised appeal may not be to your client's advantage.

2. Which issues to raise on appeal

Once you have decided that it makes sense to appeal, another decision that you will have to make before filing an appellate brief is which issues you will raise on appeal. Many appellate briefs raise only one issue, such as whether the evidence was sufficient to support a criminal conviction, while other briefs may raise dozens of issues.

In choosing which issue or issues to raise on appeal, remember that you are not required to challenge every ruling made by the trial court or agency. Experienced appellate practitioners will choose their strongest arguments and forgo those arguments that have only a small chance of succeeding for three reasons: First, a good argument buried in a host of weak arguments may be overlooked. Second, appellate judges have a lot of reading to do; if you force them to read several arguments that have little merit, they are less likely to react favorably to the one strong argument that you present. Finally, appellate courts impose length limits on briefs. If you waste words on six weak arguments, you may not have space to make that incredible winning argument on the one meritorious issue.

Notwithstanding the general advice to limit the number of issues raised on appeal, you must sometimes raise issues that you think have lit-

---

Review of Agency Decisions

As you read this chapter understand that appellate courts review decisions not just from trial courts. Appellate courts also review agency decisions, and sometimes the review of agency decisions constitutes a significant part of an appellate court's docket. Although there are some differences when an appellate court reviews an agency decision, many of the same principles discussed below apply to review of agency decisions.

So that you will have a feel for how an appeal arises from an agency decision, here is a brief description of the process.

Federal and state agencies are part of their respective executive branches. After the legislature passes a statute, often the legislature will delegate to an agency within the executive branch the authority to implement that statute. For example, Congress has delegated to the Internal Revenue Service the responsibility for implementing the tax code, and the Environmental Protection Agency implements environmental laws. States often have analogous agencies, which implement state laws. Agencies implement statutes by promulgating rules or regulations.

To enforce those regulations, agencies have authority to issue orders. Disputes often arise from those orders. For example, the Environmental Protection Agency has authority to issue permits that allow parties to discharge some material into wetlands. If the permit is denied, the party seeking the permit can challenge the EPA's decision.

The process for challenging an agency decision varies greatly from agency to agency. Some agencies have an internal process for reviewing an initial agency decision. In some agencies, that review may be before an administrative law judge and be nearly as formal as a trial. In other agencies, that review is much less formal. Still other agencies provide no review after the initial decision is made. In those cases, the initial decision is also the agency's final order.

Whatever the process may be in a given agency, once the agency issues its final order, a dissatisfied party can seek review in a state or federal appellate court, depending on whether a state or federal agency issued the order. Review of an agency's final order normally skips over the trial court and proceeds directly to an appellate court.

tle chance of success. For example, when pursuing an appeal in state court, you might identify a federal constitutional claim that has been rejected by the state intermediate appellate court in previous cases. You may, though, have reason to believe that the state supreme court or the United States Supreme Court will agree with your position. In that case, you must raise the issue in the intermediate appellate court so that it is preserved for later courts to consider. In doing so, however, the savvy practitioner will acknowledge in the intermediate court that the argument has previously been rejected by that court.

B. The Notice of Appeal

The appellate process typically begins with a notice of appeal, which in federal court must be filed within 30 days after the decision being appealed is entered in the trial court's docket.[6] The exact format of a notice of appeal will vary from jurisdiction to jurisdiction. To determine the required format in your jurisdiction, consult the appendix to the appellate rules of procedure, the court's website, or a relevant treatise. Example 5-B shows you a typical notice of appeal.

The notice of appeal is filed with either the trial court or the appellate court, depending on the rules in that jurisdiction. In addition, the notice of appeal is served on the other parties to the case. With these steps, both the court and the other parties to the case are notified that the dispute has not been finally resolved and that jurisdiction now lies with the appellate court.

After that document is filed, certain timelines begin to run and certain actions must be taken before the briefs are filed. For example, in federal court the appellant must order a transcript of the court proceedings within 14 days after the notice of appeal is filed.[7]

The Petition for Judicial Review of a Final Agency Order

When seeking judicial review of a final agency order, you would file a "petition for judicial review," which is the administrative law counterpart to a notice of appeal from a trial court decision. As with the notice of appeal, the petition for judicial review of the agency order triggers certain timelines and triggers the agency's duty to transmit relevant parts of the administrative record to the appellate court.

---

6. Fed. R. App. P. 4(a)(1)(A).
7. Fed. R. App. P. 10(b)(1).

Example 5-B · A typical notice of appeal

United States District Court for the
Southern District of Texas

Jonathan B. Wilson,	}	No. 16-10664
Plaintiff,	}	
	}	
v.	}	Notice of Appeal
	}	
	}	
Zal Medical Group, Inc.,	}	
Defendant.	}	

Notice is hereby given that Zal Medical Group, Inc., defendant, in the above named case, hereby appeals to the United States Court of Appeals for the Fifth Circuit from the final judgment entered in this action on the 7th day of March, 2016.

Gail Izaguirre

Gail Izaguirre
Attorney for Zal Medical Group
1100 Louisiana Street
Suite 410
Houston, TX 77002

C. The Record

At trial or during a hearing, the parties determine what evidence to submit to the decision maker, and the decision maker bases a decision on that evidence. That evidence, which usually consists of documents, exhibits, and a transcript of any oral testimony or argument, comprises the "record" in the case. On appeal, lawyers compile excerpts of the trial record (sometimes called an appendix) and submit it to the appellate court so that the appellate court can review the proceedings below.

The importance of the record on appeal cannot be overstated. With few exceptions, appellate courts may not consider evidence that was not before the trial court. Thus, when trying to persuade appellate courts, remember that if something is not in the record, it does not exist. References to matters that are not in the record may draw the ire of appellate judges and will detract from the persuasiveness of your argument.

Court rules differ regarding who has the responsibility for preparing the appendix or excerpt, and rules also vary regarding the contents of the appendix or excerpt. Typically, the appendix or excerpt contains only those parts of the trial record that are necessary to support the arguments made on appeal; however, some appellate courts require the full record to be transmitted.

Compiling the excerpt of record requires a little bit of thought. Lawyers tend to throw everything into the excerpt, perhaps figuring, "Better too much than too little." Although that sentiment is hard to argue with, an excerpt of record that includes virtually the entire trial court file, when the only issue on appeal is an isolated legal issue, does not inspire confidence that the lawyer is taking the necessary care in the appeal. Put that extra ounce of thought and effort into the excerpt or appendix.

Do Appellate Courts Really Care About the Record?

Yes. Here's what one California court had to say about the record:

> When practicing appellate law, there are at least three immutable rules: first, take great care to prepare a complete record; second, if it is not in the record, it did not happen; and third, when in doubt, refer back to rules one and two. In this case, the parties totally missed the appellate mark by failing to provide an adequate record for review.

Protect Our Water v. Cty. of Merced, 1 Cal. Rptr. 3d 726, 726 (Cal. Ct. App. 2003).

D. The Briefs

After the notice of appeal has been filed and the relevant parts of the record have been transmitted, the parties then submit their briefs. The different kinds of briefs that the parties file are described earlier in this chapter.

The rules of appellate procedure in each jurisdiction establish the amount of time parties have to file their briefs. In federal courts, and if no extension of time is granted, the appellant must file the opening brief (also called the "appellant's brief") 40 days after the record is filed. The respondent then has 30 days to submit a brief. In federal court, the appellant then has 14 days to file a reply brief to the respondent's brief.[8]

E. Oral Argument

After briefs are filed—often many months after briefs are filed—the parties may have an opportunity to present oral arguments to the court.

---

8. Fed. R. App. P. 31(a)(1).

Judging from movies and television, one would think that appeals are really all about oral argument. It turns out—no surprise here—that television and movies do not always depict the court system accurately. As an initial matter, many appeals are decided without oral argument; the briefs are the only opportunity the parties have to persuade the court. In addition, even for those cases in which the court hears oral argument, the briefs are almost always considered to be more important in persuading the court. Oral argument is discussed in detail in Chapter 14, *Oral Arguments*.

F. The Opinion

Finally, after briefs are submitted and after oral argument (if oral argument is permitted and if the parties elect to present oral arguments), the court will issue its opinion. The opinion is the court's explanation of its decision in an appeal.

The form of opinions varies enormously from court to court and even from case to case. The United States Supreme Court often issues opinions that run dozens or hundreds of pages in length. At the other extreme, some appellate courts issue short opinions or one-page orders that do little more than affirm or reverse a lower court's decision. Many courts also issue unpublished opinions that have little or no precedential value.

When writing an appellate brief, you should think about how you want to influence the court's opinion. For example, if you won below, you may not want the appellate court to write an opinion at all; rather, you might prefer that the appellate court summarily affirm the decision below. When writing the brief in that type of case, you would want to show that existing precedent squarely addresses all the issues raised and an analysis of those cases shows the trial court got it right. In other cases, your goal may be to convince the court to write a published opinion that will not only allow you to prevail in this case, but will also provide guidance to lower courts and litigants. Finally, there may be times when you know that you are likely to lose the appeal, but you want your brief to guide the court's analysis. In those cases, you will want your brief to help shape the court's opinion so that the opinion announces a rule that is favorable to your client's future interests, despite the loss in this particular case.[9]

G. Petitions for Reconsideration or Rehearing

If you lose an appeal in an intermediate appellate court, you might appeal to a higher court, a route that is discussed below. But, before

---

9. For an example of such a case see the discussion of *Canell v. State*, 58 P.3d 847 (Or. Ct. App. 2002), in Chapter 2, *The Ethical, Professional Advocate*.

doing so, you should consider whether to ask the intermediate appellate court to reconsider its decision (or rehear the case—the two phrases are often used interchangeably).

If you ask the intermediate appellate court to reconsider its decision, you have two options. If the court is one that sits in panels made up of fewer than all the judges on the court, you can ask the panel that decided the appeal to reconsider its decision, or you can ask all the judges of the intermediate appellate court to review the panel's decision. When all the judges on a court review a panel's decision, the review is called an "en banc review." Whether you request review by a panel of judges or by all the judges, court rules limit the circumstances in which reconsideration will be allowed.

If you ask a panel to reconsider its decision, the panel will usually do so only if a party can show that the panel failed to consider a salient fact or misunderstood the law. The Federal Rules of Appellate Procedure, for example, require that a party seeking panel reconsideration "state with particularity each point of law or fact that the petitioner believes the court has overlooked or misapprehended."[10] Many state courts have identical requirements.[11]

Thus, if you wish to persuade an intermediate appellate panel of judges to reconsider, first, look carefully at the criteria for reconsideration. If your case does not meet those criteria, do not waste your time, the court's time, and your client's money in the name of zealous representation. Appellate judges do not like petitions for rehearing that simply repeat the arguments made in the briefs. If, however, the opinion clearly shows that the court missed an important fact in the record or a point of law—one that will make a difference—a petition for rehearing may be appropriate. In that case, your goal is to carefully point out to the court what the factual or legal error is and, perhaps more importantly, why it makes a difference. Appellate courts want to correctly apply the law, but, like most of us, they occasionally make a mistake. By respectfully pointing out the mistake and explaining why a different outcome is warranted, you allow the court to fix its error and you achieve a better result for your client.

If, however, the panel that decided your case reached a legally supportable conclusion, you might consider asking all the judges of the intermediate court to review the panel's decision. However, en banc review is available in only a limited number of jurisdictions. Moreover, persuading a full court to grant en banc review is more difficult than persuading a panel to grant rehearing. For example, under the federal rules, petitions for rehearing en banc are "not favored and ordinarily will not

---

10. Fed. R. App. P. 40(a)(2).
11. *See, e.g.,* Iowa R. App. P. 6.1204(3); Wash. R. App. P. 12.4(c).

be ordered" unless you persuade the court that "en banc consideration is necessary to secure or maintain uniformity of the court's decisions" or that "the proceeding involves a question of exceptional importance."[12]

Thus, if seeking a rehearing en banc, your goal is to point out that the panel's decision is inconsistent with the decisions of other panels of the same court and that the panel's decision should be rejected in favor of the rule announced by other panels.

In summary, petitions for reconsideration or rehearing are specialized persuasive documents that are appropriate in a limited number of circumstances. By consulting the rules to determine when reconsideration will be allowed and making sure that your case meets those criteria, it is possible to obtain a better result for your client without the time or expense of seeking review in a higher court.

H. Review in a Discretionary Court

Above, we have discussed the typical appellate process as a case moves from the trial court through an appellate court. Most states, though, and the federal judiciary have two levels of appellate review: an intermediate appellate court and a supreme court.[13] Thus, after an intermediate appellate court issues its final decision in a case, a party may still request that the court of last resort—typically the supreme court—review the intermediate appellate court's decision.

We must emphasize the word "request." One of the big differences between intermediate appellate courts and supreme courts is that intermediate courts tend to be non-discretionary and supreme courts tend to be discretionary. That is, intermediate appellate courts generally have to consider every appeal that is filed, and their primary goal is to correct trial court or agency error rather than to announce rules of law. In contrast, supreme courts typically have control over which cases they review. Supreme courts usually limit their docket to those cases that represent an important issue or a conflict in the law that needs to be resolved.

Some exceptions do exist to a supreme court's ability to determine its docket. In many states, statutes will require that state's highest court to review a limited range of cases. For example, death penalty cases are often reviewed directly by the supreme court, rather than the intermediate appellate court. However, the kinds of cases that a supreme court must hear are limited. Therefore, remember that your one shot at winning may be in the intermediate appellate court; use it wisely.

---

12. Fed. R. App. P. 35(a).

13. Delaware, Maine, Montana, New Hampshire, Rhode Island, North Dakota, South Dakota, Vermont, West Virginia, and Wyoming are states without typical intermediate courts.

Be Precise!
Appellant vs. Petitioner

A party who appeals a trial court's decision and has an appeal as of right, is called an "appellant." The party responding is the "appellee" or "respondent."

By contrast, when a party seeks review in a discretionary court, the party instigating the review is called the "petitioner" not the "appellant." The instigator is called the "petitioner" because that party must petition for the right to be heard. The party responding is called the "respondent," never the appellee.

Supreme Courts

Nearly every jurisdiction designates its highest court as the "supreme" court of that jurisdiction. Exceptions, however, exist. New York and Maryland, for example, both call their highest court the "Court of Appeals." And, in New York, the trial courts are called "Supreme Courts."

For convenience, we use the term "supreme court" to refer to the highest court in a given jurisdiction.

I. Motions in Appellate Courts

Finally, many lawyers are surprised to learn that it is possible to file motions in appellate courts. As in trial courts, if you want an appellate court to take some action, you file a motion asking the court to do so. Depending on court rules, the motion should include an argument or should incorporate a separate memorandum that includes an argument. The federal rule is illustrative: "A motion must state with particularity the grounds for the motion, the relief sought, and the legal argument necessary to support it."[14]

What might you ask an appellate court to do? Just as with a trial court, the answer is that you may ask the court to do anything that is within its power and that will benefit your client. A few common examples include (1) a motion to file an overlength brief; (2) a motion for an extension of time in which to file a brief or other document; (3) a motion to dismiss based on mootness; and (4) a motion asking the court to take judicial notice. Court rules regarding motions generally are fairly specific, and you

---

14. Fed. R. App. P. 27(a)(2)(A).

should consult them before filing a motion. Most courts permit responses to motions.[15] Typically, though, appellate courts do not allow oral argument on motions.

In addition to understanding the appellate process, writing an effective appellate brief requires you to also understand several uniquely appellate concepts. These concepts include (1) appellate jurisdiction and justiciability; (2) preservation of error and plain error; (3) harmless error; (4) right for the wrong reason; and (5) standards of review. The next section explains these concepts in further detail.

V. Fundamental Appellate Concepts

Several appellate concepts shape how appellate courts handle appeals. Understanding these concepts will allow you to make an initial assessment of whether an appeal is likely to succeed and will allow you to advise your client appropriately. If you decide to proceed with an appeal, understanding these appellate concepts will also allow you to speak a language that appellate judges understand and to shape your writing to fit comfortably into the appellate setting in which it will be considered. Finally, familiarity with these concepts will also give you a deeper understanding of the many appellate opinions you will read in your legal career. What follows is a short discussion of some fundamental appellate concepts.

A. Appellate Jurisdiction and Justiciability

As with trial courts, an appellate court must have jurisdiction over a matter and the matter must be justiciable, that is, capable of being resolved by the court.

Lack of trial court or appellate court jurisdiction generally may be raised at any time, so even if the case has been tried, your most persuasive argument on appeal could be that the trial court lacked jurisdiction or that the appellate court lacks jurisdiction. You might, for instance, argue to a federal court of appeals that the federal district court never had jurisdiction over the case because the parties were adjudicating a state law matter, but were not actually citizens of different states, as re-

---

15. *See, e.g.,* Fed. R. App. P. 27(a)(3).

quired by 28 U.S.C. §1332(a)(1). Or, even if the district court had jurisdiction over the case, there might be an argument that the appellate court does not have jurisdiction because, for example, the district court never issued a "final decision," as required by 28 U.S.C. §1291.

Similarly, you should consider whether the case is justiciable, that is, capable of being decided by the court. Just as you might argue to a trial court that a dispute is not justiciable because the case is moot or is not yet ripe for adjudication, that same argument may be made to an appellate court. If, for example, events have occurred while the case is on appeal that would render any relief on appeal meaningless, the case may have become moot. If your case has become moot or is otherwise nonjusticiable, your strongest argument (as a respondent, of course) might be a procedural one: The case should be dismissed.

The point is that being aware of and thinking about jurisdiction and justiciability may provide you with persuasive arguments that are not related to the legal merits of the case. Sometimes the best argument is the simplest one.

B. Preservation of Error and Plain Error

Another important concept that occupies appellate courts is the principle known as "preservation of error." The general rule is that an appellate court will not consider a claim of error that was not raised at trial. That is, if a litigant wants to challenge a trial court's ruling on appeal, that same issue must have been brought to the trial court's attention, or the appellate court typically will not consider it. For example, if you want to argue to an appellate court that the trial court erred in admitting a piece of evidence, you must have objected to admission of the evidence in the trial court. Similarly, if you want to challenge the length of your client's prison sentence, the appellate court normally will not consider your argument unless you first raised the matter in the trial court.

Why require that a claim of error be preserved? First, the requirement promotes judicial efficiency by making the trial court aware of the claimed error when it still has a chance to take action to correct it. Second, the requirement ensures that the appellate court will have a complete record to review. For example, if the claim is that the trial court erred when it excluded a witness's testimony, challenging the exclusion at trial may allow the lawyer to describe the excluded evidence (on the record, but outside the presence of the jury). If, even in light of that description, the trial court still refuses to admit the evidence, the appellate court will know what it was that the trial court excluded. Finally—for judicial efficiency and just plain fairness—the rule prevents a litigant who notices a claimed error from "lying in the weeds," that is, waiting until after a loss to jump out and claim an error.

The Importance of Preserving a Claim of Error

Because appellate courts typically will not consider issues that were not "preserved," attorneys must think about appellate issues long before an appeal is filed. Success on appeal often hinges on trial counsel anticipating the arguments that will win on appeal and ensuring that a proper record is developed to support those arguments should an appeal follow. For an attorney who takes over a case on appeal and who sees a promising issue on which to base an appeal, nothing is more frustrating than to learn that the issue was not preserved by the trial lawyer. In that case, it may be necessary to abandon the appeal altogether or to rely only on issues that might be less persuasive. Therefore, trial lawyers should always assume that an appeal will follow and act accordingly.

Whether the action a lawyer took in the trial court was adequate to preserve the claim of error is something that appellate lawyers are happy to argue about and appellate courts are happy to write about. In fact, you may read appellate opinions in which the sole disagreement between the majority and dissent is whether a claim of error was preserved. What it takes to preserve a claim of error varies from jurisdiction to jurisdiction and from legal issue to legal issue. Nonetheless, a good guideline is that an objection or other action that may preserve a claim of error must be both timely and specific to preserve a claim of trial court error; how timely and how specific, however, varies with the context.

For our purposes, you should be aware of the following: (1) claims of error generally must be preserved for an appellate court to address them; and (2) appellate courts take the requirement seriously and many claims do not get addressed for lack of preservation. Thus, before proceeding with an appeal or raising a certain issue on appeal, you must consider whether the issue was preserved for appeal.

That said, some exceptions to the preservation requirement may allow an appellate court to address unpreserved claims. The most common exception is known as "plain error." If the trial court made a mistake that is so obvious that even a schoolchild would know it was an error, an appellate court may consider an argument based on that error. So, for example, if a trial court instructed a jury that it could convict a criminal defendant of a felony based on a preponderance of the evidence (rather than beyond a reasonable doubt) and that defendant was found guilty, that instruction would constitute plain error, and an appellate court could review the trial court's instruction to the jury despite a lack of preservation. Similarly, if a trial court refused to allow a jury trial even though one was required by the United States Constitution, an appellate court typically would address the error even if not preserved. But the trial court's foul-up must be obvious before an appellate court will be willing to treat it as plain error.

> ### Be Precise!
> ### A Note on the Phrase "Preservation of Error"
>
> Most appellate practitioners use the phrase "preservation of error"; indeed, rules of appellate procedure use the phrase. That phrase is not quite accurate. Think about it: In the lower tribunal, a lawyer does not "preserve *error*." Rather, the lawyer preserves a *claim* or *argument* that the tribunal has committed error. Accordingly, although you will often (including in this chapter) see the phrases "preservation of error" or "preserve error" used as shorthand, remember that it is just shorthand. Accordingly, rather than writing, "Counsel for plaintiff *preserved the error* by objecting to the trial court's ruling," be more precise: "Plaintiff's counsel *preserved the claim of error* by objecting to the trial court's ruling." Appellate sticklers will love you.

C. Harmless Error

Another concept relating to how appellate courts will dispose of claims of error on appeal is known as "harmless error." Consider this example: The trial court commits an error; you object, preserving the claim of error; on appeal, you raise the claim of error, make a brilliant argument, and seek reversal of the trial court's judgment. You win, right? Not necessarily. If the trial court's error—although indisputably an error—did not ultimately affect the outcome of the case, the appellate court will not reverse the decision based on the error. Thus, if one witness's testimony was admitted erroneously, but the jury heard the same information from three other witnesses, the error in admitting the first witness's testimony may be harmless. Under what circumstances an error will be considered "harmless" varies, but all appellate courts recognize the doctrine. You should consider whether an error is harmless when deciding whether to appeal and when choosing which issues to raise on appeal. In other words, no harm, no foul.

D. Right for the Wrong Reason

Another important appellate concept is known as "right for the wrong (or a different) reason." Under this principle, an appellate court may affirm a trial court's ruling, even if the trial court's reasoning was incorrect, if the trial court ultimately reached the legally correct result. Thus, when deciding whether to appeal and when considering which issues to raise on appeal, you should also consider whether the trial court was right for the wrong reason. Similarly, a respondent who is seeking to uphold a trial court's ruling should carefully consider whether there is a colorable argument that the trial court was right for the wrong reason—sometimes, that argument may be the only one available for affirmance.

> ### Right for the Wrong Reason: The Tipsy Coachman
>
> Here is a bit of colorful legal history. In Florida and Georgia, the "right for the wrong reason" rule is known as the "tipsy coachman" rule. The "tipsy coachman" label comes from a nineteenth century Georgia case, *Lee v. Porter*, 63 Ga. 345, 346 (1879), in which the Georgia Supreme Court, noting that the "human mind is so constituted that in many instances it finds the truth when wholly unable to find the way that leads to it," quoted a portion of Oliver Goldsmith's 1774 poem, *Retaliation*. That portion described "honest William . . . [h]is conduct still right, with his argument wrong . . . ."
>
> > Here lies honest William, whose heart was a mint,
> > While the owner ne'er knew half the good that was in't;
> > The pupil of impulse, it forc'd him along,
> > His conduct still right, with his argument wrong;
> > Still aiming at honour, yet fearing to roam,
> > The coachman was tipsy, the chariot drove home;
> > Would you ask for his merits? alas! he had none;
> > What was good was spontaneous, his faults were his own.

E. Standards of Review

The final—and probably most important—appellate concept addressed here is standards of review. Appellate judges live and breathe standards of review, so it is important to be familiar with the concept. In this section, you will learn what standards of review are and what different standards may apply to different cases. Then, in Chapter 11, *Constructing Appellate Briefs*, you will see how standards of review can inform your legal arguments.

Appellate standards of review can be described in various ways:

- The degree of deference that an appellate court gives to a lower tribunal's resolution of an issue
- The level of scrutiny an appellate court gives to a lower tribunal's determination
- The lens through which the appellate court will view the lower tribunal's determination

You are, no doubt, familiar with standards of review in non-legal settings. You may have asked a friend or colleague to review something you wrote to see if it is "in the ballpark." In that case, you are not asking the reviewer to tell you whether you have crossed every "t" and dotted every "i," but rather you seek a general level of scrutiny. Contrast that standard of review with the case in which you ask someone to look something over "with a fine-toothed comb." In that case, you are asking the reviewer to perform a very different type of review—a level of review with much greater scrutiny.

The sports world also has standards of review. For example, in the National Football League, a referee's initial call on the field may not be overruled absent "incontrovertible visual evidence" that the call on the field was incorrect. Such a standard gives high deference to the call on the field because it permits the call on the field to be overruled only when it is "incontrovertibly" clear that the call on the field was wrong. As a result, coaches are less likely to "appeal" decisions than if the standard were, say, "some" visual evidence.

As with standards outside the legal world, some appellate standards of review are more deferential to the trial court, while others are less deferential. Some allow the appellate court to substitute its view for that of the lower tribunal, while others require the appellate judge to say, in essence, "Well, I would not have done that, but in light of the standard of review, we cannot reverse." Before turning to specific standards of review, a few important points about standards of review are in order.

First, standards of review are tied to specific issues, not to entire cases. For example, if you are challenging a trial court's interpretation of a constitutional provision, the standard of review—de novo, as discussed below— is the same whether that issue arises in a securities regulation case or a death penalty case. That also means that different issues you raise on appeal may be (and often are) governed by different standards of review.

Second, because standards of review vary by issue you will need to research what the standard of review is for each issue you raise on appeal. Although it happens rarely, you may find an issue for which the standard of review is unsettled. If the standard of review is unsettled, you will begin your argument to the court by arguing for the standard of review that you believe is appropriate—and beneficial for your client. After presenting your argument about the appropriate standard of review, then, you will proceed to your substantive argument.

Third, standards of review are critically important. The standard of review for a given issue can affect everything from the decision whether to appeal, to your likelihood of prevailing on appeal, to how you couch your argument, to how the appellate court will think about your case. If you do not consciously consider (and set out) the proper standard of review for every issue you raise on appeal—and tie your substantive argument and relief sought to it—your brief will not have that special appellate flavor to it and the brief will be far less persuasive.

Various standards of review exist; the following discussion focuses on the most common standards of review that apply in appeals from trial court decisions. Be aware that different standards of review may apply to judicial review of agency decisions.

1. Rulings on issues of law

The most familiar standard of review is for error of law. Whether the lower tribunal correctly interpreted the law is reviewed de novo by the appellate court. That is, the appellate court determines "anew" what the correct interpretation is, and the appellate court owes no deference to the lower court's interpretation.[16] This same standard is also described by saying that the appellate court reviews the lower court's ruling "as a matter of law" or by saying that the appellate court's review is "plenary." If you lost in the court below—and assuming that you have a persuasive legal argument—this standard of review is the one under which you are most likely to prevail because under this standard the appellate court owes no deference to the lower court.

2. Factual findings

The second common standard of review relates to how the appellate court will consider the trial court's factual findings. A court is engaged in fact-finding—and not legal analysis—if its conclusion is based solely on the record, with no reference to a legal standard. For example, was the traffic light red when the pickup truck barreled through it? What exactly were the dimensions of the room in which the police officer interrogated the defendant, and how many hours did the interrogation last? Did the driver have three India Pale Ales before he jumped in his car and drove, or was it seven? The responses to all of those questions are findings of fact.

When an appellate court reviews a trial court's factual findings, the standard of review is significantly more deferential to the trial court. An appellate court will reverse a trial court's factual finding only if the trial court's findings of fact were "clearly erroneous." Under this standard, an appellate court will not re-weigh the evidence in the record. Rather, the trial court's judgment about how to resolve any conflicts in the record will stand, and the appellate court will reverse only if the trial court's factual determination is implausible, and the appellate court is left with a "firm and determined" conviction that the trial court's factual findings was a mistake.

The strong deference that appellate courts give to factual findings may affect the likelihood of your argument prevailing on appeal. If your

---

16. Although the phrase "de novo" is most commonly used as described above, de novo review may have a different meaning in different jurisdictions, so be careful to check how the phrase is used in your jurisdiction. For example, in Oregon the phrase de novo review applies to reviewing errors of fact and not errors of law:

> In Oregon, "*de novo* review" remains tied to its origins in equity cases, which appellate courts tried anew upon the record; it thus refers to the review of factual findings. The phrase is inapplicable to actions at law, such as this case, in which there is the right to a jury trial on the facts. The [United States Supreme] Court, however, uses the phrase to refer to appellate review of the trial court's legal decisions; it contrasts that standard of review with review for abuse of discretion.

Waddill v. Anchor Hocking, Inc., 78 P.3d 570, 573 (Or. Ct. App. 2003) (citation omitted).

argument on appeal depends on the appellate court finding the facts contrary to the way they were found by the trial court, you will have a steep uphill battle.

3. Discretionary rulings

The third common standard of review is for abuse of discretion. For some rulings, no rule of law provides a single correct disposition. Rather, a trial court may choose from among a number of legally justifiable actions. In those cases, unless the trial court made a choice that is outside those that are legally available, an appellate court will not disturb the trial court's choice.

The abuse of discretion standard is often applied to a trial court's decision about court processes because trial courts are permitted significant leeway when managing courtroom proceedings. Assume, for example, that a rule of civil procedure states that, upon proper request, the trial court must give a party oral argument on any motion. Assume that the rule also states that the court may determine the amount of time the party may have for oral argument. Whether a trial court chose to give a party 15 minutes or 90 minutes, the appellate court would be unlikely to consider either ruling to be in error; that choice is within the "sound discretion" of the trial court. If, on the other hand, the trial court gave a party only 30 seconds for oral argument on a complex issue, that choice might constitute an abuse of discretion. In the first instance, the trial court chose from among legally permissible options, while in the second case, the trial court's choice was outside the range that the rule permitted.

Other decisions regarding court processes to which the abuse of discretion standard of review might apply include a court's decision to grant (or deny) motions to amend a complaint; to amend a judgment; to seal court records; or to grant a continuance.

Trial courts also often have leeway with more substantive decisions. For example, Federal Rule of Evidence 403 provides that "[t]he court may exclude relevant evidence if its probative value is substantially outweighed by a danger of one or more of the following: unfair prejudice, confusing the issues, misleading the jury, undue delay, wasting time, or needlessly presenting cumulative evidence." Because weighing those considerations requires a court to choose from among more than one permissible outcome, rulings under Federal Rule of Evidence 403 are reviewed for an abuse of discretion. As a rule of thumb, if a lower court takes an action pursuant to a statute or rule stating that the court "may" do something, the action probably will be reviewed for an abuse of discretion.

Like the clearly erroneous standard for factual findings, the abuse of discretion standard of review is deferential to the lower tribunal. On balance, however, the abuse of discretion standard is probably slightly more favorable to the party who lost below than the clearly erroneous standard. An appellant may be slightly more likely to persuade an appellate court that a trial court abused its discretion than that a trial court's factual finding is clearly erroneous.

4. Mixed questions of fact and law

Things in standard-of-review land get murky when considering mixed questions of fact and law. The United States Supreme Court has "noted the vexing nature of the distinction between questions of fact and questions of law,"[17] and commentators have written volumes on the subject of the proper standard of review when the two are combined. This section addresses the issue briefly, simply to provide a feel for it.

In many cases, a trial court must perform a three-step process to resolve an issue before it. First, it must determine the facts. As you know, the standard of review for that part of the process is very deferential, and the facts as found by the trial court will not be disturbed on appeal, absent "clear error." Second, having determined the facts, the trial court must interpret a rule, a statute, a constitution, or common law to determine the appropriate rule of law. As you also know, the trial court's decision in that part of the process is entitled to no deference—it is reviewed de novo. Finally, the trial court must apply the rule it has determined to the facts it has found.

This last step—when the court applies the rule that it has discovered to the facts it has found—is the so-called mixed question of fact and law. That is the tricky part: What is the proper standard of review for that part of the process? It depends. If the application of the law to the facts in a given case is more like fact-finding, then the clearly erroneous standard applies. If, in contrast, the application is more like interpreting the law, the de novo standard applies. Unfortunately, courts and commentators may disagree about when the application of law to facts is more "fact-finding-like" and when it is more "law-interpreting-like."

Thus, if you are faced with an issue that turns on a mixed question of fact and law, do your research. Determine whether the courts in your jurisdiction have reached a conclusion. With luck, the courts will have already decided the appropriate standard of review for your issue. If not, as suggested previously, you should argue for the standard that benefits your client.

5. No articulated standard of review

Sometimes, the courts have not reached a conclusion about the appropriate standard of review. In that case, you will need to advocate that a particular standard of review should apply. In doing so, you should consider whether the particular issue is one that would better be resolved

---

17. *Pullman-Standard v. Swint*, 456 U.S. 273, 288 (1982).

by the fact finder—who is in the better position to make factual calls—
or the appellate court—which is more suited to decide legal questions.
Of course, if you won below you will hope that you can make a good
faith argument that the trial court's decision should be upheld unless it
is clearly erroneous—a standard under which you are more likely to prevail. Alternatively, if you lost below, you will similarly look for a good faith
argument that the standard of review is de novo.

Effective appellate advocacy requires an understanding of standards
of review. Often, they are obvious and undisputed; in other cases, they
are unclear and open to argument. Other cases are more complicated.
For example, what first appears to be one issue may need to be pulled apart
into several sub-issues and different standards of review will be applied
to different sub-issues depending on whether the sub-issue involves fact
finding, interpreting the law, or choosing from among legally permissible conclusions.[18] Whether obvious or complicated, standards of review
play a role in every appellate case, and you must think about them carefully when you are working on an appeal.

The discussion above provides a brief overview of the standards of
review that you will most often see in practice. Table 5-C summarizes
those standards and provides examples of when each standard would be
used. If you write appellate briefs, familiarize yourself with the other
standards of review that exist—for example, those standards that govern review of an agency's factual findings. Entire books could be and
have been written on the subject of standards of review.[19] Most importantly, remember that standards of review are critical to appellate judges.

---

18. For example, as the First Circuit Court of Appeals explained,

> The appellate standard of review for [Federal] Rule [of Evidence] 702 rul-
> ings is abuse of discretion. *Gen. Elec. Co. v. Joiner*, 522 U.S. 136, 146, 118
> S.Ct. 512, 139 L.Ed.2d 508 (1997). "This standard is not monolithic: within
> it, embedded findings of fact are reviewed for clear error, questions of law
> are reviewed de novo, and judgment calls are subjected to classic abuse-
> of-discretion review." *Ungar v. Palestine Liberation Org.*, 599 F.3d 79, 83
> (1st Cir. 2010); *see also Baker v. Dalkon Shield Claimants Trust*, 156 F.3d 248,
> 251-52 (1st Cir. 1998) (noting these three dimensions of the abuse of dis-
> cretion standard in reviewing exclusion of expert testimony).

Milward v. Acuity Specialty Prods. Grp., Inc., 639 F.3d 11, 13-14 (1st Cir. 2011).

19. *See, e.g.*, Harry T. Edwards & Linda A. Elliott, *Federal Courts Standards of
Review: Appellate Court Review of District Court Decisions and Agency Actions* (2007);
see also U.S. Ct. of App. for the 9th Cir., *Standards of Review*, http://www.ca9.
uscourts.gov/content/view.php?pk_id=0000000368 (accessed June 4, 2015) (defining and outlining standards of review in criminal and civil proceedings and in review of agency decisions).

Table 5-C · Standards of Review: Federal Courts*

STANDARD OF REVIEW	DE NOVO	ABUSE OF DISCRETION	
Type of decision under review	Question of law and some mixed questions of fact and law	Discretionary action	
Lower-court decision-maker	Trial judge	Trial judge	
Degree of deference given to lower-court decision-maker	No deference	Substantial deference	
Party typically benefitted by this standard	Appellant	Respondent	
Definition	"[W]e review the matter anew, the same as if it had not been heard before, and as if no decision previously had been rendered." *Freeman v. DirecTV, Inc.*, 457 F.3d 1001, 1004 (9th Cir. 2006). "When de novo review is compelled, no form of appellate deference is acceptable." *Salve Regina Coll. v. Russell*, 499 U.S. 225, 238 (1991).	"Under this standard, a reviewing court cannot reverse absent a definite and firm conviction that the district court committed a clear error of judgment in the conclusion it reached upon a weighing of relevant factors." *Valdivia v. Schwarzenegger*, 599 F.3d 984, 988 (9th Cir. 2010). "An abuse of discretion occurs where the district court clearly erred or ventured beyond the limits of permissible choice under the circumstances." *Wright ex rel. Trust Co. of Kan. v. Abbott Labs., Inc.*, 259 F.3d 1226, 1233 (10th Cir. 2001). "Under an abuse of discretion standard, a trial court's decision will not be disturbed unless the appellate court has a definite and firm conviction that the lower court made a clear error of judgment or exceeded the bounds of permissible choice in the circumstances. That is to say, we will not alter a trial court's decision unless . . . the court's decision was an arbitrary, capricious, whimsical, or manifestly unreasonable judgment." *Id.* at 1235-36 (citations and internal quotation marks omitted).	
Examples	Motions for summary judgment; constitutional questions; statutory interpretation; mootness, ripeness, and standing; contract interpretation.	Amount of Rule 11 sanctions; attorney's fees; courtroom management and discovery issues (such as whether to grant a motion for continuance or whether to grant a motion to compel the production of documents); injunctions; temporary restraining orders.	

* Professor Terri Pollman, University of Nevada, Las Vegas William S. Boyd School of Law, created the original version of this chart. Numerous other professors within the legal writing community have since updated and modified it.

CLEARLY ERRONEOUS	SUBSTANTIAL EVIDENCE	ARBITRARY AND CAPRICIOUS
Question of fact	Question of fact	Agency resolution of a question of fact
Trial judge	Jury	Administrative law judge
Significant deference	Extreme deference	Extreme deference
Respondent	Respondent	Respondent
A reviewing court "will not reverse a lower court's finding of fact simply because [it] would have decided the case differently. Rather, a reviewing court must ask whether, on the entire evidence, it is left with the definite and firm conviction that a mistake has been committed." *Easley v. Cromartie*, 532 U.S. 234, 242 (2001) (citations and internal quotation marks omitted). "If the district court's account of the evidence is plausible in light of the record viewed in its entirety, the court of appeals may not reverse it even though convinced that had it been sitting as the trier of fact, it would have weighed the evidence differently. Where there are two permissible views of the evidence, the factfinder's choice between them cannot be clearly erroneous." *Anderson v. Bessemer City*, 470 U.S. 564, 573-74 (1985). *See generally* Fed. R. Civ. P. 52(a)	When evidence is supported by substantial evidence, it means that there is "more than a mere scintilla. It means such relevant evidence as a reasonable mind might accept as adequate to support a conclusion." *Richardson v. Perales*, 402 U.S. 389, 401 (1971) (quoting *Consolidated Edison Co. v. NLRB*, 305 U.S. 197, 229 (1938)). The "unsupported by substantial evidence" is more deferential than the "clearly erroneous" standard. *Stern v. Marshall*, 131 S. Ct. 2594, 2627 (2011), *reh'g denied*, 132 S. Ct. 56.	The absence of a rational connection between the facts found and the choice made. There should be a clear error of judgment; an action not based upon consideration of relevant factors and so is arbitrary, capricious, an abuse of discretion or otherwise not in accordance with law or if it was taken without observance of procedure required by law. *Natural Resources Defense Council, Inc. v. United States EPA*, 966 F.2d 1292, 1297 (9th Cir. 1992)
Findings of fact made by a trial court.	A finding of fact from a jury, or a finding of fact made by an administrative agency under an Administrative Procedure Act adjudication or formal rulemaking.	A government agency's resolution of a question of fact decided by informal rulemaking under the Administrative Procedure Act.

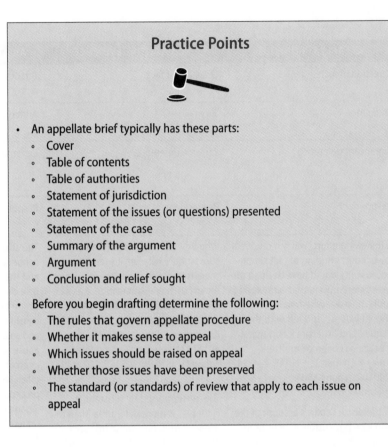

Practice Points

- An appellate brief typically has these parts:
  - Cover
  - Table of contents
  - Table of authorities
  - Statement of jurisdiction
  - Statement of the issues (or questions) presented
  - Statement of the case
  - Summary of the argument
  - Argument
  - Conclusion and relief sought

- Before you begin drafting determine the following:
  - The rules that govern appellate procedure
  - Whether it makes sense to appeal
  - Which issues should be raised on appeal
  - Whether those issues have been preserved
  - The standard (or standards) of review that apply to each issue on appeal

Chapter 6

Themes for Persuasive Arguments

Developing a persuasive argument depends on telling a cohesive story about the law, the facts, and the conclusion that the court should adopt. Developing a theme is one way in which attorneys create a cohesive, compelling narrative for the court.[1] This chapter explains what a theme is, the purpose of having a theme, how to develop a theme, and how to integrate that theme into your argument.

I. The Purpose of a Theme

A "theme" is some unifying idea that quickly and simply explains why the court should rule in your client's favor. A brief to the court—whether at the trial level or on appeal—will usually address multiple claims. Each of those claims is, in turn, supported by a series of distinct legal arguments. A theme links the law and facts in those otherwise distinct legal arguments in a way that justifies the end that your client seeks.

---

1. Although many people use "theory of the case" and "theme" interchangeably, they are a bit different. The theory of the case is your comprehensive plan for convincing the judge or the jury to rule in your client's favor. You develop your theory of the case when preparing for trial. *See* John Korzen, *Make Your Argument: Succeeding in Moot Court and Mock Trial* 153 (2010); Thomas A. Mauet, *Trials: Strategy, Skills, and the New Powers of Persuasion* 8 (2d ed. 2009) ("[T]he theory of the case . . . is simply each party's version of what really happened."). Your theme is a quick and simple explanation or summation of the overarching theory of the case.

A coherent theme counter-balances a problem that can arise when trying to tell a compelling legal story. A compelling legal story must account for all the relevant facts and law. A compelling legal story is, therefore, detailed and often lengthy. Keeping track of those details can be difficult. A theme can help the judge organize and make sense of the details within your story by providing a bottom line to which all those details connect.

One well-known theme comes from the trial of the legendary football star and actor O.J. Simpson: "If it [the glove] doesn't fit, you must acquit." That single, catchy sentence explained the crux of O.J. Simpson's argument. Simpson was accused of killing his estranged wife and a local restaurant server at her home. Part of the evidence against him included a bloody glove found on Simpson's estate, and a matching glove found at the crime scene. In a surprising move, prosecutors had Simpson try on the exhibit during trial, but the glove did not fit. From that event, the defense latched on to a winning theme of the case, and Simpson was later acquitted of murder.

More often, legal themes are not nearly as catchy as the one presented to the jury in the O.J. Simpson trial. In fact, many scholars warn against the use of a catchy theme because it can alienate the judge and undermine your credibility.[2] Thus, in developing a theme for your argument, be careful not to undermine your credibility by choosing a theme that is too simplistic or that sacrifices substance for flash.

II. Developing a Theme

Lawyers will look for a theme in one of three places: in the procedural legal standard, in a policy underlying the law, or in a social good or value that is at stake. Thus, as you develop a theme, look closely at those three areas.

A. Based on Procedural Law

Judges examine legal issues within their procedural posture. For that reason, your theme will most often be based on the legal standard for the issue before the court. For example, if you are opposing a motion for summary judgment, you will likely build a theme around the standard for denying a motion for summary judgment, as in Table 6-A. If you want to overturn a jury verdict, you would build a theme around that standard, as in Table 6-B. Both themes emphasize the applicable standard, which often is more compelling to the court than the catchy O.J. Simpson theme.

---

2. *See* Korzen, *supra* note 1, at 40-43.

Table 6-A • **Developing a theme to oppose a motion for summary judgment**

The case	You want to argue that summary judgment should not be granted.
Legal standard	Summary judgment may be granted only if "there is no genuine dispute as to any material fact and the movant is entitled to judgment as a matter of law." Fed. R. Civ. P. 56(a).
Theme	There *is* a "material issue of fact" and, therefore, summary judgment is inappropriate.
Technique	As frequently as possible (1) state that a genuine issue of fact exists and that the fact is material, and (2) prove the dispute by pointing to contradictory factual assertions and prove that the factual dispute is material by explaining the relationship between the fact and the legal standard. Thus, the summary judgment standard becomes the touchstone to which you will return because it governs how the court will decide the issue.

Table 6-B • **Developing a theme to overturn a jury verdict**

The case	You want to argue that the court should overturn a jury's verdict.
Legal standard	A judgment of acquittal must be entered for any offense for which the evidence is insufficient to sustain a conviction. Fed. R. Crim. P. 29. Evidence must be viewed in the light most favorable to the winning party. United States v. Augustine, 663 F.3d 367, 373 (8th Cir. 2011).
Theme	Even considering the evidence in the light most favorable to the winning party, the evidence does not support the verdict.
Technique	In the conclusion for every element, and as frequently as otherwise possible, (1) state that the evidence does not support the element, and (2) prove the evidence does not support the element by bringing forward all the evidence put forward by the winning party and explaining why it cannot support the element. Thus, the standard for a judgment of acquittal becomes the touchstone to which you will return.

B. Based on Substantive Law and Its Underlying Policy

Themes may also arise out of the substantive law and the policies, or reasons, for that law. Take, for example, the case *Oregon v. Ashcroft*.[3] In that case, the State of Oregon passed a statute that permitted physician-assisted suicide. The U.S. Attorney General then issued an interpretive regulation that would allow the federal government to revoke the license of any physician who dispensed a controlled substance sufficient for a person to commit suicide under the state statute. If that interpretive regulation went into effect, it would prevent all physician-assisted suicides in Oregon. Thus, the State of Oregon sought to enjoin the United States Attorney General from enforcing his interpretive regulation.

Table 6-C shows how the U.S. Attorney General might approach the argument for a motion to dismiss, and Table 6-D shows how the State of Oregon might approach its brief in response.[4] As you can see, the U.S. Attorney General can emphasize his statutory authority to regulate controlled substances, and the State of Oregon can emphasize a State's authority to regulate medical practice. Note that, although both perspectives are valid, they emphasize different laws and the reasons for those laws.

C. Based on a Social Good or Value

Themes can also relate to an important social goal or shared, core value. Themes can emphasize that a decision will promote (or undermine) an ideal, such as fairness, justice, individual autonomy, individual responsibility for damages caused, or the public's health, safety, or welfare. Themes can also emphasize core values about our legal or political system, such as efficiency in the administration of justice, separation of powers between branches, or the appropriate allocation of authority between states and the federal government.[5]

For example, advocates in the *Bush v. Gore* litigation developed themes that focused on core values about our political and legal system. In *Bush v. Gore*, the candidates for President of the United States disputed which candidate had earned Florida's electoral votes in the 2000 general election. Before the United States Supreme Court, the legal questions were whether the Florida Supreme Court's decision was consistent with certain federal statutes and the Federal Constitution. Although the legal questions fo-

---

3. 192 F. Supp. 2d 1077 (D. Or. 2002), *aff'd*, 368 F.3d 1118 (9th Cir. 2004), *aff'd*, *Gonzales v. Oregon*, 543 U.S. 1145 (2005).

4. Tables 6-C and 6-D are based on Brief for Appellants, 368 F.3d 1118 (9th Cir. 2004) (No. 02-35587), and Appellee's Brief of the State of Oregon, 368 F.3d 1118 (9th Cir. 2004) (No. 02-35587), respectively.

5. Ellie Margolis, *Teaching Students to Make Effective Policy Arguments in Appellate Briefs*, 9 Perspectives 73, 75 (Winter 2001).

Table 6-C · Developing a theme for a motion to dismiss based on the substantive law

The case	The State of Oregon passed a statute that permitted physician-assisted suicide. Citing his authority under the Controlled Substances Act, the U.S. Attorney General issued an interpretive regulation that would allow the U.S. Attorney General to revoke the licenses of physicians who prescribed drugs sufficient for an individual to commit suicide under the state statute. Among other things, the interpretive regulation stated that, "assisting suicide is not a 'legitimate medical purpose' within the meaning of [the Controlled Substances Act and its regulations]." 66 Fed. Reg. 56,607-02 (Nov. 9, 2001). The state and several private parties filed a complaint that sought to enjoin the Attorney General from enforcing that interpretive regulation. You are an Assistant U.S. Attorney seeking to dismiss that complaint.
Legal standard	Under the Controlled Substances Act, "[a] prescription for a controlled substance . . . must be issued for a legitimate medical purpose." 21 C.F.R. § 1306.04 (2015). The Attorney General has the authority to promulgate "rules and regulations . . . relating to the registration and . . . distribution and dispensing of controlled substances." *Id.* § 801.
Theme	The Controlled Substances Act permits the distribution of controlled substances for only a "legitimate medical purpose" and assisted suicide is not a "legitimate medical purpose."
Technique	In the brief, emphasize the everyday and historical understanding of "medicine" as "healing" and that Congress delegated to the Attorney General authority to regulate controlled substances. In this case, the U.S. Attorney General properly used that authority.

cused on the intersection of federal and state laws and the Florida Supreme Court's interpretation of those laws, the parties developed themes that focused on what was at stake in the litigation. As illustrated in Table 6-E, George W. Bush argued that, if the Florida Supreme Court's decision stood, the rule of law would be ignored and "electoral chaos" would ensue. By contrast, and as illustrated in Table 6-F, Albert Gore focused on the "legitimacy of public power" and "respecting the intent of the electorate."[6]

---

6. Table 6-E is based on Brief for Petitioner, *Bush v. Gore*, 531 U.S. 98 (2000) (No. 00-949). Table 6-F is based on Brief of Respondent Albert Gore, Jr., *Bush v. Gore*, 531 U.S. 98 (2000) (No. 00-949) (emphasis in the original).

Table 6-D • Developing a theme opposing the motion to dismiss based on the substantive law

The case	Same scenario as in Table 6-C, but you are an Assistant Attorney General for the State of Oregon, and you are arguing against the motion to dismiss and in favor of an injunction.
Legal standard	The clear statement doctrine: When "Congress intends to alter the 'usual constitutional balance between the States and Federal Government,' it must make its intention to do so 'unmistakably clear in the language of the statute.'" *Will v. Mich. Dept. of State Police*, 491 U.S. 58, 65 (1989) (quoting *Atascadero State Hosp. v. Scanlon*, 473 U.S. 234, 242 (1985)). Historically, states have retained the authority to regulate the practice of medicine.
Theme	The U.S. Attorney General's interpretive regulation is an unwarranted federal intrusion into the sovereign interests of Oregon, the medical practice of its physicians, and end-of-life decisions.
Technique	In the motion, emphasize the state's historical right to regulate medical practice and that, in enacting the Controlled Substances Act, Congress meant to regulate drug trafficking, not medical practice. Thus, the U.S. Attorney General overreached his authority under the Controlled Substances Act.

D. Based on Undisputed Law, Facts, or Values

Whatever the inspiration for your theme may be, remember that it must be consistent with the law and facts relevant to the argument. In fact, to the extent that you can incorporate facts or concepts that are not in dispute, your theme is more likely to be accepted. For example, in Tables 6-A and 6-B, which illustrated themes based on a procedural legal standard, no one can dispute the standard for summary judgment or overturning a jury verdict. Similarly, in Tables 6-C and 6-D the themes were based on the substantive law—the Controlled Substance Act and the clear statement doctrine, respectively. The themes in Tables 6-E and 6-F rely on core values that everyone would agree are "good" values—the importance of following the rule of law and that, in an election, every vote should count. In each case, the theme is founded on a law or principle that is not in dispute.

III. When to Develop a Theme

Attorneys develop their themes at different times. Many attorneys begin to think about a theme as part of their theory of the case at the beginning. It develops as they get to know their client and research the

Table 6-E · Developing a theme that focuses on a policy or social value that is at stake

The case	After a close general election in 2000, the Florida Supreme Court ordered a statewide manual recount of all votes. Petitioner argued that ordering such a recount violated federal law. Specifically, the petitioner argued that ordering a statewide recount violated the U.S. Constitution's guarantee to equal protection because each county had different recount procedures and, therefore, votes might be counted differently in different counties. In addition, the petitioner argued that in ordering the recount, the Florida Supreme Court established procedures that differed from those legislatively authorized, and in so doing the Florida Supreme Court inappropriately exercised legislative power.
Theme	"This case is the quintessential illustration of what will inevitably occur in a close election where the rules for tabulating ballots and resolving controversies are thrown aside after the election and replaced with judicially created *ad hoc* and *post hoc* remedies .... The Florida Supreme Court has not only violated the Constitution and federal law, it has created a regime virtually guaranteed to incite controversy, suspicion, and lack of confidence not only in the process but in the result that such a process would produce."
Technique	Petitioner returns to this theme throughout the brief. A few examples are provided below.
	Statement of the case: "The thirty-three days since the election have been characterized by widespread turmoil resulting from selective, arbitrary, changing, and standardless manual recounts."
	Argument: "The decision below therefore ushers in a regime that cannot possibly be supported by any reasonable reading of the contest statute or any other provision of the Florida Election Code. The authority to count votes, entrusted by the Legislature to county officials subject to limited judicial review, has now been seized by the state judiciary ...."
	Argument: "The Florida Supreme Court's decision is a recipe for electoral chaos. The court below has not only condoned a regime of arbitrary, selective and standardless manual recounts, but it has created a new series of unequal after-the-fact standards. This unfair, new process cannot be squared with the Constitution."

Petitioner's theme suggests that the decision of the Florida Supreme Court to order manual recounts violates the rule of law and, if upheld, will undermine confidence in federal elections and in the government.

Table 6-F · Developing a theme that focuses on a policy or social value that is at stake

The case	Same case as in Table 6-E, above. Respondent argues that the Florida Supreme Court has properly exercised judicial review of Florida election law.
Theme	"This case raises the most fundamental questions about the legitimacy of political power in our democracy. In this case, the Court will decide whether the Electors for President of the United States, and thus the President of the United States himself, will be chosen by ascertaining the actual outcome of the popular vote in Florida in the election of November 7, 2000, or whether the President will instead be chosen without counting all the ballots lawfully cast in that state."
Technique	**Introduction:** "The question is whether this Court may properly override Florida's own state-law process for determining the rightful winner of its electoral votes in this Presidential election. Such intervention would run an impermissible risk of tainting the result of the election in Florida — and thereby the nation. For this Court has long championed the fundamental right of all who are qualified to cast their votes "and to have their votes counted."
	Argument: The Florida Supreme Court's order does nothing more than place the voters whose votes were not tabulated by the machine on the same footing as those whose votes were so tabulated. In the end, all voters are treated equally: Ballots that reflect their intent are counted.
	Argument: "[P]etitioners would have the Court abruptly end the counting altogether and *toss out lawfully cast ballots that have been, and are now being, counted.* That is an absurd and unprecedented response . . . , and one that surely is not required by the U.S. Constitution."
	Argument: "The only due process right even arguably implicated by this case is the right of voters to have their ballots counted . . . ."

To create a theme, the respondent steps back from technical arguments about whether the Florida Supreme Court's order is consistent with federal law to remind the court that the value at stake is respect for the intent of the voters.

facts and law surrounding the case. Often, though, a theme does not fully emerge until they have researched the law and developed their arguments. At that point, the attorney has a full grasp of the law and facts. Also at that point, the attorney can take a step back to reflect on the argument and develop a cohesive theme consistent with the theory of the case.

Do not worry too much if a theme is not immediately evident. Often when you begin working on an argument, you will not know what the theme will be. As you continue to write and think about a case, the key legal or moral principle will likely reveal itself. You may not see a theme early on, but one may emerge after you have started organizing your arguments or developing the strengths and weaknesses of your case. As you wrestle with your case's legal and factual minutiae, if you find yourself saying, "What's *really* going on here is ..." you have likely found your theme. Once a theme has emerged—be it a legal standard or something more "catchy"—you can go back and make sure you have integrated the theme into the structure of your legal argument.

Practice Points

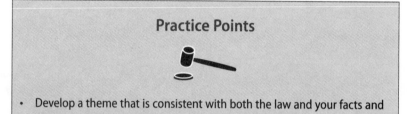

- Develop a theme that is consistent with both the law and your facts and reminds the court why you win.

- Lawyers often develop themes from examining the procedural legal standard, a policy underlying the substantive law, or a social value that is at stake.

- When developing a theme, remember that the court is more likely to accept your theme to the extent that you can incorporate facts or concepts that are not in dispute.

- Continue to develop and refine your theme as you write.

Chapter 7

Organizing Persuasive Arguments

The previous chapters have provided you with background necessary for the writing process. In the previous chapters you have learned about the nature of persuasion, the ethics and professionalism required of an advocate, and the litigation process (Chapters 1 through 3). You have been introduced to the trial motion and the appellate brief (Chapters 4 and 5), and you have begun to think about what underlying themes might exist within your client's case (Chapter 6). Now, we turn to the heart of the matter: the arguments you will present to a court. After researching the law and understanding the facts of your client's case, you are likely to begin the drafting process

The drafting process begins by thinking about how to organize the various claims and arguments you intend to present to the court. This chapter addresses how to organize those claims and arguments.

This chapter is broken down into several sections. The first section, § 7.1, addresses how to organize multiple claims and multiple arguments. Most legal arguments involve multiple arguments, and often, multiple claims. Thus, § 7.1, *Organizing Claims and Arguments*, will be applicable to almost any argument you make. The sections that follow address how to organize particular legal arguments. Some arguments depend more on analogical arguments, some on rule-based arguments, and others on a factor analysis. Of course, some briefs rely on all three. The remaining sections of this chapter—§ 7.2 through § 7.5—explain how to organize your legal arguments whether those arguments depend on analogical arguments, rule-based arguments, a factor analysis, or some combination. We recommend that you focus on those sections that are necessary to developing your particular argument.

As you read this chapter and the individual sections within it, you will likely notice two guiding principles emerge: First, no matter what your argument, use a traditional structure. Lawyers—and, therefore, judges—share certain ingrained expectations about how information will be presented. If your writing conforms to those expectations, your arguments will be easier for the judge to follow and to absorb. The more your writing deviates from those expectations, the more likely the judge will struggle to follow your argument. The sections that follow describe traditional organizational structures.

Second, whenever possible, help your reader see your organization by explicitly stating how the argument ahead is organized. As an advocate, you want to carry your reader along with your argument. A judge, surprised by new information, will have to stop, go back, and figure out how it all fits together. You have just lost the judge. To avoid losing the judge along the way, be explicit about your organization.

Finally, as you read, you may notice that the information is already familiar to you. The organizational structures you use when writing to a court are by and large the same organizational structures you use when writing an objective, interoffice memo. The purpose of this chapter is to show how those very same organizational structures can be used to present a persuasive argument.

Organizing Claims and Arguments

The first step in developing the argument section of a brief is to determine the order in which you will present the claims or defenses you are raising and the order of the arguments within each claim. In addition, you will want to make that order and the reason for that order clear to the court. When the court can easily follow the order of your arguments, you make it easier for the court to understand and absorb your arguments. Thus, in addition to explaining how to order your claims and arguments, this section of the book also addresses how to make that organization clear to the court.

I. Organizing Multiple Claims

A "claim" is an assertion of a right that, if proved, entitles a party to relief. Usually, litigation involves multiple claims arising from a single event. If a party fails to raise all the claims arising from a single event, that party can be barred from raising that claim later. Thus, most litigation includes multiple claims. For example, an employment dispute might raise claims of breach of contract and a variety of tort claims such as intentional infliction of emotional distress, discrimination based on gender, and invasion of privacy. Usually, the different claims are governed by different law.

If you represent the responding party, you will likely respond to the claims, arguing that they are unsupported by the law or facts, and you may also have defenses to the claims. You may argue that the court lacks jurisdiction, which would be a defense to the entire claim, or you might argue that the statute of limitations has run on a particular claim. Defenses, like the initial claims, often are each governed by different law.

Thus, whether you are the moving party or the responding your party, you will likely have to decide the order in which to address each claim or defense.

A. Order Your Claims

With respect to ordering claims or defenses, the default rule is simple: Address your strongest claim or defense first. First impressions count, and you want the court's first impression to be that your arguments are strong.

That rule—that you should state your strongest argument first—is sometimes forgotten when you are writing a responding motion or brief. In that case, your opponent has set out a series of claims and chosen how to order those claims. You may be inclined to simply follow the structure established by your opponent's opening motion or brief. Do not fall into that trap! Instead, run your own race. Think about the defenses or counter-claims *you* want to present and determine the order that will be most effective. Then, present your counter-claims or defenses in that order.

Of course, every rule has its exception. Sometimes logic requires that one claim be addressed before others. For example, procedural issues—such as the court's jurisdiction or a statute of limitations—must be presented before the substantive claims are presented because the court cannot address the substantive issues until the procedural issues are resolved. In that situation, present the procedural issue first.

B. Tell the Reader the Order of Your Claims

As discussed above, you want to make your organizational scheme easy for the court to see and follow. You can do that by alerting the court to the order in which you are addressing the claims or defenses.

In fact, any time one unit of analysis breaks down into smaller units of analysis, you should alert your reader to that analytical fork in the road. In a persuasive document, the argument section is the largest analytical unit. That argument section often addresses several claims. When the argument section—the largest analytical unit—breaks down into individual claims—smaller analytical units—you will must alert the court to that analytical divide.

A roadmap sentence will do the job. A "roadmap sentence" (or sentences) is any sentence (or group of sentences) that explains the number of smaller units that lie ahead. For example, the roadmap sentences in Example 7.1-A identify the claims that will be addressed within the argument section. In that example, the roadmap sentences are conclusions. Using conclusions to identify the issues is a persuasive tactic because it begins the process of shaping the court's thinking about the outcome of the case. Example 7.1-B illustrates a one-sentence roadmap.

Example 7.1-A • Two sentences create a roadmap for an argument section

---

ARGUMENT

Defendants John Ashcroft, in his official capacity as United States Attorney General, and Asa Hutchinson, in his official capacity as Administrator of the Drug Enforcement Agency, hereby oppose Plaintiffs' motion for a preliminary injunction. That injunction would prohibit the Attorney General from enforcing the Controlled Substances Act, 21 U.S.C. §§ 801-971, against doctors who prescribe federally controlled substances to help patients commit suicide. As explained below, the State of Oregon, the principal plaintiff in this case, lacks standing to seek an injunction against the enforcement of federal law against private parties and should therefore be dismissed from the case. Moreover, Plaintiffs cannot sustain their burden of showing both a likelihood of success on the merits and irreparable injury absent a preliminary injunction.

The last two sentences (shaded) provide a roadmap by identifying the two claims that will be addressed in the argument section.

Notice that those two sentences are stated as conclusions. Reread those last two sentences imagining that they were written instead as "the first issue is whether" and "the second issue is whether." Which formulation is more persuasive?

I. The State of Oregon lacks standing to seek an injunction; thus, the complaint must be dismissed.

The State of Oregon lacks standing to enjoin the Federal Government from enforcing federal law against private parties . . . .

Example 7.1-B • One sentence creates a roadmap for the argument section

---

ARGUMENT

The plaintiff's complaint must be dismissed for two reasons: The complaint fails to state a claim, and the statute of limitations has run.

The first sentence (shaded) provides a roadmap.

The text before the colon would, by itself, also be a roadmap sentence. However, the writer likely thought the sentence would be more powerful if the reasons were explained.

I. Plaintiff's complaint must be dismissed because Plaintiff's complaint fails to state a claim on which relief can be granted.

Plaintiff's complaint must be dismissed because Plaintiff has failed to allege conduct that is "extreme and outrageous," a necessary element of the tort.

II. Organizing Multiple Legal Arguments Within a Single Claim

After determining the order in which you will address each claim or defense, you will have to determine how to organize their constituent parts. Each claim or defense is usually governed by rules that can be broken down into elements or factors. Thus, your next organizational task is to determine the order in which to address those constituent elements or factors and to describe that organizational choice to the court.

A. Order the Arguments Within a Claim

The typical organizational structure you are likely to choose depends on whether your claim is composed of elements or factors. Below, we discuss each in turn.

1. Elements

An "element" is a condition that *must* be proved for a party to succeed in its claim. For example, to establish a claim of negligence, the plaintiff typically must prove five elements: a duty, a breach of that duty, factual causation, proximate (or legal) causation, and harm. Usually, the elements are recited in that order. Because the elements are usually recited in that way, your default assumption should be to present them in that order.

Although you will usually present your arguments in their commonly recited order, you should consider whether another order is better. If, for example, you are counsel to a defendant accused of negligence and your research tells you that your strongest argument is that the plaintiff cannot prove harm, you might start there.

Remember, though, that if you present your arguments in an order different from the order in which the elements appear in the governing rule, you will want to explain the different order to the judge in the roadmap section of that claim, as explained below in Part II.B, *Use a Roadmap Section to Tell the Reader the Order of Your Arguments*.

2. Steps

A "step" is also an element; a step, however, is an element that must be addressed within a particular sequence. That is, when a claim is composed of steps, courts have established a particular order in which the elements are to be addressed.

One common area in which you will see arguments structured around steps is in any argument involving employment discrimination or retaliation. Often, to prove that she has been discriminated against, a plaintiff will have to, first, prove a *prima facie* case of discrimination. That is, the plaintiff will have to introduce evidence that she was discriminated against because of some protected characteristic (such as race or gender) or because of some protected action (such as whistle-blowing). In the next step, the employer must come forward with some legitimate, nondiscriminatory reason for taking the action about which the plaintiff is complaining. Finally, and in the step necessary for the plaintiff to win, she must prove that the ostensibly legitimate reason provided by the defendant is "mere pretext."

When a claim is composed of steps, the organization is easy: Follow the sequence the court has established.

3. Factors

In contrast to an element or step, a "factor" is a condition that is weighed to determine an outcome. When an argument is dependent on factors, no one factor must be present for a party to win. Rather, to reach a conclusion, the decision-maker will assess the strength of each factor and the degree to which each factor weighs in favor of or against a particular conclusion.

For example, to determine whether a party entered into a prenuptial agreement voluntarily, a court may consider a variety of factors including when the agreement was signed, whether the parties had adequate opportunity to consult with a lawyer, the relative sophistication of the parties, and whether the assets of each party were sufficiently disclosed.[1] No one factor is determinative of the outcome. Rather, all the relevant facts are considered, and the decision-maker determines whether the agreement was entered into voluntarily based on the relative weight of the different factors.

When an analysis depends on factors, you are likely to find that the organization is less obvious. Because factors are weighed against one another to reach a conclusion, factors are connected in a way that elements are not. This connection among factors creates organizational challenges. Ultimately, you will have to choose between addressing all the factors in a single argument or addressing each factor in its own argument. Section 7.5, *Structuring Factor Analyses*, discusses in more detail these different organizational patterns and how to choose between them. For now, understand that a factor analysis can be addressed as either one legal argument, which will addresses all the factors in combination, or as multiple legal arguments, in which each argument addresses just one factor.

If you address a factor analysis with multiple legal arguments, then you must decide which factor to address first. The advice for ordering a multi-factor analysis is the same as for ordering a multi-element analysis. As a default, address the factors in the same order in which they are

---

1. *In re Rudder*, 217 P.3d 183, 194 (Or. Ct. App. 2009).

explained in the governing rule. If, however, one factor is a particularly dominant factor that is likely to swing the analysis in your client's favor, you will likely want to address that factor first.

Again, if your arguments occur in an order different from the order explained in the governing rule, take a moment to explain the different order to the court in the roadmap section to that claim, as explained below.

B. Use a Roadmap Section to Tell the Reader the Order of Your Arguments

Once you have chosen the order in which you will present the elements or factors within a claim, you must explain that order to the court by providing a roadmap section. A "roadmap section" is a more extensive form of roadmapping that differs from the roadmap sentences described above. A roadmap section is used when the smaller units of analysis share some governing law. Figure 7.1-C on the facing page illustrates when you might use a roadmap section as opposed to roadmap sentences.

> **A Roadmap Section Is Not an Argument**
>
> A roadmap section tells your reader what arguments you will be making later in the motion or brief and the order in which you will be making them. The introduction does not provide the necessary legal and factual foundation to actually make the arguments.

A roadmap section is always necessary at the beginning of a claim that is composed of more than one element or when a factor analysis addresses the factors one-by-one. A typical roadmap section to a claim includes up to five parts.

- The conclusion about the claim,
- The governing rule for the claim, which identifies the constituent elements or factors,
- A statement identifying any of the smaller elements or factors that will *not* be addressed in a full legal argument and an explanation of why,
- A roadmap of the remaining elements or factors that will be addressed with full legal arguments, and
- A conclusion regarding what you will show about each element or factor for the claim as a whole.

Each part is designed to give the court a look at the landscape ahead so that it can better follow your arguments.

Although a roadmap section has up to five parts, you do not always need all five parts. The remainder of this section briefly explains the parts and describes when you are more or less likely to employ them.

1. Conclusion

A roadmap section begins with a conclusion for two reasons. First, a conclusion tells the court where you are headed with the series of arguments that follow, and it provides one more opportunity to remind the court of what you hope will be its ultimate conclusion. Thus, the roadmap section provides both an organizational and a persuasive op-

Figure 7.1-C · Roadmap sections and roadmap sentences

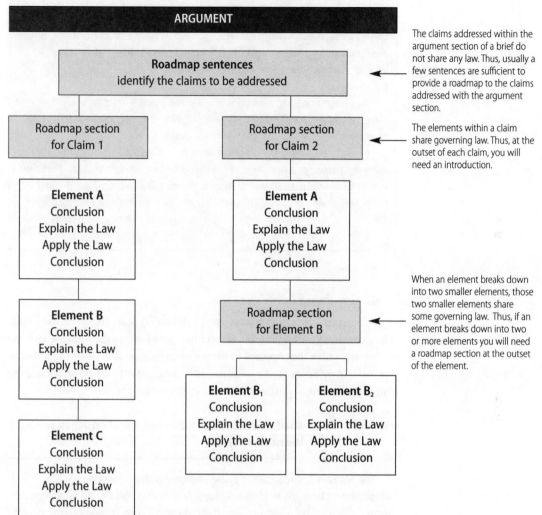

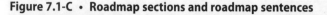

portunity. Despite the importance of an initial conclusion, some attorneys choose not to include a conclusion at the outset because it may repeat an immediately preceding point heading.

Repeating an initial conclusion in the point heading and at the outset of your argument can, however, be effective. A court may want to read just the point headings, or the court may choose to skip the point headings and read just the text. Because you do not know which way a judge will read your argument, it's best to include a conclusion at the outset even if it asserts the same idea that is in the point heading. Why lose an opportunity to help organize and persuade the court? To avoid having the same sentence verbatim, you may choose to repeat the conclusion with slightly different phrasing.

Roadmap sentences vs. roadmap sections

Roadmap sections and roadmap sentences have similar functions. Both alert your reader that a larger analytical unit breaks down into smaller analytical units. Whether you use one or the other depends on the circumstances

You use a roadmap section whenever the smaller units of analysis share some governing law. Thus, any time an argument breaks down into one or more elements or factors, you will need a roadmap section.

By contrast, you use a roadmap sentence to explain any idea that has different parts. For example, you could use a roadmap sentence to alert the reader to the number of claims in an argument. Those claims are distinct ideas, but share no governing law. Similarly, you could use a roadmap sentence to alert the reader to a court's analysis that has several parts.

---

2. Governing rule

After stating the conclusion, you will usually state the governing rule. The governing rule identifies the elements or factors that follow and explains any rules that applies to *all* the elements or factors in the governing rule. Any rules that relate to just one element or factor should be contained in the argument about that element or factor.

Example 7.1-D · Roadmap section includes additional explanation about the governing rule

---

The Workers' Compensation Board improperly denied workers' compensation benefits to Mr. Mark Floyd, and its decision should be reversed. Under California law, a person injured during an off-duty recreational activity is entitled to workers' compensation if the activity was a reasonable expectancy of employment. Cal. Lab. Code Ann. § 3600(a)(9) (West 2003). An activity is a

Governing rule explained.

reasonable expectancy of employment if (1) the employee subjectively believed he was required to participate in the activity and (2) the employee's belief was objectively reasonable. *Meyer v. Workers' Comp. Appeals Bd.*, 204 Cal. Rptr. 74, 76 (Ct. App. 1984). In assessing whether an activity is a reasonable expectancy of

Additional information about how courts interpret governing rule.

employment, California courts liberally construe the statute in favor of extending benefits. Cal. Lab. Code Ann. § 3202 (West 2003).

In this case, Mark Floyd subjectively believed he was required to participate in the paddleball game and his belief was objectively reasonable. He is therefore entitled to workers' compensation benefits.

In Example 7.1-D, the roadmap section appropriately explains that a California statute is liberally construed. That explanation is provided in the introductory paragraph because that rule of construction is relevant to both elements of the governing rule. By contrast, it would not be appropriate to explain in the introductory paragraph anything about how a court determines if a subjective belief is reasonable because that explanation applies to only the second element. Those more specific rules that are focused on just one element should be explained in the argument about whether the plaintiff's belief is reasonable.

Because the governing rule identifies all the elements or factors in that claim, the governing rule is itself a roadmap of the possible arguments ahead. When reading the governing rule, a judge will intuitively break that rule down into its elements or factors. The judge will then expect that each element or factor will be addressed with a full legal argument. If you are not going to meet that expectation, alert the judge.

3. Disposing of uncontested elements or factors

An element or factor named in the governing rule will not warrant a full legal argument if that element is clearly met, is not disputed, or the factor clearly weighs in favor of one party. When you are the moving party and an element is clearly met or a factor clearly weighs in your favor, you may want to quickly establish the element or the factor[2] in the roadmap section and then move on, as in Example 7.1-E.

Example 7.1-E · Roadmap section disposes of elements that are clearly met

---

Rabbi Davis cannot be compelled to testify. Under New York law, a "minister of any religion," is prohibited from disclosing a "confidence made to him in his professional character as a spiritual advisor," if the privilege has not been waived. N.Y.C.P.L.R. § 4505 (McKinney 2007). The statute is construed liberally to encourage people to feel comfortable in talking with their ministers. *In re Fuhrer*, 419 N.Y.S.2d 426, 430 (N.Y. Sup. Ct. 1979). In this case, the defendant, ◄ Ms. Schlomberger, has not waived her privilege. Moreover, as explained in his affidavit, Rabbi Davis is an ordained rabbi, and the senior rabbi at Beth El Israel Synagogue. Rabbi Davis thus qualifies as a "minister of any religion." Thus, the only questions before this court are (1) whether the conversation between Rabbi Davis and the defendant was confidential and (2) whether Rabbi Davis was acting in his professional character as a spiritual advisor. As explained

Here, the moving party disposes of two elements — "waiver" and "minister of any religion" — because both are clearly met and there will be no dispute about them.

The moving party then maps the remaining argument.

---

2. When an element is clearly met or a factor clearly favors your client, you may decide to establish that element or factor in the roadmap section and then move on. However, for persuasive effect you may decide to nevertheless address the factor or element in a separate legal argument. Doing so may emphasize the strength of your case. Especially with factors, you may want to create a single argument for each factor. Because factors are weighed against each other and courts may consider the strength of each factor, you may want to take the opportunity to elaborate on the extent to which the factor weighs in your client's favor.

below, all the evidence shows that the conversation was confidential and that, during that conversation, Rabbi Davis was acting in his capacity as a minister. Thus, Rabbi Davis cannot be compelled to testify against Ms. Schlomberger.

In addition, an element or factor does not warrant a full legal argument when you must concede the element or factor or the moving party has already conceded that element or factor. Conceding a part of an argument is, of course, a delicate task. You do not want to strengthen the opposing party's position by emphasizing weaknesses in your own position. Thus, when you must concede an element or factor, sometimes the best route is to simply focus the court's attention on what is at issue, rather than discussing what is not at issue, as in Example 7.1-F.

Example 7.1-F · Roadmap section focuses on disputed elements only

---

Mr. McCabe is entitled to an order of dismissal because the evidence, viewed in the light most favorable to the State, is not legally sufficient to prove that Mr. McCabe is guilty of burglary in the first degree. To establish burglary in the first degree, the state must prove that the defendant "knowingly enter[ed] or remain[ed] unlawfully in a dwelling with intent to commit a crime therein," and as is relevant to this case, "when, in effecting entry or while in the dwelling or in immediate flight therefrom, he . . . [was] armed with explosives or a deadly weapon . . . ." N.Y. Pen. Code § 140.30(1) (2010).

By failing to contest two elements—whether the house was a dwelling and whether he was armed—the defendant has conceded those elements.

As explained more fully below, the evidence is not legally sufficient to show that Mr. McCabe "knowingly entered or remained unlawfully" in Ms. McCabe's home or that he "intend[ed] to commit a crime" either when entering or remaining in her home. Ms. McCabe had previously provided Mr. McCabe with a key to her home and, as he had often done before, while waiting for Ms. McCabe to return home, Mr. McCabe ate some of the food in the home, while waiting for Ms. McCabe to return home. These facts are insufficient to prove burglary in the first degree.

Alternatively, you may decide to more explicitly concede a factor or element as in Example 7.1-G.

Example 7.1-G · Roadmap section disposes of a set of factors that the party must concede and then focuses on the factors in dispute

---

Competitive cheer, as it is structured at Central State University of Utah, is not a sport for purposes of Title IX compliance. To determine whether an athletic opportunity constitutes a sport, the Office of Civil Rights examines the activity's program structure and administration, and then the activity's competitive opportunities. In balancing these factors, the Office of Civil Rights has urged that more weight be given to an activity's competitive opportunities.

In *Beidiger v. Quinnipiac*, the only case yet to consider whether cheer is a sport, the court followed this approach giving particular weight to the availability of competitive opportunities, noting that the quality of competition is "highly important, if not essential, to the varsity experience." 728 F. Supp. 2d 62, 100 (D. Conn. 2010). In this case, the parties agree that the program structure and ⟵ administration of competitive cheer at Central State are sufficient. However, Central State cannot show that the competitive opportunities are sufficient to provide its program with the competition "essential to the varsity experience." For that reason, competitive cheer cannot currently be considered a sport for purposes of assessing a university's compliance with Title IX.

> Plaintiff concedes that Central State's program and administration of competitive cheer is sufficient to comply with Title IX requirements for determining which activities constitute an athletic opportunity.
>
> After disposing of factors that must be conceded, plaintiff maps the arguments that remain.

By contrast, if the opposing party must concede an element or factor, you may take a moment to emphasize that point, as in Example 7.1-H.

Example 7.1-H • Roadmap section notes that the opposing party has conceded factors and then addresses factors in dispute

Competitive cheer at Central State University of Utah is a sport for purposes of Title IX compliance. The Office of Civil Rights assesses six factors to determine whether an activity is a sport. The first three factors assess the program's structure and administration. The remaining three factors assess the activity's competitive opportunities. These factors were developed to allow a university to expand its athletic program by including sports "not yet recognized by governing athletic organizations" such as the NCAA. Each activity is assessed on a case-by-case basis.

Plaintiff concedes the first three factors. First, Plaintiff concedes that Central State provides its cheer team with an operating budget, support services, and coaching staff equivalent to that of other established teams. Second, Plaintiff concedes that Central State recruits competitive cheerleaders and provides them athletic scholarships consistent with established varsity athletes. Third, Plaintiff concedes that Central State provides its cheer team with practice opportunities equivalent to opportunities provided to its established teams.

> Introduction emphasizes that the plaintiff has conceded that a series of factors weigh in favor of the defendant.

Because an analysis of the remaining three factors shows that Central State's competitive cheer team also has sufficient competitive opportunities, competitive cheer at Central State should be deemed a sport for purposes of Title IX compliance.

Finally, if all the elements or factors in the governing rule need to be supported by a legal argument, you will not dispose of any component of the governing rule.

4. Mapping the remaining arguments

Next, you will want to consider whether you need to map the remaining arguments. You will need to map the remaining arguments under two circumstances.

First, you will need to map the remaining arguments if you have disposed of an element or factor. For example, if an element or factor is clearly met and therefore unlikely to be contested (as in Example 7.1-E) or if one of the parties has conceded the element or factor (as in Example 7.1-G), then you will want to set out which elements or factors remain. Mapping the remaining arguments helps to reorient the court because a judge may have difficulty remembering which elements or factors remain in play. Providing a roadmap will allow a judge to keep reading rather than going back to the governing rule to figure out what remains.

Second, you will need to map the remaining arguments if you have changed the order of the arguments from the order in which they were presented in the governing rule. As this chapter explained earlier, if one element or factor presents a particularly strong argument for your client, you may want to argue that element or factor first. If so, you will want to make sure that the judge is prepared to read the arguments in a different order from the one the governing rule established, as in Example 7.1-I.

If either of those two circumstances exist, then you will map the remaining arguments. When you "map" the remaining arguments, you are simply using "roadmap sentences," described above in Part I.B, to explain the order of the remaining arguments.

Example 7.1-I · Map the remaining arguments

Serving raw fish and meats to diners is an ultra-hazardous activity, and Bellisimo Food Corporation must be held strictly liable for the damages that resulted from that activity. Under Illinois law, the court, not a jury, determines whether an activity is ultra-hazardous. *See Miller v. Civil Constructors, Inc.*, 651 N.E.2d 239, 244 (Ill. App. Ct. 1995). In its determination, the court must analyze six factors to determine whether an activity is ultra-hazardous:

1. The existence of a high degree of risk of some harm to the person, land, or chattels of others;
2. The likelihood that the resulting harm will be great;
3. The inability to eliminate the risk by exercise of reasonable care;
4. The extent to which the activity is not a matter of common usage;
5. The inappropriateness of the activity to the place where it is carried on; and
6. The extent to which the activity's value to the community is outweighed by its dangerousness.

The introduction alerts the court that the argument will address the third factor first and explains why.

Id. Of the above factors, Illinois courts give the third factor—the inability to eliminate risk by exercise of reasonable care—the most weight. *Id.* All six factors weigh in favor of finding that serving raw fish and meats is an ultra-hazardous activity. However, because the third factor is weighted most heavily, the analysis begins there.

If, however, you have not disposed of any part of the governing rule and if you will address each part of the governing rule in the same order in which it was identified in the governing rule, then the governing rule will itself act as a roadmap and there is no need to create a second roadmap.

5. Final conclusion

Finally, in a persuasive argument, your roadmap section should include a final conclusion about what you will prove about the remaining elements or factors, or about what you will prove about the claim as a whole. Doing so will remind the court of the direction you are headed and the conclusion you want the court to reach.

III. Introducing Sub-Arguments

Just as a roadmap section explains the order in which you will address the arguments within a claim, you will sometimes need a roadmap section to explain the order in which you will address sub-arguments. Whenever an element or step within a claim breaks down into two or more smaller elements or factors, you will need a roadmap section to alert the court of the structure ahead. Figure 7.1-C, above, illustrates where you would place a second roadmap section in the event that one element splits into two smaller elements or factors.

The potential parts of a roadmap section mid-claim are the same as those for a roadmap section at the outset of the claim: A conclusion (to that element), the governing rule (for that element), dispose of any sub-elements that will not be addressed, and state the conclusion for the element. Figure 7.1-C, above, illustrates an argument with a roadmap section in the middle of a single claim, as does Example 7.1-J.

Example 7.1-J · A roadmap section mid-claim

B. Mr. Floyd's subjective belief that he was expected to play paddleball with his supervisor was objectively reasonable.

Mark Floyd reasonably believed that he was expected to participate in the paddleball game with his supervisor. To determine whether an employee's subjective belief is objectively reasonable, California courts usually weigh three factors: (1) whether the employer was involved in the activity, (2) whether the employer benefited from the activity, and (3) whether the employer pressured the employee to participate. *Meyer v. Workers' Comp. Appeals Bd.*, 204 Cal. Rptr. 74, 76 (Ct. App. 1984). In this case, Fitness Functions was involved with the paddleball game; Fitness Functions benefited from the game; and, given the circumstances, Mr. Floyd felt pressured to join the game.

IV. Organizing a Single Legal Argument

Once you have introduced a single claim and identified the elements or factors that make up that claim, you must then structure the individual arguments that address each element or factor. The parts of a single legal argument and their order are no different when writing a persuasive brief to a court than when writing an objective memorandum. That single legal argument is made up of four parts:

- A conclusion
- An explanation of the law
- An application of the law
- A final conclusion.

You may have learned this argument structure by using a mnemonic such as IRAC, CREAC, CREXAC, or CRRPAP. All of those mnemonics describe the same structure, albeit with different vocabulary, as illustrated in Table 7.1-K. Example 7.1-L illustrates that structure in a very short motion to dismiss.

Table 7.1-K · One legal argument; various mnemonics

	IRAC	CREAC	CREXAC	CRRPAP
Conclusion	Issue	Conclusion	Conclusion	Conclusion
Explain the law	Rule	Rule	Rule	Rule
		Explanation	Explanation	Rule Proof
Apply the law	Application	Application	Application	Application
Conclusion	Conclusion	Conclusion	Conclusion	Prediction

Example 7.1-L · A single legal argument

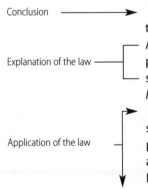

Conclusion →

    This case is moot and should, therefore, be dismissed. A case is moot if there is no justiciable controversy. *State v. Hauskins,* 281 P.3d 669, 672 (Or. Ct. App. 2012). A justiciable controversy exists only when the interests of the

Explanation of the law →

parties to the action are adverse and the court's decision in the matter will have some practical effect on the rights of the parties to the controversy. *McIntire v. Forbes,* 909 P.2d 846, 850-51 (Or. 1996) (internal quotation marks omitted).

Application of the law →

    This case is moot because Ms. Peterson has already received that which she sought—the return of her two dogs, Peaches and Tango, which were previously seized by a Klamath County animal control officer. The attached agreement, which Ms. Peterson signed, demonstrates that Ms. Peterson's dogs, Peaches and Tango, have been returned and are once again residing in the

Peterson household. Because the appellant has received that which she sought, the parties no longer have any interests that are adverse and any ruling by the Court would have no practical effect. The case should be dismissed as moot. ◄— Final conclusion

---

Judges, like other attorneys, will expect to see legal arguments structured in this same way. Accordingly, you will reduce confusion and make your arguments easier for a judge to absorb if you, too, structure each legal argument in this way: conclusion, explanation of the law, application of the law to facts, and conclusion.

Developing the arguments within your brief is a multi-step process. The first step is to simply determine a framework within which your arguments will sit. This section of the book, *Organizing Claims and Arguments*, provides guidance so that you can develop a framework appropriate for the claims or defenses you will present. It also provides guidance so that you can make your organizational choices known to the court.

After you order your claims or defenses and order the individual legal arguments that make up the claim, the next step is to begin developing the individual legal arguments within each claim. Sections 7.1 through 7.5 address how to structure each legal argument, whether that argument is based on analogical or rule-based reasoning.

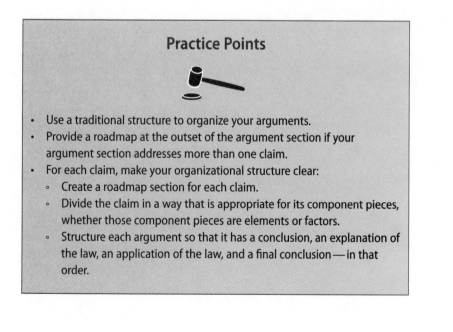

Practice Points

- Use a traditional structure to organize your arguments.
- Provide a roadmap at the outset of the argument section if your argument section addresses more than one claim.
- For each claim, make your organizational structure clear:
  - Create a roadmap section for each claim.
  - Divide the claim in a way that is appropriate for its component pieces, whether those component pieces are elements or factors.
  - Structure each argument so that it has a conclusion, an explanation of the law, an application of the law, and a final conclusion — in that order.

Structuring Analogical Arguments

Analogical reasoning is the hallmark of "thinking like a lawyer." An analogical argument asserts that a client's case raises the same legal issue as a prior case and is factually similar to that case. It then asserts that, because of the factual similarity, the same legal outcome is warranted in a client's case. Alternatively, an analogical argument can assert that a client's case is factually distinct and, because of the distinction, the prior case should not direct the outcome in the client's case. Either way, the heart of an analogical argument is a factual comparison to a prior case. Once the comparison is established, the legal outcome follows.

A persuasive analogical argument follows the same structure as an objective analogical argument. That structure is outlined in Table 7.2-A, and Example 7.2-B allows you to see that structure in action.

Table 7.2-A · An analogical argument's typical structure

Basic Framework	Analogical argument
Conclusion	• Conclusion
Explain the law	• Explain rules relevant to the element or factor being examined. • Explain factually similar prior cases that address the same legal issue. Your description should focus on the facts, holding, and rationale that led the court to reach its conclusion about the element or factor being examined.

Apply the law	• Compare the prior case to client's case.
	  ◦ If the prior case and your client's case are similar
	    ▪ Establish the factual similarity, and
	    ▪ Establish the legal outcome that results from the similarity.
	  ◦ If the prior case and your client's case are distinguishable
	    ▪ Establish factual distinction, and
	    ▪ Explain that, therefore, the precedent is inapplicable and an alternative conclusion is warranted.

Conclusion	• Conclusion

Example 7.2-B · An analogical argument

Conclusion

The explanation of the law begins here.

The rules explain, among other things, the factors that the court must consider.

The case illustrations — *In re Rudder* and *Coward* — address all the factors that the court considered and then explain how the court weighed those factors to reach its conclusion.

Persuasive case illustrations have the same parts as objective case illustrations. Notice that the writer begins each case illustration with a hook (shaded), explaining the point the court should learn from the prior case. The writer then explains the trigger facts, the court's reasoning about those facts, and the court's holding.

The trial court correctly concluded that Ms. Moran did not voluntarily execute the premarital agreement. A wife voluntarily executes a premarital agreement only if she signs the agreement without being coerced, intimidated, or unduly pressured. *In re Rudder*, 217 P.3d 183, 193 (Or. Ct. App. 2009). In addition, she must have "some modicum" of knowledge of the terms of the agreement and the property affected. *Id.* at 194. To determine whether the wife entered the agreement voluntarily and had the appropriate degree of knowledge, courts look at a variety of factors: (1) the timing of the agreement in relation to the wedding, (2) whether the assets were sufficiently disclosed, (3) the relative sophistication of the parties, and (4) whether the complaining party had adequate opportunity to consult with independent counsel. *Id.*

A wife does not enter a premarital agreement voluntarily if the agreement is provided one day before the wedding, the agreement does not disclose assets, the wife is unsophisticated, and an attorney is not present. *Id.* at 194-95. In the *Rudder* case, the husband, an electrician, and the wife, a cosmetologist who had owned a beauty salon, discussed in general terms a pre-marital agreement a few weeks before the wedding. *Id.* at 194. The husband's attorney drafted the agreement, which the wife first saw the day before leaving for the wedding. Although she had asked that her attorney be present when she signed the agreement, her attorney was not. Her husband urged her, "[g]o ahead and just sign it. The wedding is on." *Id.* After reading through the agreement, which did not list all the husband's assets or their value, the wife signed the agreement. *Id.* On these facts, the court determined that the circumstances created a coercive environment. *Id.* In discussing the wife's relative business sophistication, the court of appeals agreed with the trial court that "although . . . [the] wife had some experience in business matters, that experience was limited and she was relatively unsophisticated in financial matters." *Id.* at 195. Therefore, the wife did not enter into the agreement voluntarily. *Id.*

By contrast, an experienced businesswoman who has an opportunity to know her husband's assets and is provided with an agreement more than two weeks in advance, can enter into the premarital agreement voluntarily. *In re Coward*, 582 P.2d 834, 835 (Or. Ct. App. 1978). In the *Coward* case, the couple signed the pre-marital agreement seventeen days before the wedding. *Id.* At that time, the husband's attorney advised the wife to seek independent counsel. *Id.* The wife, who had worked as a bookkeeper and assisted her husband with his financial affairs, declined to speak with an attorney and signed the agreement. *Id.* The court concluded that the wife had had sufficient opportunity to consult with an attorney, was an experienced businesswoman, and was aware of her husband's property. *Id.* Accordingly, the court held that the wife voluntarily signed the pre-marital agreement. *Id.* at 836. Although the 1978 *Coward* case was decided before the 1987 enactment of Oregon Revised Statute § 108.725, the legislature intended § 108.725 to codify existing case law; therefore the *Coward case* still stands as an example of "voluntariness." *See Rudder*, 217 P.3d at 192.

Ms. Moran did not enter into her premarital agreement voluntarily. She is an unsophisticated businesswoman who had limited time before the wedding to review the document. Moreover, the agreement did not disclose her future husband's assets, and she was unable to consult with an attorney.

> The application begins here.

These facts are similar to the facts in *Rudder*, in which the court found the agreement was not signed voluntarily. First, in both cases the agreement was signed within days of the wedding. In *Rudder*, it was one day before the wedding, and in this case, it was five days. Although Ms. Moran had a few more days to consider the agreement, the time span created pressure. In *Rudder*, the pressure was evidenced by the husband's urging the wife, "[g]o ahead and just sign it. The wedding is on." In this case, Ms. Moran stated that, "she didn't want to wait to find an attorney, not with so many people traveling so far." Thus, in this case, as in *Rudder*, the shortened time span created pressure and did not leave adequate time to consult with an attorney. Moreover, like the wife in *Rudder*, Ms. Moran is not a sophisticated businesswoman. As an office manager she has the approximate business experience of a cosmetologist who owned a beauty salon, and the *Rudder* court decided that the business-owner was not a sophisticated business person. In addition, Ms. Moran, like the wife in *Rudder*, was not told the value of her husband's assets. Finally, although Ms. Moran was advised to speak with an attorney, that one fact should not outweigh the other facts that are similar to the facts in *Rudder*. Those facts show a pressured environment in which Ms. Moran did not have sufficient time to fully assess the agreement. For these reasons, this Court should reach the same conclusion that the *Rudder* court did: The agreement was not entered into voluntarily.

> Note the careful fact-to-fact comparison. For each comparison, the writer first asserts what is similar. (The overt statement of similarity is underlined.) The writer then describes the specific facts that prove that similarity exists.
>
> The writer is also careful to use parallel structure when describing similar facts to bring out the similarities between the client's case and the *Rudder* case.
>
> Finally, the last sentence explains how these similarities lead to a particular conclusion.
>
> These are all the same devices used to create an effective objective analogical argument.

Defendant's reliance on *Coward* is misplaced. The wife in *Coward* had previously reviewed her husband's finances; thus, she understood the value of her husband's assets. In this case, no evidence indicates that Ms. Moran was aware of the value of her husband's assets. Her lack of knowledge of her husband's assets, the lack of evidence that her job as an office manager would allow her to assess the value of his assets, and the compressed time span of only five days in which to decide whether to sign the agreement support the trial court's conclusion that she signed in an coercive environment. She, therefore, did not sign voluntarily.

> Addressing a counter-argument

> Final conclusion

As you can see, the same structure that effectively develops an objective analogical argument also effectively develops a persuasive analogical argument.[1]

An analogical argument is often the strongest argument you can develop because an analogical argument relies on stare decisis. "Stare decisis" is the principle that a court should reach the same conclusion as a prior court when presented with the same legal issue and the same facts

---

1. Should you want to review in more detail how to construct an effective analogical argument, review section 8.2 in *A Lawyer Writes*. *See* Christine Coughlin, Joan Malmud Rocklin & Sandy Patrick, *A Lawyer Writes: A Practical Guide to Legal Analysis* 135-49 (2d ed. 2013).

as presented in the prior case. This principle will almost always persuade a court to follow its own precedent.

Although an analogical argument is a powerful tool, sometimes you do not need all the strength of an analogical argument and sometimes you have no similar prior case to rely on. In those circumstances, as § 7.3 explains in greater detail, a rule-based argument is appropriate.

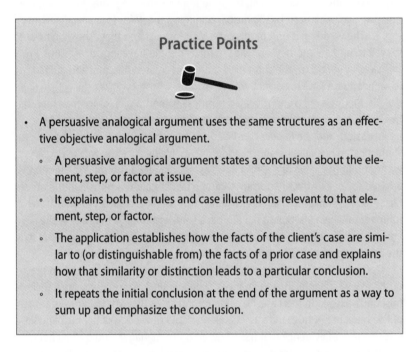

Practice Points

- A persuasive analogical argument uses the same structures as an effective objective analogical argument.

  ○ A persuasive analogical argument states a conclusion about the element, step, or factor at issue.

  ○ It explains both the rules and case illustrations relevant to that element, step, or factor.

  ○ The application establishes how the facts of the client's case are similar to (or distinguishable from) the facts of a prior case and explains how that similarity or distinction leads to a particular conclusion.

  ○ It repeats the initial conclusion at the end of the argument as a way to sum up and emphasize the conclusion.

Structuring Rule-Based Arguments

I.   A Simple Rule-Based Argument
II. Statutory Construction Arguments
III. Policy Arguments
IV. Syllogisms

In addition to relying on analogical arguments, attorneys also rely on rule-based arguments. In a rule-based argument, an attorney asserts that a conclusion is warranted by comparing the facts of a client's case directly against a legal standard (i.e., the rule). Such an argument follows the structure in Table 7.3-A.

Table 7.3-A • A rule-based argument's typical structure

Basic Framework	Rule-based argument
Conclusion	• Conclusion
Explain the law	• Explain the rules relevant to the element or factor being examined.
Apply the law	• Apply the rules to the facts of your client's case.
Conclusion (if necessary)	• Conclusion

I. A Simple Rule-Based Argument

A very simple rule-based argument might look like the argument in Example 7.3-B. In the example, notice how key language from the rule is repeated in the application. That juxtaposition of key concepts from the rule against facts from the client's case is the technique that makes a rule-based argument persuasive.

Example 7.3-B • An effective rule-based argument uses the language of the rule in the application

---

The rule is explained here. Its key concepts are highlighted.

    This case is moot and should, therefore, be dismissed. A case is moot if there is no justiciable controversy. *State v. Hauskins,* 281 P.3d 669, 672 (Or. Ct. App. 2012). A justiciable controversy exists only when the interests of the parties to the action are adverse and the court's decision in the matter will have some practical effect on the rights of the parties to the controversy. *McIntire v. Forbes*, 909 P.2d 846, 850-51 (Or. 1996) (internal quotation marks omitted).

The application begins here. Notice how the key concepts are repeated and aligned with the facts.

    This case is moot because Ms. Peterson has already received that which she sought—the return of her two dogs, Peaches and Tango, which were previously seized by a Klamath County animal control officer. The attached agreement, which Ms. Peterson signed, demonstrates that Ms. Peterson's dogs, Peaches and Tango, have been returned and are once again residing in the Peterson household. Because the appellant has received that which she sought, the parties no longer have any interests that are adverse and any

Final conclusion

ruling by the Court would have no practical effect. The case should be dismissed as moot.

Example 7.3-C • A rule-based argument that does not use the language of the rule in the application is less effective

---

The rule is explained here. Its key concepts are highlighted.

    This case is moot and should, therefore, be dismissed. A case is moot if there is no justiciable controversy. *State v. Hauskins,* 281 P.3d 669, 672 (Or. Ct. App. 2012). A justiciable controversy exists when the interests of the parties to the action are adverse and the court's decision in the matter will have some practical effect on the rights of the parties to the controversy. *McIntire v. Forbes*, 909 P.2d 846, 850-51 (Or. 1996) (internal quotation marks omitted).

The application begins here. Notice how the key concepts are **not** *repeated.*

    Ms. Peterson has already received that which she sought. The only relief Ms. Peterson sought was the return of her two dogs, Peaches and Tango, which were previously seized by a Klamath County animal control officer. The attached agreement, which Ms. Peterson signed, demonstrates that Ms. Peterson's dogs, Peaches and Tango, have been returned and are once again residing in the Peterson household. Because the appellant has received that which she sought, no ruling by the Court is necessary, and the case should be dismissed as moot.

    Repeating key language from the rule in the application, as in Example 7.3-B, allows the court to easily see how the facts of the case align with the rule and lead to the desired outcome. In Example 7.3-C, however, counsel did not rely on the language of the rule in her analysis. Do you see how Example 7.3-C is less compelling because the application does not re-integrate key language from the rule?

An attorney relies on a rule-based argument in one of several situations. Sometimes a sufficiently similar prior case does not exist. In that case, the attorney has no choice but to develop a rule-based argument.

Attorneys will also develop a rule-based argument when the legal issue is simple and unlikely to be contested. In that case, the attorney does not need the firepower of an analogical argument, and a rule-based argument will usually establish the point much more efficiently than an analogical argument. Why waste your time and the court's time comparing detailed facts, when the point can be made effectively and much more quickly?

Finally, in some cases, the facts of your particular case are not relevant or necessary to the resolution of the legal issue in dispute. For example, in a statutory construction argument, the specific facts of a client's case are not central to the argument because the question revolves around the meaning of the statutory language and the legislature's intent when it enacted the statute. In such a case, a method of argument in which the facts are central would be inapt.

Table 7.3-A, above, illustrates a very simple rule-based argument. However, rule-based arguments are also used to present more complex arguments. In particular, statutory construction arguments and policy-based arguments are, at their heart, rule-based arguments. Although more complex, the persuasiveness of those arguments also depends on showing the court how key concepts from a legal standard line up against other evidence. Let's look.

II. Statutory Construction Arguments

In a statutory construction argument, the parties are asking a court to determine the meaning of particular words in a statute.[1]

As mentioned above, a statutory construction argument is a more complex rule-based argument. In a simple rule-based argument the rule and its meaning is known. Thus, the court's—and the advocate's—only task is to apply that rule to the facts. In a statutory construction argument the rule is a statute, and that statute is susceptible to more than one interpretation. Your task is two-fold. First, you must argue to the court what the legislature intended the statute to mean when the legislature enacted the statute. Then, you must apply that clarified rule to the facts of your case. Both steps involve rule-based reasoning. Let's look at each step more closely.

The first step—arguing how a rule should be understood—constitutes the bulk of a statutory construction argument. In this first step, you must help the court determine the legislature's intent when it enacted the

---

1. Although this section refers to "statutory" construction, the concepts it discusses apply similarly to construing administrative rules, ordinances, and constitutional provisions.

statute. Because courts are repeatedly asked to construe the meaning of a statute, most jurisdictions have developed a particular methodology to determine the legislature's intent. Although the steps vary somewhat from jurisdiction to jurisdiction, most courts use the same tools. First, the court will analyze the plain meaning of the text. Next, the court will analyze the text in context—that is, the court will analyze the text in light of the larger statutory scheme. Finally, the court will consider other evidence of the legislature's intent when enacting the statute, such as statements made at committee hearings or during floor debates.[2]

At each of these steps, a court might use a "canon of construction" to assess the meaning of a statute. A canon of construction is simply a traditional way that words, a sentence, or a paragraph are to be understood. Figure 7.3-D provides some common canons of construction that courts use.

Table 7.3-D · Textual canons of construction[3]

1. **Canon regarding the plain meaning rule**
   - "If language is plain and unambiguous it must be given effect."

2. **Canons regarding specific words**
   - "May" is permissive; "shall" is "mandatory."
   - "And" is conjunctive; "or" is "disjunctive."
     - Example: "fruits, seeds, nuts, vegetables, honey, sheep, cattle, pigs, *and* poultry." A person must produce all of these things to come under the statute. Change "and" to "or," and a person would have to produce only one of them.

3. **Canons regarding ambiguous modifiers**
   - "A modifier or exception applies only to the last antecedent in a phrase or list."
     - Example: "Employees shall be paid base wages, environmental hazard pay, and overtime <u>as determined by the lead agency to be consistent with private sector practices</u>." Under this canon, the underlined phrase modifies only "overtime," the last antecedent; if, however, a comma had followed the word "overtime" the underlined phrase would have modified all three kinds of compensation listed.

4. **Canons regarding lists of things**
   - **Noscitur a sociis:** Interpret an ambiguous word in a list by the company it keeps, that is, in light of the surrounding words.
     - Example: "pigs, cattle, sheep, and poultry." Does "poultry" include exotic birds?

---

2. For a more complete discussion of statutory construction arguments, *see* Christine Coughlin, Joan Malmud Rocklin & Sandy Patrick, *A Lawyer Writes: A Practical Guide to Legal Analysis* 181-97 (2d ed. 2013).

3. These examples of canons have been frequently used over the years. The original source of the examples is unknown.

- **Ejusdem generis:** General, catch-all phrases at the end of a list are construed to mean the same kind or type as the rest of the list. If "motor vehicle" is defined as a "car, truck, or any other self-propelled vehicle not designed for running on rails," does it include an airplane? A motorized scooter?
- **Expressio unius, exclusion alterius:** The enumeration of specific things implies the exclusion of all others. If the word is not in, then it is meant to be out.
    ◦ Example: "rain, sleet, and hail" excludes snow.

5. **In pari materia:** Statutes with the same subject or purpose should be read together to effectuate that purpose.
    - Example: A statute setting out the punishment for kidnapping should be read in conjunction with a statute setting out sentencing guidelines for felonies.

A statutory construction argument is, essentially, a series of nested rule-based arguments. Example 7.3-E provides a statutory construction argument.[4] It highlights some of the key rules and shows how those key rules are then applied to the statutory text and other evidence before the court.

Example 7.3-E • A statutory construction argument

ARGUMENT

The indictment against Mr. Hidalgo must be dismissed because Arizona's anti-human smuggling statute was never meant to be used to prosecute individuals who were smuggled. Under Arizona's anti-human smuggling statute, it is "unlawful for a person to intentionally engage in the smuggling of human beings for profit or commercial purpose." Ariz. Rev. Stat. Ann. § 13-2319 (2010). In human smuggling, there are only two "person[s]" involved: the smuggler (also known as the "coyote") and his human cargo. The question before this Court is whether the person to be prosecuted under this statute is only the smuggler or whether the person to be prosecuted also includes the human cargo.

To answer that question, this Court must construe the word "person." When construing the text of a statute, Arizona courts must ascertain the legislature's intent when it enacted the statute and give effect to that intent. *Wyatt v. Wehmueller,* 806 P.2d 870, 872 (Ariz. 1991). To do so, Arizona courts begin their analysis with the plain text of the statute. *State v. Christian,* 66 P.3d 1241, 1243 (Ariz. 2003). The plain text of the statute is the "best and most reliable" indication of a statute's meaning. *Id.* If the court finds the plain text of § 13-2319 ambiguous, the court may next look to the text in context, the legislative history of the statute, and the historical context of the statute. *Id.*

This paragraph is the roadmap section for the statutory construction argument. The roadmap section explains that the governing rules for this analysis are Arizona's rules of statutory construction. The arguments that follow each address one step in Arizona's rules of statutory construction.

4. A special thanks goes to Professor Anne Villella at Lewis & Clark School of Law who developed this issue and to Alexis Curry who drafted an earlier version of this example.

In this case, the text in context, its legislative history, and the historical context surrounding enactment of the statute all establish that the legislature never intended the prosecution of the human cargo. Accordingly, Mr. Hidalgo should not be prosecuted under § 13-2319, and the charges should be dismissed.

A. The plain text of Arizona Revised Statute § 13-2319(a) limits the scope of the statute to "persons" in the business of smuggling human beings.

The plain text of § 13-2319(a) limits application of the statute to the smuggler, and not his human cargo. When analyzing the plain text of a statute, Arizona courts must give "each word, phrase, clause and sentence . . . its natural, obvious, and ordinary meaning" such that no other part of the statute is rendered "void, inert, redundant or trivial." *Arpaio v. Steinle III*, 35 P.3d 114, 116 (Ariz. Ct. App. 2001); *Stein v. Sonus, USA, Inc.*, 150 P.3d 773, 776 (Ariz. Ct. App. 2007). When a word is undefined by the statute, Arizona courts turn to any established and widely used dictionary to determine the natural and obvious meaning of a term. *Helvetica Servicing, Inc. v. Pasquan*, 277 P.3d 198, 205 (Ariz. Ct. App. 2012).

The most natural and obvious meaning of a "person . . . smuggling . . . for profit or commercial purpose" limits this statute to the prosecution of smugglers, not the smuggler's human cargo. Where smuggling is concerned, as explained above, a "person" is either the smuggler or his cargo. Neither "profit" nor "commercial purpose" is defined by statute, but both limit the "person" who can be prosecuted to the smuggler, and not the individual migrant.

First, the ordinary meaning of the phrase "for profit" limits the person who can be prosecuted to those in the business of smuggling. "Profit" is widely understood as "net income . . . from the conduct of business." *Webster's Third New International Dictionary* 1811 (2002); *see also The American Heritage Dictionary* 989 (5th ed. 2009) (defining profit as "financial gain from a . . . business activity"). Therefore, a "person" who smuggles "for profit" is one who seeks a "net income" from the "business" of smuggling. Only the coyote is seeking income from the smuggling. And only the coyote—not the individual migrant—is in the business of smuggling. Thus, the phrase "for profit" limits the "person" who can be prosecuted to the smuggler, and not the individual migrant.

Next, the ordinary meaning of the phrase "for . . . commercial purpose" similarly limits the person who can be prosecuted. "Commercial" means "of or relating to 'commerce.'" *Webster's Third New International Dictionary* at 594. "Commerce" refers to "an exchange of goods . . . especially on a large scale between different countries." *Id.* The human cargo hopes to be smuggled once. By contrast, the coyote is involved in the exchange of goods on a large scale. Again, the statutory text shows that the Arizona legislature chose to impose criminal sanctions on the person who repeatedly profits from a smuggling operation, not the human cargo.

To read the statute as imposing criminal liability on individual migrants would, effectively, render the phrases "for profit" and for "commercial purpose" void and inert. As explained above, the individual migrant is not seeking to

---

The plain language argument is the first rule-based argument. It includes several other embedded rule-based arguments.

The first paragraph begins with a conclusion to the plain language analysis. It then explains the rules with respect to how the court should interpret the plain language of the text.

The shading below allows you to see how this rule is applied in the context of Arizona's anti-smuggling statute.

This next rule-based argument is embedded within the plain language argument.

Again, it begins with a conclusion (in the sentence that begins "First, ..."). It then explains the relevant rules, which are underlined.

You can see how key aspects of the rule are repeated, here, in the application.

This next argument is the second ruled-based argument embedded within the plain language argument.

Again, it begins with a conclusion (in the sentence that begins "Next, ..."). It then explains the relevant rules, which are underlined.

You can see how key aspects of the rule are repeated in the application.

profit or engage in the activity commercially. Thus, to extend the reach of the statute to permit the prosecution of individual migrants would be to ignore the words "for profit" and "commercial purpose," which limit the "person" to be prosecuted under the statute. Such a reading would contravene the legislature's intent.

Thus, the plain meaning of the statutory section demonstrates that human cargo falls outside the intended scope of § 13-2319(a). Accordingly, this Court should dismiss Count I of the indictment against Mr. Hidalgo.

> The plain language argument ends here with the application of the rule (shaded) and a final conclusion.

If this Court nevertheless concludes that the meaning of the word is ambiguous, this Court may also look at the text in context and the statute's legislative history. Both examinations lead to the same conclusion: The Arizona legislature did not intend to subject individual migrants to criminal prosecution.

B. The text of § 13-2319(a) read in context also demonstrates a legislative intent to make § 13-2319(a) a tool for prosecuting organized crime, not individual migrant activity.

> The text-in-context argument addresses the second step in Arizona's method of statutory construction.

The heading of § 13-2319(a) also evidences a legislative intent to criminalize organized crime, not individual migrant activity. When examining the text in context, <u>the court may consider the headings of the statute to aid the interpretation of the statute and to ascertain legislative intent</u>. *State v. Hauser,* 105 P.3d 1158, 1161 (Ariz. 2005). Chapter 23 of the Arizona Criminal Code is entitled "Organized Crime, Fraud and Terrorism." Ariz. Rev. Stat. Ann. § 12-2301 (2005). This <u>heading</u> shows that when enacting § 13-2319, the legislature intended to target organized crime, fraud, or terrorism, and not individual migrant activity.

> Conclusion
>
> Rules
>
> Application
>
> Conclusion

C. The legislative history of § 13-2319(a) also demonstrates a legislative intent to target organized crime, not individual migrant activity.

> The legislative history argument addresses the next step in Arizona's method of statutory construction.

The legislative history of § 13-2319 also shows that the legislature was focused on criminalizing the conduct of the smuggling organization and not the conduct of the individual migrant. When the bill that became § 13-2319 was first drafted, it focused exclusively on criminalizing human trafficking. Ariz. Fact Sheet, S.B. 1372, 2005 Reg. Sess. (2005). Thus, the legislative history focuses on human trafficking. *Id.* <u>In discussing human trafficking, the legislature distinguished between the "traffickers" who received "illicit profits" and those who were trafficked.</u> *Id.* Accordingly, the bill subjects traffickers to prosecution and incarceration, while those who are trafficked may, under the statute, receive restitution. *Id.* Thus, the statute from its inception <u>distinguished between those who organize the movement of others and those who were moved and treated those two groups differently.</u> *See id.* The Judiciary Committee then added to the bill the provision that also criminalizes "smuggling for profit or commercial purpose." *Id.* Given that the statute had consistently <u>distinguished between those organizing the movement of others and those who were moved</u>, the most consistent understanding of the text that criminalizes "smuggling for profit or commercial purpose" is that it, too, <u>distinguishes between those who organize the movement of others and those</u>

> The description of what the legislature intended when it enacted the statute acts as the rules that are then applied.
>
> The application integrates the key idea from the explanation of what the legislature was thinking when enacting the law.
>
> Conclusion

who are moved. Accordingly, the legislative history suggests that the legislature contemplated criminalizing the conduct of only the smuggler, not the person who was smuggled.

D. Finally, the historical context of § 13-2319(a) also demonstrates a legislative intent to target organized crime, not individual migrant activity.

The historical background to § 13-2319 also supports the interpretation that the legislature intended to target organized crime, and not human cargo. In 2005, the year § 13-2319 was passed in Arizona, the United States Government Accountability Office reported to Congress that "[p]eople smuggling is a huge and highly profitable business worldwide, involving billions of dollars annually." Colleen DiSanto, *Alien Smuggling Along the Arizona-Mexico Border*, 43 Ariz. Att'y, Jan. 2007, at 29. At that time, the "volume and sophistication" of human smuggling rings had increased dramatically, and Arizona, which shares a border with Mexico, was already feeling the great weight of <u>human smuggling by trafficking organizations</u>. *Id*. The same year § 13-2319 was enacted, <u>Arizona declared a state of emergency due to the severe financial burden from jailing thousands of illegal immigrants</u>. *Id*. at 32. This historical background makes it unlikely that the Arizona legislature intended individual migrant activity to be treated as a class four felony because it would increase <u>jail time</u> for smuggled migrants. A more natural interpretation of § 13-2319, given this historical background, is that the statute is intended to target the members of the <u>trafficking organizations who were responsible for the severe financial burdens</u> placed on the State of Arizona.

In sum, the text, the text in context, its legislative history, and the historical context surrounding enactment of the statute of § 13-2319 all support the interpretation that people in the business of human smuggling, not their human cargo, are the intended target of the statute. Accordingly, Mr. Hidalgo should not be prosecuted under § 13-2319 because he was merely the commodity from which other criminal organizations profit. The statute does not extend to cover Mr. Hidalgo's conduct, and the Court should dismiss the indictment against him.

Margin notes:

When construing a statute, Arizona courts will consider the historical context in which a statute was enacted. Thus, this last step considers the historical context.

Conclusion

The writer explains the historical context in which the statute was enacted. Note how ideas from that explanation are then incorporated into an argument about how the statute should be interpreted.

The last paragraph is the final conclusion to the statutory construction argument.

What makes a statutory construction argument more complex is that it usually involves a series of rule-based arguments, and often some of those rule-based arguments are nested within other rule-based arguments.

Figure 7.3-F provides a graphic representation of the arguments in Example 7.3-E above. That figure should help you see how the larger statutory construction argument is actually composed of a series of rule-based arguments, some of which are nested. Then, Examples 7.3-G and 7.3-H, extract individual rule-based arguments from the larger argument in Example 7.3-E so that you can look at them individually.

Example 7.3-G shows excerpts from the "plain language argument," highlighting the aspects that make it a rule-based argument. Example

Figure 7.3-F · A statutory construction argument graphically represented as a series of rule-based arguments

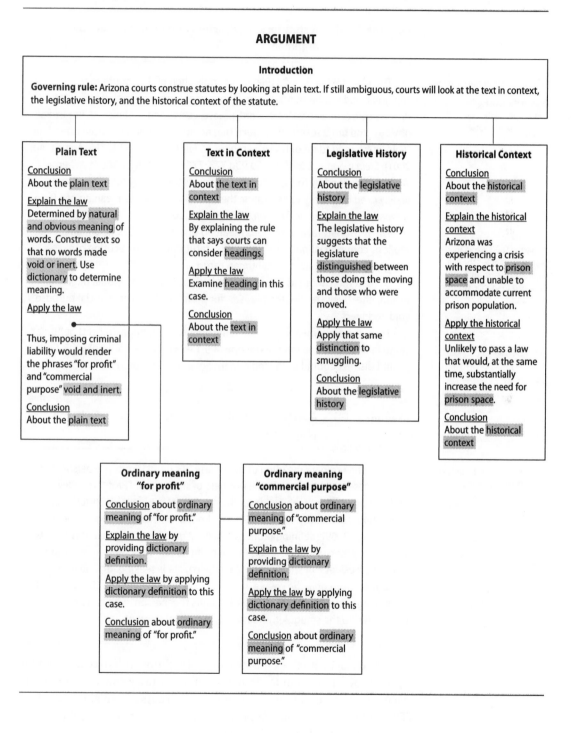

7.3-H is a set of smaller arguments nested within the plain language argument, which is also a rule-based argument.

Example 7.3-G · A statutory construction argument as a rule-based argument

Conclusion about the plain text

Explain the law: Explain how courts analyze the plain meaning of a statutory text.

The plain text of § 13-2319(a) limits application of the statute to the smuggler, and not his human cargo. When analyzing the plain text of a statute, Arizona courts must give "each word, phrase, clause and sentence . . . its natural, obvious, and ordinary meaning" such that no other part of the statute is rendered "void, inert, redundant or trivial." *Arpaio v. Steinle III*, 35 P.3d 114, 116 (Ariz. Ct. App. 2001); *Stein v. Sonus, USA, Inc.*, 150 P.3d 773, 776 (Ariz. Ct. App. 2007). When a word is undefined by the statute, Arizona courts turn to any established and widely used dictionary to determine the natural and obvious meaning of a term. *Helvetica Servicing, Inc. v. Pasquan*, 277 P.3d 198, 205 (Ariz. Ct. App. 2012).

Apply the law: Each of these paragraphs applies the law regarding how to analyze the plain text to specific words in the statute.

The most natural and obvious meaning of a "person . . . smuggling . . . for profit or commercial purpose" limits this statute to the prosecution of smugglers, not the smuggler's human cargo . . . .

To read the statute as imposing criminal liability on individual migrants would, effectively, render the phrases "for profit" and for "commercial purpose" void and inert . . . .

Conclusion about the plain text

Thus, the plain meaning of the statutory section demonstrates that human cargo falls outside the intended scope of § 13-2319(a). Accordingly, this Court should dismiss Count I of the indictment against Mr. Hidalgo . . . .

Example 7.3-H · A statutory construction argument as a rule-based argument

Conclusion about the ordinary meaning of "for profit"

Explain the rule: dictionary definition

Application of the dictionary definition to the statute

Conclusion about the ordinary meaning of "for profit"

First, the ordinary meaning of the phrase "for profit" limits the person who can be prosecuted to those in the business of smuggling. "Profit" is widely understood as "net income . . . from the conduct of business." *Webster's Third New International Dictionary* 1811 (2002); *see also The American Heritage Dictionary* 989 (5th ed. 2009) (defining profit as "financial gain from a . . . business activity"). Therefore, a "person" who smuggles "for profit" is one who seeks a "net income" from the "business" of smuggling. Only the coyote is seeking income from the smuggling. And only the coyote, not the individual migrant, is in the business of smuggling. Thus, the phrase "for profit" limits the "person" who can be prosecuted to the smuggler, and not the individual migrant.

Table 7.3-I compares the structure of a simple rule-based argument against the more complex structure of a statutory construction argument. As you can see, most of your work occurs in explaining the law. That is because you and opposing counsel are actually arguing about how the law should be understood.

Table 7.3-I · Comparing the structure of a simple and complex rule-based argument

Basic Framework	A simple rule-based argument	A statutory construction argument
Conclusion	Conclusion	Conclusion
Explain the law	Explain the rules	**Explain the statutory language (as you understand it).** **Explain the jurisdiction's methodology for construing a statute.** **Rule-based argument 1 (plain meaning)** Conclusion about the plain meaning of the statute's text Rules regarding the plain meaning **Nested rule-based argument 1A** **Conclusion** about the meaning of a particular word or phrase **Rules** that allow you to reach that conclusion **Application** of those rules **Conclusion** **Nested rule-based argument 1B** **Conclusion** about the meaning of a particular word or phrase **Rules** that allow you to reach that conclusion **Application of** those rules **Conclusion** Application of plain meaning rules to the text of the statute Conclusion about the plain meaning **Rule-based argument 2 (text in context)** Conclusion about the text within its context Rules regarding how to construe the text of the statute within its context Application of those rules to the text and surrounding provisions Conclusion about the text in context **Rule-based argument 3 (legislative history)** Conclusion about the legislature's intent as drawn from legislative record Any rules about how legislative record should be read, including quotes from the legislative history that establish the legislature's intent Application of those rules to the legislative record. Conclusion about the legislature's intent as drawn from the legislative record **Conclusion stating how the statute should be understood**
Apply the law	Apply the rule to the facts of your client's case	**Apply the statute as you have proposed that it should be understood to the facts of your client's case.**
Conclusion (if necessary)	Conclusion	**Conclusion**

In reviewing Table 7.3-I, keep in mind several points. First, the table above offers an example of a statutory construction argument. As mentioned above, different jurisdictions have different methods for construing statutes. Any statutory construction argument you develop must follow the analytical method of that jurisdiction. As a result, make sure you research what types of statutory construction arguments are used in your jurisdiction. For example, in Example 7.3-E, the statutory construction argument addresses the historical background of the statute because Arizona courts will consider that aspect. Table 7.3-I does not show that step because many statutory construction arguments do not include historical background. Similarly, the number of nested arguments will vary from argument to argument.

Second, notice that all of the "action" in a statutory construction argument occurs in the explanation of the law. That is because in a statutory construction argument, you will need to make a series of rule-based arguments simply to establish your position about how the statute should be construed. Once you have finished arguing how the statutory language should be understood, you have one final rule-based argument to make. That final rule-based argument is applying the statute—as you believe it should be understood—to the facts of your client's case.

Finally, remember that when developing a statutory construction argument you will use all the same skills that you use when developing a rule-based argument: state the rule; then apply that rule to the evidence before the court, whether that evidence is the text of the statute, the surrounding text, or the legislative record.

III. Policy Arguments

Policy arguments also rely on rule-based reasoning. A "policy" is a means of achieving a "broader moral, philosophical, or social goal[] behind a law."[5] A policy argument asserts that a particular outcome is warranted because such an outcome would be consistent with a particular goal that is beneficial to society. In a policy argument, a lawyer asserts that a favorable decision by the court will lead to positive moral, philosophical, or social outcomes while the opposite decision will generate negative moral, philosophical, or social ramifications. A policy argument may have the flavor of, "If you don't agree with our argument, it will be the end of the world as we know it."

In Example 7.3-J, the lawyer representing the state argues that a police search should be upheld, in part, because doing so protects police

---

5. Coughlin, *supra* note 2, at 173-80.

officer safety. (In that example, the social goal is police officer safety.) The policy is to allow "considerable latitude" in searches of criminal suspects to protect the officers' safety. That policy is applied to potential outcomes in the case. If the court upholds the search, so the argument goes, police officer safety will be protected. If the court does not uphold the search, police officer safety will be at risk.

Example 7.3-J · A policy argument considers whether certain social goods will be achieved in light of the court's decision

Finally, the officer's search was appropriate because it occurred within the "considerable latitude" given to police officers when their safety is at stake. This Court has observed in the officer safety context that an officer's judgment in the field should not be "second-guessed":

Conclusion

The explanation of the law begins here.

In a policy argument, the explanation of the law explains the public good that is at stake.

> [I]t is not our function to uncharitably second-guess an officer's judgment. A police officer in the field frequently must make life-or-death decisions in a matter of seconds. There may be little or no time in which to weigh the magnitude of a potential safety risk against the intrusiveness of protective measures. An officer must be allowed considerable latitude to take safety precautions in such situations.

A public policy argument is stronger when the explanation of the policy cites to a case or other authority that recognizes that public good.

State v. Bates, 747 P.2d 991, 994 (Or. 1987).

That admonition recognizes that, because police work is inherently dangerous, an officer engaged in otherwise lawful activity should not have to choose between continuing to engage in that activity and placing his or her life at risk. Giving weight to those concerns, a reviewing court's "inquiry therefore is limited to whether the precautions taken were reasonable under the circumstances as they reasonably appeared at the time that the decision was made." *Id.*

As the Court of Appeals correctly explained, the admonition not to "second-guess" an officer's judgment is a "method of analysis, not an apologia." *State v. Miglavs*, 63 P.3d 1202, 1209 (Or. Ct. App. 2003). As such, it must be followed, not merely recited.

Here, the precaution the officers took was reasonable under the circumstances as they reasonably appeared at the time. The defendants were known to associate with a gang whose members regularly carry weapons. The officers engaged in a pat down to protect themselves against those possible weapons. Even if the question was a close one — which it is not — this Court should err on the side of giving the officers latitude in the situation and should conclude that the trial court properly denied Defendant's motion to suppress evidence discovered during the pat-down search.

The application of the rule to the facts of this case begins here.

Note how the application relies on the same language used to explain the policy. Doing so helps the court see how the sought after conclusion is consistent with the public good described above.

Table 7.3-K compares the structure of a policy-based argument with a rule-based argument so that you can see the similarity between the two.

Table 7.3-K · Comparing the structure of a simple rule-based argument and a policy-based argument

Basic framework	A simple rule-based argument	A policy-based argument
Conclusion	• Conclusion	• Conclusion
Explain the law	• Explain the rule(s)	• Explain the policy that is at stake.
Apply the law	• Address whether the standard articulated in the rule is met in light of the facts of the case.	• Address whether the moral, social, or philosophical good articulated in the policy will be achieved if the court reaches the conclusion you seek.
Conclusion	• Conclusion	• Conclusion

IV. Syllogisms

Although rule-based arguments are, in theory, simple, in practice they can be difficult to execute. For that reason, here is an alternative way of thinking about rule-based arguments: the syllogism. A "syllogism" is an argument structure in which a conclusion is derived from two other premises. Those two premises are (1) the major premise and (2) the minor premise. The "major premise" is usually a broad statement of general applicability. The "minor premise" is a more particular statement that is related to the major premise. The "conclusion" should follow logically from the major and minor premises.[6]

Although the syllogism provides a different way of thinking about rule-based arguments, the syllogism should result in the same kind of structure. If rule-based arguments seem hard to grasp and a different or additional explanation would be helpful, then you might want to think in terms of syllogisms.

Example 7.3-L is a classic syllogism and illustrates the major premise, minor premise, and conclusion drawn from them.

Example 7.3-L · A classic syllogism

Major premise:	All humans are mortal.
Minor premise:	All Greeks are humans.
Conclusion:	All Greeks are mortal.

---

6. James A. Gardner, *Legal Argument: The Structure and Language of Effective Advocacy* 4 (2d ed. LexisNexis 2007).

Rule-based arguments are syllogisms.[7] In a rule-based argument, the rule is the major premise. For lawyers, a rule is an assertion of general applicability. When cited to a binding authority, that rule has a force that is difficult to controvert. The "minor premise" is the evidence from your case against which the standard is applied. A minor premise is most effective when it presents evidence that is also difficult to controvert. The conclusion results from the application of the undisputed major premise (the rule) to the undisputed minor premise (facts or other evidence in the case).

Let's look back at two rule-based arguments, provided here in Examples 7.3-M and 7.3-N, to see how they fall within the structure of a syllogism.

Example 7.3-M · A rule-based argument as a syllogism

This case is moot and should, therefore, be dismissed. A case is moot if there is no justiciable controversy. *State v. Hauskins,* 281 P.3d 669, 672 (Or. Ct. App. 2012). A justiciable controversy exists when the interests of the parties to the action are adverse and the court's decision in the matter will have some practical effect on the rights of the parties to the controversy. *McIntire v. Forbes,* 909 P.2d 846, 850-51 (Or. 1996) (internal quotation marks omitted).

Major premise is shaded.

This case is moot because Ms. Peterson has already received that which she sought. The only relief Ms. Peterson sought was the return of her two dogs, Peaches and Tango, which were previously seized by a Klamath County animal control officer. The attached agreement, which Ms. Peterson signed, demonstrates that Ms. Peterson's dogs, Peaches and Tango, have been returned and are once again residing in the Peterson household. Because the appellant has received that which she sought, the parties no longer have any interests that are adverse and any ruling by the Court would have no practical effect. The case should be dismissed as moot.

Minor premise is underlined.

Final conclusion. For purposes of effective writing, conclusion is repeated.

Example 7.3-N · A rule-based argument as a syllogism

First, the ordinary meaning of the phrase "for profit" limits the person who can be prosecuted to those in the business of smuggling. "Profit" is widely understood as "net income . . . from the conduct of business." *Webster's Third New International Dictionary* 1811 (2002); *see also The American Heritage Dictionary* 989 (5th ed. 2009) (defining profit as "financial gain from a . . . business activity"). Therefore, a "person" who smuggles "for profit" is one who seeks a "net income" from the "business" of smuggling. Only the coyote is seeking income from the smuggling. And only the coyote—not the individual

Major premise (shaded) is established.

Minor premise is underlined.

---

7. Analogical arguments can also be understood more or less in terms of syllogisms. *See id.* at 7-9. The syllogistic structure is usually more helpful when constructing rule-based arguments than it is when constructing analogical arguments. Thus, this discussion about syllogisms is limited to rule-based arguments.

Final conclusion. For purposes of effective writing, conclusion is repeated.

<u>migrant — is in the business of smuggling.</u> Thus, the phrase "for profit" limits the "person" who can be prosecuted to the smuggler, and not the individual migrant.

Thinking about your arguments as a syllogism can also help strengthen your arguments. Once you determine your major and minor premise, you can examine each, asking how that premise might be attacked. Asking that question can help you shore up your argument before you present it to the court. Moreover, you can subject opposing counsel's argument to that same scrutiny and determine where its weaknesses might lurk.

Practice Points

- A persuasive rule-based argument uses the same structure as an objective rule-based argument.

  - A persuasive rule-based argument states a conclusion about the element, step, or factor at issue.

  - It explains the rule relevant to that element, step, or factor.

  - The application juxtaposes the key concepts from the rule against the facts from the client's case. Juxtaposing the key concepts from the rule against the facts is the technique that makes a rule-based argument persuasive.

  - A persuasive rule-based argument repeats the initial conclusion at the end of the argument as a way to sum up and emphasize the conclusion.

- A statutory construction argument follows that same pattern; however, the explanation of the law becomes an argument about what the statutory text means. The argument about what the statutory text means — is developed through a series of rule-based arguments.

- A policy argument follows the same structure as a simple rule-based argument. The "rule" is an assertion about what would be good for society, and the application shows that the outcome your client seeks is consistent with that societal good.

- A syllogism is another way to think about a rule-based argument. Examining your rule-based arguments as a syllogism is another way to test the logic of your argument.

Using Rule-Based and Analogical Arguments Together

In the preceding sections, rule-based arguments and analogical arguments were discussed separately; however, rule-based and analogical arguments can be used together to create a single legal argument. Usually, when using them in combination, you will first rely on the rule-based argument and then shore up that argument with one or more analogies to prior cases.

The advantage of using the two different kinds of argument in combination is that you get the benefits of both. The rule-based argument allows you to focus on the broader legal principles and tell a cohesive story about how the court should apply the law to your client's case. The analogies that follow add strength to that story by showing that previous courts have come to the same conclusion that you want the current court to reach.

Example 7.4-A provides an example of an argument that uses rule-based and analogical reasoning.

Example 7.4-A • An argument that relies on both rule-based and analogical reasoning

---

Officers Brown and Cockerham had a reasonable suspicion that justified a protective frisk of the defendant. Whether a suspicion is reasonable depends on the inferences drawn from the particular circumstances confronting the officer viewed in light of the officer's experience. *See State v. Ehly*, 854 P.2d 421, 430 (Or. 1993) (citing *Terry v. Ohio*, 392 U.S. 1, 21-22, 27-30 (1968)). An "intuitive sixth sense" or "instinct" cannot "form the entire basis for 'reasonable suspicion.'" *State v. Valdez*, 561 P.2d 1006, 1010-11 (Or. 1977). Rather, an officer must be able to point to specific and articulable facts that give rise to a reasonable inference that the person might pose an immediate threat. *See Ehly*, 854 P.2d at 430. An officer need not show that the threat was "more likely than not." Or. Rev. Stat. 131.005(11) (defining "probable cause"). An officer must simply have a reasonable belief that a circumstance may exist or that a particular event might occur. *See State v. Stanley*, 935 P.2d 1202, 1204 (Or. 1997). In other words, for a protective frisk to be justified, an officer must only show that the particular circum-

The shaded text shows the key ideas from the rules, which will later be applied to the facts.

147

stances gave rise to a reasonable belief that the defendant might pose an immediate threat.

To establish a reasonable belief that the defendant might pose an immediate threat, officers may rely on their knowledge that the defendant associates with a known dangerous person or that the person is connected with an activity that involves weapons. For example, in *Ehly*, this Court determined that officers had reasonable suspicion to conduct a protective search. *Ehly*, 854 P.2d at 432. In that case, officers knew that the defendant was a drug user and that "many people who use illegal narcotics possess guns." *Id.* at 430. Moreover, the officers also knew that defendant was "running" with a person who carried weapons. *Id.* Because the defendant was rummaging through a gym bag with his hands concealed and did not respond to the officer's suggestion to dump out the contents of the bag, this Court concluded that it was reasonable for one of the officers to dump the contents of the bag out on the motel room bed. *Id.*

Officers must, however, rely on more than the defendant's "looks" when that "look" does not reasonably connect the defendant to a criminal or threatening activity. For example, in *Valdez*, this court held that police officers lacked reasonable suspicion to stop a person who was dressed in a blue leisure suit and shiny black shoes, had a "real neat" Afro, and looked "real sharp." *Valdez*, 561 P.2d at 1010. Although the police officers thought the defendant looked like a "typical pusher," the court disagreed, stating that "[n]eedle scars on forearms may legitimately speak of possible criminal activity in drugs, but shined shoes, sharp clothes, a neat Afro, and staring at a police officer do not say much." *Id.* at 1010-11. Similarly, in *Bates*, this court held that the officers had not established reasonable suspicion when all that the officers could point to was that the defendant was a self-described "Indian" who had long hair, a beard, was wearing a leather jacket, and looked suspicious. *State v. Bates*, 747 P.2d 991, 994 (Or. 1987).

Officers Brown and Cockerham can point to specific, articulable facts that gave rise to a reasonable suspicion that the defendants posed an immediate threat. First, the officers knew that the defendant was associated with the 18th Street Gang. Defendant was wearing a shirt with the phrase "18th Street" printed on it, and his companion had a tattoo under his eye, which is a tattoo that is associated with membership in the 18th Street Gang. In addition, both men had shaved heads and were wearing baggy gang-style clothes. Thus, the officers knew that the defendant was associated with the 18th Street Gang.

Second, the officers knew that members of the 18th Street Gang were dangerous, often carrying concealed weapons. In fact, one of the officers had encountered a gang member in the parking lot of the same apartment complex who, on a pat-down search, was found to have a weapon concealed in the waistband of his pants under a baggy shirt. Another officer had personally removed weapons from several 18th Street Gang members in that same neighborhood. Indeed, he had found a gun on a gang member "just previously to this incident." Thus, the officers knew that members of the 18th Street Gang carried weapons and posed a danger to the officers, and they knew that the defendant was associated with that gang and its activities.

Margin notes:

A case illustration of *State v. Ehly* establishes the rule that the writer wishes to rely on later and will provide the basis for an analogical comparison.

The writer provides a case illustration of *Valdez* and *Bates* as a defensive move. These are cases the defense is likely to rely on; thus, the writer must show how these cases are distinguishable.

The rule-based argument begins here and continues into the next paragraph. Do you see how the writer re-integrates key ideas from the rule into the analysis of the facts? In that way, the writer shows how the law, when applied to the facts, establishes a particular outcome.

Based on these facts, the officers had reason to believe that the defendant might pose an immediate threat. In fact, the officers relied on the same kinds of facts that established reasonable suspicion in *Ehly*. Just as the officer in *Ehly* relied on the defendant's drug activity, an activity that often involves weapons and therefore poses a danger to others, the officers in this case relied on the defendant's gang membership, an activity that often involves weapons and also poses a danger to others. Moreover, just as the officers in *Ehly* relied on the defendant's association with a person who was known to carry weapons, the officers in this case relied on the defendant's association with a group of people—the 18th Street Gang—who were known to carry weapons. Finally, just as the officers in *Ehly* were concerned for their safety because the defendant was rummaging through a bag (a place where a gun could be concealed) and they could not see his hands, the officers in this case were concerned because the defendant's waistband was concealed and was a place where a handgun could be concealed. Thus, the officers in this case relied on the same kinds of facts as did the officers in *Ehly* and, accordingly, had reasonable suspicion to pat down the defendant.

The writer then analogizes to Ehly. *The analogy asserts that because the facts described above established reasonable suspicion in that case, similar facts should establish reasonable suspicion here.*

For these same reasons, the officers relied on far more than simply the defendant's "looks." In *Valdez* and in *Bates*, the "look" that the officers relied on—a blue leisure suit, shiny black shoes, and a "neat Afro" in *Valdez* and long hair, a beard, and a leather jacket in *Bates*—could not be particularly associated with a weapons-related activity or with a particular group of people who regularly carry weapons. By contrast, here, the "look" at issue established a reasonable suspicion of gang activity and membership in the 18th Street Gang. Both the association with gang activity generally and the association with a particular gang known to carry weapons are specific, articulable facts that raise a reasonable suspicion that the defendant might pose an immediate threat.

Here, the writer distinguishes Valdez *and* Bates.

Practice Points

- Lawyers sometimes combine a rule-based and an analogical argument.

- Such an argument allows the writer, in the rule-based argument, to tell a story about how the law applies to the facts and, in the analogical argument, to show that the conclusions are supported by precedent.

- When using both a rule-based and analogical argument, the more general rule-based argument should precede the more specific analogical argument.

Structuring Factor Analyses

I.   Factors Analyzed as a Single Legal Argument
II. Factors Analyzed in Multiple, Distinct Legal Arguments
III. Choosing an Organizational Structure for a Factor Analysis

---

As mentioned in section § 7.1, *Organizing Claims and Arguments*, organizing a factor analysis presents particular organizational challenges. That is because, in a factor analysis, the court reaches its conclusion by weighing the factors against each other. The presence or absence of any one factor is not determinative; rather, the court will consider the degree to which the factors weigh in favor of one conclusion as compared to the degree to which the factors weigh in favor of the opposite conclusion. Because factors are weighed against one another, the relationships among factors are different from the relationships among elements.

When an analysis depends on factors, the organizational structure may not be obvious. The connection among factors creates organizational challenges. Ultimately, you will have to choose between addressing all the factors in a single argument or addressing each factor in its own argument.[1] This section describes both possibilities and explains how to choose between the two.

I. Factors Analyzed as a Single Legal Argument

The first way you might organize a factor analysis is to address all the factors and how they should be weighed in one legal argument. Schematically, such an organization would look like Figure 7.5-A.

---

1. Occasionally, attorneys will group related factors together. Such a case presents a third organizational choice. To keep the discussion simple, this section focuses on the two most common organizational structures.

Figure 7.5-A · A factor analysis organized into one legal argument

Conclusion about the factor analysis

Explain the Law about the factor analysis

- <u>Rules</u> will name the factors the court will consider and describe any general principles about those factors.

- <u>Case illustrations</u> will show how courts have previously weighed *all* the relevant factors to reach a conclusion.

Apply the Law to the Facts

- <u>Rule-based arguments</u> will step through each factor, examining the degree to which each factor is present.

- <u>Analogical arguments</u> will compare the degree to which each factor is present in this case as compared to a prior case to reach a conclusion about whether the current case is like or not like a prior case. Because you will be comparing a group of factors in a prior case to a group of factors in a current case, the comparison will likely be complex, and you will have to work hard so that you don't lose your reader.

Conclusion about the factor analysis

If you choose to organize your factor analysis in one legal argument, the most challenging aspect will likely be writing case comparisons. If you use one legal argument to address all factors, then your comparison will have to address *all* the factors that the court considered in the prior case and compare the relevant facts for each factor to the analogous facts in your client's case. Thus, the case comparison will be complex, and you will have to take care so that the court does not lose track of your argument.[2]

In Example 7.5-B you can see how you might organize a factor analysis in one legal argument. Pay particular attention to how the lawyer carefully walks the court though the comparison of the current case to a prior case.

---

2. *A Lawyer Writes*, pages 143 through 149, provides many useful techniques to help a reader through a difficult case comparison. Christine Coughlin, Joan Malmud Rocklin & Sandy Patrick, *A Lawyer Writes: A Practical Guide to Legal Analysis* 143-47 (2d ed. 2013).

Example 7.5-B · A factor analysis organized into one legal argument

The trial court correctly concluded that Ms. Moran did not voluntarily execute the pre-marital agreement. A wife voluntarily executes a pre-marital agreement only if she signs the agreement without being coerced, intimidated, or unduly pressured. *In re Rudder*, 217 P.3d 183, 193 (Or. Ct. App. 2009). In addition, she must have "some modicum" of knowledge of the terms of the agreement and the property affected. *Id.* To determine whether the wife entered the agreement voluntarily and had an appropriate degree of knowledge, courts look at a variety of factors: (1) the timing of the agreement in relation to the wedding, (2) whether the assets were sufficiently disclosed, (3) the relative sophistication of the parties, and (4) whether the complaining party had adequate opportunity to consult with independent counsel. *Id.* at 194.

A wife does not enter a pre-marital agreement voluntarily if the agreement is provided one day before the wedding, the agreement does not disclose assets, the wife is unsophisticated, and an attorney is not present. *Id.* at 194-95. In *Rudder*, the husband, an electrician, and the wife, a cosmetologist who had owned a beauty salon, discussed in general terms a pre-marital agreement a few weeks before the wedding. *Id.* at 194. The husband's attorney drafted the agreement, which the wife first saw the day before leaving for the wedding. Although she had asked that her attorney be present when she signed the agreement, her attorney was not. Her husband urged her, "[g]o ahead and just sign it. The wedding is on." *Id.* After reading through the agreement, which did not list all the husband's assets or their value, the wife signed the agreement. *Id.* On these facts, the court determined that the circumstances created a coercive environment. *Id.* In discussing the wife's relative business sophistication, the Court of Appeals agreed with the trial court that "although . . . [the] wife had some experience in business matters, that experience was limited and she was relatively unsophisticated in financial matters." *Id.* at 195. Therefore, the wife did not enter into the agreement voluntarily. *Id.*

By contrast, an experienced businesswoman who has an opportunity to know her husband's assets and is provided with an agreement more than two weeks in advance can enter into the premarital agreement voluntarily. *In re Coward*, 582 P.2d 834, 835 (Or. Ct. App. 1978). In that case, the couple signed the pre-marital agreement seventeen days before the wedding. *Id.* At that time, the husband's attorney advised the wife to seek independent counsel. *Id.* The wife, who had worked as a bookkeeper and assisted her husband with his financial affairs, declined to speak with an attorney and signed the agreement. *Id.* The court concluded that the wife had been given sufficient opportunity to consult with an attorney, was an experienced businesswoman, and was aware of her husband's property. *Id.* Accordingly, the court held that the wife voluntarily signed the pre-marital agreement. *Id.* at 836. Although the 1978 *Coward* case was decided before the 1987 enactment of Or. Rev. Stat. § 108.725, the legislature intended § 108.725 to codify existing case law; therefore the *Coward case* still stands as an example of "voluntariness." *See Rudder*, 217 P.3d at 192.

Conclusion

The explanation of the law begins here.

The rules explain, among other things, the factors that the court must consider.

The case illustrations—*In re Rudder* and *In re Coward*—address all the factors that the court considered and then explain how the court weighed those factors to reach its conclusion.

The application begins here.

Here, Ms. Moran did not enter into her premarital agreement voluntarily. She is an unsophisticated businesswoman who had limited time before the wedding to review the document. Moreover, the agreement did not disclose her future husband's assets, and she was unable to consult with an attorney.

These facts are similar to the facts in *Rudder*, in which the court found the agreement was not signed voluntarily. First, in both cases the agreement was signed within days of the wedding. In *Rudder*, it was one day before the wedding, and in this case, it was five days. Although Ms. Moran had a few more days to consider the agreement, the time span created pressure. In *Rudder*, the pressure was evidenced by the husband's urging the wife, "[g]o ahead and sign it. The wedding is on." In this case, Ms. Moran stated that, "she didn't want to wait to find an attorney, not with so many people traveling so far." Thus, in this case, as in *Rudder*, the shortened time span created pressure and did not leave adequate time to consult with an attorney. Moreover, like the wife in *Rudder*, Ms. Moran is not a sophisticated businesswoman. As an office manager she has the approximate business experience of a cosmetologist who owned a beauty salon, and the *Rudder* court decided that the business-owner was not a sophisticated business person. In addition, Ms. Moran, like the wife in *Rudder*, was not told the value of her husband's assets. Finally, although Ms. Moran was advised to speak with an attorney, that one fact should not outweigh the other facts that are similar to the facts in *Rudder*. Those facts show a pressured environment in which Ms. Moran did not have sufficient time to fully assess the agreement. For these reasons, this Court should reach the same conclusion that the *Rudder* court did: The agreement was not entered into voluntarily.

Defendant's reliance on *Coward* is misplaced. In *Coward*, the wife had previously reviewed her husband's finances; thus, she understood the value of her husband's assets. In this case, there is no evidence that Ms. Moran was aware of the value of her husband's assets. Her lack of knowledge of her husband's assets, the lack of evidence that her job as an office manager would give her sufficient experience to assess the value of his assets, and the compressed time span of only five days she had in which to make a decision support the trial court's conclusion that she signed in an coercive environment. Ms. Moran did not sign voluntarily.

In the application, you can see the lawyer carefully walk through each factor that was important to the prior court and compare the relevant facts from the prior case to the facts in Ms. Moran's case.

Final conclusion

II. Factors Analyzed in Multiple, Distinct Legal Arguments

Although a factor analysis can be organized in one legal argument, sometimes the better choice is to break out the individual factors and create one legal argument for each factor, as in Figure 7.5-C.

Example 7.5-C · A factor analysis organized by factor

Roadmap to Factor Analysis

Factor 1

State a **conclusion** about the degree to which factor 1 weighs in favor of the desired outcome.

Explain the law about factor 1.

- Rules will focus on only those rules relevant to factor one.

- Case illustrations will be limited to a prior court's analysis of factor 1. The case illustrations may be difficult to write because you will have to pick out the facts and reasoning that the court relied on to reach a conclusion about factor 1. All facts and reasoning related to other factors should be eliminated.

Apply the law of factor 1.

- Rule-based arguments will compare the facts relevant to factor 1 to the rules above.

- Analogical arguments will compare the facts of this case to those of a prior case, but only with respect to factor 1.

State a **conclusion** about the degree to which factor 1 weighs in favor of the desired outcome.

Factor 2

State a **conclusion** about the degree to which factor 2 weighs in favor of the desired outcome.

Explain the law about factor 2.

- Rules will focus on only those rules relevant to factor two.

- Case illustrations will be limited to a prior court's analysis of factor 2. The case illustrations may be difficult to write because you will have to pick out the facts and reasoning that the court relied on to reach a conclusion about factor 2. All facts and reasoning related to other factors should be eliminated.

Apply the law of factor 2.

- Rule-based arguments will compare the facts relevant to factor 2 to the rules above.

- Analogical arguments will compare the facts of this case to those of a prior case, but only with respect to factor 2.

State a **conclusion** about the degree to which factor 2 weighs in favor of the desired outcome.

Factor 3

State a **conclusion** about the degree to which factor 3 weighs in favor of the desired outcome.

Explain the law about factor 3.

- Rules will focus on only those rules relevant to factor three.

- Case illustrations will be limited to a prior court's analysis of factor 3. The case illustrations may be difficult to write because you will have to pick out the facts and reasoning that the court relied on to reach a conclusion about factor 3. All facts and reasoning related to other factors should be eliminated.

Apply the law of factor 3.

- Rule-based arguments will compare the facts relevant to factor 3 to the rules above.

- Analogical arguments will compare the facts of this case to those of a prior case, but only with respect to factor 3.

State a **conclusion** about the degree to which factor 3 weighs in favor of the desired outcome.

Weigh conclusions to reach final conclusion

If you choose this second structure, illustrated in Figure 7.5-C, in which each factor is addressed in a separate legal argument, you will likely face two challenges.

First, your case illustrations will have to be carefully drafted because each case illustration will focus on only one factor. In their opinions, courts sometimes carefully delineate their determination about each factor, but sometimes they do not. Thus, you will have to review the relevant prior decisions and extract the court's analysis about each individual factor. Depending on how explicitly it analyzed individual factors, this step could be very easy to do or very difficult.

The other challenge in presenting a factor analysis is determining the conclusion that you can reach about a single factor. Remember that a factor analysis depends on assessing the weight of each factor and then weighing all the factors against each other. Thus, when you are finished analyzing a factor, the only conclusion you can reach is whether that factor weighs in favor of a particular outcome. Factors are not "satisfied" or "met." Rather, they weigh—perhaps strongly or not so strongly—in favor of or against an outcome. So, you will need to structure your conclusion about each factor carefully.

Finally, if you use one legal argument to analyze each factor, you will have an additional step. After analyzing each factor, you will need a final paragraph that weighs all the factors against each other. This paragraph will not be structured as a typical legal argument because there should be no additional law to explain. Rather, you will take the conclusions that you reached with respect to each individual factor and explain how those conclusions weigh in favor of your client's desired outcome.

In Example 7.5-D you can see how you might organize a factor analysis by creating one legal argument for each factor. Look at the conclusions that the lawyer reaches with respect to each factor, and then take a look at the last paragraph, which brings together the conclusions for each factor to reach an overall conclusion.

Example 7.5-D · A factor analysis organized into one legal argument for each factor[3]

The introduction describes the factors that must be analyzed.

B. Mr. Floyd's subjective belief that he was expected to play paddleball with his supervisor was objectively reasonable.

Mark Floyd reasonably believed that he was expected to participate in the paddleball game with his supervisor. To determine whether an employee reasonably believed he was required to participate in an activity, California courts usually weigh three factors: (1) whether the employer was involved in the activity, (2) whether the employer benefited from the activity, and (3) whether the

---

3. Professor Leslie Oster of Northwestern University School of Law first developed this legal argument.

employer pressured the employee to participate. *Meyer v. Workers' Comp. Appeals Bd.*, 204 Cal. Rptr. 74, 76 (Ct. App. 1984). In this case, an analysis of all three factors shows that Mr. Floyd reasonably believed that he was required to play paddleball as part of his job.

1.   Fitness Functions was involved in the paddleball game.

Fitness Functions was involved in the paddleball game because it provided all the resources necessary for employees to play the game. When an employer subsidizes the activity, courts have routinely found the employer to be involved in the activity. *See, e.g. Ezzy v. Workers' Comp. Appeals Bd.*, 194 Cal. Rptr. 90, 95 (Ct. App. 1983); *Meyer*, 204 Cal. Rptr. at 77. For example, in *Ezzy*, the court held that an employer was involved with an after-hours softball game when the employer had subsidized the game. 194 Cal. Rptr. at 95. There, a part-time law clerk was injured after joining members of the law firm in an after-hours softball game. *Id.* The law firm paid for all equipment, t-shirts, refreshments, and an awards banquet. *Id.*

Only when the employer has not contributed any resources to the activity will courts find minimal involvement under this factor. *See, e.g. Meyer*, 204 Cal. Rptr. at 77. For example, in *Meyer*, the court held that the employer was only "minimally involved" in a weekend rafting trip. *Id.* The court explained that although a supervisor had invited other employees to go rafting and stay at his house on a river, no evidence showed that the employer had subsidized the trip. *Id.*

Whether an activity occurs on an employer's property does not affect whether an employer was involved. *See e.g. Todd v. Workers' Comp. Appeals Bd.*, 243 Cal. Rptr. 925, 927 (Ct. App. 1988). As the *Todd* court explained, "the statute does not differentiate between recreational activities on and off the employer's premises." *Id.* at 927.

In this case, Fitness Functions was involved because it provided all the resources necessary for the game to occur. In fact, Fitness Functions provided more resources than the employer in *Ezzy*, which was determined to be involved. In *Ezzy*, the employer provided equipment and t-shirts and hosted a banquet. Similarly, here, Fitness Functions allowed Ms. Randolph to purchase paddleball equipment with money from her expense account. In addition, Fitness Functions paid for and installed the paddleball court. In *Ezzy*, although the employer held a banquet, the employer did not actually build a softball field. By building the paddleball court and providing the equipment, Fitness Functions was "involved" with the activity.

For these same reasons, Fitness Functions's involvement goes beyond the involvement in *Meyer*, where a supervisor invited employees to go rafting together, but the employer provided no other resources. Although Ms. Randolph similarly invited the employee, Mark Floyd, to play, Fitness Functions provided additional resources to facilitate the paddle ball games, whereas the employer in *Meyer* provided none. Because Mr. Floyd can show employer involvement greater than in both *Meyer* and *Ezzy*, Fitness Functions was involved in the paddleball game.

Conclusion about factor 1 — whether Fitness Function was "involved." The explanation of the law for factor 1 begins immediately after the conclusion.

The law is then applied.

2. Fitness Functions also benefited from the paddleball game.

Fitness Functions also benefited from Ms. Randolph's paddleball games because they were a means to generate camaraderie. One benefit an employer
may derive from employee participation in a recreational activity is improved
"cooperation, spirit, morale, and camaraderie." *Ezzy*, 194 Cal. Rptr. at 95. To determine whether an activity builds employee camaraderie, California courts
have looked at (1) the employer's intention to create a spirit of camaraderie, (2)
the activity's regularity, and (3) the number of employees involved. *See id.* For
example, in *Ezzy*, the court concluded that there was substantial employer benefit from an employee's participation in a law firm softball team. In that case, a
partner testified that the games were "good for office spirit." *Id.* at 92. The
games were played according to a schedule, and the office also had a schedule
of practices. *Id.* Partners, other members of the firm, and some secretaries
played, and all firm employees received a team t-shirt and were invited to a
final banquet. *Id.* at 91. By contrast, in *Meyer*, the court held that the benefit to
an employer from a "last minute get together" of a "few salesman" and their
wives was "speculative and remote." *Meyer*, 204 Cal. Rptr. at 77.

The law is then applied.

In this case, Fitness Functions benefited from the paddleball game through
improved office camaraderie. Mr. Floyd's case is like *Ezzy*. First, the employers
in both cases intended to create a spirit of camaraderie through employee participation. In *Ezzy*, a partner stated the games were "good for office spirit." Similarly, in Mr. Floyd's case, Ms. Randolph stated that she played paddleball
regularly with employees because "[i]t's a great way to get to know my employees" and she thought "people work better together when they're also friends
and know each other in ways other than work." Second, in both cases the activity was played regularly. In *Ezzy*, the softball games and practices followed a
schedule. In Mr. Floyd's case, although there was no schedule, Ms. Randolph ac-
knowledged that she played regularly and estimated that she plays with other
employees between two and three times a week. Finally, in both cases, a wide
array of employees were involved. In *Ezzy*, the team included members of the
firm as well as secretaries. In Mr. Floyd's case, Ms. Randolph stated she plays
with "people who report to [her,]" "people above [her,]" and "people in other de-
partments." Because his supervisor expected a benefit from employee participation and because the games were played regularly with numerous
employees, Fitness Functions, like the law firm in *Ezzy*, benefited from employee
participation in the paddleball game.

A final conclusion about factor 1

For these same reasons, the paddleball game is distinct from the last
minute get together of a few salesmen in *Meyers*. Accordingly, Fitness Functions benefited from the paddleball games, and this factor weighs in favor of
finding that his subjective belief was objectively reasonable.

3. Mr. Floyd can show he was pressured to play paddleball.

Mark Floyd was also pressured to play paddleball with Ms. Randolph . . . .

* * *

Thus, this factor also weighs in favor of concluding that Mr. Floyd's subjective belief was reasonable.

4. Weighing all three factors, Mr. Floyd's belief that he was expected to play paddleball was objectively reasonable.

Based on the above facts, Mr. Floyd's subjective belief that he was expected to play paddleball with his supervisor was objectively reasonable. Fitness Functions was involved with the game by providing the court and equipment necessary to play. Fitness Functions also benefited from employee participation in the paddleball game because it provided Ms. Randolph an opportunity to build relationships with her employees in a manner with which she was comfortable. Finally, given Mr. Floyd's status as a probationary employee, his recent employment reviews, and the advice of the human resources officer that playing paddleball would help his relationship with Ms. Randolph, Ms. Randolph's invitation to play created pressure. Thus, all the relevant factors tend to show that Mr. Floyd reasonably believed he was expected to play, and the decision of the Workers' Compensation Board of Appeals should be reversed.

Moreover, this Court has repeatedly stated that California worker's compensation laws are to be construed liberally to benefit the employee. For all of these reasons, Mr. Floyd should be compensated for the injuries he sustained in the course of his work for Fitness Functions.

> After all the factors are analyzed individually, the factors are weighed together to reach a final conclusion.

III. Choosing an Organizational Structure for a Factor Analysis

When you are faced with a factor analysis, choosing whether to structure the analysis as a single legal argument or multiple legal arguments is often a difficult decision. In fact, you may begin to write under one structure only to find that, actually, the other structure may work better.

At first your decision may be largely influenced by how the courts have analyzed the factors in the past. If the prior decisions tend to focus on the ultimate outcome and leave individual factors unexplained, it may be very difficult for you to pull apart the analysis and explain the law one factor at a time. In that situation, you may decide to explain the law as the courts have—analyzing all the facts relevant to all the factors in a single legal argument.

Sometimes, however, the courts have analyzed the factors individually, or (even if they haven't) you can pull apart the court's analysis and address the factors individually. In those cases, you have a choice: You can analyze all the facts relating to each factor in one legal argument or you can create individual arguments for each factor. After addressing each factor individually, a final paragraph at the end will weigh the factors together.

Whenever you have the choice of how to present a factor analysis— and as you gain more experience it is more and more likely that you will have that choice—you should consider what will be most persuasive to the court. Sometimes, if you have a series of factors, all of which you can argue weigh in your favor, it can be persuasive to have a series of shorter arguments, each of which ends, "This factor, too, weighs in favor of finding for my client." The repetition of factor after factor weighing in your client's favor has a persuasive effect. On the other hand, if you analyze all the factors in a single argument, you have other persuasive opportunities. When analyzing all the factors in a single argument, you will have more facts to work with in one place. The greater range of facts may afford you with more choices about how to order the facts, thus allowing you greater opportunity to arrange the facts in the most favorable light.

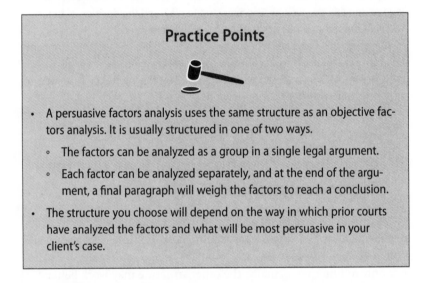

Practice Points

- A persuasive factors analysis uses the same structure as an objective factors analysis. It is usually structured in one of two ways.

    ○ The factors can be analyzed as a group in a single legal argument.

    ○ Each factor can be analyzed separately, and at the end of the argument, a final paragraph will weigh the factors to reach a conclusion.

- The structure you choose will depend on the way in which prior courts have analyzed the factors and what will be most persuasive in your client's case.

Chapter 8

Developing Persuasive Arguments

I.   Begin with Your Conclusion
II. Explain the Law Persuasively
     A. Rules
         1. Explain existing rules from your client's perspective
         2. Develop rules that advance your client's argument
         3. Acknowledge unfavorable rules in a favorable way
     B. Case Illustrations
         1. Highlight helpful facts
         2. Create hooks for your case illustrations
         3. Acknowledge unfavorable cases in a favorable way
III. Apply Your Persuasive Explanation of the Law to the Facts
     A. Developing your Application
     B. Responding to your Opponent's Analysis
IV. End with a Final Conclusion

As you saw in the last chapter, attorneys use the same structures to organize their writing whether they are writing objectively or persuasively. This chapter focuses on what does change when you write persuasively. Although you will use the same structures, the content of your arguments will subtly shift. In all instances, the purpose of that shift is to make it easier for the court to rule in favor of your client.

That shift to persuasion is a subtle shift. When advocating for a particular outcome, neither the law nor the facts suddenly change. As discussed in Chapter 2, *The Ethical, Professional Advocate*, "it is what it is," and you must work within the confines of the law and the facts. Moreover, if you stretch the law or facts too far, you are likely to undermine every effort at persuasion because the court will no longer trust you.

Although you must accept the law and facts as they are, you can present both so that they more readily allow the court to reach the outcome you seek. This chapter, *Developing Persuasive Arguments*, and the next chapter, Chapter 9, *Refining Persuasive Arguments*, provide you with techniques to do just that. This chapter focuses on developing the substance

161

of a persuasive legal argument, while the next chapter addresses how to fine-tune that substance.

In developing the substance of a persuasive argument, this chapter looks at each component part of a legal argument—the conclusion, the explanation of the law, the application, and the final conclusion—and addresses how each can be developed to present your client's case in the most persuasive way and make it easier for a court to find in your client's favor.

I. Begin with Your Conclusion

A persuasive legal argument should begin with a conclusion. That conclusion should state the decision you believe the court should reach regarding the element or factor at issue.

Stating your conclusion at the outset of your argument has at least two persuasive functions. First, stating your conclusion tells the judge where you are going and, therefore, helps the judge follow your argument. An argument that is easier to follow is more likely to be absorbed and accepted. In addition, stating your conclusion at the outset is likely to provide repetition about a key point. You will also state your conclusion in a point heading and at the end of your argument. That repetition helps your main idea stick in the judge's head.

Occasionally, you may choose to omit the initial conclusion and begin an argument with a statement of the issue before the court. For example, if your introduction and a point heading already state the conclusion, stating it again may seem overly repetitive. When in doubt, though, state your conclusion about the element or factor in dispute and take advantage of its persuasive effect.

II. Explain the Law Persuasively

Although you will likely begin with a conclusion, and the conclusion is your first persuasive step, the real work begins with explaining the law. Many attorneys think that explaining the law is the easy part. You simply look up the law and write down what you find. If, however, you think that the real work of developing arguments begins when the law is applied to the current case, you will lose significant persuasive opportunities. In particular, you will lose the opportunity to present the law in a way that is most favorable to your client. You will also lose the opportunity to prime the court so that it is receptive to the analysis that will follow. Thus, do not wait. Begin persuading as soon as you begin explaining.

The next two sections address how to present rules and case illustrations persuasively. Although the two sections explain rules and case illustrations separately, keep in mind that, when your argument includes both rules and case illustrations, the two must work together.

A. Rules

You can use several techniques to present legal rules in a persuasive light. First, you can present existing rules so that they state the law from your client's perspective. Second, you can develop new rules that will advance your argument. Finally, you can address unfavorable rules in a way that minimizes their negative impact.

1. Explain existing rules from your client's perspective

As mentioned above, too many attorneys explain the rules to the court in the same way that they read the rules. You, however, can do more than merely cut and paste the rules as you found them. As you set out a rule, think about how you can emphasize those parts of the rule that are most helpful to your position. Although no set formula dictates how to do that, here are a few techniques to get you thinking.

First, you should consider whether to state a rule positively or negatively. If you are arguing that a standard is met, then frame the rule so that it explains when the required standard is met. By contrast, if you are arguing that a standard is not met, then frame the rule so that it explains when the standard is not met.

Take, for example, the rule for summary judgment. If you represent the moving party and argue that the court should grant summary judgment on your client's behalf, you should emphasize when summary judgment *must* be granted. By contrast, if you represent the non-moving party, you will want to emphasize when summary judgment must *not* be granted. Table 8-A shows the rule for summary judgment and how opposing counsel might present that same rule in two different ways. Note that the rule is the same under either version; what has changed is how the rule is presented.

Table 8-A · Explaining the summary judgment standard consistently with your client's position by stating when the standard is met or not met

The rule as written	"The court shall grant summary judgment if the movant shows that there is no genuine dispute as to any material fact and the movant is entitled to judgment as a matter of law." Fed. R. Civ. P. 56(a).
The moving party	Summary judgment must be granted if there is no issue of material fact and the moving party is entitled to judgment as a matter of law. Fed. R. Civ. P. 56(a).
The non-moving party	Summary judgment may not be granted if there is an issue of material fact. Fed. R. Civ. P. 56(a).

> **What "must" a court do?**
> When using the auxiliary verb "must," choose your subject carefully. Although lawyers often state what "must" happen under the law, a judge may be put off if you assert what the court "must" do. Thus, explain what "must" happen under the law, but urge the court to do what it "should."

You can use the same technique with more substantive rules. If you are alleging discrimination, explain when discrimination takes place. If you are defending against a charge of discrimination, explain when a party does not discriminate under the law, as in Table 8-B.

Table 8-B • **Explaining a substantive rule consistently with your client's position by stating the rule positively or negatively**

The rule as written	"A recipient which operates or sponsors interscholastic . . . athletics shall provide equal athletic opportunity for members of both sexes. In determining whether equal opportunities are available the Director will consider, among other factors: (1) Whether the selection of sports and levels of competition effectively accommodate the interests and abilities of members of both sexes . . . ." 34 C.F.R. 106.41(c)(1).
Plaintiff	A university discriminates against its female students if it fails to effectively accommodate the interests and abilities of its female students. 34 C.F.R. 106.41(c)(1); *Roberts v. Colo. St. Bd. of Agric.*, 998 F.2d 824, 828 (10th Cir. 1993).
Defendant	A university complies with Title IX if it effectively accommodates the interests and abilities of its female students. 34 C.F.R. 106.41(c) (1); *Roberts v. Colo. St. Bd. of Agric.*, 998 F.2d 824, 828 (10th Cir. 1993).

Similarly, your explanation of the rule can emphasize the breadth or the narrowness of a standard. Compare the explanations of the standard for granting summary judgment in Table 8-C. Notice how the non-moving party uses the word "only" to suggest that summary judgment should be granted in limited circumstances.

Table 8-C • **Explaining the summary judgment standard consistently with your client's position by emphasizing the breadth or narrowness of a standard**

The moving party	Summary judgment **must** be granted if there is no issue of material fact and the moving party is entitled to judgment as a matter of law. Fed. R. Civ. P. 56(a).
The non-moving party	Summary judgment may be granted **only** if there is no issue of material fact and the moving party is entitled to judgment as a matter of law. Fed. R. Civ. P. 56(a).

Finally, consider the order in which you present the rules. Usually, attorneys begin by explaining the most broadly relevant rule and then discussing more specific aspects of the rule. The judge will be confused if you begin with specific parts of a rule and then present the rule more broadly.

Sometimes, however, you might have some opportunity to choose which rules to present first. Consider, for example, how two different parties might present the rules regarding whether a defendant's encounter with a police officer was "mere conversation" or was a "stop" that needs to be justified by reasonable suspicion. The defendant would like to argue that the encounter was a stop and, therefore, had to be justified by reasonable suspicion. He would likely begin by discussing what constitutes a stop, as in Example 8-D. By contrast, the state would likely begin by describing what constitutes "mere conversation" because the state wants to focus the court's attention on that legal standard, as in Example 8-E. Notice that ultimately both parties describe the same law, but the order in which they describe the relevant rules differs because they wish to emphasize different aspects of the law.

Example 8-D • Defendant's explanation of the rules emphasizes when an encounter is a stop

When a police officer stops a citizen, evidence gathered during the course of that stop is not admissible against that citizen unless the stop was justified by reasonable suspicion. *State v. Spenst*, 662 P.2d 5, 6 (Or. Ct. App. 1983). A police officer "stops" a citizen if that person's liberty is restrained, by physical force or a show of authority, by a peace officer lawfully present in any place. Or. Rev. Stat. § 131.605(6); *State v. Warner*, 901 P.2d 940, 942 (Or. Ct. App. 1995). More generally, a person's liberty may be restrained if an individual believes his liberty has been restrained and that belief is objectively reasonable. *Warner*, 901 P.2d at 942. To determine whether a person reasonably believes his liberty was restrained, a court will consider the totality of the circumstances. *State v. Wenger*, 922 P.2d 1248, 1251 (Or. Ct. App. 1996). Only if, under the totality of the circumstances, a person could not reasonably believe his liberty was restrained, is the encounter "mere conversation." *See, e.g., State v. Smith*, 698 P.2d 973, 975 (Or. Ct. App. 1985).

> The defendant, who wants to focus on when a "stop" occurs, begins his explanation of the law by discussing the requirements for a valid stop. A reader's attention, even the attention of an attentive judge, wanes over time. Thus, ideas at the outset receive more focused attention, and it advances your argument to explain first those ideas that you want to emphasize.

Example 8-E • The state's explanation of the rules emphasizes when an encounter is mere conversation

Under Oregon law, citizens can have different encounters with police officers. When an encounter is "mere conversation," evidence an officer acquires during the encounter is admissible against the defendant. *State v. Shelton*, 796 P.2d 390, 392 (Or. Ct. App. 1990).

An encounter is "mere conversation" if, under the totality of the circumstances, a person could not reasonably believe his liberty is being restrained.

> The state, by contrast, wants to focus on when an interaction with a law enforcement agent is "mere conversation." Thus, the state begins its explanation with that idea, giving more emphasis to the idea that some encounters are only "conversation" and not stops.

See, e.g., State v. Smith, 698 P.2d 973, 975 (Or Ct. App. 1985). By contrast, if a person reasonably believes his liberty is being restrained, he is "stopped." Or. Rev. Stat. § 131.605(6); *State v. Warner*, 901 P.2d 940, 942 (Or. Ct. App. 1995). Any evidence obtained during that stop is admissible only if the stop was justified by reasonable suspicion. *State v. Spenst*, 662 P.2d 5, 6 (Or. Ct. App. 1983).

To determine whether an encounter is "mere conversation" or a "stop," the court considers the totality of the circumstances. *State v. Wenger*, 922 P.2d 1248, 1251 (Or. Ct. App. 1996).

---

2. Develop rules that advance your client's argument

Presenting rules consistently with your client's perspective may involve developing rules that will advance your analysis. You might think of the law as settled and believe that you should not "create" new law. Although reasonable, that kind of thinking will limit your usefulness to your client. Within the settled law—and usually within the settled case law—there exist patterns of judicial or legislative thinking. Before they are articulated, those patterns are sometimes called "implicit rules." As an advocate, one of the ways you can help your client is to make those implicit rules explicit. By making implicit rules explicit, you will provide the court with a way to reach a conclusion that is consistent with the currently existing law. And courts want their decisions to be consistent with the existing law.

Of course, all sorts of patterns exist in the law and only some are relevant and helpful. To make sure that you are drawing out relevant and helpful patterns, you need to (1) formulate a possible rule and then (2) evaluate that rule. To formulate a possible rule, you must first identify a pattern in the cases that seems to explain why courts reach their conclusions and, second, craft a rule from the pattern that encompasses both the prior cases and your client's case. Crafting the rule may require you to explain the rule more broadly or more narrowly.

After you have formulated a possible rule, then you must evaluate the rule to make sure that it is wise to use. To evaluate the rule, ask yourself these two questions:

- Is my proposed rule consistent with all the other law that governs this issue?
- If so, does my proposed rule make common sense?

These two questions are important because, if your proposed rule is not consistent with other applicable authorities, then you are not providing the court with an easy way to rule in your favor. Moreover, and perhaps not surprisingly, judges prefer rules that make sense.

Let's look at how you might develop a rule that advances your client's position. Take, for example, the case in which two police officers conducted a safety frisk and found an unregistered, concealed gun. The officers have stated that the reason they conducted the safety frisk was that the defendants were wearing clothing that suggested they were members of a gang. The officers knew that members of this gang often carried weapons and, therefore, they conducted the safety frisk.

Now imagine you are the prosecutor, and you wish to argue that the officer's safety frisk was justified. You begin by reviewing the cases. You read a variety of cases, two of which are excerpted in Table 8-F.

You then begin to formulate a possible rule. From the cases, you notice two things. First, in past cases in which safety frisks were permitted, the defendant had been with a dangerous person. That's a problem for you. In the current case, no known gang member was actually present when the officers arrived. So, a rule that "a safety frisk can be supported if the defendant is *with* a dangerous person at the time of the stop" would not be helpful to your position. You will have to explain the pattern in slightly broader terms. For example, you could argue that officers are permitted to conduct safety frisks if the defendant "associates with" someone dangerous. That explanation of the law accurately reflects past decisions, but it does so in a way that supports your client's position.

Second, you notice that in past cases, police officers presented evidence that the stop related to an activity that involved weapons. Arguably, the protective search in this case was related to an activity that involved weapons. In this case, the officers conducted a safety frisk because they believed the defendants were associated with a gang. Being a member of a gang is an activity that often involves weapons.

Table 8-F · Formulating an explicit rule from implicit rules in case law

Case	Holding	Facts
State v. Stanley	Safety frisk upheld	The defendant was suspected of robbing a bank. The officers testified that those who commit robberies often carry weapons. The defendant was with a man who, during the course of the stop, acted aggressively by grabbing the officer's hand.
State v. Ehly	Safety frisk upheld	The defendant was known to be a drug user, and officers testified that drug users often possess guns. The officer had just seen another man leave the motel where the officers were currently confronting defendant. The man who had just left was known to use guns and was friends with the defendant. Finally, the defendant's hands were concealed.
Proposed rule	To establish a reasonable suspicion for a protective search, officers may rely on their knowledge that the defendant associates with a known dangerous person or that the person is connected with an activity that involves weapons.	

You have now developed a proposed rule: "To establish a reasonable suspicion for a protective search, officers may rely on their knowledge that the defendant associates with a known dangerous person or that the person is connected with an activity that involves weapons."

Now, you need to evaluate the rule. First, you must make sure that no other case rejects the very rule you are proposing. In addition, you would want to consider whether your proposed rule is consistent with the other rules, case law, and policies that govern this area of the law. For example, you know that an officer must have reasonable suspicion for a frisk and that reasonable suspicion must be supported by "clearly articulable facts." Is this an example of a clearly articulable fact, and not a hunch? Arguably, it is. Officers can explain the facts that lead them to believe that the defendants were associated with a dangerous group. Thus, this proposed rule is consistent with at least one other rule.

If your proposed rule is consistent with existing law, you will want to ask yourself the final question. Does your proposed rule make sense? Answering that question requires some knowledge about this area of the law and some imagination. You want to imagine other situations in which the court might be faced with someone "associated with" a dangerous person. Would a frisk still be justified in those circumstances? Suppose the defendant and someone known to carry a gun were on the same basketball team and were, therefore, wearing the same uniform. The defendant would be "associated with" a dangerous person. Would a frisk be warranted in that case? Of course not. But that case can be distinguished because the association is not one that involves the danger. By considering other scenarios the court might face in the future, you can determine whether the proposed rule is likely to appeal to a court.

Once you have formulated and then evaluated the rule, you can finally include it in your explanation of the law, as in Example 8-G.

Example 8-G · Developing a favorable rule from case law

The proposed rule is stated in the first sentence. The case illustrations that follow prove that case law supports the proposed rule.

> To establish a reasonable suspicion for a protective search, officers may rely on their knowledge that the defendant associates with a known dangerous person or that the person is connected with an activity that involves weapons. For example, in *Ehly*, this Court determined that officers had reasonable suspicion to conduct a protective search. *Ehly*, 854 P.2d at 431. In that case, officers knew that the defendant was a drug user and that "many people who use illegal narcotics possess guns." *Id.* at 430. Moreover, the officers also knew that defendant was "running" with a person who carried weapons. *Id.* Because the defendant was rummaging through a gym bag with his hands concealed and did not respond to the officer's suggestion to dump out the contents of the bag, this Court concluded that it was reasonable for one of the officers to dump the contents of the bag onto the motel room bed. *Id.; see also Stanley*, 935 P.2d at 1204 (finding reasonable suspicion because the defendant was suspected of robbing a bank; officers knew that those engaged in a possible robbery may carry weapons; and the defendant associated with a man who, during the course of the stop, acted aggressively by grabbing the officer's hand).

Notice that in Example 8-G the statement of the rule is followed by case illustrations. When making an implicit rule explicit, be sure to provide the court with all the information it will need to see the same pattern in the law that you do. For that reason, when making an implicit rule explicit, state the rule, and then provide case illustrations that will prove your understanding of the law is accurate.

Of course, opposing counsel is likely to follow the same steps and, if at all possible, explain the preceding case law in a way that will be helpful to his client. As explained below, one technique attorneys use in formulating a favorable rule is to state the rule more broadly or more narrowly.

In this case, the prosecutor has described the law more broadly to provide maximum opportunity for the court to uphold the stop. By contrast, defendant's counsel will propose a narrower rule that would restrict an officer's right to stop and frisk a citizen. Defendant's counsel will argue that a police officer can consider a defendant's association with another person as a basis for a frisk only if the other person was present or recently present.

Thus, in the same case, the lawyers may very well explain the prior case law more broadly or more narrowly, as suggested in Table 8-H. Doing so is good advocacy.

Table 8-H · Prior case law explained more broadly or more narrowly

Case	Holding	Facts
State v. Stanley	Safety frisk upheld	The defendant was suspected of robbing a bank. The officers testified that those who commit robberies often carry weapons. The defendant was with a man who, during the course of the stop, acted aggressively by grabbing the officer's hand.
State v. Ehly	Safety frisk upheld	The defendant was known to be a drug user, and officers testified that drug users often possess guns. The officer had just seen another man leave the motel where the officers were currently confronting defendant. The man who had just left was known to use guns and was friends with the defendant. Finally, the defendant's hands were concealed.
Prosecutor's proposed rule	To establish a reasonable suspicion for a protective search, officers may rely on their knowledge that the defendant associates with a known dangerous person or that the person is connected with an activity that involves weapons.	
Defendant's narrower rule	A police officer may not conduct a safety frisk merely because a person has a relationship with someone who is known to be dangerous. Such a relationship, by itself, does not provide a sufficient connection to a dangerous activity such that it would support a protective search.	

Developing rules from patterns in case law is as much art as it is science. To help you get a better feel for it, look at another example.

Imagine that, now, your clients are a four-year-old child and her parents. The four-year-old struck an elderly pedestrian while the four-year-old was riding her bicycle. The estate of the elderly pedestrian sued the four-year-old and her parents.[1] You would like to argue that, as a matter of law, a four-year-old cannot be held liable for negligence. Unfortunately, the case law is not entirely clear on that point. Some prior cases hold that four-year-olds, as a matter of law, cannot be held liable for negligence. Other cases, however, hold that four-year-olds can be held liable for negligence and that a jury should decide whether a particular four-year-old was negligent. Of course, you do not want the case to go to the jury; you want it dismissed. How can you shape your description of the law to provide the court with an easy way to dismiss the case?

Reviewing the cases, as illustrated in Table 8-I, you might see that some cases were dismissed when the court held that the child could not, as a matter of law, be negligent. In those cases, the child was under the parent's supervision. Thus, you begin to consider a rule that says, "A four-year-old child under the supervision of a parent cannot, as a matter of law, be held liable for negligence."

Table 8-I · Formulating a rule from implicit patterns in case law

Case	Holding	Facts
Ehrlich v. Marra	4-year-old not liable as a matter of law	Child of 4 years and 10 months "under direction of mother" was crossing the street when hit by car.
Romanchuk v. County of Westchester	4-year-old not liable as a matter of law	Child of 4 years and 11 months "under the direct supervision and control of the father" was sledding when accident occurred.
Boyd v. Trent	4-year-old not liable as a matter of law	Child of 4 years had climbed to front seat where mother permitted her to stay. Child distracted mother, and a car accident resulted.
Camardo v. New York State Railways	Question for the jury	Child of 4 years and 10 months walking home from school, unaccompanied by adult, when accident occurred.
Defendant's proposed rule	A four-year-old child under the supervision of her parents cannot, as a matter of law, be held liable for negligence.	

---

1. Based on *Menagh v. Breitman*, Index No. 107856/09 (NY S. Ct. N.Y. Co. 2010).

Again, before deciding to rely on that rule, you would have to check every case to make sure no court allowed a negligence claim against a four-year-old when a parent was present at the time of the accident. If there were such a case, you would either need to abandon the proposed rule or acknowledge the case as an outlier that is inconsistent with the majority of decisions.

Finally, you would need to ask yourself whether this proposed rule makes sense. Arguably, it does. When a parent is present, the parent is in charge and making decisions. Under those circumstances, you could argue, the child should not be liable for injuries.

Thus, you might explain the law as in Example 8-J.

Example 8-J · Including a favorable rule from case law in your explanation of the law

With respect to claims of negligence brought against infants, this Court has consistently held that a four-year-old child, who is under the supervision of an adult, is incapable of negligence. For example, in *Ehrlich v. Marra*, this Court held that a child of four years and ten months could not be found guilty of contributory negligence. 300 N.Y.S.2d 81, 82 (N.Y. App. Div. 1940). In that case, the child had been crossing the street "at the direction and under the supervision of his mother" when he was struck by a car. *Id.*

Similarly, in *Romanchuk v. County of Westchester,* this Court held that a child "then several days short of his fifth birthday . . . must be deemed, as a matter of law, to have been free of contributory negligence" in a sledding accident. 337 N.Y.S.2d 926, 927 (N.Y. App. Div. 1972). In that case, the court noted that the child was "under the direct supervision and control of the father" when the father placed the child on a sled and the child then coasted down a slope by himself. *See id.*

Most recently, in *Boyd v. Trent*, this Court again held that a four-year-old, could not be held liable for negligence. 746 N.Y.S.2d 191, 193 (N.Y. App. Div. 2002). In that case, the parent was also present. *Id.* The four-year-old had extricated herself from her car seat and made her way to the front of the car where her mother, who was driving, permitted her to remain. *Id.* Soon thereafter the mother failed to negotiate a turn and collided with another car. This Court held that the four-year-old was "incapable of being held liable for negligence." *Id.*

> The proposed rule is stated in the first sentence. The case illustrations that follow prove that case law supports the proposed rule.

Again, opposing counsel is likely to review the same prior case law and recommend a different rule. Although the defendant's lawyer will argue for a strict rule, that four-year-olds under the supervision of an adult can never be found to be negligent, plaintiff's counsel is likely to look at the same case law and derive a more permissive rule. Plaintiff's counsel is likely to emphasize those instances when a jury is allowed to consider whether a four-year-old is negligent and may propose this rule: "With respect to four-year-olds no bright-line rule exists; rather, a jury is permitted to determine whether a four-year-old was negligent."

In each case, the lawyer is doing her job: providing a way for the court to rule in favor of that lawyer's client. Some people find this process uncomfortable. To some, it seems odd that lawyers can look at the same law and argue that the law should be understood in two very different ways. That, however, is how the law develops. Opposing counsel look at the prior case law and advocate different, but reasonable, ways for the court to understand that prior case law. The court may choose one of the proposed rules to follow, or the court may see the law in yet another way and modify the rules proposed by counsel when it issues its decision. As an advocate, your role is to explain one reasonable interpretation of the existing law.

3. Acknowledge unfavorable rules in a favorable way

The theme of this chapter (and this book) is that as an advocate your job is to provide a way for the court to rule in your client's favor. To do so, you sometimes must acknowledge unfavorable, relevant law and show the court why the outcome you seek is still appropriate. In fact, you should consider your explanation of unfavorable law to be an opportunity. It is an opportunity to explain why, despite anything opposing counsel might say, you still win. And, in addition to being a way to produce the most persuasive argument, acknowledging unfavorable rules is your ethical duty.[2]

Take for example the scenario in which you are a prosecutor trying to uphold a frisk based in part on the officer's observation that the defendant was wearing clothes that associated the defendant with a gang. (The scenario is described above in the text accompanying Tables 8-F and 8-H.) The unfavorable rule for your position is that an officer cannot base reasonable suspicion for a frisk on the suspect's appearance. Of course, in your case, the officers had, arguably, done just that. They had conducted a safety frisk based on the clothes the defendants were wearing. By acknowledging that rule in your explanation of the law, you will begin the process of disposing of opposing counsel's argument. In particular, by acknowledging that the rule exists, you are implicitly saying, "I know about that rule. I'm not scared of it. And it does not preclude the outcome I seek."

Example 8-K demonstrates how you might draft an explanation of the law that also addresses unfavorable law. You might state, as in Example 8-K, that an officer cannot conduct a safety frisk based on a defendant's looks *if* those looks do not reasonably connect the defendant to a dangerous activity. Framed that way, you have created an opportunity

---

2. Model R. of Prof'l Conduct R. 3.3(a)(2) ("A lawyer shall not knowingly . . . fail to disclose to the tribunal legal authority in the controlling jurisdiction known to the lawyer to be directly adverse to the position of the client and not disclosed by opposing counsel.").

to argue that the safety frisk was justified because, in this case, the clothes were reasonably connected to a dangerous activity.

Example 8-K • An explanation of law that acknowledges unfavorable law

Officers Brown and Cockerham had a reasonable suspicion that justified a protective frisk of the defendant. Whether a suspicion is reasonable depends on the inferences drawn from the particular circumstances confronting the officer viewed in light of the officer's experience. *See State v. Ehly*, 854 P.2d 421, 430 (Or. 1993)(citing *Terry v. Ohio*, 392 U.S. 1, 21-22, 27-30 (1968)). An "intuitive sixth sense" or "instinct" cannot "form the entire basis for 'reasonable suspicion.'" *State v. Valdez*, 561 P.2d 1006, 1010-11 (Or. 1977). Rather, an officer must be able to point to specific and articulable facts that give rise to a reasonable inference that the person might pose an immediate threat. *See Ehly*, 854 P.2d at 430. An officer need not show that the threat was "more likely than not." *See* Or. Rev. Stat. 131.005(11) (defining "probable cause"). An officer must simply have a reasonable belief that a circumstance may exist or that a particular event might occur. *See State v. Stanley*, 935 P.2d 1202, 1204 (Or. 1997). In other words, for a protective frisk to be justified, an officer must show only that the particular circumstances gave rise to a reasonable belief that the defendant might pose an immediate threat.

> The explanation of the law begins here. It describes general principles about which both parties would agree.

To establish a reasonable belief that the defendant might pose an immediate threat, officers may rely on their knowledge that the defendant associates with a known dangerous person or that the person is connected with an activity that involves weapons. For example, in *Ehly*, this Court determined that officers had reasonable suspicion to conduct a protective search. *Ehly*, 854 P.2d at 431. In that case, officers knew that the defendant was a drug user and that "many people who use illegal narcotics possess guns." *Id.* at 430. Moreover, the officers also knew that defendant was "running" with a person who carried weapons. *Id.* Because the defendant was rummaging through a gym bag with his hands concealed and did not respond to the officer's suggestion to dump out the contents of the bag, this Court concluded that it was reasonable for one of the officers to dump the contents of the bag onto the motel room bed. *Id.*

> Here, the explanation of law asserts a rule that the State wants to rely on later — that officers can take into account dangerous activities or dangerous people that the defendant is associated with.

Officers must, however, rely on more than the defendant's "looks" when that "look" does not reasonably connect the defendant to a criminal or a dangerous activity. For example, in *Valdez*, this court held that police officers lacked reasonable suspicion to stop a person who was dressed in a blue leisure suit and shiny black shoes, had a "real neat" Afro, and looked "real sharp." *Valdez*, 561 P.2d at 1010. Although the police officers thought the defendant looked like a "typical pusher," the court disagreed, stating that "[n]eedle scars on forearms may legitimately speak of possible criminal activity in drugs, but shined shoes, sharp clothes, a neat Afro, and staring at a police officer do not say much." *Id.* at 1010-11. Similarly, in *Bates*, this court held that the officers had not established reasonable suspicion when all that the officers could point to was that the defendant was a self-described "Indian" who had long hair, a beard, was wearing a leather jacket, and looked suspicious. *State v. Bates*, 747 P.2d 991, 994 (Or. 1987).

> The explanation of the law acknowledges an unfavorable rule — that officers cannot rely on the way defendants look.

Do not wait for your opponent to explain the unfavorable rule or, worse, for the court to find the unfavorable rule on its own. If you know that a rule is relevant and implicated by the facts of the case, your client will be best served if you present that law couched in your client's favor. Never ignore unfavorable law and hope the court will not notice it. The court will notice. And then both your client and your reputation will suffer.

B. Case Illustrations

In addition to presenting rules in the most persuasive way, you will also want to present case illustrations of those rules in the most persuasive way.[3]

1. Highlight helpful facts

Just as you want to shape rules so that the rules reflect your perspective, you also want to shape your explanation of the cases that illustrate those rules. With respect to cases, your argument will ultimately rely on comparing the facts of a prior case to the facts of your client's case. You will usually argue either that your client's case is like the prior case and the same outcome is warranted, or you will argue that your client's case is distinguishable from the prior case and, therefore, the prior case is not precedent for the current case.

To support that ultimate argument, you will want to carefully draft the case illustrations you provide in your explanation of the law. In particular, you will want your case illustration to highlight those facts in the prior court's analysis that will support your argument. Drafting a case illustration to support your argument is a straightforward task when the facts that you want to highlight were clearly central to the court's analysis.

Sometimes, however, you want to base your argument on a factual similarity or distinction that was not obviously central to the prior court's analysis (i.e., the fact is mentioned in the statement of the facts, but the court does not mention it when analyzing the particular legal issue). In that case, you need a process for determining whether the factual comparison or distinction you would like to draw is a good one. That process is very similar to the process for determining whether a proposed rule is a good one. With respect to factual comparisons, you need to determine the comparison you would like to make and then evaluate that comparison. Evaluating the comparison requires you to ask the same questions as with proposed rules:

- Is the proposed similarity or distinction consistent with all other relevant law?
- Does the proposed similarity or distinction make sense?

---

3. Note that some legal arguments will have no case illustrations, e.g., rule-based arguments.

Consider again the case of the four-year-old bicyclist who ran into an elderly pedestrian. Imagine, this time, that you represent the estate of the elderly woman who was struck by the four-year-old cyclist. Your client, the estate of the elderly woman, would like to sue the four-year-old (and her parents) for negligence. Many cases say that the question of negligence goes to the jury. One case, however, holds differently. The court in *Romanchuk* held that a four-year-old child who had been involved in a sledding accident could *not*, as a matter of law, be held liable for contributory negligence.

In reviewing the *Romanchuk* case, you notice that the sledding accident took place in an area designated for sledding. You question whether that fact could be the basis of distinguishing the *Romanchuk* case. After all, in your client's case, the four-year-old was not in a designated bicycling area; rather, the child was on a city street. Thus, you have identified a possible distinction.

Now you must evaluate that distinction. Is the fact that the accident in the *Romanchuk* case occurred in a designated sledding area a reasonable basis on which to distinguish the case? To answer that question, you would first need to review all the other prior cases to determine whether there is a case in which the court held that a child who injured another person in a designated play area could not be held liable for negligence.

Assuming you find no such cases, you will need to ask yourself whether that distinction is a reasonable one on which the court could distinguish the case. Arguably, it is. When a child is in a designated play area, the child is paying less attention and should not be held liable for an injury that occurs in an area designated for that purpose. By contrast, in an area not designated for that purpose, it is appropriate for a child to be held more accountable.

Assuming that the distinction makes sense, then you simply need to craft a case illustration that highlights the fact that, later, will form the basis of your case comparison, as seen in Example 8-L.

Example 8-L · Plaintiff highlights facts that will support a helpful distinction

---

In the *Romanchuk* case, the child was sledding in a park designated for that activity when the child was struck by a parks department vehicle. *Romanchuk v. Westchester Ct.*, 337 N.Y.S.2d 926, 926 (N.Y. App. Div. 1972). The key fact in that case was not the child's age or the parent's supervision. Rather, the key fact was that the child was sledding "in an area of the park where such activities were permitted." *Id.* Thus, the jury could reach only one conclusion, that whoever was sledding in that area, regardless of age or parental supervision, was not contributorily negligent. *See id.*

For the plaintiff, the key fact is that the child was sledding in an area designated for sledding. Note how that fact is emphasized in the topic sentence and again in the second textual sentence.

Because determining which facts to focus on can sometimes be challenging, consider one more example. In this example, you will see how following the steps described above might help you avoid making an unpersuasive argument.

Imagine that you are prosecuting a defendant for unlawful possession of a controlled substance. Police officers found the drugs when they stopped a car that looked like a stolen car. The officer checked the defendant's identification and registration and quickly discovered that the car belonged to the defendant and was not stolen. At the same time, the officers also checked the companion's identity. That check took longer because the companion lacked identification. So as not to make the whole stop a complete waste of time, the officer also asked the defendant whether any drugs were in the car. The defendant said that there were. The officer found the drugs in a subsequent search. All told, the stop lasted twenty minutes. The defendant will argue that the evidence should be suppressed because the stop was too long. Of course, as the prosecutor, you would like both the defendant's admission and the drugs found in the car to be admitted into evidence.

During your research, you find a case, the *Wolfe* case, which has remarkably similar facts. You particularly like the court's analysis, which is provided in Example 8-M.

Example 8-M • An excerpt from a prior case: which facts to focus on?

In *Wolfe*, the stop lasted twenty-seven minutes, and the court held that the stop lasted for a reasonable period of time. You want to argue that twenty minutes is also a reasonable period of time for a stop. Can you rely on *Wolfe* for that argument?	"An officer may detain an individual only for the time reasonably necessary to accomplish the purpose of the stop. [Officer] Truedson testified that he detained defendant and his companion for approximately 27 minutes in order to question them about their activities in the neighborhood, check their identity and fill out a field contact report documenting the stop. He testified that, normally, if an individual has identification, he would spend ten minutes per individual to verify identity, check his record and fill out a field identification card. In this case, it took him longer, however, because defendant's companion did not have any identification. We hold that the stop did not extend for longer than reasonably necessary to accomplish the purposes of the stop." —*State v. Wolfe*, 763 P.2d 154, 156 (Or. App. 1988).

You consider making the argument that because the twenty-seven-minute stop in *Wolfe* was appropriate, a twenty-minute stop must also be appropriate.

Such a comparison would be unpersuasive. As discussed above, you need to make sure that the comparison you rely on is consistent with other authority. In this case, the rule cited by the court in *Wolfe* is that the stop must be no longer than the time "reasonably necessary to accomplish the purpose of the stop." Thus, whether a stop is reasonable is tied to the purpose of the stop, not just how long the stop lasts. By focusing on the twenty-seven minutes as a bright-line rule, your analysis would be in conflict with the governing statute, which requires only reasonableness as compared to the purpose of the stop.

Looking again at the court's analysis, you might realize that the court did not say that ten minutes was always reasonable (that was the police officer's testimony). That fact was not actually important to the court's analysis. The important fact was that twenty-seven minutes was reasonable when the defendant's companion had no identification because the purpose of the stop was to "question them about their activities in the neighborhood [and] check their identity."

Thus, before explaining prior case law, take a moment to think about which facts will be most useful to your ultimate analysis. If those facts were not central to the prior court's analysis, take another moment to consider whether emphasizing those facts—and, therefore, suggesting that those facts were important in the prior case—would be consistent with the surrounding law. If so, go ahead and shape your explanation of the law so that it advances your client's case.

2. Create hooks for your case illustrations

A "hook" is a sentence that introduces a case illustration. It states the specific legal point the case represents. In doing so, a hook focuses the judge's attention and explains why the judge should bother reading about the case.

If you have developed an implicit rule, that rule can be used as a hook to introduce those cases that support the proposed rule. In the examples above that illustrated how to draw out an implicit rule, the final text uses the implicit rule as the hook to those case illustrations. Examples 8-N and 8-O, below, reproduce excerpts of those examples and point out the hooks.

Notice that the hooks for the case illustrations explain exactly what the attorney wants the court to learn from those cases. In that way, the hooks help to shape how the courts will think about the governing case law.

Example 8-N • A hook for a series of case illustrations shapes the court's thinking about those cases

With respect to claims of negligence brought against infants, this Court has consistently held that a four-year-old infant, who is under the supervision of an adult, is incapable of negligence. For example, in *Ehrlich v. Marra*, this Court held that a child of 4 years and 10 months could not be found guilty of contributory negligence. In that case, the child had been crossing the street "at the direction and under the supervision of his mother" when he was struck by a car. 300 N.Y.S.2d 81, 82 (N.Y. App. Div. 1940). Similarly, in *Romanchuk v. Westchester County,* this Court held that a child "then several days short of his fifth birthday . . . must be deemed, as a matter of law, to have been free of contributory negligence" in a sledding accident. 337 N.Y.S.2d 926, 927 (N.Y.

A thoughtfully explained rule acts as a hook for a series of case illustrations. The hook shapes how the court should think about the cases that follow.

App. Div. 1972). In that case, the court noted that the child was "under the direct supervision and control of the father" when the father placed the child on a sled and the child then coasted down a slope by himself. *See id.*

Example 8-O · Hooks for case illustrations tell the court the rule it should follow

---

This hook, like the hook in 8-N, explains an implicit rule and guides the court to think about the case illustration that follows in a particular way.

To establish a reasonable belief that the defendant might pose an immediate threat, officers may rely on their knowledge that the defendant associates with a known dangerous person or that the person is connected with an activity that involves weapons. For example, in *Ehly*, this Court determined that officers had reasonable suspicion to conduct a protective search. *Ehly*, 854 P.2d at 432. In that case, officers knew that the defendant was a drug user and that "many people who use illegal narcotics possess guns." *Id.* at 430. Moreover, the officers also knew that the defendant was "running" with a person who carried weapons. *Id.* Because the defendant was rummaging through a gym bag with his hands concealed and did not respond to the officer's suggestion to dump out the contents of the bag, this Court concluded that it was reasonable for one of the officers to dump the contents of the bag onto the motel room bed. *Id.*

This hook allows the prosecutor to frame a rule that is important to the defendant's argument. The hook frames the rule in a way that will be helpful later. In Example 8-Q, below, you can see how this explanation of the *Valdez* case later helps the writer to distinguish the *Valdez* case.

Officers must, however, rely on more than the defendant's "looks" when that "look" does not reasonably connect the defendant to a criminal or a dangerous activity. For example, in *Valdez*, this court held that police officers lacked reasonable suspicion to stop a person who was dressed in a blue leisure suit and shiny black shoes, had a "real neat" Afro, and looked "real sharp." *Valdez*, 561 P.2d at 1010. Although the police officers thought the defendant looked like a "typical pusher," the court disagreed, stating that "[n]eedle scars on forearms may legitimately speak of possible criminal activity in drugs, but shined shoes, sharp clothes, a neat Afro, and staring at a police officer do not say much." *Id.* at 1010-11.

To see how powerful a hook can be, consider alternative, less persuasive hooks. The hook in Example 8-P still states a point that the court should draw from reading the case illustration that follows. However, by focusing on the holding rather than on the legal principle, the hook does less to advance the client's argument.

Example 8-P · A case illustration with no hook

Less carefully crafted hooks, not surprisingly, do less to advance your argument before the court.

Many cases have held that a four-year-old cannot be found guilty of contributory negligence. For example, in *Ehrlich v. Marra*, this Court held that a child of 4 years and 10 months could not be found guilty of contributory negligence. In that case, the child had been crossing the street "at the direction and under the supervision of his mother" when he was struck by a car. 300 N.Y.S.2d 81, 82 (N.Y. App. Div. 1940). Similarly, in *Romanchuk v. Westchester County*, this Court held that a child "then several days short of his fifth birthday . . . must be deemed, as a matter of law, to have been free of contributory negligence" in a sledding accident. 337 N.Y.S.2d 926, 927 (N.Y. App. Div. 1972). In that case, the court noted that the child was "under the direct supervision and control of the father" when the father placed the child on a sled and the child then coasted down a slope by himself. *See id.* . . .

Other cases have held that a four-year-old can be found guilty of contributory negligence . . . .

---

3. Acknowledge unfavorable cases in a favorable way

Just as you should never ignore an unfavorable rule, never ignore an unfavorable, relevant case hoping opposing counsel and the court will not notice it. Ignoring relevant precedent is unethical. Besides, the chances are too great that the judge or opposing counsel will find the case.

Instead, take the opportunity to describe that authority on your terms. Doing so provides you with the advantage of being the first to shape the court's understanding of the law. For example, if you plan to distinguish a prior case from your client's case, describe the prior case and highlight those facts that distinguish it from your client's case. If you plan on disposing of a case by arguing that the law is trending away from the analysis in the prior decision, your explanation of law should highlight that trend. Again, your explanation of the law should provide the foundation for the argument you will make.

Finally, addressing unfavorable law will also improve your credibility with the court. If you voluntarily come forward and address unfavorable law the court will begin to think of you as a trustworthy advocate who will fully address all the issues the court must confront. As explained in Chapter 1, *The Nature of Persuasion*, a trustworthy lawyer is a more persuasive lawyer.

III. Apply Your Persuasive Explanation of the Law to the Facts

Now that you have explained the relevant law, you must apply that law to your client's case to explain why the outcome you seek is justified under the law. Applying the law requires two steps: First, you must apply the law as you have asserted it should be applied. Second, you must explain why an opposing analysis is incorrect.

A. Developing Your Application

Explaining how the court should apply the law to your client's facts should be fairly straightforward. The hard work is actually writing an explanation of the law that is specifically crafted to support your application. Remember that the explanation of the law and the application should reflect each other. If you explain the law so that it supports your ultimate argument, all you need to do now is show how that same set of rules and case law apply to your client's case.

The key to matching your application to your explanation is to use the same language in both sections of your argument. In Example 8-Q, you can see how re-using the language from the explanation of the law in the application allows the writer to show how her argument is supported by the law.

Example 8-Q • An effective application re-uses the language used in the explanation of the law.

The shaded text is key language in the explanation of the law. Note the key language that is shaded, and then look for that same language in the application.

Officers Brown and Cockerham had a reasonable suspicion that justified a protective frisk of the defendant. Whether a suspicion is reasonable depends on the inferences drawn from the particular circumstances confronting the officer viewed in light of the officer's experience. *See State v. Ehly*, 854 P.2d 421, 430 (Or. 1993) (citing *Terry v. Ohio*, 392 U.S. 1, 21-22, 27-30 (1968)). An "intuitive sixth sense" or "instinct" cannot "form the entire basis for 'reasonable suspicion.'" *State v. Valdez*, 561 P.2d 1006, 1010-11 (Or. 1977). Rather, an officer must be able to point to specific and articulable facts that give rise to a reasonable inference that the person might pose an immediate threat. *See Ehly*, 854 P.2d at 430. An officer need not show that the threat was "more likely than not." *See* Or. Rev. Stat. 131.005(11) (defining "probable cause"). An officer must simply have a reasonable belief that a circumstance may exist or that a particular event might occur. *See State v. Stanley*, 935 P.2d 1202, 1204 (Or. 1997). In other words, for a protective frisk to be justified, an officer must show only that the particular circumstances gave rise to a reasonable belief that the defendant might pose an immediate threat.

Here, the explanation of the law asserts a rule that the State wants to rely on later—that officers can take into account dangerous activities or dangerous people that the defendant is associated with.

To establish a reasonable belief that the defendant might pose an immediate threat, officers may rely on their knowledge that the defendant associates with a known dangerous person or that the person is connected with an activity that involves weapons. For example, in *Ehly*, this Court determined that officers had reasonable suspicion to conduct a protective search. *Ehly*, 854 P.2d at 431. In that case, officers knew that the defendant was a drug user and that "many people who use illegal narcotics possess guns." *Id.* at 430. Moreover, the officers also knew that defendant was "running" with a person who carried weapons. *Id.* Because the defendant was rummaging through a gym bag with his hands concealed and did not respond to the officer's suggestion to dump out the contents of the bag, this Court concluded that it was reasonable for one of the officers to dump the contents of the bag onto the motel room bed. *Id.*

The explanation of the law acknowledges a rule that the opposing party—the defendant—will likely rely on to argue that the police officer's frisk was illegal.

Officers must, however, rely on more than the defendant's "looks" when that "look" does not reasonably connect the defendant to a criminal or a dangerous activity. For example, in *Valdez*, this court held that police officers lacked reasonable suspicion to stop a person who was dressed in a blue leisure suit and shiny black shoes, had a "real neat" Afro, and looked "real sharp." *Valdez*, 561 P.2d at 1010. Although the police officers thought the defendant looked like a "typical pusher," the court disagreed, stating that "[n]eedle scars on forearms may legitimately speak of possible criminal activity in drugs, but shined shoes, sharp clothes, a neat Afro, and staring at a police officer do not say much." *Id.* at 1010-11. Similarly, in *Bates*, this court held that the officers had not established reasonable suspicion when all that the officers could point to was that the defendant was a self-described "Indian" who had long hair, a beard, was wearing a leather jacket, and looked suspicious. *State v. Bates*, 747 P.2d 991, 994 (Or. 1987).

Officers Brown and Cockerham can point to specific, articulable facts that gave rise to a reasonable suspicion that the defendants posed an immediate threat. First, the officers knew that the defendant was associated with the 18th Street Gang. Defendant was wearing a shirt with the phrase "18th Street" printed on it, and his companion had a tattoo under his eye, which is a tattoo that is associated with membership in the 18th Street Gang. In addition, both men had shaved heads and were wearing baggy gang-style clothes. Thus, the officers knew that the defendant was associated with the 18th Street Gang.

Second, the officers knew that members of the 18th Street Gang were dangerous, often carrying concealed weapons. In fact, one of the officers had encountered a gang member in the parking lot of the same apartment complex who, on a pat-down search, was found to have a weapon concealed in the waistband of his pants under a baggy shirt. Another officer had personally removed weapons from several 18th Street Gang members in that same neighborhood. Indeed, he had found a gun on a gang member "just previously to this incident." Thus, the officers knew that members of the 18th Street Gang carried weapons and posed a danger to the officer, and they knew that the defendant was associated with that gang and its activities.

Based on these facts, the officers had reason to believe that the defendant might pose an immediate threat. In fact, the officers relied on the same kinds of facts that established reasonable suspicion in *Ehly*. Just as the officer in *Ehly* relied on the defendant's drug activity, an activity that often involves weapons and therefore poses a danger to others, the officers in this case relied on the defendant's gang membership, an activity that often involves weapons and also poses a danger to others. Moreover, just as the officers in *Ehly* relied on the defendant's association with a person who was known to carry weapons, the officers in this case relied on the defendant's association with a group of people—the 18th Street Gang—who were known to carry weapons. Finally, just as the officers in *Ehly* were concerned for their safety because the defendant was rummaging through a bag (a place where a gun could be concealed) and they could not see his hands, the officers in this case were concerned because the defendant's waistband was hidden and was a place where a handgun could be concealed. Thus, the officers in this case relied on the same kinds of facts as did the officers in *Ehly* and, accordingly, had reasonable suspicion to pat down the defendant.

For these same reasons, the officers relied on far more than simply the defendant's "looks." In *Valdez* and in *Bates*, the "look" that the officers relied

The shaded text echoes the key language used in the explanation of the law.

on — a blue leisure suit, shiny black shoes, and a "neat Afro" in *Valdez* and long hair, a beard, and a leather jacket in *Bates* — could not be particularly associated with a weapons-related activity or with a particular group of people who regularly carry weapons. By contrast, here, the "look" at issue established a reasonable suspicion of gang activity and membership in the 18th Street Gang. Both the association with gang activity generally and the association with a particular gang known to carry weapons are specific, articulable facts that raise a reasonable suspicion that the defendant might pose an immediate threat.

Remember, though, as you write, you refine your thinking. As a result, you will need to return to your explanation of the law after you draft your application to ensure that the words you use in your explanation of the law and your application are consistent. Doing so will make it easy for the court to see how the law that you have explained supports the arguments that you are making.

B. Responding to Your Opponent's Analysis

The aspect of persuasive writing that is most different from objective writing is addressing weaknesses that give rise to an opposing analysis. You must address those weaknesses without emphasizing them — a balancing act that is not always easy to accomplish. Thus, this section addresses *how* to address the weaknesses and then *where* to address the weaknesses.

With respect to how to address weaknesses (and the counter-analyses that they spawn), the key is to address the weakness from your client's perspective and not from your opponent's perspective.

Often when we think about a weakness in a case, we think about how our opponent will exploit a certain facet of the law or a certain fact. Thus, we tend to think about weaknesses from our opponent's perspective. As a result, a common impulse is to first explain a weakness from our opponent's perspective and then explain why that perspective is incorrect. To the extent possible, you should avoid that first step — explaining the weakness from your opponent's perspective. Instead, skip right to the second step — explaining the weakness from your perspective. Compare Examples 8-R and 8-S.

Example 8-R is less effective because in that example the plaintiff's attorney first explains the defendant's argument. In doing so, the attorney inadvertently emphasizes the defendant's argument — in essence, making defendant's argument for him. You should not help your opponent in that way.

Example 8-R · Less effective approach: highlighting your opponent's argument

Defendant carves out an exception for four-year-olds who are supervised by an adult. Defendant has pointed to three cases, *Ehrlich, Trent,* and *Romanchuk.* In those cases, the courts have held that, as a matter of law, the four-year-old could not be held liable for negligence. *Ehrlich v.* Marra, 300 N.Y.S.2d 81, 82 (N.Y. App. Div. 1940); *Boyd v. Trent,* 746 N.Y.S.2d 191, 193 (N.Y. App. Div. 2002); *Romanchuk v. Westchester Cnty.,* 337 N.Y.S.2d 926, 927 (N.Y. App. Div. 1972). In each of those cases, a parent was present when the alleged negligent act took place. *Ehrlich,* 300 N.Y.S.2d at 82 (parent present when child crossed street and was struck by car); *Boyd,* 746 N.Y.S.2d at 193 (parent present when child extricated herself from her car seat, moved to the front seat, and contributed to a car accident); *Romanchuk,* 337 N.Y.S.2d. at 928-928 (parent present when child went sledding and hit another at the bottom of the slope). On that basis, Defendant concludes that when a parent is present and supervising a child, the child cannot be found guilty of negligence as a matter of law.

Plaintiff addresses a weakness by first explaining that weakness.

Although each of those cases did conclude as a matter of law that a four-year-old could not be held liable for negligence, such a conclusion is a minority conclusion. The majority of courts that have considered the issue have concluded that a four-year-old can be held liable for negligence. *See e.g., Sun Jeong Koo v. St. Bernard,* 392 N.Y.S.2d 815, 816 (Sup. Ct. Queens Cnty. 1977) (considering *Ehrlich* but rejecting a bright-line rule in negligence case against a child of 4 years and 10 months); *Searles v. Dardani,* 347 N.Y.S.2d 662, 665 (Sup. Ct. Albany Cnty. 1973) (considering *Ehrlich,* but concluding that jury should decide whether a child of four and a half years was negligent); *Republic Ins. Co. v. Michel,* 885 F. Supp. 426, 433 (E.D.N.Y. 1995) (considering *Ehrlich,* but concluding that a four-and-a-half year old could be liable for negligence).

After explaining the weakness, counsel turns to her counter-argument.

Thus, the bright-line rule first expressed in *Ehrlich,* and then followed in *Trent* and *Romanchuk* represents a minority view. The majority view in this jurisdiction is that a jury is permitted to decide whether a four-year-old is liable for negligence.

The fix for an argument that begins with your opponent's position, as in Example 8-R, is easy: Just skip over your description of the opposing position. In Example 8-S, you can see how plaintiff's counsel can rewrite the argument so that the defendant's argument is not emphasized and just go straight to explaining how the plaintiff sees things.

Example 8-S · More effective: present the argument from your perspective only

The majority view in this jurisdiction is that a four-year-old can be held liable for negligence. *See, e.g., Sun Jeong Koo v. St. Bernard,* 392 N.Y.S.2d 815, 816 (Sup. Ct. Queens Cnty. 1977); *Searles v. Dardani,* 347 N.Y.S.2d 662, 665 (Sup. Ct. Albany Cnty. 1973); *Republic Ins. Co. v. Michel,* 885 F. Supp. 426, 433

Here, plaintiff's counsel has removed his explanation of opponent's argument and moves directly to explaining why defendant's explanation of the law is incorrect.

(E.D.N.Y. Feb 23, 1995). Any attempt to carve out an exception for four-year-olds who are supervised by an adult is unsupported by the weight of authority. In asserting that novel rule, the defendant relies on *Romanchuk, Ehrlich,* and *Trent.* Although each of those cases did conclude as a matter of law that a four-year-old could not be held liable for negligence, the courts that have considered the issue since then have rejected the bright-line rule relied on in those cases and concluded that a four-year-old can be held liable for negligence. *See e.g., Sun Jeong Koo,* 392 N.Y.S.2d at 816 (considering *Ehrlich,* but rejecting a bright-line rule in negligence case against a child of four years and 10 months); *Searles,* 347 N.Y.S.2d at 665 (considering *Ehrlich,* but concluding that a jury should decide whether a child of four-and-a-half years was negligent); *Republic Ins. Co.,* 885 F. Supp. at 433 (considering *Ehrlich,* but concluding that a four-and-a-half year old could be liable for negligence). No court has considered, let alone followed, *Trent* or *Romanchuk.* Thus, the bright-line rule first expressed in *Ehrlich,* and then followed in *Trent* and *Romanchuk* represents a minority view. This court should conclude—as all recent courts have concluded—that a jury can determine whether a four-year-old was negligent.

Admittedly, when drafting an argument, you may find it easier to first draft your opponent's argument and then respond to it, as in Example 8-R. Doing so may help you clarify your opponent's argument and write a more effective response. But that is your *draft*. In the final product, eliminate as much of your opponent's argument as possible so that the court reads about the issue only from your client's perspective.

With respect to *where* to address a weakness, you will ordinarily respond to a counter-analysis after you have presented your primary analysis. The judge will expect to see your argument first, so when you apply the law, first explain your analysis before explaining why an alternative analysis is unwarranted.[4]

IV. End with a Final Conclusion

End each legal argument by stating the conclusion you want the court to reach about the element or factor being examined, as in Example 8-T. The last sentences of your argument are in positions of emphasis, so clearly and concisely state the idea you want the court to walk away with. Be sure to make your conclusion explicit.

---

4. Some weaknesses are less significant and do not need to be addressed with a full counter-analysis. Less significant weaknesses can be addressed with a dependent clause, as discussed in Chapter 9, *Refining Persuasive Arguments.*

Example 8-T • A final conclusion

... Both the association with gang activity generally and the association with a particular gang known to carry weapons are specific, articulable facts that raise a reasonable suspicion that the defendant might pose an immediate threat. For these reasons, the police officers properly stopped the defendant and conducted a safety-frisk. The unregistered weapon the officers found during that frisk is admissible.

Practice Points

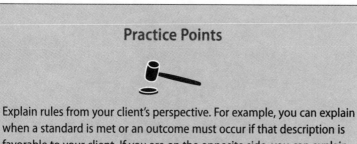

- Explain rules from your client's perspective. For example, you can explain when a standard is met or an outcome must occur if that description is favorable to your client. If you are on the opposite side, you can explain when a standard is not met or an outcome may not occur.

- Consider whether past cases yield a rule that will help your client's argument. If such a rule exists, test that rule to make sure it is consistent with all prior law and makes sense in the real world. If it does, explain that rule to the court.

- Acknowledge unfavorable rules, but demonstrate that, despite that rule, the outcome your client seeks is still the most reasonable outcome.

- Use a hook to introduce case illustrations and explain to the court what rule it should draw from a prior case.

- Acknowledge unfavorable cases; then, distinguish them.

Chapter 9

Refining Persuasive Arguments

After you have developed the substance of your arguments, you will then want to review your arguments to ensure that each part is presented as persuasively as possible. To present arguments as persuasively as possible, attorneys use a variety of writing techniques. These techniques emphasize why the outcome their client seeks is a correct and preferable outcome compared to the one opposing counsel seeks. These techniques, while helpful, are not magical. They will not cause you to prevail if the law and facts are not on your side. If, however, you have an argument that could win, these techniques make it easier for the court to see why your argument should win.

I. Core Concepts

Before turning to specific writing techniques, this chapter focuses on a few core concepts. If you understand these core concepts, you will find it easier to adjust the specific writing techniques to the particular argument you are drafting.

A. Assert Your Point. Then, Provide Details.

To write persuasively, you must be clear about the point you wish to make. A judge must first know what you are arguing for before the judge can decide whether to agree with you.

Lawyers, though, sometimes get distracted. Legal arguments are chock full of details—details about rules, about prior cases, about the client's case. Lawyers sometimes get so absorbed in the detail that they forget to tell the judge the point of all those details. Those lawyers will lose the judge in the details.

Instead, explain your point before providing supporting details. Explain why the details are important. Doing so will help focus the judge's attention and make it easier for the judge to work her way through the details.

In fact, to effectively communicate your argument you will need to repeatedly assert your point. You will need to assert your large, overarching point—that is, the ultimate legal conclusion you want the court to adopt. But you will also need to clearly assert those smaller points that support your larger argument. Lawyers assert their point—and explain the purpose of the details that follow in—numerous places. For example,

- A **point heading** asserts the conclusion the judge should reach after reading the more detailed arguments in that section.

- A **conclusion** at the outset of a legal argument explains the conclusion the judge should reach after reading the more detailed explanation and application of the law.

- A **thesis sentence** at the beginning of a paragraph explains the point the judge should take away after reading the details explained within the paragraph.

- A **hook** at the beginning of a case illustration explains the legal principle a court should derive after having read the particulars of a prior case.

Asserting your point before providing details has numerous benefits. It tells the judge what is to come. When you tell your reader what is to come, your reader feels more comfortable because she will have context for the argument. She is no longer stumbling in the dark wondering in which direction she is heading. Feeling comfortable and oriented, your reader is better able to absorb the argument.

Second, when you tell the judge where you are going and then actually go there you gain the judge's trust. The judge knows she can count on you to do what you say you will do. A judge who trusts you is one who is more likely to accept the information you provide.

Finally, explaining your point in advance of the detail shapes the way the judge will absorb the details. If you tell the judge your point, she will then read the detail trying to match the detail to the point you have said you are going to make. By first stating your point, you give the judge a framework on which to hang the details. As the judge matches details to your stated point, those details will come together in the way you and your client see those details. Of course, a judge reads critically and may have other ideas than the one explained. Still, the judge will at least be encouraged to consider seeing the details in the way you and your client see them. Thus, by clearly stating your point before the supporting details, you begin the process of shaping how the judge will view the upcoming information.

Too many writers do not recognize when a mass of detail is in need of a clearly stated point. If you are one of those writers, you will leave the judge struggling in the dark and looking for direction; you will lose an opportunity to gain the judge's trust; and you will have missed an opportunity to shape those details in the way you want the judge to see it. Worst of all, without your guidance, the judge may reach an entirely different conclusion than the one you wanted.

Accordingly, this chapter highlights locations within your argument that are likely in need of a sentence that explains the point of all the detail to follow.

B. Use Location to Your Advantage

One of the best ways to emphasize your point is to put your point where the judge is most likely to see and process it. When reading text, most readers' eyes—including judges' eyes—tend to fall and rest on a few positions of emphasis. Thus, many of the techniques below are based on the idea that you should put information where a judge is most likely to see it and absorb it. In particular, review your point headings, the first sentence of each paragraph, and the last sentence of each paragraph. Those are locations where the judges' eyes will rest. Take advantage of that fact and use those locations for the information you want to emphasize. Similarly, use those locations where the judges' eyes are less likely to rest to disclose information that is less helpful to you. Thus, disclose unhelpful information in the middle of a paragraph and in the middle of sentences, where that information will receive less emphasis.

C. Be Explicit

The last core concept is to "be explicit." In other words, consider talking directly to the judge and state what you are up to. Judges appreciate candor, and being explicit helps gain their trust.

For example, if you are about to launch into a five-page detailed discussion of the relevant case law, tell the judge what you are about to do and why, as in Example 9-A. By giving such an explanation, the judge knows that she should settle in and expect a lot of facts, and she will appreciate that you have explained why you are troubling her with the factual minutiae.

Example 9-A · Be explicit

The discussion of the cases that follows is necessarily fact-intensive because the standard this Court must apply is a "totality of the circumstances" standard.

Similarly, tell the court when you will address matters out of the normal order, as in Example 9-B. By doing so, you have told the court that it should expect something different and that you are doing something different to benefit the court.

Example 9-B · Be explicit

Although normally a court will consider the merits of a legal argument first, this brief begins with a discussion of harmless error because the case is most efficiently resolved on that basis.

In short, be explicit about where your argument is going and why—especially, if you are about to do something unexpected or particularly difficult to absorb. By explicitly stating what you are doing, you help the judge follow your argument and you enhance your credibility with the court.

With these core concepts in mind, let's turn to specific writing techniques.

II. Persuasion Through Point Headings

One of the first locations where a judge's eyes will rest will be on your point headings. Moreover, a judge is likely to return to your point headings if he needs an overview of your argument, or if he is searching for particular information. Thus, construct your point headings so that they emphasize the main points you want the court to accept.

To create persuasive point headings in your argument, follow these guidelines. First, in your argument section, create assertive point headings that tell the judge the conclusion you want the court to reach and the reasons the court should reach that conclusion. Second, create point headings that work together and provide an outline of your argument. Third, keep your point headings short. Fourth, use point headings to divide the argument into readable chunks. Finally, create polished point headings in a traditional format so that they make your brief look professional and credible.

A. Create Assertive Point Headings

An assertive point heading has up to two parts:

1. The action you want the court to take or the conclusion you want the court to adopt, and

2. The primary reason the court should take that action or adopt that conclusion.

Of the point headings you will craft, you will need to think most carefully about the main point headings designated by Roman numerals. Those point headings designate a new claim. They should, therefore, assert the procedural action that you want the court to take with respect to that claim. Compare Example 9-C with 9-D. Example 9-C is the more effective opening point heading because it tells the court the procedural action it should take.

Example 9-C · A main point heading that asserts the procedural action the court should take

---

I. Plaintiffs' complaint should be dismissed because the ADEA does not permit disparate impact claims.

Example 9-D · A main point heading that does not assert the procedural action the court should take

---

I. The ADEA does not permit disparate impact claims.

Although as a general rule you should use point headings to assert the legal conclusions that you want the court to adopt, occasionally you may opt for descriptive point headings. Descriptive point headings are appropriate—not surprisingly—when the purpose of a section is to describe rather than to assert a legal argument, as in Example 9-E. (Descriptive point headings are also appropriate in statements of fact, but that idea will be addressed in more detail in Chapter 12, *Statements of Fact and of the Case.*)

Example 9-E · A descriptive point heading

I.   Oregon's method of statutory construction

B. Coordinate Your Point Headings

Because more than one element or factor will be argued within each claim, attorneys use sub-headings to alert the reader to each new element, factor, or part of an argument. These sub-headings, together with the main point heading, should be coordinated so that, together, they provide an overview of the arguments that support the claim. In longer motions and in all appellate briefs, you will see the point headings and sub-headings gathered together in a table of contents. Gathering the point headings and sub-headings in a table of contents not only helps the court find particular parts of your argument, it also allows the court to see the overarching structure of your argument. Example 9-F illustrates how a main point heading and its sub-headings can provide an overview of your argument.

Example 9-F · Example of a main point heading and supporting sub-headings

I.   Plaintiffs' complaint should be dismissed because the ADEA does not permit disparate impact claims.

    A. The text of the ADEA precludes disparate impact claims.

        1. Section 4(a) of the ADEA, which prohibits discrimination "because of age," prohibits only intentional discrimination.

        2. Section 4(f) of the ADEA, which permits employers to consider "reasonable factors other than age," precludes a discrimination claim based on the impact of an employment decision.

    B. The legislative history confirms that disparate impact claims are not cognizable under the ADEA.

C. Use Short Point Headings

In drafting point headings, your goal should be for the reader to be able to look down and quickly absorb the point heading's conclusion. Thus, pay attention to the length of the heading. A point heading that is too long will be difficult to absorb. How long is too long? No definitive answer exists, but here are some guidelines.

First, a point heading that sits on a single line is easiest to absorb. If your point heading is more than three lines, the point heading may be perceived as a forbidding block of text and your reader is less likely to wade through it. Thus, keep your point heading short.

Second, use multiple point headings if you have a complex idea that cannot be expressed in a single line. You will not always be able to draft a precise point heading that sits on a single line. You may need more than one line—or maybe several lines—to fashion a complete and accurate point heading. If a point heading is becoming too long for the reader to absorb its meaning, consider stating the conclusion you want the court to reach in one point heading and the reasons for that conclusion in sub-headings as in Example 9-F, above.

Finally, consider whether the point heading *needs* both the conclusion and the reasons for that conclusion. Sometimes, you may want to sacrifice completeness for conciseness. You will notice that in Example 9-F not all the point headings state the conclusion counsel wants the court to adopt and the reason the court should adopt that conclusion.

Different practitioners have different ideas about when a point heading becomes too long and the importance of including both your conclusion and the primary reason the court should adopt that conclusion. If you are working with a more senior attorney, follow the senior attorney's preference; likewise, if you are writing to a judge who you know prefers a particular style, follow that judge's preference.

Generally, most judges and attorneys prefer short point headings. We recommend aiming for one to two lines and not going beyond three lines. Your goal is to keep the point headings short, but choose words that convey as much substance as possible.

D. Divide the Text into Readable Chunks

When drafting point headings, one question that sometimes comes up is how frequently to insert a point heading. As a general rule, you should have a point heading before each dispositive issue. If those issues break down such that you have a single legal argument for each element or factor, you should include a point heading for each argument that addresses a single element or factor. Whether to sub-divide an argument addressing a single element or factor further depends on how long the legal argument is. Point headings should break text into readable chunks, both to give your reader a break and to help your reader return to your argument and find specific information. However, do not include so many point headings that the text becomes choppy.

E. Use a Professional, Easy-to-Read Format

Point headings can also help provide a professional look to your argument if they are formatted effectively. Although variation exists in how attorneys format their point headings, we recommend this format:

- **Numbering.** Each dispositive legal issue is given a Roman numeral. Sub-issues are identified with a capital letter, an Arabic number, a lower case letter, and then a lower-case Roman numeral.

- **Single space.** Each heading and sub-heading is single-spaced.

- **Punctuate properly.** If your point heading is a full sentence—and in your argument section usually all of your point headings will be full sentences that assert a conclusion—use proper punctuation, which includes a period at the end of the heading or sub-heading.

- **Hanging indent.** If your point heading wraps to a second line, the first letter of the second line should appear under the first letter of the point heading. (This bulleted list uses hanging indent. The first letter of the second line appears under the first letter of the first line. The second line does not extend to the left under the bullet.)

- **Use bold.** Point headings should be in bold so that they stand out from the text and are easy to see. Italicized text tends to slow the reader down and, therefore, is less effective. Nonetheless, italicize if your workplace or court custom requires that you do so.

- **ALL CAPS?** TRADITIONAL POINT HEADINGS USE ALL CAPS FOR POINT HEADINGS OF DISPOSITIVE ISSUES. ALL CAPS ARE, HOWEVER, MORE DIFFICULT TO READ. SO, AVOID THEM IF YOU CAN. NONETHELESS, IF YOUR WORKPLACE OR COURT REQUIRES ALL CAPS FOR MAIN HEADINGS, THEN ADHERE TO THOSE GUIDELINES.

- **Initial Caps.** A Point Heading Using Initial Caps Capitalizes the First Letter of Most Words in the Point Headings. Typography Experts Now Recommend Against Using Initial Caps Because That Format Is More Difficult to Read and Tends to Slow the Reader Down.

- ***Do not combine typeface alterations.*** *Headings become especially hard to read when the writer combines two or more typeface alterations.*

The format described above will create point headings that are both professional-looking and easy-to-read. Example 9-G illustrates that format.

Example 9-G • Professional, easy-to-read point headings

I.   Each dispositive point heading has a Roman numeral.

    A.   An outline should not have an "A" without a "B" or a "1" without a "2."

    B.   However, when your argument has only one dispositive point, you may have a "I" without a "II."

        1.   Hanging indents make your point headings look polished.

        2.   Create a hanging indent by positioning the first word of the second line under the first word of the first line.

            a.   Experts in typography have recommended changes to traditional formats.

                i.   Avoid "all caps," which is difficult to read and slows the reader down.

                ii.   Avoid italicized text, which is difficult to read and slows the reader down.

            b.   Use bold instead, which will make the point heading pop from the page.

    C.   Assertive point headings are complete sentences with final punctuation.

Although we recommend the format described above and illustrated in Example 9-G, if you work in a very traditional office or jurisdiction, you may need to follow a more traditional format. The most traditionally formatted point headings will be formatted as in Example 9-H.

Example 9-H • Traditionally formatted point headings

I.   EACH DISPOSITIVE POINT HEADING STILL HAS A ROMAN NUMERAL, BUT YOU WILL USE ALL CAPS AND THE TEXT MAY BE BOLDED AS WELL.

    A.   The First Sub-Heading Will Use Initial Caps and May Be Bolded As Well.

        1.   In the next sub-heading, the text is bolded, but, like any other sentence, only the first letter of the point heading is capitalized.

        2.   Hanging indents still make your point headings look polished.

a. <u>The next sub-heading will, again, use ordinary capitalization, but the text will likely be underlined.</u>

    i. You can see a trend in the formatting.

    ii. Each sub-heading is formatted with less emphasis than the previous heading to reflect the smaller ideas contained in each sub-heading.

b. <u>Again, never have an "A" without a "B"; however, when your argument has only one dispositive point, you may have a "I" without a "II."</u>

B. Assertive Point Headings are Complete Sentences With Final Punctuation.

III. Paragraph-Level Persuasion

The techniques for persuading at the paragraph level are straightforward and can be explained quickly. Do not let the brevity of the discussion suggest that these techniques are somehow less important. Although simple, these techniques are powerful. Their appropriate use will provide organization and direction to your reader and will be critical to the effective presentation of your argument.

A. The Thesis Sentence

Within the argument section of your memorandum of law or brief, every single paragraph should begin with a thesis sentence. That's right: every single paragraph.

A "thesis" is a proposition put forward for consideration—one that the speaker intends to prove. A thesis sentence is a sentence in which that proposition is stated. As explained earlier in this chapter, a thesis sentence is one way in which a writer guides the reader and shapes the information to come. An effective thesis sentence tells the reader the point you plan to make in that paragraph. By telling the reader the point you intend to make, your reader will have an easier time absorbing the details within the paragraph. In the best motions and briefs, the thesis sentences for each paragraph form a skeletal outline of the argument you are presenting to the court.

Compare the paragraph in Example 9-I, which uses a thesis sentence, and the paragraph in Example 9-J, which does not. Notice how the thesis sentence in Example 9-I tells the court the conclusion it should reach after reading the paragraph. In doing so, the thesis sentence shapes the way the court absorbs the information provided in the paragraph.

> **Thesis vs. Topic Sentences**
>
> Whereas a thesis sentence asserts a proposition that the text that follows will support, a topic sentence merely describes the kind of information that follows. A topic sentence asserts no point.
>
> Lawyers prefer thesis sentences over topic sentences because each paragraph should be structured to make a point.

Example 9-I • More effective approach: a thesis sentence that asserts the point the paragraph will prove

.... An officer establishes reasonable suspicion to search a suspect if the officer can point to specific and articulable facts that give rise to a reasonable inference that the person might pose an immediate threat. *See State v. Ehly*, 854 P.2d 421, 430 (Or. 1993).

To establish a reasonable belief that the defendant might pose an immediate threat, officers may rely on their knowledge that the defendant associates with a known dangerous person or that the person is connected with an activity that involves weapons. For example, in *Ehly*, this Court determined that officers had reasonable suspicion to conduct a protective search. *Id.* at 432. In that case, officers knew that the defendant was a drug user and that "many people who use illegal narcotics possess guns." *Id.* at 430. Moreover, the officers also knew that defendant was "running" with a person who carried weapons. *Id.* Because the defendant was rummaging through a gym bag with his hands concealed and did not respond to the officer's suggestion to dump out the contents of the bag, this Court concluded that it was reasonable for one of the officers to dump the contents of the bag onto the motel room bed. *Id.* at 432.

With a strong thesis sentence, the judge knows the writer's primary assertion and what point the paragraph will prove. Here, the thesis sentence also acts as a hook for the case illustration.

Example 9-J • Less effective approach: a paragraph with no thesis sentence

.... An officer establishes reasonable suspicion to search a suspect if the officer can point to specific and articulable facts that give rise to a reasonable inference that the person might pose an immediate threat. *See State v. Ehly*, 854 P.2d 421, 430 (Or. 1993).

For example, in *Ehly*, this Court determined that officers had reasonable suspicion to conduct a protective search. *Id.* at 432. In that case, officers knew that the defendant was a drug user and that "many people who use illegal narcotics possess guns." *Id.* at 430. Moreover, the officers also knew that defendant was "running" with a person who carried weapons. *Id.* Because the defendant was rummaging through a gym bag with his hands concealed and did not respond to the officer's suggestion to dump out the contents of the bag, this Court concluded that it was reasonable for one of the officers to dump the contents of the bag out on the motel room bed. *Id.* at 432.

The writer omits the thesis sentence and jumps directly into the facts of a case. By not providing a thesis sentence, the lawyer has lost an opportunity to focus the court's attention on the legal proposition that is important in that case.

B. The Middle of the Paragraph

When you have information that is less favorable to your client but that you either have to disclose (because you are ethically bound to) or that you choose to disclose (to frame it in a more favorable light), put it in the middle. Put it in the middle of a section, in the middle of a paragraph, or in the middle of a sentence. As discussed above, information in the middle gets less attention. Examples 9-K, 9-L, and 9-M show the difference between a paragraph that puts damaging information in the middle, beginning, or end of a paragraph. Which structure minimizes the damaging information the most?

Example 9-K · Damaging information buried in the middle of the paragraph[1]

Here, the writer embeds the damaging information (the fact that Moore's blood alcohol level was far in excess of the permitted level of .08 percent) in the middle of the paragraph, a position that will de-emphasize that information.

The facts in this case, even when viewed most favorably for the plaintiff, failed to establish any "substantial evidence" of Moore's intoxication. Although Moore's blood alcohol level was .13, she did not demonstrate any outward signs of intoxication. Her speech was not slurred. She appeared to be in control of her body. She did not have the odor of alcohol. Because Moore exhibited none of these symptoms, Defendant Soto could not have known she was intoxicated.

Example 9-L · Damaging information at the beginning of the paragraph

Here, the damaging fact is at the beginning of the paragraph, a position that tends to highlight the information.

Although Moore's blood alcohol level was .13, she did not demonstrate any outward signs of intoxication. Her speech was not slurred. She appeared to be in control of her body. She did not have the odor of alcohol. Because Moore exhibited none of these symptoms, Defendant Soto could not have known she was intoxicated. Therefore the facts in this case, even when viewed most favorably for Plaintiff, failed to establish any "substantial evidence" of Moore's intoxication.

Example 9-M · Damaging information at the end of the paragraph

Here, the damaging fact is in the last sentence. Although the last sentence receives less attention than the first sentence, it still receives more attention than the middle of the paragraph.

The facts in this case, even when viewed most favorably for Plaintiff, failed to establish any "substantial evidence" of Moore's intoxication. She did not demonstrate any outward signs of intoxication. Her speech was not slurred. She appeared to be in control of her body. She did not have the odor of alcohol. Because Moore exhibited none of these symptoms that would support her blood alcohol level of .13, Defendant Soto could not have known she was intoxicated.

---

1. The examples in 9-K, 9-L, and 9-M were adapted from class materials prepared by Professor John Korzen, Wake Forest University School of Law.

C. Final Sentences

The thesis sentence tells your reader the proposition you intend to prove in the paragraph. Often, you will want to return to that point in the last sentence of the paragraph. Doing so closes the loop by establishing that you have now proved what your thesis sentence said you would prove. In addition, and as noted at the outset of this chapter, a reader's eyes tend to rest on (and the reader tends to absorb) the first and last sentences of a paragraph, so the last sentence is an ideal place to remind the reader of the conclusion you believe the reader should reach.

Look at Example 9-N. In that example, you can see how a final sentence repeating the paragraph's thesis helps drive home the point you want to make.

Example 9-N • Repeating assertion in the final sentence

Officer Ephgrave's interaction with defendant Adams was mere conversation, and not a stop because the defendant could not reasonably believe his liberty was ever restrained at any point during his encounter with Officer Ephgrave. Like the officer who asked for identification in *Gilmore*, here Officer Ephgrave wanted to learn if Adams was involved in the bank robbery. In addition, as in *Gilmore* where the officer only requested information but did not alter the defendant's course, Officer Ephgrave did not alter Adams's course or prevent him from leaving. Officer Ephgrave asked Adams if he was planning to leave, to which Adams responded that he was not. Further, Officer Ephgrave said he would move his car whenever Adams needed to leave. According to Officer Ephgrave, Adams said, "Oh, okay. No problem." Therefore, Officer Ephgrave did not prevent Adams from leaving nor did he alter Adams's course. Accordingly, Adams could not reasonably believe that his liberty was restrained; the statement was mere conversation.

> The final sentence re-asserts the conclusion, thereby driving home the point of the paragraph.

Although having a final sentence that repeats the original thesis is helpful, occasionally such a sentence is overly repetitive or adds length unnecessarily. In those instances, omit the final, repetitive sentence. In most cases, though, hammer home your point by restating your thesis in the final sentence of a paragraph.

D. Coherence Throughout

Finally, each paragraph must be coherent. A "coherent" paragraph is a paragraph in which the ideas flow logically, one from the next. When a paragraph is coherent, a judge is more likely to follow your logical path to the conclusion you wish him to reach. By contrast, when a paragraph lacks coherence, a judge is more likely to stumble along, veer off your intended path, and arrive at a different conclusion.

A variety of techniques will help create a coherent paragraph. First, as mentioned above, start each paragraph with a thesis sentence that asserts the point that will be established in that paragraph. Then, check each sentence in that paragraph to ensure that the sentences that follow are about that same idea.[2]

Finally, follow an order that will be logical to a law-trained reader. What will be "logical" to a law-trained reader will depend on the paragraph you are drafting. Throughout this book, we have described logical orders that lawyers expect. Here, we want to emphasize the order in which to present rules and the order in which to present case illustrations.[3]

With respect to rules, generally, your rules should be explained with the broadest concept first. Rules are refined and explained in more detail as you move through a paragraph. Then, use a bridge to connect one rule to the next. You can create a bridge between sentences by taking a key word or phrase from one sentence and repeating that key word or phrase at the beginning of the very next sentence that follows. In Examples 9-O and 9-P, you can see the difference between an explanation of rules that uses bridging language and one that does not.

Example 9-O · A coherent explanation of rules will often use "bridging language"

The shaded text highlights bridging language. Notice how each sentence begins with an idea expressed in the previous sentence.

A university complies with Title IX if it provides equal athletic opportunities to both sexes. 34 C.F.R. § 106.41(c) (2015). Whether equal athletic opportunities exist depends on an analysis of ten factors. *Id.* at 106.41(c)(1)-(10). However, an institution's failure to comply with the first factor is sufficient to constitute a violation of Title IX. *Mansourian v. Regents of U. of Cal.*, 602 F.3d 957, 965 (9th Cir. 2010).

The first factor requires an institution to "effectively accommodate" the interests of its students. An institution can effectively accommodate the interests of its students if it meets any one part of a three-part test. Under that test, an institution can comply with Title IX if it . . .

---

2. The idea that each sentence within a paragraph should relate to the same idea is also called "paragraph unity."

3. Other logical orders that lawyers might expect to see in a paragraph are (1) the order described for a roadmap paragraph, explained in § 7.1, *Organizing Claims and Arguments*; (2) the order described for an analogical argument, described at § 7.2, *Structuring Analogical Arguments*; and (3) the order in which a statutory construction argument is presented, described in § 7.3, *Structuring Rule-Based Arguments*.

Example 9-P · The lack of "bridging language" makes the logic of a paragraph more difficult to follow

---

A university complies with Title IX if it provides equal athletic opportunities to both sexes. 34 C.F.R. § 106.41(c) (2015). The conclusion rests on an analysis of ten factors. *Id.* at 106.41(c)(1)-(10). However, an institution's failure to comply with the first factor is sufficient to constitute a violation of Title IX. *Mansourian v. Regents of U. of Cal.*, 602 F.3d 957, 965 (9th Cir. 2010).

An institution can "effectively accommodate" the interests of its students if it meets any one part of a three-part test. An institution can comply with Title IX if it . . .

Notice how the connection between ideas is more difficult to follow without bridging language.

For case illustrations, follow this standard order: Begin with a hook that explains the legal principle that the following case will illustrate. Next, explain the facts. Usually, chronological order is the best order for facts; although on occasion you may prefer a topical organization.[4] Be sure to provide *all* the facts relevant to the court's decision before moving on. The final two steps are to state the court's holding and the court's reasoning (if the court provides reasoning beyond the relevant facts). Often, lawyers will end with the court's holding because it offers a nice summary at the end, but you can end on either the court's holding or the court's reasoning, whichever most emphasizes the point you want to make.

Rules and case illustrations do not always form independent paragraphs, but when they do, the above organizational principles will help provide logical coherence to your paragraph.

Finally, use appropriate transitions. Occasionally, a writer will add a transitional word, but the selected transitional word does not accurately describe the relationship between ideas. Compare Examples 9-Q and 9-R. Can you see how the wrong transitional word can disrupt the logical flow of your argument? Table 9-S will help you select an appropriate transitional word if you are unsure which transitional word will best connect two ideas.

Example 9-Q · The correct transition allows your reader to understand the relationship between ideas

---

Plaintiffs can establish actual possession by showing that they used the land as an owner would use that particular type of land. *Zambrotto v. Superior Lumber Co.*, 4 P.3d 62, 65 (Or. Ct. App. 2000). Courts focus on the type of use for which the land is suited and do not necessarily focus on the amount of activity. *Id.* For example, in one past case plaintiffs established actual possession by showing that they used the property in the same way they did their adjoining

---

4. For more on chronological versus topical organizations, see Chapter 12, *Statements of Fact and of the Case.*

land. *Davis v. Park*, 898 P.2d 804, 806-07 (Or. Ct. App. 1995). In another case, plaintiffs proved actual possession by building a fence and planting vegetation. *Slak v. Porter*, 875 P.2d 515, 518 (Or. Ct. App. 1994).

Example 9-R • An incorrect transition confuses

"In addition" is not an appropriate transition because the sentence that follows does not add to the law. The sentence that follows provides an example of the rule just stated.

"By contrast" is also inappropriate because the sentence is another similar example of the rule that courts focus on the type of activity.

Plaintiffs can establish actual possession by showing that they used the land as an owner would use that particular type of land. *Zambrotto v. Superior Lumber Co.*, 4 P.3d 62, 65 (Or. Ct. App. 2000.) Courts focus on the type of use for which the land is suited and do not necessarily focus on the amount of activity. *Id.* In addition, in one past case plaintiffs showed that they used the disputed land as an owner would by showing that they used the property in the same way they did their adjoining land. *Davis v. Park*, 898 P.2d 804, 806-07 (Or. Ct. App. 1995). By contrast, plaintiffs in another case proved actual possession by building a fence and planting vegetation. *Slak v. Porter*, 875 P.2d 515, 518 (Or. Ct. App. 1994).

Table 9-S • Transitions[5]

Introduce	**Add**	**Contrast**	**Sequence**	**Emphasize**
First	Again	However	First, second,	Certainly
Initially	Moreover	Although	third . . .	Above all
To begin	Additionally	But	Initially	Indeed
The first reason	Similarly	Yet	Then	Especially
Primarily	Also	Unlike	Finally	Accordingly
In general	Likewise	In contrast	Before	Since
Alternatively	Further	Nevertheless	Next	Not only . . .
A further reason		Nonetheless	Last	but also
		Rather		
Connect	**Exemplify**	Despite	**Restate**	**Conclude**
Because	For example	Instead	That is	Finally
Thus	For instance	Still	In other words	As a result
As a result	To illustrate	On the other	More simply	Thus
Thereby	In particular	hand	As noted	Therefore
Therefore	Namely			In short
Hence	Specifically			Consequently

---

5. Excerpted from L. Oates, A. Enquist & K. Kunsch, *The Legal Writing Handbook: Analysis, Research, and Writing*, 613-22 (3d ed. 2002), and supplemented by Bryan A. Garner, *Legal Writing in Plain English: A Text with Exercises* 68 (2001).

IV. Sentence-Level Persuasion

Just as paragraphs can be shaped to present your arguments more or less persuasively, individual sentences can be shaped to present information more or less persuasively.

A. Beginning, Middle, and End

The same locational guidelines that apply to paragraphs apply to sentences. Readers tend to absorb information at the beginning and end of sentences; readers pay less attention to information in the middle.

Compare Examples 9-T and 9-U. Can you see how the same information in different locations is emphasized differently? Thus, think carefully about where you locate information within a sentence.

Example 9-T · Damaging information at the beginning of the sentence

Even with a blood alcohol level of .13, Moore did not demonstrate outward signs of intoxication such as having slurred speech or smelling of alcohol.

Here, the damaging information appears at the beginning of the sentence, which is a point of emphasis.

Example 9-U · Damaging information in the middle of the sentence

Moore did not demonstrate signs of intoxication consistent with a blood alcohol level of .13 because her speech was not slurred and she did not smell of alcohol.

Here, the negative information appears in the middle of the sentence, a place where it will receive less emphasis.

B. Subjects and Verbs

Another focal point of a sentence is the subject and verb. Readers naturally want to know "who did what," and they will consciously or subconsciously seek out that information first. You can make it easier for the judge to find that information if you follow the steps below.

1. Place the subject and verb close together and at the beginning of the main clause

You will make the information in your sentences easier to absorb if you place the subject and verb of the sentence at the beginning of the main clause and if you place the subject and verb close together. Compare Examples 9-V and 9-W. In the first example, Example 9-V, the subject and verb (shaded) are far apart. In the second example, Example 9-W, they are close together. Can you see how, as a result, the sentence in the first example is more difficult to absorb?

Example 9-V · Subject and verb far apart

The police officer, believing that it was suspicious that the defendant's vehicle sped up after the police officer began following it, pulled the defendant's vehicle over.

Example 9-W · Subject and verb close together

The police believed that it was suspicious that the defendant's vehicle sped up after the police officer began following it. The police officer, therefore, pulled the defendant's vehicle over.

As Examples 9-V and 9-W indicate, often, when the subject and verb of a sentence are far apart, one way to fix the problem is to remove the information that separates the subject and verb and put it into its own sentence.

2. Prefer the active voice

As a general rule, you should write using the active voice.

The active voice is best understood in comparison to the passive voice.[6] In the active voice, the subject is the "be-er" or the "do-er" of the sentence. By contrast, in a sentence written in the passive voice the subject is neither a "be-er" nor a "do-er." Rather, the subject is acted on by another force.[7]

Example 9-X is written in the active voice, while Examples 9-Y and 9-Z are written in the passive voice. In the first example, Example 9-X, the supervisor is the subject of the sentence, and he is the "do-er" because he dismisses the plaintiff from his job. Because the subject is the "do-er," that sentence is in the active voice. By contrast, in the next two examples, Examples 9-Y and 9-Z, the plaintiff is the subject, but is not doing anything. Rather, something is happening to the plaintiff by the supervisor, in Example 9-Y, and by some unnamed source in Example 9-Z. Thus, those two sentences are written in the passive voice.

Example 9-X · Active voice

The plaintiff's supervisor then dismissed the plaintiff from his job.

Example 9-Y · Passive voice

The plaintiff was then dismissed from his job by his supervisor.

---

6. Remember that "passive voice" is different from "past tense." "Past tense" refers to *when* an action occurs. "Passive voice" refers to *who* did the action.

7. Capital Community College, *Guide to Grammar & Writing*, http://grammar.ccc.commnet.edu/grammar/passive.htm (last visited Oct. 9, 2015).

Example 9-Z · Passive voice

The plaintiff was then dismissed from his job.

Although, usually, you should prefer to clearly name "who did what," there are times when you do not want to call attention to "who did what." For example, if you represent an automobile driver following an accident with a cyclist, you may want to de-emphasize the role of your client (the driver), by using the passive voice, as in Example 9-aa. Other times, your client may have done something appropriate but distasteful, such as fire an employee. Again, you might use the passive voice, as in Example 9-bb. In both of those cases, the passive voice puts the actor (your client) in the background and the action in the foreground.

Example 9-aa · Appropriate passive voice

The cyclist was hit in the intersection.

Example 9-bb · Appropriate passive voice

Ms. Jones was then fired.

Finally, you may have to use the passive voice when you do not know who did what. For example, you may need to refer to a report, but the record does not disclose who prepared the report. In that case, you may have no choice but to use the passive voice.

Although passive voice has its uses, remember that the active voice is usually easier for your reader to absorb and makes for more evocative and stronger writing, both of which help persuade. Thus, prefer the active voice.

Verb Choice Makes a Difference!

Word choice can affect both the reader's perception and memory. In a 1974 experiment, psychologists Elizabeth Loftus and John Palmer showed a film of an auto accident to study participants. Some participants were asked how fast they thought the cars were going when they "hit" each other. Other groups were asked, respectively, how fast the cars were going when they "smashed into" each other, "collided with" each other, "bumped into" each other, or "contacted" each other. The results were impressive: The average speed estimate by those who were asked how fast the cars were going when they "smashed into" each other was nearly ten miles per hour faster than the estimate by those who were asked how fast the cars were going when they "contacted" each other.

The Loftus and Palmer study demonstrates that your choice of wording can have a significant impact on the reader's perception of what happened.

3. Prefer evocative verbs

When selecting verbs, go for strong verbs that show action. In Example 9-aa, for instance, the sentence could be rewritten with active verbs for punch. Saying the driver collided, hit, bumped, or crashed into the cyclist elevates the impact and visual image in the sentence. Unless, of course, you represent the driver, in which case, less evocative verbs will serve your client better.

4. Avoid "it is" and "there are"

For all the reasons stated above, avoid the "it is" or "there is" structure in a sentence when the "it" and the "there" do not actually refer to a specific subject. We often use the phrases "it is" and "there are" when we speak, but that structure creates weak writing. Those phrases obscure the subject of the sentence by creating a false subject ("it" or "there"); they use a weak verb, "is" or "are"; and they often create a wordier sentence. Compare the sentences in Example 9-cc. Which version of each sentence is stronger?

Example 9-cc · Avoid "it is" and "there are"

Version 1:   It is likely the defendant posted the information after her conversation with the seller.

Version 2:   The defendant likely posted the information after her conversation with the seller.

Version 1:   There are five factors that the court considers.

Version 2:   The court considers five factors.

---

5. Use a noun instead of "it"

Another good rule of thumb is to eliminate the word "it" altogether, and use a noun instead. "It" can create confusion or ambiguity when the reader is not clear which noun "it" refers to. For example, look at this sentence: "The tractor-trailer hit the bridge, but it was not damaged." What was not damaged—the truck or the bridge? Be clear in your writing—replace "it" with a noun.

C. Dependent Clauses

Dependent clauses are a wonderful way to acknowledge less favorable information. A dependent clause is a group of words that have a subject and verb but cannot stand alone. In Example 9-dd the shaded text is a dependent clause. The important point about dependent clauses is that the actual subject and verb of the sentence are located elsewhere.

As mentioned above, readers naturally look for the subject and verb of a sentence. Thus, the subject and verb of a sentence receive more attention. By putting information in a part of the sentence that is separate from the subject and verb, you will de-emphasize that information. Compare the two different versions of the sentence in Example 9-dd. Can you see how the emphasis shifts depending on which information is placed in the dependent clause? Choose the structure that works best for your argument.

Example 9-dd • The dependent clause receives less emphasis

Version 1: Although Moore's blood alcohol level was .13, she did not demonstrate any outward signs of intoxication.

Version 2: Although she did not demonstrate any outward signs of intoxication, Moore's blood alcohol level was .13.

Be careful, though, about putting a dependent clause in the first sentence of a paragraph. The first sentence of a paragraph is emphasized. Thus, you will undo your efforts to de-emphasize information if that information appears at the beginning of a paragraph.

D. Short Sentences

Short sentences add punch. Use them. Sparingly.

Example 9-ee • Too many short sentences

Officer Ephgrave pulled into the lot. He parked his car behind the defendant's car. The defendant yelled to move the car. Officer Ephgrave walked over to the defendant. He asked if the defendant was planning to leave. The defendant said, "No, I'm going to sit a little longer." Officer Ephgrave said no other parking slots were available. Ephgrave said he could move. The defendant said, "Oh, okay. No problem."

Although we love a punchy, short sentence, a short sentence has punch only when placed in contrast to longer sentences. Thus, if every sentence you use is short and punchy, the resulting read will be bumpy, like riding a bike over cobblestones, as in Example 9-ee. A short sentence has a stronger effect if interspersed among longer, flowing sentences. The short sentences in Examples 9-ff and 9-gg are much more effective.

Example 9-ff · Contrast a long sentence with a short punchy sentence[8]

By 2000, the investigation of the helicopter-conversion industry was winding down, with disappointing results for Wales and the U.S. Attorney's Office. Only one case remained.

Example 9-gg · Contrast a long sentence with a short punchy sentence

---

The firm, called Intrex Helicopters, which was based at Powell's home, was renovating a single helicopter for civilian use. Still, the stakes were substantial.

V. Persuasion through Quotations

When used appropriately, quotations can be used for persuasive effect. When used inappropriately, quotations disrupt your writing and clutter your prose.

To achieve persuasive effect and avoid quotation-clutter, you should, as a general rule, avoid quoting a text. Too often attorneys are not confident enough in their own analytical skills to explain what a court said or did and why. In motions and briefs written by those lawyers, you will see one quotation right after the next, with the tone, style, and word choice changing sentence-by-sentence. Such motions and briefs not only shout "Lazy!" and "This writer refuses to think!," they also are very difficult to read. As a state supreme court justice once stated, "Quotations are no substitute for analysis."[9] Instead, as a general rule, take the time to understand the law and explain it in a cohesive, straight-forward manner.

That said, when used thoughtfully, quotations can be persuasive.

A. Quote When Specific Words Matter

One good reason to quote text is because the specific wording matters to the legal argument. For example, attorneys will usually quote a governing statute so that the court knows the exact language of the statute. Similarly, if a witness's statement is important to the analysis, that statement should be quoted so that the reader knows what the witness actually said—as opposed to your characterization of what the witness said. Likewise, quote the contract when the contractual language

---

8. Jeffrey Toobin, *An Unsolved Killing*, The New Yorker, Aug. 6, 2007, at 43, 48. This example was brought to our attention by Ross Guberman, *Legal Writing Pro: Lessons from* The New Yorker, http://www.legalwritingpro.com/articles/D09-new-yorker.php (last visited Oct. 14, 2015).

9. Former Oregon Supreme Court Justice W. Michael Gillette to one of the authors.

is the subject of the dispute. On those occasions when the precise words matter, quoting text will emphasize the precision with which you are addressing the text and the care you are taking to accurately represent the facts.

B. Quote for Emphasis

Quotations are also effective when used to link your explanation of the law to your application. Sometimes a court will explain its reasoning in such an evocative way and in a way that so perfectly suits your client's case that you want to provide that quote in your explanation of the law. That's great. But if you provide that quote in only your explanation of the law, you are losing an opportunity. That quote will be most persuasive if you then repeat it in your application. By re-integrating that quote (or a key part of that quote) in your explanation of the law, you will be helping your reader to see how your analysis is exactly consistent with the analysis in prior case law. Table 9-hh provides an example.

Table 9-hh • Weaving a quotation into your analysis

Original quotation from *Richards v. Sandusky Community Schs.*, 102 F. Supp. 2d 753, 763 (E.D. Mich. 2000)	"The only evidence provided by plaintiff that would support a contention that she was 'about to report' defendants' alleged health and safety violations is the fact that plaintiff received the appropriate paperwork from OSHA. Plaintiff, however, admitted that she never completed the paperwork. (Richards Dep. at 63). This fact, by itself, falls drastically short of the clear and convincing proof required under the [Whistle-blowers' Protection Act]."
Quotation in the explanation of the law	In *Richards*, the court held that the plaintiff could not prove that she was "about to report" a violation. In that case, the plaintiff first reported a possible health violation internally to her employer. *See Richards v. Sandusky Community Schs.*, 102 F. Supp. 2d 753, 755, 763 n.14 (E.D. Mich. 2000). Then, she contacted OSHA and received the appropriate paperwork to file a complaint. *Id.* at 763 n.14. The plaintiff never completed the paperwork. *Id.* at 763. The *Richards* court held that this evidence was insufficient to prove that the plaintiff was "about to report" a violation. *Id.* In fact, the court held that the evidence fell "drastically short of the clear and convincing proof required." *Id.*
Quotation integrated into the application	Mr. Conway, like the plaintiff in *Richards*, reported the violation internally, to his supervisor, but he did nothing further. Although Mr. Conway went online and downloaded the necessary paperwork, this action is exactly like going to OSHA and receiving, but never filling out, the appropriate paperwork. As the *Richards* court explained, such action falls "drastically short of the clear and convincing proof required."

C. Avoid Block Quotes, but If You Must Use Them, Assert Your Point First

As a general rule, most careful writers would say, "Avoid block quotations." The reason: Most readers tend to skip over them because the dense text is difficult to read. Thus, if you must cite to a long portion of a case or some statutory material, try to integrate that text into your sentences, quoting only key sections or phrases of the source.

Sometimes, however, you cannot avoid a block quotation, for example if you need to cite to a statutory section in its entirety or if a large portion of a record needs to be presented in one block in your argument. When you cannot avoid the block quotation, explain the point of the quotation just before the quotation. By explaining the point of the quotation, your reader will be encouraged to read the quotation to see if, in fact, the quotation supports that point.

Examples 9-ii and 9-jj show how an explanatory sentence can make the advocate's point easier to understand. The quotation is from the legislative history to a statute that permits the revocation of a person's driver's license when that person has been convicted of driving under the influence of intoxicants "for a third time." In a brief, a state assistant attorney general wants to use the legislative history to argue that the statute should be construed so that the phrase "for a third time" is understood to permit a revocation when a person has been convicted of "three or more" DUIs. In Example 9-jj, notice how the sentence that precedes the block quote makes it easier to understand the point the assistant attorney general wants to make.

Example 9-ii · A block quotation without its point explained

When Representative Barker carried the bill on the House floor, he stated the following:

> Under the current law, someone convicted of driving under the influence of intoxicants does not permanently lose their driving privileges until after their fourth conviction. This means that after the initial DUI arrest, which often results in a diversion program, someone has to be convicted four more times to lose their privileges. As an Oregonian and the father of two daughters, I find this to be unacceptably tolerant towards such reckless behavior.

Example 9-jj · A block quotation with its point explained

When Representative Barker carried the bill onto the House floor, he stated that waiting until a fourth DUI conviction to revoke a driver's license was unacceptable:

> Under the current law, someone convicted of driving under the influence of intoxicants does not permanently lose their driving privileges until after their fourth conviction. This means that after the initial DUI arrest, which often results in a diversion program, someone has to be convicted four more times to lose their privileges. As an Oregonian and the father of two daughters, I find this to be unacceptably tolerant towards such reckless behavior.

In addition to providing an explanatory sentence before the quotation, consider also providing a sentence immediately after the quotation to sum up or further explain the point of the quotation. When a reader jumps over a block quote, the reader's eye often lands on the first text after the block quote. Thus, you can also emphasize your point by summarizing it in the text immediately after the block quote.

Because readers have difficulty extracting the point from a block of text, if you must use a block quote, help your reader: Explain the point the reader should have taken away had the reader actually read the block quote.

A Judge's Thoughts on Block Quotes

"Block quotes, by the way, are a must; they take up a lot of space but nobody reads them. Whenever I see a block quote I figure the lawyer had to go to the bathroom and forgot to turn off the merge/store function on his computer. Let's face it, if the block quote really had something useful in it, the lawyer would have given me a pithy paraphrase."

The Hon. Judge Kozinski
U.S. Court of Appeals, 9th Cir.
The Wrong Stuff
1992 BYU L. Rev. 325, 329

VI. Persuasion through Citations

The techniques discussed above will help you refine the substance of your argument. As a general rule, your argument should be made in the text, which the court will read, and not through citations, which many readers skip over. However, effective use of citations can bolster the argument that you make in the text.

A. Build Credibility Through Citations

As we explained in Chapter 2, *The Ethical, Professional Advocate*, and again in Chapters 4 and 5, *Motion Practice* and *Appellate Practice*, respectively, you should always conduct yourself so that you are perceived as a professional and credible lawyer. Citations, though tedious, are one of those places where you can reinforce the idea that you are a professional, credible attorney. Simply do two things. First, many jurisdictions have local rules that establish how to cite in that jurisdiction. Follow those rules. Second, be accurate. Be certain that your citation is, in fact, directing the court to the proper authority and the proper page within that authority. No need to make the court's job more difficult by giving the judge a citation to nowhere.

In addition to conveying your credibility, citations can provide more substantive support for your argument, thus making it more persuasive.

B. Emphasize the Weight of Authority

Citations, first, emphasize the binding authority for your argument. As a general rule, attorneys choose cases from the same jurisdiction and from the highest court possible. The citation will then reveal that the case is binding on the courts below.

Sometimes, though, questions arise about which authority will best emphasize the binding nature of the authority. For example, when a legal proposition is frequently stated, you may wonder whether to cite the first case to have stated the proposition or a more recent case. Citing the earliest case highlights the point that the proposition has ancient roots, but may leave the reader wondering whether the proposition still holds true. Whether to cite the earliest case, the latest case, or a combination depends on the point you want to make in the text. For example, if your text emphasizes that a rule of law was first recognized decades ago, the appropriate citation is to the first case, as in Example 9-kk.

Example 9-kk • Citing to an early case to emphasize the historical roots of a doctrine

When determining the custody of a child, Minnesota has historically declared a preference for the natural parents of the child. *See State v. ex rel. Larson v. Halverson,* 127 Minn. 387, 389-89 (1914) (holding that a natural's parent's rights of custody and control are a "paramount" consideration).

By contrast, if you want to emphasize the applicability of a principle without particularly emphasizing its history, use a current case and the citation signal, "e.g.," as in Example 9-ll. The citation signal "e.g." means "for example" and is used to indicate that the cited case is just one of many cases that support a proposition.[10]

---

10. ALWD & Coleen M. Barger, *ALWD Guide to Legal Citation* 252-56 (5th ed. 2014) (R. 35); *The Bluebook: A Uniform System of Citation* 19-22 (Columbia L. Rev. Ass'n et al. eds., 20th ed. 2015) (R. B1.2).

Example 9-ll • Citing to a current case to focus on current law

---

When determining the custody of a child, Minnesota prefers the child be placed with a natural parent. *See, e.g., Durkin v. Hinich,* 442 N.W.2d 148, 152-153 (Minn. 1989) ("[T]here is a presumption in custody determinations that a natural parent is fit to raise his or her own child.").

Finally, if you want to emphasize both the ancient roots of a proposition and that it is still good law, you can cite to both the first case and a recent application of the rule, as in Example 9-mm.

Example 9-mm • Citing to both an early and current case to emphasize continuity of policy

---

When determining the custody of a child, Minnesota has historically and to this day expressed its preference that a child be placed with the child's natural parents. *See State v. ex rel. Larson v. Halverson,* 127 Minn. 387, 389-89 (1914) (holding that a natural parent's rights of custody and control are a "paramount" consideration); *In re Custody of N.A.K.,* 649 N.W.2d 166, 175 (Minn. 2002) (concluding that upon the death of a custodial parent, custody will be awarded to the non-custodial parent unless that assumption is overcome by "extraordinary circumstances").

C. Show a Trend Through Citations

If you want to establish a trend in the law or argue that a majority of courts have reached a conclusion that you want the court to reach in your client's case, a string cite may be the simplest, most direct way of establishing that point. A string cite, when combined with parentheticals, can quickly establish a trend without having to describe the facts of each case in detail.

Take for example the case in which the estate of an elderly woman sued a four-year-old bicyclist and her parents after the four-year-old collided with the elderly woman. Counsel for the elderly woman wanted to establish that the majority of courts did allow for the possibility that a four-year-old could be negligent by using a string cite after describing the lead case. Thus, the attorney drafted the text in Example 9-nn in which the attorney asserts that the majority of courts allow for four-year-olds to be sued and then supports that assertion with a string cite.

Example 9-nn • Using string cites to show a trend in the law

The *Comardo* decision, which concludes that a jury must assess the culpability of a four-year-old, has been consistently followed since that case was decided in 1928. *See Chandler v. Keene,* 168 N.Y.S.2d 788, 791(N.Y. App. Div. 1957) (holding that a jury properly decided whether a child of four years and eleven months was contributorily negligent); *Weidenfeld v. Surface Transp. Corp. of N.Y.*, 55 N.Y.S.2d 780, 783 (N.Y. App. Div. 1945) (same regarding a four-year-old child); *Sun Jeong Koo v. St. Bernard*, 392 N.Y.S.2d 815, 816 (N.Y. Sup. Ct. 1977) (same regarding a child of four years and ten months); *Searles v. Dardani*, 347 N.Y.S.2d 662, 665 (N.Y. Sup. Ct. 1973) (same regarding a child of four and a half years); *Republic Ins. Co. v. Michel*, 885 F. Supp. 426, 433 (E.D.N.Y. 1995) (same regarding a child of four years and four and a half months); *Redmond v. City of New York*, 447 N.Y.S.2d 434, 434 (N.Y. 1981) (same regarding a child of four years and ten months).

As you can see, though, string cites can be difficult to read because they, essentially, create a long block of text, and readers tend to skip over long blocks of text. Moreover, a string cite is useful only if the point of law that you are discussing is in controversy. If your opponent is likely to agree that courts have adopted a particular point of law, then a string cite is simply a waste of space and of the court's time. Thus, use string cites sparingly.

If you wish to assert a point of law that is uncontroversial and is stated by a number of authorities, consider using the signal "e.g.," which means "for example," rather than a string cite. When many cases state the same proposition and the opposing party is unlikely to dispute the proposition, you can simply choose one case that states the proposition and precede the citation with "e.g.," as in Example 9-oo. The abbreviation "e.g." tells the reader that the case you have chosen to cite is just one of several that state the same proposition.

Example 9-oo • Using "e.g." to present a common and undisputed proposition

---

When a district court grants an injunction based on its interpretation of a statute, this Court's review is de novo. *See, e.g., Edina Educ. Ass'n v. Bd. of Educ. of Indep. Sch. Dist. No. 273*, 562 N.W.2d 306, 311 (Minn. App. 1997) (reviewing de novo injunction based on interpretation of Data Practices Act).[11]

D. Use Explanatory Parentheticals Effectively

An explanatory parenthetical is a part of a citation that is used to help a reader understand the citation's significance.[12] When you assert a propo-

---

11. Adapted from *Williams v. Nat'l Football League*, 794 N.W.2d 391, 395 (Minn. Ct. App. 2011).

12. See the *ALWD Guide to Legal Citation*, *supra* note 10, at 328-31 (R. 37), or *The Bluebook: A Uniform System of Citation*, *supra* note 10, at 5-6 (R. B1.3), for details about how to incorporate explanatory parentheticals.

sition that depends on synthesizing the holdings from a series of cases, parentheticals can be an effective way to prove the asserted proposition without delving into the specific facts and holdings of each case you have reviewed. For example, parentheticals can be used to great effect to establish a trend in the law. Both Example 9-nn and Example 9-pp use parentheticals to show that a series of courts have reached the conclusion that the writer wants the court to reach in this case.

Example 9-pp • Parentheticals used to establish a trend[13]

Plaintiff's claim must fail because the First Amendment does not allow a citizen to avoid paying taxes because she objects to government policy. *Adams v. Comm'r*, 170 F.3d 173, 182 (3d Cir. 1999) ("Plaintiffs engaging in civil disobedience through tax protests must pay the penalties incurred as a result of engaging in such disobedience."); *United States v. Rowlee*, 899 F.2d 1275, 1279 (2d Cir. 1990) ("The consensus of this and every other circuit is that liability for a false or fraudulent return cannot be avoided by evoking the First Amendment[.]"); *Welch v. United States*, 750 F.2d 1101, 1108 (1st Cir. 1985) ("[N]oncompliance with the federal tax laws is conduct that is afforded no protection under the First Amendment[.]"); *United States v. Ness*, 652 F.2d 890, 892 (9th Cir. (1981) ("Tax violations are not a protected form of political dissent.").

Parentheticals should be used for less important ideas, not the primary points of your analysis. Great points can get lost in a mass of citations, and even the most engaged readers tend to skip over a string of citations with parentheticals. Thus, your argument must appear in the text and not in citations. To test whether you have used parentheticals effectively, read your motion or brief without the citations and their parentheticals to see whether you have also made your point within the text.

The techniques in this chapter should help fine-tune your brief so that a court can see why your substantive arguments should win. Although these techniques cannot eradicate undesirable law or facts, they can help emphasize why the outcome your client seeks is a correct and preferable outcome to the one opposing counsel seeks.

---

13. From *Greene v. I.R.S.*, No. 1:08–CV–0280, 2008 WL 5378120, at *5 (N.D.N.Y. Dec. 23, 2008).

Practice Points

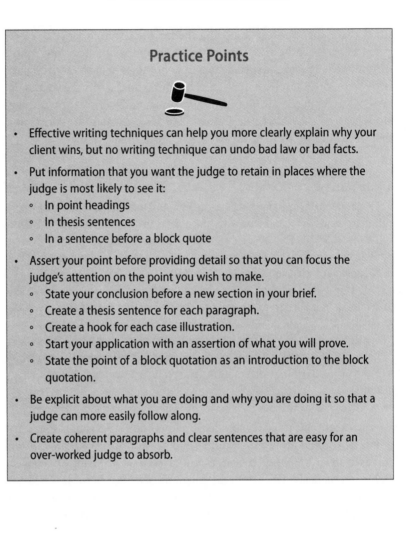

- Effective writing techniques can help you more clearly explain why your client wins, but no writing technique can undo bad law or bad facts.

- Put information that you want the judge to retain in places where the judge is most likely to see it:
  - In point headings
  - In thesis sentences
  - In a sentence before a block quote

- Assert your point before providing detail so that you can focus the judge's attention on the point you wish to make.
  - State your conclusion before a new section in your brief.
  - Create a thesis sentence for each paragraph.
  - Create a hook for each case illustration.
  - Start your application with an assertion of what you will prove.
  - State the point of a block quotation as an introduction to the block quotation.

- Be explicit about what you are doing and why you are doing it so that a judge can more easily follow along.

- Create coherent paragraphs and clear sentences that are easy for an over-worked judge to absorb.

Chapter 10

Constructing Motions and Supporting Memoranda of Law

The last several chapters have discussed how to build a persuasive argument. If your case is being heard by a trial court, that argument will be presented to the court through a motion and a supporting memorandum of law. This chapter addresses how to construct that motion and a memorandum of law, whether the memorandum of law supports the motion or opposes the motion.

We have already discussed the first step in effectively presenting a trial motion and its accompanying memorandum of law. Chapter 4, *Motion Practice*, explains that to produce an effective motion and memorandum of law, you must research the rules that govern the form of the motion and its accompanying memorandum of law. Those rules include your jurisdiction's procedural rules, the court's local rules, and any standing orders issued by the judge before whom you will appear.

If you have not researched those rules already, you need to do so now before you begin constructing your motion and memorandum of law. Once you find those rules, you must follow them carefully. As explained in Chapter 4, a judge is likely to have more confidence in — and thus more likely to be persuaded by — a motion and supporting memorandum of law that follow the rules over a submission that does not. If the recommendations in this chapter conflict with the rules that govern in your jurisdiction, always follow the rules that govern in your jurisdiction.

After determining the rules that govern your motion or memorandum of law, you should next consider your audience.

I. Your Audience: The Trial Judge

The primary audience for your motion and its supporting memorandum of law is, of course, a trial judge. Trial judges often work with a law clerk who assists the judge by researching the law and producing draft opinions. Some law clerks have worked with a judge for years and have vast experience in analyzing legal problems. Other law clerks are hired directly out of law school and may have only a few months of experience before reviewing your motion.

The trial judge and her law clerk have one trait in common: They are busy. For example, one New York court estimated that a judge assigned to hear civil motions for one week will hear "upwards of 650 motions."[1] Thus, pare your memorandum of law to its essentials, and present your argument simply, clearly, and directly. Your goal should be to help the judge *quickly* decide your motion in your favor.

Sometimes you may be able to learn more about the judge who will be hearing your case or your motion. In some jurisdictions, a single judge is assigned to hear pre-trial motions and another judge will preside over the trial. In other jurisdictions, a judge will be assigned to the entire case and will, therefore, also hear your pre-trial motions. When you know the judge who will be hearing your motion, take the time to determine whether that judge has standing orders that govern motions submitted to that judge, and be sure to consult more experienced colleagues. Colleagues will often have invaluable information about the preferences of a particular judge.

II. The Motion

As explained in Chapter 4, *Motion Practice*, a motion is a request to a court that it take some action. A motion typically has four parts: (1) a caption, (2) a statement of the party's request, (3) a brief statement of the grounds for that request, and (4) the attorney's signature. Examples

---

1. *Judge Assignments*, NY Courts, http://www.courts.state.ny.us/courts/nyc /civil/ assignmentsdef.shtml (last visited Feb. 15, 2015).

10-A and 10-B will remind you of what those typical parts look like. (You previously saw these examples in Chapter 4, *Motion Practice*, as Examples 4-A and 4-B.) This chapter then discusses each part in turn.

Example 10-A • A motion to suppress

IN THE CIRCUIT COURT OF THE STATE OF OREGON
FOR LANE COUNTY

THE STATE OF OREGON,	)	
	)	Case No. 21-15-18156
Plaintiff,	)	
	)	DEFENDANT'S MOTION TO
vs.	)	SUPPRESS EVIDENCE
	)	
TRAVIS Z. TREATSKY,	)	
	)	ORAL ARGUMENT REQUESTED
	)	
Defendant.	)	EST. TIME: 30 MINUTES
	)	

Caption

Local rules explain how to request a hearing. In this case, the request is made in the caption.

The defendant, through his attorney, Jordan R. Silk, moves this Court for the following orders:

1. An order suppressing any and all evidence of the field sobriety tests performed by the defendant on May 21, 2015, and

2. An order suppressing all evidence of the breath test performed by the defendant on May 22, 2015.

The statement of the relief defendant seeks

This motion is based on the attached memorandum of law and is, in the opinion of counsel, well founded in law and not made or filed for the purpose of delay.

DATED this _____ day of November, 2015.

This motion cross-references a memorandum of law, which explains the grounds for relief. That memorandum is provided in Chapter 4, at Example 4-C.

Jordan R. Silk
OSB # 105031
Lane County Public Defender's Office
555 Willamette Street
Eugene, OR 97401
Appearing for Defendant

Sign motions with care. Your signature indicates that you believe the motion is supported by both the facts of the case and the law.

Example 10-B · A motion to dismiss

United States District Court
For the District of Utah

KATELYN MASON and	:	Civil Action No. 14 CV 921
JENNIFER WELCH, individually	:	
and on behalf of those	:	
similarly situated,	:	DEFENDANT'S MOTION TO
	:	DISMISS PLAINTIFF
-	:	WELCH'S COMPLAINT
Plaintiffs,	:	
	:	
v.	:	
	:	
CENTRAL STATE UNIVERSITY	:	
OF UTAH,	:	
	:	
Defendant.	:	MAY 5, 2015

Pursuant to Federal Rule of Civil Procedure 12(b)(6), defendant Central State University of Utah hereby moves to dismiss that portion of the Complaint that relates to plaintiff Jennifer Welch because plaintiff Welch lacks standing.

Specifically, all claims asserted by plaintiff Welch must be dismissed because plaintiff Welch, by her own allegations, did not suffer any present or past injury, and she cannot establish future injury because she is graduating this year. For these reasons, and as explained more fully in the attached memorandum of law, she lacks standing to bring her Title IX claim.

Therefore, defendant Central State University of Utah respectfully requests that this Court grant its Motion to Dismiss Plaintiff Welch's Complaint.

Hepworth & Peterson LLP

By: _____
Justin Hepworth, Esq.
jhepworth@wiggin.com
Federal Bar No. ut01386
350 Lake Street
Provo, UT 84601
Phone: (203) 363-7512
Fax: (203) 262-7676
Attorney for Defendant

> **Reminder: Motion Is Not a Verb**
>
> A party *never* "motions" for summary judgment; a party "moves" for summary judgment. A party does not "motion" the court to dismiss plaintiff's complaint; a party "moves" for the court to dismiss the complaint.

A. Caption

The caption to a motion appears at the top of the motion and provides procedural details of the motion. It identifies the name and division of the court in which the case is proceeding, the parties, and the file number.

The caption also includes the title of the motion. The attorney who drafts the motion will create its title. No list of acceptable titles exists. Rather, you must create a title that clearly identifies the purpose and scope of the motion. In a case involving a single plaintiff and a single defendant, the title might be as simple as "Defendant's Motion for Summary Judgment" or as in Example 10-A, "Defendant's Motion to Suppress Evidence." If a case involves multiple parties and the motion has a more limited scope, however, the title would need to be more specific. For example, a title might read, "Defendant Vasco's Motion to Dismiss Count Two of Plaintiff Siegel's Complaint" or, as in Example 10-B, "Defendant's Motion to Dismiss Plaintiff Welch's Complaint."

Your firm or organization will likely have a template for the caption that complies with the local court rules. Even so, take time to make sure the information in the caption is correct, that names are spelled correctly, and that the caption is neat in appearance.

B. Statement of the Relief Requested

You submit a motion to ask a court to act on your client's behalf. Thus, the body of the motion states the action you seek to take. That action may be to ask the court to dismiss the case, to extend a filing date, or to suppress certain evidence.

C. Legal Grounds for the Relief Requested

The statement of the grounds supporting the motion is short and simple. Usually, a motion will simply state the statutory basis, such as "Federal Rule of Civil Procedure 12(b)(6)" for a motion to dismiss, or it might reference a statute or legal principle that a party has violated. If the statement of the grounds supporting the motion requires more detailed legal analysis, you should attach a separate memorandum of law in support of the motion.

D. Signature

You must sign and date any motion that you submit. Local rules will also usually require that you provide contact information directly under your signature. Take note when you sign a motion: You are confirming that the motion is not frivolous, not intended to harass, and not intended to delay the proceedings.[2]

III. The Memorandum of Law

In addition to the motion, you will have to explain why the motion should be granted. If the request is anything other than a ministerial request, that explanation will be a legal argument that explains the relevant law and applies the facts of the case to that law. The legal argument will be presented in a document that, depending on the jurisdiction, may be called a "memorandum of law," a "brief," a "memorandum of points and authorities," or something else entirely.[3]

Whatever the name, the document usually has four parts: (1) a caption, (2) an introduction, (3) a statement of facts, (4) the argument, and (5) the conclusion. The purpose of this chapter is to look at those parts in detail.

A. Caption

The caption for a brief supporting a motion is identical to the caption for the motion itself—except for the title. With respect to the title, take care to coordinate the brief's title to the title of the motion. The brief should begin with a phrase like "Memorandum in Support of" or "Brief in Support of" and then repeat *exactly* the title of the motion. Compare the titles of the motion in Example 10-A and the caption for the supporting brief in Example 10-C. You can see that the title for the memorandum in Example 10-C is generated by simply adding "Memorandum in Support of" to the title of the motion, "Defendant's Motion to Suppress Evidence." The names of documents can get long,

---

2. *See, e.g.,* Fed. R. Civ. P. 11(b).

3. This book assumes two separate documents—a motion *and* a brief or memorandum in support of that motion. Not all motions, though, come with a separate supporting memorandum of law. Some jurisdictions merge the motion and the legal argument into a single document, and some ministerial requests require no supporting argument. To keep things simple, this text assumes that the motion you are drafting will have two parts—the motion and a supporting brief or memorandum of law.

especially in complex cases, but you will make the court's job easier by repeating the name of the motion in all documents supporting that motion.

Example 10-C • A memorandum of law in support of a motion to suppress

---

IN THE CIRCUIT COURT OF THE STATE OF OREGON
FOR LANE COUNTY

THE STATE OF OREGON,	)	
	)	Case No. 21-15-18156
Plaintiff,	)	
	)	
vs.	)	MEMORANDUM IN SUPPORT
	)	OF DEFENDANT'S MOTION
TRAVIS J. TREATSKY,	)	TO SUPPRESS EVIDENCE
	)	
Defendant.	)	
_____	)	

B. Introduction

Most memoranda begin with an introduction that provides an overview of and context for the arguments that are to follow. The name of the introduction varies from jurisdiction to jurisdiction. It might be called an "Introduction," a "Preliminary Statement," a "Summary of the Argument," the "Statement of the Nature of the Matter Before the Court," or something else entirely. Check your jurisdiction's local rules or consult colleagues to determine the local custom.

Whatever the introductory material is called, it usually establishes the nature of the litigation, the procedural posture of the case, and the type of motion before the court. In some jurisdictions, the introductory material also presents a quick preview of the arguments.

In those jurisdictions in which the introduction describes only the nature of the litigation, the procedural posture, and the type of motion before the court, the introduction usually has a more objective tone, as in Example 10-D.

Example 10-D • An introduction describing the procedural posture, nature of the case, and motion before the court

INTRODUCTION

The "nature of the case" is identified by stating that Ms. Stark filed a complaint alleging that Michigan's Whistle-blowers' Protection Act protects her from being fired.

On November 29, 2015, Plaintiff Julie Stark was dismissed from her employment with defendant Michigan Power & Electric Company (MPE). Immediately after her dismissal, Ms. Stark filed a complaint alleging that Michigan's Whistle-blowers' Protection Act protected her from discharge. This motion for summary judgment seeks to dismiss her Whistle-blowers' claim because no material issues of fact exist, and as a matter of law, Ms. Stark cannot prove that she was engaged in an activity protected by Michigan's Whistle-blowers' Protection Act.

Both the "procedural posture" and the "type of motion" before the court are identified by explaining that this motion is a motion for summary judgment.

If you are in a jurisdiction that provides a short preview of the arguments, your introduction might look like Example 10-E.

Example 10-E • An introduction that also previews the argument

INTRODUCTION

The "nature of the case" is a criminal prosecution for bank robbery.

Defendant Paul Adams's statement to an undercover police officer should be admitted into evidence at his trial for bank robbery. The State of Oregon filed charges against Adams for an alleged bank robbery on August 15, 2015. Adams was arraigned on August 20, 2015. He has pleaded not guilty, and the trial is set for September 16, 2015.

The "procedural posture" and the "type of motion at issue" is a motion to suppress in advance of trial.

Shortly after the robbery, Adams spoke to an undercover police officer. That statement implicated him in the robbery. Defendant Adams now moves to suppress that statement. Oregon law, however, allows a defendant's statement to be admitted into evidence where, as here, the statement was made during "mere conversation" with a police officer. Because Adams's statement was made during a conversation and not during a police stop, his statement should be admitted into evidence, and defendant's motion to suppress should be denied.

This motion also explains why the motion should be denied.

In jurisdictions that permit or require an overview of the arguments, practices vary with respect to the degree of advocacy displayed in the introduction. Example 10-E provides a fairly objective preview of the argument before the court. Example 10-F, by contrast, is both a more complete summary of the arguments and more aggressively persuasive.

Example 10-F • An introduction that previews the arguments more fully and more aggressively

In some jurisdictions introductory procedural information is placed before the section labeled "introduction." The "introduction" then provides an overview of the argument. As always, check your local rules and research local customs.

Defendant Central State University of Utah moves this Court pursuant to Federal Rule of Civil Procedure 56(a) to enter judgment for Central State University of Utah as a matter of law and dismiss the complaint brought by Nicole Hermann and Jennifer Welch.

INTRODUCTION

Plaintiffs' action under Title IX of the Education Amendment of 1972 fails because the University complies with Title IX. Central State University of Utah made the difficult decision to eliminate its women's golf team after the State of Utah cut funding to the University by thirty percent. Thus, the University was forced to sell its golf course. However, after eliminating the women's golf team, the University established a women's competitive cheer team of twenty-four players, expanding its women's athletic program by twelve positions.

Central State University complies with Title IX because it has a history and continuing practice of program expansion. The addition of the women's cheer team is yet one more step in that history of expanding opportunity. Since Central State University began its women's athletic program in the 1970s, the University has more than doubled the number of athletic opportunities available to its female students. The competitive cheer team is yet one more addition to this history and continuing practice of program expansion because it, too, increases the number of equal athletic opportunities available to women.

Because Central State University can show a history and continuing practice of program expansion, the University is in compliance with Title IX and is entitled to judgment as a matter of law.

Especially in those jurisdictions in which attorneys preview the arguments to come, the introduction plays an important persuasive role. It sets forth your vision of the precise legal question and the most important facts the judge should consider while reading your brief. And, of course, the introduction is the first part of the memorandum that the judge will read.

Although the introduction can (and should) play a persuasive role, the tone should still be reasonable. Introductions framed too passionately can trigger heightened skepticism in a judge. By presenting yourself as a reasonable advocate, the judge will be more likely to trust the path you are encouraging the court to take.

C. Statement of Facts

The statement of facts typically follows the introduction. Chapter 12, *Statements of Fact and of the Case*, provides detailed advice about constructing a persuasive statement of facts, and we recommend that you review that chapter when writing your statement of facts.

D. Argument

The argument section is, of course, the heart of the memorandum, and it will likely require the greatest portion of your time and effort as you are constructing your memorandum. Accordingly, this book devotes three chapters to developing and refining your persuasive arguments.

Those chapters are Chapter 7, *Organizing Persuasive Arguments*; Chapter 8, *Developing Persuasive Arguments*; and Chapter 9, *Refining Persuasive Arguments*. We recommend that you return to those chapters as you develop your argument in support of your motion.

E. Conclusion

In most instances, the conclusion of a brief consists of a simple request for the relief the plaintiff seeks. (For that reason, the conclusion is also sometimes called the "prayer for relief.") This section is very short, often consisting of only one sentence in which you respectfully request that the court take the requested action or rule in your favor on the issues presented, as in Example 10-G.

Example 10-G · Traditional conclusion

CONCLUSION

For the reasons stated in this memorandum of law, Defendant respectfully requests that this Court grant Defendant's motion for summary judgment.

Sometimes attorneys use the conclusion to quickly summarize the argument made in the brief, as in Example 10-H.

Example 10-H · Short, summary conclusion

CONCLUSION

Because evidence of Mr. Treatsky's performance of field sobriety tests and from the breath test were obtained in violation of Article I, Section 9 of the Oregon Constitution, this Court should suppress all such evidence.

F. Signature

Like the motion, the brief must be signed and dated by the lawyer submitting the motion and brief. Again, sign with care. Your signature confirms that your arguments are non-frivolous and are supported by the law and facts.[4]

---

4. *E.g.*, Fed. R. Civ. P. 11.

Practice Points

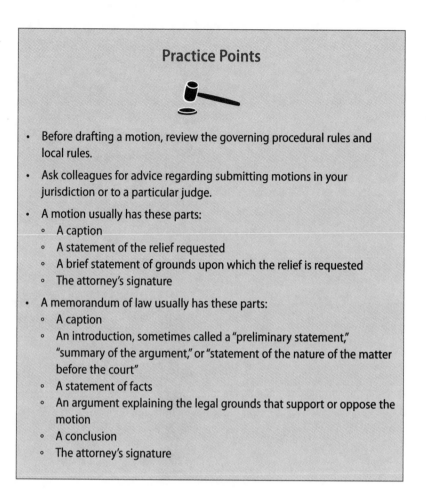

- Before drafting a motion, review the governing procedural rules and local rules.

- Ask colleagues for advice regarding submitting motions in your jurisdiction or to a particular judge.

- A motion usually has these parts:
  - A caption
  - A statement of the relief requested
  - A brief statement of grounds upon which the relief is requested
  - The attorney's signature

- A memorandum of law usually has these parts:
  - A caption
  - An introduction, sometimes called a "preliminary statement," "summary of the argument," or "statement of the nature of the matter before the court"
  - A statement of facts
  - An argument explaining the legal grounds that support or oppose the motion
  - A conclusion
  - The attorney's signature

Chapter 11

Constructing Appellate Briefs

I. Appellant's Brief
   A. Cover
   B. Table of Contents
   C. Table of Authorities
   D. Statement of Jurisdiction
   E. Issue (or Question) Presented
      1. The components of an effective issue presented
      2. One or more sentences?
      3. Incorporating the standard of review
   F. Statement of the Case
   G. Summary of the Argument
   H. Argument
   I. Conclusion and Relief Sought
II. Respondent's Brief
III. Appellant's Reply Brief

This chapter now turns to what often is thought of as the quintessential example of persuasive legal writing: the appellate brief. Chapter 5, *Appellate Practice*, first introduced the appellate brief. That chapter provided you with an image of what an appellate brief looks like and then introduced you to your appellate court audience and the rules and concepts that govern appeals. This chapter now returns to the appellate brief to look more closely at each part and how each part can be used to advance your argument.

As discussed in Chapter 5, *Appellate Practice*, you must begin by examining the appellate court rules. Just as the rules will prescribe the appropriate procedure for the appeal, they also will specify the requirements for the brief. Rules of appellate procedure will tell you everything from the proper color for the brief cover, to the required font, to the size of the margins.[1]

---

1. *See, e.g.*, Fed. R. App. P. 32(a)(2) (color of brief cover); Fed. R. App. P. 32(a)(5)(A) (requiring 14-point font size for appellate briefs); Fed. R. App. P. 32(a)(4) (requiring one inch margins on all sides).

Complying with the rules will make your brief more persuasive.[2] Why? First, it shows the reader that you know how to, and make the effort to, find and follow rules. Following the rules enhances your credibility with the court, and the more credible you appear, the more likely the judges will be open to the argument that you have drafted.

Second, following the rules reduces distractions. Judges are very busy, and they read many briefs. They expect the brief to look a certain way, to have the sections in a certain order, and to contain all the information required by the rules. To the extent that a brief does not do those things, the judges have to work harder to follow it and will have less mental energy to devote to the legal argument. The easier you make your brief to digest, the less heartburn it will cause the judges.

Persuasive writing directed to appellate courts is generally no different from other persuasive writing: It must be focused, concise, accurate, and credible. The prettiest typeset brief with a fancy cover will get you nowhere unless the contents are persuasive. Conversely, if your brief looks like something that the dog just dragged in, it will be less persuasive. As in other contexts in which you are attempting to persuade, a polished, professional presentation of a persuasive argument is best.

I. Appellant's Brief

Now, let's look at the particular sections of the brief. Usually, an appellate brief includes these components:

- Cover
- Table of contents
- Table of authorities
- Statement of jurisdiction
- Statement of the issues (or questions) presented
- Statement of the case
- Summary of the argument
- Argument
- Conclusion

To be honest, some components of an appellate brief are pretty dry and do not create much opportunity for creativity. Other components—primarily the issue presented, the statement of facts, and of course, the argument—let you really strut your analytic and writing skills. But all aspects of the brief are important. To the extent that the dry, constrained parts of the brief are not properly prepared, the reader will be less positively inclined toward a brilliant argument. To be persuasive, an argument must be served

---

2. Chapter 4, *Motion Practice*, also explains how following the rules makes your brief more persuasive. If you have already read Chapter 4, *Motion Practice*, you may have already heard this point. It is repeated here because the point bears emphasis.

up right. Put another way, the obligatory, formulaic parts of the brief are to the argument as a picture frame is to a work of art. A good frame enhances, but does not distract from, the work; an ugly frame can ruin the whole effect. Below, you will see how each section of the appellate brief offers an opportunity, no matter how small, to persuade the court.[3]

A. Cover

Briefs have covers and, traditionally, they are colored. Typically, the appellant's or petitioner's brief has a blue cover and the respondent's brief has a red cover. The appellant's reply brief has a gray cover; amicus curiae briefs sport a green cover. In fact, appellate practitioners and judges often refer to briefs by their color. So, in the hallways of an appellate court you may hear someone say, "I have the blue brief and the red brief; do you know if they filed a gray brief?" In addition to prescribing the color of the cover, the rules set out what information is required to be included, and where it should be placed on the cover. Usually, the cover will state the name of the court hearing the appeal, the parties to the case, the docket number, the court from which the appeal is being taken, and the names of the attorneys and their contact information.[4]

The cover is the first place to begin persuading. If you scrupulously follow the rules, the judge's first impression will be that you are professional and competent, and that you know what you are doing.

B. Table of Contents

Like any other table of contents, the table of contents in an appellate brief lists all the sections of the brief and the page on which each section begins. In an appellate brief, the table of contents is created by listing—verbatim—all the point headings and subheadings found within your brief and the page on which those point headings and subheadings can be found. As discussed in Chapter 9, *Refining Persuasive Arguments*, point headings should read as an outline of your argument. Thus, if you have constructed effective headings in your brief, the table of contents will serve as a summary of your argument.

The table of contents is particularly important because it is the very first place the judges will be exposed to your legal argument. If, for example, the first heading under the argument section in the table of con-

---

3. This chapter discusses the typical components of an appellate brief. This discussion does not address one section required in the federal circuit courts, but not usually required in state appeals: a corporate disclosure statement. *See* Fed. R. App. P. 26.1(a) (requiring that "[a]ny nongovernmental corporate party to a proceeding in a court of appeals must file a statement that identifies any parent corporation and any publicly held corporation that owns 10% or more of its stock and states that there is no such corporation").

4. *See, e.g.*, Fed. R. App. P. 32(a)(2).

tents is, "Plaintiff never objected to admission of the toxicologist's report, so his claim of error is unpreserved," the judges are already thinking that this appeal may have a simple answer: "lack of preservation."

The table also serves utilitarian functions, which will bring the judges back to your table of contents over and again. For example, as the judges are considering your case, they are likely to address one issue at a time. As the judges consider each issue, they will use the table of contents to find that section of your brief. In addition, if the judges lose track of your argument, they are likely to come back to the table of contents to get an overview of your argument. Thus, the table of contents is not just the first place where the judges will see your argument, it is likely to be the place where they return repeatedly and are exposed to your argument again and again.

For those reasons, your table of contents should always present a persuasive summary of your argument. For example, it is hardly ever appropriate to produce a table of contents that has no subheadings between "Argument" and "Conclusion." As you can imagine, judges do not find that form of table of contents useful, and you have lost a prime opportunity to persuade.

Compare the table of contents in Example 11-A with the tables of contents in Examples 11-B and 11-C. Which is more likely to persuade the judges that your analysis is correct? Which table of contents will be easier for the judges to use? Importantly, which table of contents is more likely to convince the judges that you think carefully about the details?

Example 11-A · A table of contents without an effective overview of the argument fails to persuade

---

TABLE OF CONTENTS

Page

These subheadings do not actually explain the party's legal argument. Rather they assert specific sub-points within the argument. By failing to connect these sub-points to the larger legal conclusions, the table of contents misses an opportunity to persuade.

Example 11-B · A persuasive table of contents

Read the point headings under "ARGUMENT" to see how the point headings provide a clear summary of the argument.

Notice also how the table of contents has a crisp look to it. That crisp look is achieved by using consistent tabs (each level is indented an additional 1/2 inch); by using hanging indents, which are explained in Chapter 9, *Refining Persuasive Arguments*, at Example 9-G; and by leaving a column of white space (interrupted only by leader dots) between the text of each point heading and the page numbers.

Example 11-C · A carelessly formatted table of contents fails to persuade

---

Inconsistent formatting makes the table look sloppy. Judges are apt to think that a sloppy brief is a prelude to sloppy thinking.

Page numbers do not line up.

The initial indentation at each level of the outline — after the Roman numeral, the capital letter, and the Arabic numeral — is inconsistent.

When the text of a point heading comes out as far as the page number, the page number is more difficult to see. Why make the judge's job more difficult?

When a point heading is a complete sentence, use final punctuation.

Bold and all caps are used inconsistently. Compare "VI. ARGUMENT" with "**VII. Conclusion.**"

TABLE OF CONTENTS

<u>Page</u>

C. Table of Authorities

The table of authorities is one of those dry sections of the brief. The table of authorities simply lists every authority that you rely on in your brief. Often, as the court is considering your case, the court will want to see how you addressed a particular case, statute, or other authority. The table of authorities allows the court to easily find where you have addressed each authority.

As with a table of contents, a professional-looking table of authorities will persuade the judges that you know the rules and pay attention to detail. Like other parts of the brief, the form the table takes typically is specified in the appellate rules.[5] While the table is often produced by support staff or computer programs, you must still make sure that it is accurate and looks good. Your name will be on the brief. Thus, you are ultimately responsible for everything between the covers of the brief—and for the covers themselves. The same consistency in formatting that makes a table of contents look professional and credible will also make your table of authorities (and you) look professional and credible. To see the difference between a professionally and unprofessionally presented table of authorities, compare Example 11-D with Example 11-E.

---

5. *See, e.g.*, Fed. R. App. P. 28(a)(3) (explaining that a table of authorities should have "cases (alphabetically arranged), statutes, and other authorities—with references to the pages of the brief.").

Example 11-D · A professionally presented table of authorities

TABLE OF AUTHORITIES

Cases

<u>Page</u>

In a professionally presented table of authorities, authorities are grouped by kind of authority, e.g., cases are listed separately from constitutions and statutes. Within each kind of authority, the individual authorities are listed alphabetically.

Consistent formatting and effective use of white space make a table easy to read.

Compare with Example 11-E. Note that the blank line between each authority and space between the citations and the page numbers (where only the leader dots appear) make the information easy to pick out.

Of course, all citations must be accurate.

Traditionally, as a courtesy, practitioners provided parallel citations so that attorneys could find an authority no matter which reporter was available. Court rules may dictate whether parallel cites are required.

Notice that no pinpoint page numbers are given. These citations are to an authority generally and not to a particular page within the authority.

Reid v. Georgia,
    448 U.S. 438, 100 S. Ct. 2752,
    65 L. Ed. 2d 890 (1980)... 23

State v. Bates,
    304 Or. 519, 747 P.2d 991 (1987) 2, 9, 14, 17, 20, 21, 24, 25, 26, 28

State v. Ehly,
    317 Or. 66, 854 P.2d 421 (1993)............ 16, 17, 18, 19, 20, 21, 22, 25

State v. Goodman,
    328 Or. 318, 975 P.2d 458 (1999)................................... 19

State v. Gulley,
    324 Or. 57, 921 P.2d 396 (1996).................................... 16

State v. Miglavs,
    186 Or. App. 420, 63 P.3d 1202,
    rev. allowed, 335 Or. 479 (2003) 10, 14, 15, 27, 28

State v. Valdez,
    277 Or. 621, 561 P.2d 1006 (1977).................... 17, 18, 20, 21, 24

Terry v. Ohio,
    392 U.S. 1, 88 S. Ct. 1868,
    20 L. Ed. 2d 889 (1968)... 17

United States v. Bignoni-Ponce,
    422 U.S. 873, 95 S. Ct. 2574,
    45 L. Ed. 2d 607 (1975)... 17

Constitutional and Statutory Provisions

Or. Const., Art. I, § 9.. 2, 14, 15, 16

Or. Rev. Stat. § 131.005(11)... 16

Or. Rev. Stat. § 166.250(11) 9

Other Authorities

4 Wayne R. La Fave, *Search and Seizure: A Treatise on the Fourth*
    Amendment (3d ed. 1996) 15, 23, 24

Webster's Third New Int'l Dictionary (unabridged ed. 1993) 24

Example 11-E · A table of authorities that is not professionally presented

TABLE OF AUTHORITIES
Cases

<u>Page</u>

State v. Bates, 747 P.2d 991 (1987) . . . . *passim*

State v. Ehly, 317 Or. 66, 854 P.2d 421 (1993) . . . . *passim*

State v. Goodman, 328 Or. 318, 975 P.2d 458 (1999) 19

State v. Gulley, 324 Or. 57, 921 P.2d 396 (1996) 16

State v. Miglavs, 186 Or. App. 420, 63 P.3d 1202, *rev. allowed,* 335 Or. 479 (2003)
. . . . 10, 14, 15, 27, 28

State v. Valdez, 277 Or. 621, 561 P.2d 1006 (1977) 17, 18, 20, 21, 24

Terry v. Ohio, 392 U.S. 1, 422 U.S. 873, 95 S. Ct. 2574, 45 L. Ed. 2d 607 (1975). 17

United States v. Bignoni-Ponce, 422 U.S. 873, 95 S. Ct. 2574, 45 L. Ed. 2d 607
(1975) 17

Reid v. Georgia, 448 U.S. 438, 100 S. Ct. 2752, 65 L. Ed. 2d 890 (1980) 23

Constitutional and Statutory Provisions

Or. Const., Art. I, § 9 . . . . 2, 14, 15, 16

Or. Rev. Stat. § 131.005(11) 16

Or. Rev. Stat. § 166.250(11) 9

OTHER AUTHORITIES

4 Wayne R. La Fave, *Search and Seizure: A Treatise on the Fourth Amendment* (3d
ed. 1996) 15, 23, 24

Webster's Third New Int'l Dictionary (unabridged ed. 1993) 24

One good way to frustrate a judge and the judge's staff is to make your brief more difficult to use. Here, the lawyer has done just that in the following ways:

- Providing inaccurate citations (compare the *Terry* and *Bignoni-Ponce* cites)

- Providing inconsistent citations

- Failing to correctly alphabetize the list (where is *Reid v. Georgia*?)

- Failing to list the pages where the judge can find arguments citing *Bates* and *Ehly*

- Making the table difficult to read because citations and page numbers overlap and the absence of white space between each authority makes each authority difficult to pick out

Additionally, because your goal in providing a table of authorities is to be helpful to the court, whenever possible avoid using the term *"passim." Passim* is a Latin word meaning "throughout," "frequently," or "here and there."[6] A table of authorities may use the word *passim* rather than provide specific page numbers when an authority appears so frequently in a brief that listing every page on which that authority appears would be more overwhelming than helpful. No uniform rule exists about when to use *passim* as opposed to listing specific pages, but many courts discourage the use of *passim.*[7] Simply keep in mind what will be most helpful to the court, and then make your decision. As a rule, judges will likely find it more helpful to see the exact pages in which you have cited an authority, even if you have cited the authority frequently.

---

6. *The American Heritage Dictionary* 1323 (3d ed. 1992).

7. *See, e.g.*, Or. R. App. P. 5.35(3) ("Reference to '*passim*' or '*et seq.*' in the index of authorities is discouraged.").

D. Statement of Jurisdiction

The federal rules require a statement of jurisdiction. In this section, you must state the basis for the district court's jurisdiction, the basis for the appellate court's jurisdiction, the relevant dates demonstrating that the appeal is timely, and the basis for claiming that the judgment or order appealed from is appealable,[8] as in Example 11-F. Often, the easiest way to provide this information is in chronological order. For example, of the events that need to happen to establish appellate jurisdiction, the district court must first have jurisdiction, so describe that first. Then, the district court must enter a judgment or appealable order, so describe that next. And so on. As with the other sections discussed above, to make this section persuasive, make it complete, concise, and error-free.

Example 11-F · Statement of jurisdiction

The district court had jurisdiction of this action under 28 U.S.C. §§ 1331 and 1346(a)(2) (2012). The district court granted plaintiff's motion for summary judgment and entered a permanent injunction on June 10, 2015. Defendants filed their notice of appeal on July 5, 2015, within the 30-day time limit allowed by Federal Rule of Appellate Procedure 4(a)(1)(A). This court has jurisdiction under 28 U.S.C. § 1291 (2012), which provides for review of all final decisions of district courts.

The trial court's jurisdiction is established in the first sentence.

The court's appellate jurisdiction is established in the second and last sentences. Under 28 U.S.C. § 1291, federal courts of appeals have jurisdiction from all final decisions of district courts. Summary judgment and a permanent injunction are final decisions.

The timeliness of the appeal is established by stating the rule establishing a 30-day timeline for filing the notice of appeal (Fed. R. App. P. 4(a)(1)(B)), the date of the final decisions, and the date the notice of appeal was filed.

E. Issue (or Question) Presented[9]

Finally, in the issue (or question) presented you have an opportunity to write some beautiful prose, foreshadowing your argument or arguments. Here, you must begin to put some careful thought into how you want to pitch your case. "In law," Supreme Court Justice Frankfurter explained, "the right answer usually depends on putting the right question."[10]

The issue presented serves several functions. First, it tells the court what legal issue is presented by the appeal. For example, it may tell the court that the very specific question in the case is not whether violent video games are bad for children, but whether, under the First Amendment, a state is required to demonstrate a direct causal link between violent video games and physical and psychological harm to minors before the state

---

8. Fed. R. App. P. 28(a)(4).

9. The terms "issue presented" and "question presented" are used interchangeably. Choose the phrase that is used in your jurisdiction. Also, if more than one issue is raised in the appellate brief, make your chosen term plural, as in "issues presented" or "questions presented."

10. *Estate of Rogers v. Comm'r*, 320 U.S. 410, 413 (1943) (Frankfurter, J.).

can prohibit the sale of the games to minors.[11] Because it precisely defines the legal issue the court is to consider, the issue presented is a prime opportunity for persuasion.

Second, the issue presented section allows you to frame that issue in an advantageous way.[12] A good issue presented will concisely present a legal issue with just enough facts to give it context and to persuade. To persuade, the question presented should suggest an answer that is favorable to your client. Some appellate lawyers will specifically aim for a question presented that leads to a "yes" answer, believing that creating a question that leads to a "yes" answer has the most persuasive value.

Finally, after reading the issue presented, a judge should be intrigued; she should be motivated to read the rest of the brief to discover your argument about what the answer should be.

Questions Presented in Objective vs. Persuasive Writing

You have probably already figured this out, but the questions presented in objective writing, such as a memo, are very similar to the questions presented in persuasive writing, such as a brief. In both cases, the question presented must be concise and accurate and describe the key facts on which the issue will turn.

The difference between the two lies in the dual function of the question presented in an appellate brief. In an appellate brief, the question presented not only narrows the issue and informs the reader, but also is an opportunity to begin persuading.

---

1. The components of an effective issue presented

An effective issue presented will usually have three parts:

- The controlling law
- The determinative facts
- The legal conclusion that is at issue

One easy way to present all three parts of an effective issue presented is in the "Under-Does-When" format.[13]

---

11. *See Brown v. Entm't Merchants Ass'n*, 564 U.S. ___ , 131 S. Ct. 2729 (2011).

12. For a more detailed discussion about effectively constructing a question presented, see Christine Coughlin, Joan Malmud Rocklin & Sandy Patrick, *A Lawyer Writes: A Practical Guide to Legal Analysis* 216-24 (2d ed. 2013).

13. We believe the originators of this format are Laurel Currie Oates, Anne Enquist, & Kelly Kunsch, *The Legal Writing Handbook: Analysis, Research, and Writing* (1st ed. 1993).

> **Under** the controlling law
>
> **Does/Is/Can** the legal conclusion result
>
> **When** the determinative facts occur

You can see each of these parts in Example 11-G.

Example 11-G · An effective question presented in three parts

---

Under Wisconsin state common law, which requires specificity in contracts, does an apple grower breach his contract when an apple grower contracts to supply 10,000 bushels of Scarlet Gala apples to a distributer, but delivers only Royal Gala apples?

Of the three parts necessary for an effective question presented, the most critical—and often most difficult—is the selection of determinative facts. Those facts can suggest the "yes" or "no" answer that is favorable to your client. And it is the facts that provide you with the opportunity to leave the court intrigued about the arguments that will follow. Selecting those facts can, however, be difficult because you cannot include every determinative fact. Doing so would create an overly long and unreadable question presented. Rather, you must select those facts that are *most* determinative and favorable to your client, and you must describe those facts accurately and precisely.

You can see how Example 11-G above has effectively framed the issue. After reading Example 11-G, you may suspect that the answer is "yes." You likely know that the law requires "specificity in contracts." You also know from the facts given that the contract specified Scarlet Gala apples, yet no Scarlet Gala apples were delivered—only Royal Gala were. Thus, this question presented persuades while it explains the legal issue the court must address.

Should You Use "Whether" in Your Question Presented?

Many commentators suggest that you should not begin your question presented with the word "whether." As a general matter, beginning a sentence with "whether" often leads to long and convoluted sentences that will be difficult for the judge to read. But practices vary, and you should look at briefs filed by experienced practitioners in the court in which you are appearing. Moreover, there is one major exception to this advice: the Supreme Court of the United States. Traditionally, and continuing today, in the Supreme Court, the question presented begins with "whether."

2. One or more sentences?

Traditionally, the issue presented was written as a single sentence; however, in crafting the issue presented, you may have the option to use multiple sentences. If your local rules and customs allow, and if the question presented does not reasonably fit into one sentence, consider using more than one sentence to present the question. Compare the two versions of the same question presented, provided in Examples 11-H and 11-I.[14]

Example 11-H • **A weak question presented: too much information forced into one sentence**

Whether, when the legislature amends the law so that a sentence may ◄——— Under this rule, extend to a youth defendant's 25th birthday, when previously it could extend only to the youth defendant's 21st birthday, and the youth defendant here was found guilty of violating a provision of the juvenile code before the law was   when these facts occur, amended, but who was committed to juvenile detention until his 25th birthday after the amendment, that sentence violates the *ex post facto* clauses of the ◄——— does this conclusion result? Oregon Constitution.

Example 11-I • **An effective question presented: information is divided into sentences of reasonable length**

The Oregon Constitution prohibits a retroactive increase in "punishment" ◄— Under this rule, for a "crime." In 1994, the defendant was sentenced to juvenile detention until his 21st birthday — the maximum time then allowed under Oregon's juvenile code. In 1995, the legislature allowed juvenile sentences to extend to a   when these facts occur, juvenile's 25th birthday. In 1997, the juvenile court committed the defendant to juvenile detention until his 25th birthday. Was the four-year increase to ◄——— does this conclusion result? defendant's sentence an increase in "punishment" for a "crime" such that it violates Oregon's constitution?

The second version, Example 11-I, is preferable because it is written in understandable sentences of reasonable length. Moreover, it still contains all the same information that is included in the single-sentence "under-does-when" format.

3. Incorporating the standard of review

Finally, in framing the issue presented, consider the relevant standard of review. Framing the issue presented in terms of the relevant standard of review shows the court that you recognize the importance of

---

14. The questions presented in Examples 11-H and 11-I are derived from *State ex rel. Juvenile Dep't v. Nicholls*, 87 P.3d 680 (Or. Ct. App. 2004).

standards of review and reminds the court what the relevant standard is. Consider Example 11-J. By framing the issue in terms of an abuse of discretion, the writer immediately has the court leaning in his favor. After reading the question presented in Example 11-J, the judge likely will be thinking two things: "This lawyer speaks my language!" and "It will take a lot to convince me that the lower tribunal abused its discretion."

Example 11-J · Incorporating the standard of review

Oregon Uniform Trial Court Rule 5.050 provides, "There must be oral argument if requested by the moving party in the caption of the motion or by a responding party in the caption of a response," but gives the court discretion in determining the time allowed for the argument. The court granted 15 minutes for oral arguments on the question of whether the defendant would be permitted to substitute counsel two days before trial was to begin. Did the trial court abuse its discretion in allowing 15 minutes for oral argument?

You are most likely to incorporate the standard of review into your question presented when you won below (thus, you are the respondent) and the applicable standard requires deference to the trial court. For example, if you won below and the appellate court will review for an abuse of discretion or for clear error, reminding the appellate court of the deferential standard of review will tilt the question presented in your favor.

Because appellate judges are so familiar with the de novo standard for questions of law, appellate practitioners are less likely to incorporate the standard of review in the question presented when the standard of review is de novo. Nonetheless, if you lost below, and you want to emphasize that the question before the appellate court must be resolved with no deference to the lower tribunal, you should consider referring to the de novo standard in your question by, for example, using the phrase "as a matter of law."

If the applicable standard of review is debatable and you intend to argue that a certain standard should apply, you should draft a question presented devoted solely to that issue.

F. Statement of the Case

Appellate rules also require a statement of the facts, a statement of the case, or both.[15] Those sections explain the facts—both historical and procedural—that are relevant to the issues on appeal. Chapter 12, *Statements of Fact and of the Case,* discusses how to draft those sections.

---

15. *See, e.g.,* Fed. R. App. P. 28(a)(6).

G. Summary of the Argument

Most appellate court rules require a summary of the argument or arguments in the brief. The following provision is typical: "[An appellant's brief must contain] a summary of the argument, which must contain a succinct, clear, and accurate statement of the arguments made in the body of the brief, and which must not merely repeat the argument headings[.]"[16]

The summary should not be so long that it simply repeats the argument. Nor should it be so short that it does not give the judge a flavor of the argument ahead. The summary should be a readable, succinct summary of your argument. If the brief raises a number of issues, it may be appropriate to have separate summaries of argument for each issue.

Example 11-K is a summary of one argument.

Example 11-K · Summary of argument

Because the trial court correctly refused to give the defendant's requested jury instruction, this court should affirm the defendant's convictions.

After the jury began deliberations, the defendant tendered a jury instruction to the court. The proposed instruction would have told the jurors that they had to agree on the "specific factual theory alleged in each . . . count."

For several reasons, the court correctly refused to give the instruction. First, the proposed instruction referred to only two counts, when in fact, the jury had three counts before it; the proposed instruction would have confused the jury. Second, each of the three counts of sexual abuse was very fact-specific; because the jurors acquitted the defendant on two counts and convicted him only of one, they must have agreed on the underlying facts. Finally, although the jurors must agree generally about what occurred, the requirement of jury unanimity does not require agreement on factual details. Here, the only possible fact about which the jurors could have disagreed is whether the defendant touched the victim over her clothes or under them. That fact is not a material element of sexual abuse.

Thus, the trial court correctly refused to give the requested instruction, and this court should affirm the trial court's judgment of conviction.

The summary, which generally does not include citations to the record or to authority, describes the legal argument the judge will be considering. The summary primes the argument, making the full argument easier for the judge to digest.

Practitioners differ as to whether they prefer to write the summary before or after they have written the argument. You may choose to use the summary to outline your argument, writing it before drafting the complete argument. Doing so allows you to see your argument in its purist form, without supporting authority or detail. Alternatively, you may write your argument first, and then simply summarize it. Whichever ap-

---

16. Fed. R. App. P. 28(a)(7).

proach you choose, you must be sure that, in finalizing the brief, the summary and the argument are consistent. If the summary of argument has not been updated to reflect changes that you have made to the argument, you will have a confused judge on your hands.

H. Argument

You have finally reached the part of the brief in which you will perform your persuasive magic. Remember that by this time, the judge has seen the cover of your brief; the table of contents and the summary of the argument, both of which give an overview of the case; a statement of the issues presented; and the statement of the case, which presents the facts as you see them. If you have correctly prepared those parts of the brief, the judge will arrive at your legal argument knowing what the case is about, knowing what arguments she is about to read, and knowing that she is dealing with an intelligent, trustworthy lawyer. In short, she should be predisposed to be convinced.

Two earlier chapters, Chapter 8, *Developing Persuasive Arguments*, and Chapter 9, *Refining Persuasive Arguments*, explain in detail how to build a persuasive legal argument, whether for a trial motion or an appellate brief. No matter the format, your argument should be organized, concise, well-written, and supported by citations to the record (for factual assertions) or to authorities (for legal assertions). The argument section should include headings and, because those same headings will make up the table of contents, they should be descriptive and persuasive. You should use transitions, correct grammar, engaging sentence and paragraph structure, and accurate punctuation. In short, the argument section should be a professional, persuasive, easy-to-read chunk of persuasive prose.

One special aspect of appellate brief arguments deserves discussion. As you may remember, standards of review are important to appellate courts. Accordingly, incorporating the standard of review into your arguments is helpful. Indeed, the federal rules require that, in your argument, you identify the standard of review. Specifically, the rule states that, "for each issue, a concise statement of the applicable standard of review (which may appear in the discussion of the issue or under a separate heading placed before the discussion of the issues)" must be included.[17]

But, making the standard of review work *for* you is better than just setting it out in a separate section. The next several examples illustrate

---

17. Fed. R. App. P. 28(a)(8)(B); *see also, e.g.,* Or. R. App. P. 5.45(5) (requiring that the appellant's brief "identify the applicable standard or standards of review, supported by citation to the statute, case law, or other legal authority for each standard of review").

how to incorporate the standard of review into your argument. Consider Examples 11-L and 11-M, two versions of the same assertion, with a subtle difference.

Example 11-L • A less effective assertion because it does not incorporate the standard of review

---

The trial court erred in granting summary judgment in favor of the defendants on the ground that the statute does not violate the First Amendment.

Example 11-M • A more effective assertion because it incorporates the standard of review

---

The trial court erred as a matter of law in granting summary judgment in favor of the defendants on the ground that the statute does not violate the First Amendment.

Both statements assert that the trial court erred. The second one, however, inserts the phrase "as a matter of law." That phrase subtly reminds the appellate court that the trial court's ruling is reviewed de novo, with no deference to the trial court's view. That is, the phrasing reminds the court that the standard of review is relatively favorable to the appellant, and it shows the court that you know the standard of review. The phrasing demonstrates that you are speaking the same language as the appellate judges.

Here is another example. Suppose that you represent a defendant who won the jury trial below. During that trial, the trial court decided to exclude the plaintiff's evidence under Federal Rule of Evidence 403 on the ground that its probative value was substantially outweighed by the danger of unfair prejudice. The plaintiff is now appealing. Now compare Examples 11-N, 11-O, and 11-P. Those examples show three versions of a statement you might make in response to the plaintiff's brief claiming that the trial court erred in excluding the evidence:

Example 11-N • Assertion, but no reference to the standard of review

---

The trial court did not err in excluding the evidence under Federal Rule of Evidence 403.

Example 11-O • Assertion with direct reference to the standard of review

---

The trial court did not abuse its discretion in excluding the evidence under Federal Rule of Evidence 403.

Example 11-P · Assertion with a reminder about what the standard of review means

---

Although this court or another court might have ruled differently, the trial court did not abuse its discretion in excluding the evidence under Federal Rule of Evidence 403.

The first version, Example 11-N, is adequate. It states your position.

The second version, Example 11-O, is better. It includes the standard of review when it says that "[t]he trial court did not abuse its discretion." By incorporating the "abuse of discretion" language, Example 11-O reminds the appellate judge that a great deal of deference is owed to the trial court's decision.

The third version, Example 11-P, is a more forceful way of including the standard of review. As you will recall, an issue is reviewed for an abuse of discretion when the issue could be resolved in a number of permissible ways, and the only question is whether the trial court chose one of several permissible resolutions. Thus, by reminding the appellate judge that "this court or another court might have ruled differently," Example 11-P also reminds the court that the standard of review is abuse of discretion and that a great deal of deference is owed to the trial court's decision.

What makes the third version, Example 11-P, the most effective is that it talks to the appellate judge like a real person. That version addresses what the appellate judge might be thinking—"I sure wouldn't have ruled that way"—but reminds the judge of her responsibility—that the ruling below cannot be reversed simply because she would not have ruled that way. Thus, Example 11-P translates the legal standard, "abuse of discretion," into what it means for the appellate judge as she wrestles with the appeal before her.

Once you have decided to incorporate the standard of review, the question is where to do so. Because the standard of review is usually coupled with the conclusion you are seeking under that standard, the best place to remind the court of the standard of review is anywhere that you would assert the conclusion to that legal issue. As discussed in Chapter 9, *Refining Persuasive Arguments*, the three places where you will most often assert a conclusion is in a point heading at the outset of an argument, the topic sentence that begins an argument, and the final sentence that sums up an argument.

Consider incorporating the standard of review into those three places. Doing so (1) enhances your credibility by showing the court that you understand the importance of standards of review; (2) strengthens your argument if the standard of review is favorable to your position; and (3) forces both you and the court to focus on the legal issue in light of the standard of review.

I. Conclusion and Relief Sought

The final section of the brief is the conclusion and relief sought. As with some of the other parts of the brief, this section often receives too little attention. Spending a few extra minutes to carefully think about this section and to draft it accordingly will enhance your brief and avoid confusion regarding what you really want the court to do.

The look of this section varies among appellate courts. In some courts, this part of the brief consists of something like the summary of argument, followed by a request for relief, as in Example 11-Q.

Example 11-Q · Conclusion that summarizes and states relief sought

In conclusion, this court should reverse Defendant's conviction. As explained above, the trial court erred in denying Defendant's motion to exclude the evidence of Defendant's mental illness on the ground that it was irrelevant. But even if the court upholds Defendant's conviction, it should reverse and remand for resentencing. That is so because, for the reasons set out above, Defendant's sentence is cruel and unusual in violation of the Eighth Amendment.

In other courts, the conclusion is simply another formulaic section, often consisting of a single sentence, as in Example 11-R or 11-S.

Example 11-R · Formulaic conclusion and request for relief

For the foregoing reasons, the trial court's judgment should be reversed.

Example 11-S · Another formulaic conclusion and request for relief

Therefore, the judgment should be reversed.

Check the rules, ask for sample briefs from your colleagues, or search for briefs written by well-respected attorneys in your jurisdiction to determine how this section should look.

Think carefully about what relief you seek from the court and make sure (1) that the court can grant the requested relief in light of its authority and the procedural posture of the case and (2) that the relief sought is consistent with the arguments made in the brief. For example, asking the appellate court to simply "reverse the judgment" is not always appropriate. Your request may be to vacate the judgment, to modify the judgment, to remand for reconsideration, or to remand for entry of an order directing a party to take a certain action.

Whether you write a short summary followed by a request for relief, or you simply make a request for relief, put some thought into what relief you are requesting. If the only argument in your brief is that the trial court erred in the sentence it imposed in a criminal case, the only relief you can request is a remand for a revised sentence. Your conclusion should not assert, "Defendant's convictions should be reversed." In short, make sure that your request for relief follows from the arguments in the brief.

II. Respondent's Brief

After the appellant files an opening brief, the respondent can respond with her argument. Most of the same parts discussed above will also be included in a respondent's brief. Many courts, however, allow a respondent to accept parts of the appellant's brief and not repeat those parts in the respondent's brief. The federal rules, for example, state that, unless the respondent is dissatisfied with the appellant's statement, a respondent's answering brief need not include the jurisdictional statement, the statement of the issues, the statement of the case, or the statement of the standard of review.[18]

Some lawyers are loath to "accept" anything that their opponents have proposed. As a result, respondents often repeat those parts of the appellant's brief, with no substantive changes. You should not do that. If you accept certain parts of the appellant's brief, you serve a number of goals. First, you save space in your brief that can be devoted to persuasive writing, rather than repetition. Second, you help yourself and the court pinpoint where the disagreement is. For example, if you accept the appellant's statement of the case, everyone is on the same page about which facts will be relevant to the appeal. Third, accepting parts of the appellant's brief saves the judge time and energy. If the judge does not have to spend time determining whether your slightly different statement of jurisdiction means that you really disagree or if you are just being overzealous, the judge has more energy to consider your argument.

Although a respondent's brief need not include all the sections that the appellant's brief includes, it should be largely self-contained. Judges often read briefs away from their offices and in pieces. Thus, your respondent's brief should stand on its own. For example, instead of simply stating that appellant's argument is wrong, make sure to give sufficient context so that the judge will remember the argument that you are rebutting. The goal is to achieve a good balance between redundancy and self-containment.

---

18. Fed. R. App. P. 28(b).

III. Appellant's Reply Brief

The other common type of brief is the reply brief, that is, the brief an appellant files in response to the respondent's brief. Reply briefs are not always allowed as a matter of right.[19] Before assuming that you can file a reply brief, check the rules. In addition, an appellant should never "save" an argument for the reply brief. The appellant should make his arguments in the opening brief. The reply brief should be used only to address points made in the respondent's brief that were not addressed in appellant's opening brief.

Reply briefs may be useful to respond to the following types of arguments that a respondent makes: that the case has become moot after your opening brief was filed; that a claim of error raised in your opening brief is not preserved or that the claimed error is harmless; that a new authority, which came out after you filed your opening brief, supports the respondent's position; or that the record supports a different view of the facts from that set out in your opening brief.

Finally, do not file a reply brief unless you have something to say. If your reply brief will merely reiterate the points you made in your appellant's brief, do not file one; the court will be grateful.[20]

---

19. For example, under the Oregon Rules of Appellate Procedure, the appellant in a criminal case is not allowed to file a reply brief without leave of court. Or. R. App. P. 5.70(3)(a). Other jurisdictions may have similar rules.

20. In fact, some advocates suggest that not responding is a sign of strength because it suggests the other party has not come up with any arguments that weaken your position. Other appellate advocates, however, disagree, pointing out that it is helpful to get the last word in. They also suggest that if an appellant does not file a reply brief, judges will assume that the appellant agrees with the respondent. However, we suggest that to avoid burdening the court with unnecessary reading, avoid filing a reply if you have nothing further to add.

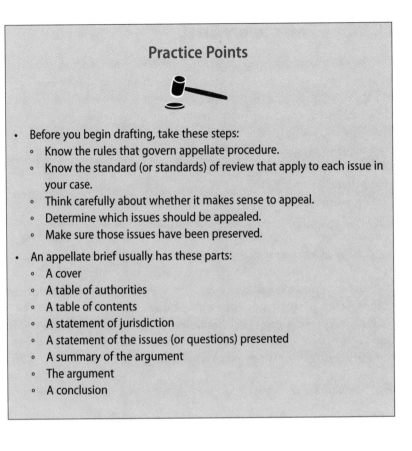

Practice Points

- Before you begin drafting, take these steps:
  - Know the rules that govern appellate procedure.
  - Know the standard (or standards) of review that apply to each issue in your case.
  - Think carefully about whether it makes sense to appeal.
  - Determine which issues should be appealed.
  - Make sure those issues have been preserved.

- An appellate brief usually has these parts:
  - A cover
  - A table of authorities
  - A table of contents
  - A statement of jurisdiction
  - A statement of the issues (or questions) presented
  - A summary of the argument
  - The argument
  - A conclusion

Statements of Fact and of the Case

At the heart of every legal issue lies a story. The word "story" does not refer to fiction. Rather, you are explaining the factual story that gave rise to the controversy before the court. Your role is to present a commanding narrative that will help the court view the facts from your client's vantage point.

In explaining your client's story, you have two goals. First, you are laying the factual foundation for the legal argument that will follow. You will need to explain all the facts that will be relevant to the court's analysis of the legal issue, and you will need to explain those facts with scrupulous accuracy. That means you must include all legally relevant facts, whether those facts hurt or help your client.

In explaining those facts, you have a second goal. Your second goal is to have the judge see the story from your client's perspective. You will want to make the busy judge care about your client. If you remember from Chapter 1, *The Nature of Persuasion,* the statement of facts lets you take advantage of a powerful mode of persuasion—*pathos*, that is, persuading by appealing to the audience's emotions. Although the emotional appeal will be subtle, you can influence how the judge connects with your client. You can highlight those facts that make your client seem reasonable and sympathetic and place difficult facts in context. In fact, if your client's story is explained effectively, the judge should be inclined to rule in favor of your client before he has even read the legal arguments.

To meet those goals, you will need to make deliberate choices about how you frame the conflict, portray the parties, and organize the story. This chapter addresses those deliberate choices.

I. Statements of Fact vs. Statements of the Case

The section of your brief in which you present your client's story will usually be designated as either the "statement of facts" or the "statement of the case." Whether you present a statement of facts, a statement of the case, or both will depend on the rules in your jurisdiction.

Some jurisdictions ask for both a statement of facts and a statement of the case. If the rules call for both, then the statement of facts will describe the historical facts—the conflict between the parties up until the time the case entered the court system—and the statement of the case will describe the procedural facts—those facts that relate to the case once it entered the court system.[1]

Sometimes, though, the court rules will ask for only a statement of facts or only a statement of the case. If so, then you will explain both the historical facts and the procedural facts in that one section.

---

1. The section that describes procedural facts sometimes has names other than statement of the case. For example, some jurisdictions require that procedural facts be explained in a "statement of the nature of the matter before the court" or through a "preliminary question."

Accordingly, you should read the procedural and local rules in your jurisdiction before you begin writing to determine whether the court will expect both a statement of facts and a statement of the case or whether one section will contain both the historical and procedural facts.

For convenience, we will refer to the "statement of facts" throughout. The same advice applies no matter the name of the section.

II. Present the Conflict and Your Client

Before you draft, take a step back and consider the role of "conflict" and "character" in your client's story. If you took a literature class in high school or college, you may remember that the three main elements of any good story are character, conflict, and resolution.[2] Those elements also come into play in drafting a persuasive and engaging statement of facts.

A. Frame the Conflict

The conflict that gave rise to your client's case may very well fall into one of several traditional kinds of conflicts. Thinking about the kind of conflict that exists in your case may give you new ways of thinking about your client, the problem before you, and how to present your client and your client's problem to the court. Chart 12-A lists some traditional kinds of conflicts found in stories.

Chart 12-A · Traditional kinds of conflicts[3]

- Person versus Nature
- Person versus Society (or Society versus Person)
- Person versus Self
- Person versus Machine
- Person versus Person
- Person versus God

Your story will likely present one of these conflicts. For example, say you represent a student with autism in a claim against the public school system. The heart of your client's claim is that the school is not pro-

---

2. Much has been written in recent years about the power of story in legal analysis. This chapter touches on those ideas only briefly. For more information on the topic, consider these resources: Brian J. Foley & Ruth Anne Robbins, *Fiction 101: A Primer for Lawyers on How to Use Fiction Writing Techniques to Write Persuasive Facts Sections*, 32 Rutgers L.J. 459 (2001); Ruth Anne Robbins, Steve Johansen, & Ken Chestek, *Your Client's Story* 87-119 (2013).

3. Foley & Robbins, *supra* note 2, at 472.

viding sufficient opportunities for the student in the mainstream class-room, in violation of a federal statute. In that case, you might frame the conflict as "person versus machine." Here, your client, the child with autism, is the person, and the machine is the behemoth school system that grinds forward without considering the individual needs of each student.

On the other hand, if you represented the school system, you would frame the conflict very differently. Then, you might frame the conflict as "person versus society," but your client, the school system, would be the person. You would humanize the school system by presenting it as a collection of people who do care, but who lack the financial and human resources to meet the needs of one student at the expense of hundreds or thousands of others. You would present the battle as one against a society that does not adequately fund education or give educators the resources they need to help individuals.

Too often, attorneys default to the most common conflict, "person versus person." Although that conflict nearly always exists in litigation, that framework may not lead a judge to intuitively side with your client. In a "person versus person" conflict one person must be portrayed as the hero and the other as the villain.[4] A judge, however, usually knows that neither party is entirely hero or villain. If the judge does not immediately agree with your portrayal, your narrative will have lost its power.

Although you probably will not explicitly name the kind of conflict that exists in your client's case, assessing the type of conflict may provide a valuable perspective that will help you use facts in the case in the most advantageous way. To assess the type of conflict, answer the following questions before you draft a statement of facts.

- What kind of conflict would best fit this story?
- What facts illustrate this conflict?
- If you must use "person versus person," what facts can you use to present the story in the most reasonable and objective way without overly glorifying one side or vilifying the other?

Once you have assessed how the conflict can best be framed, you are ready to think about how to portray your client and the other characters in the story.

B. Cast the Characters

In addition to a conflict, every legal story also has a cast of characters—major players and minor players.[5] The major player is the "pro-

---

4. *Id.*
5. *See id.* at 466-67; Robbins, Johansen, & Chestek, *supra* note 2, at 2; Ruth Anne Robbins, *Harry Potter, Ruby Slippers and Merlin: Telling the Client's Story Using*

tagonist," or the good guy, and the "antagonist," or the bad guy with whom the good guy is in conflict. Attorneys usually want to cast clients as the protagonists, or the good guys; at a minimum, they do not want their clients to be perceived as the bad guys.

When casting the story's characters, take the same thoughtful approach as you did when framing the conflict in the story. Although no character is completely a hero or villain, you may be able to cast your client in one of these traditional heroic roles, such as Warrior, Creator, Caregiver, Everyperson, Outlaw, Seeker, or Innocent.[6]

Think about what heroic archetype qualities you want to highlight. Then think about what facts support those characterizations. Do the same for the other major characters in the story, avoiding the blatant labels of villain or bad guy.

As you think about the characters in your story, answer these questions for each major player.

- What heroic archetype labels may best fit this character?
- What facts support this archetype label?
- What facts contradict or erode this label?
- What are this character's strengths or flaws?

Although we encourage you to think about your conflict and your client in heroic terms, that process is to get you thinking. Remember that the next step is to find the facts that will lead the judge to see your client and the conflict in a way that most benefits your client. You will never write, "My client is 'every man' in a conflict against machine." Rather, you will state facts that will allow a judge to reach that conclusion on his own. The rest of this chapter explains how to find and shape those facts.

III. Decide Which Facts to Include

As mentioned above, as you are thinking about the conflict and the role your client plays in the conflict, you will need to cull the record to find the facts that will make your perspective evident to the court.

As you read through the entire record, make a list of the facts that appear to be relevant. Include both positive ones that help your client's position and negative ones that undermine your client's position. You can then use this list to help you categorize and label your facts as well as to assess their value in the story.

---

the Characters and Paradigm of the Archetypal Hero's Journey, 29 Seattle U. L. Rev. 767 (2006).

6. Robbins, Johansen, & Chestek, *supra* note 2, at 777-78.

Usually, your facts will fall into three categories: legally significant facts, background facts, and emotional facts.

A. Include All Legally Significant Facts

When drafting a statement of facts, begin by focusing on the "legally significant facts." Legally significant facts are the facts necessary for the court to resolve the legal issues in the case. These facts may sometimes be called "key facts," "determinative facts," or "critical facts." No matter what name is used, these facts are the ones on which the court's decision will turn.

Your statement of the facts must include *all* legally significant facts, whether those facts help or hurt your client. If you omit a negative fact, you lose the opportunity to present that fact in context and minimize its impact. Moreover, the judge will see the negative facts anyway when reading the opposing party's brief and examining the record or supporting documents. Your work will be more credible and trustworthy if the judge sees that you have forthrightly presented *all* the facts. Instead of running from negative facts, take advantage of the opportunity to present the negative facts in a way that supports your theory of the case.

To ensure that you have included every legally significant fact, begin, as mentioned above, by reviewing the record. In addition, re-read your own argument. Highlight every fact that you relied on and make sure that that fact is in your statement of facts. Remember, judges do not like to be surprised, so be sure to include all the facts where the judge expects to see in them—in the statement of facts.

Finally, consider whether your statement of facts should point out the absence of a legally significant fact. Sometimes pointing out the absence of a fact can be helpful to your client. For example, in an intentional infliction of emotional distress case, the plaintiff must establish that he suffered "severe" emotional distress. As the defendant, you might point out that the plaintiff never contacted a doctor or therapist for treatment regarding his emotional distress. Later, you would argue that the absence of a visit to a doctor or therapist demonstrates that the plaintiff did not suffer severe emotional distress and that, therefore, the claim should fail. In such a case, the absence of a fact is important to note.

B. Include Enough Background Facts to Provide Context

Background facts are facts that explain the context in which the controversy takes place. Background facts allow the court to understand your client's situation and how the conflict arose; they provide a frame for the details necessary to resolve the case. Provide enough background facts for the legally significant facts to make sense. That said, be selective about the background facts that you include. Judges assume that the statement of facts focuses on legally significant facts. Including too many background facts will distract and confuse the judge about which facts are actually relevant to the legal issues.

In all forms of written communication, readers absorb a message when they are provided with context before detail; so too with statements of facts. Present the facts with enough contextual information so that the court can understand the detail.

C. Include Emotional Facts Selectively

Emotional facts are a kind of background fact that cause a reader to feel positively toward one party or negatively toward another; that is, they invoke *pathos*. Emotional facts are not necessary to resolve the legal issues, but they may help the judge understand what motivated a party to act or react in a particular way. Often, the judge will connect with your client through the emotional facts you choose.

Although emotional facts may help a judge sympathize with or understand your client better, you must choose your emotional facts with care. Too many emotional facts, especially when those facts seem irrelevant to the legal issues, may make a judge skeptical of the brief's objectivity. Accordingly, when constructing a persuasive statement of facts, choose emotional facts selectively.

Consider Examples 12-B and 12-C. Both offer openings to a statement of facts in which the primary issue is whether a university violated Title IX when it eliminated its women's golf team. The opening in Example 12-B provides background facts that help put the plaintiff, a member of the golf team, in a positive light and the university in a negative light.

Example 12-C attempts to do the same thing, but by spending too much time on facts that are not relevant to the legal issues, the emotional facts ultimately detract from the narrative.

Example 12-B • Choosing emotional facts to support the story

Plaintiff Katelyn Mason is a scholarship student who came to Defendant Central State University of Utah to play on its varsity golf team. Mason Depo. 8. Less than a year after Ms. Mason arrived, Central State eliminated the women's golf team. Blasher Depo. 15. The University plans to replace golf with a sport not yet recognized by the National College Athletic Association (NCAA): cheerleading. *Id.* at 22. Ms. Mason is now seeking to enjoin Central State from eliminating its golf team on the ground that eliminating golf and replacing it with cheerleading would violate Title IX. Am. Compl. 8.

In the 1970s, Title IX prompted Central State to establish its women's athletic program . . . .

Example 12-C · Too many emotional facts detract from the story

Again, the emotional facts are those that put Ms. Mason in a positive light and the university in a negative light; however, the extent of those details is likely to annoy a judge because the judge will struggle to understand their relevance and wonder why her time is being wasted.

For example, the plaintiff's status as an "A" student, her role as president of her class, the colleges that recruited her, and her golfing record both before and during college add details that are unnecessary and, together, will bog the judge down.

Plaintiff Katelyn Mason came to Defendant Central State University of Utah to play on its varsity golf team. Mason Depo. 8. Before arriving at Central State, Ms. Mason was an "A" student, president of her class, and a noted golf player. *Id.* at 9. She had won first place in the 2012 and the 2013 U.S. Juniors Invitational, and she had won second place at the Junior Ryder Cup in Perthshire, Scotland. *Id.* For all of these reasons, Ms. Mason was heavily recruited by other colleges and universities, including Williams College, The University of Hawaii, and Stanford University. *Id.* at 10-11. Nevertheless, she chose to attend and play golf for Central State. *Id.* at 11. Once at Central State, she had a successful year, contributing to the varsity golf team's 10-1 record and leading the team to its second-place finish at the NCAA Golf Championship. *Id.* at 12.

Despite the success of the golf team, Central State decided to eliminate the women's golf team after Ms. Mason had played for just one season. Blasher Depo. 15. The University decided to replace golf with a sport not yet recognized by the National College Athletic Association (NCAA): cheerleading. *Id.* at 22. A wide range of students and alumni protested the decision; the University nevertheless moved ahead, eliminated the golf team, and replaced it with a cheerleading team. *Id.* at 25-28. Ms. Mason is now seeking to enjoin Central State from eliminating its golf team on the ground that eliminating golf and replacing it with cheerleading would violate Title IX. Am. Compl. 8.

In the 1970s, Title IX prompted Central State to establish its women's athletic program . . . .

In addition to being selective about the emotional facts that you include, be sure to stick to the facts. Because emotional facts attempt to place one's client in a sympathetic light, some lawyers make the mistake of providing their opinion about their client (and the opposing party) rather than stating the facts. A lawyer's opinion or characterization of the facts is far less persuasive than the facts themselves; indeed, your opinion about the facts has no place in a statement of facts. Example 12-D attempts to provide the same background facts as Example 12-B, but instead Example 12-D (in the shaded text) states the writer's opinion about the facts.

Example 12-D · State the facts, not your opinion about the facts

Plaintiff Katelyn Mason is a gifted student and junior golf player. She came to Defendant Central State University of Utah to play on its varsity golf team. Mason Depo. 10-11. Less than a year after Ms. Mason arrived, Central State suddenly and inexplicably eliminated the women's golf team. Blasher Depo. 15. The University plans to replace golf with an activity that is not even a recognized sport: cheerleading. *Id.* at 22. Ms. Mason is now seeking to enjoin Central State from eliminating its golf team on the ground that eliminating golf and replacing it with cheerleading would violate Title IX. Am. Compl. 8.

In the 1970s, Title IX prompted Central State to establish its women's athletic program . . . .

For a good example of a brief that uses background and emotional facts selectively, look again at the brief of John Roberts in the *"Red Dog Mine"* case mentioned in Chapter 1. Without choosing overtly-emotional facts or inserting his opinions and characterizations, Roberts firmly establishes the economic importance of the mine to the remote community in a subtle way.

> Operating 365 days a year, 24 hours a day, the Red Dog Mine is the largest private employer in the Northwest Arctic Borough, an area roughly the size of the State of Indiana with a population of about 7,000. The vast majority of the area's residents are Inupiat Eskimos whose ancestors have inhabited the region for thousands of years. The region offers only limited year-round employment opportunities, particularly in the private sector . . . . Prior to the mine's opening, the average wage in the borough was well below the state average; a year after its opening, the borough's average exceeded that of the State.[7]

Roberts selected these facts with care. After reading this passage, a judge will undoubtedly realize than any decision adverse to the mine will negatively impact the people who live there. Thus, with a subtle use of *pathos*, his phrasing creates a commanding narrative that helps the legal reader connect to that litigant's side of the story.

In sum, be selective about the emotional facts you include, particularly when your purpose for using those facts is to paint your client in a positive light or to cast the opposing party's actions in an undesirable light. Moreover, when you do include such facts, be sure to stick to the facts rather than characterizing or inserting your opinion about those facts.

D. Include Procedural Facts

Together, the legally significant facts, the background facts, and the emotional facts tell your client's story from your client's perspective. In addition to that story, you will also need to tell the story of the case once it entered the court system. As with any story, the procedural story will be better told if you are selective. Once litigation begins, attorneys file a variety of different pleadings, they engage in discovery, and they file motions that address issues large and small. You do not want to detail all of it.

---

7. From Brief for Petitioner, *Alaska, Dept. of Environmental Conservation v. U.S. E.P.A*, 540 U.S. 461 (2004), available at 2003 WL 2010655 (citations omitted); *see also* Ross Guberman, *Five Ways to Write Like John Roberts*, http://www.legalwriting pro.com/articles/john-roberts.pdf.

Rather, simply highlight those points along the way that brought you to the current brief you are filing with the court. Thus, if you are drafting a motion for summary judgment, the only procedural history you might include is that the plaintiff filed a complaint and, after discovery, the defendant is now filing a motion for summary judgment. By contrast, if the case went to trial and the current dispute is whether the jury verdict should stand, you would likely note that a complaint was filed (in a civil case), that the case went to the jury, and that the verdict was returned. You would not note a motion for summary judgment, unless the motion for summary judgment raised the same issue that the current motion involves. Finally, if you are drafting an appellate brief, your statement of the procedural facts would identify each trial court decision that you believe was in error.

Notice that in drafting the procedural facts you again have the opportunity to persuade. Compare Examples 12-E and 12-F. Both examples point out the key procedural events: plaintiff filed a complaint, defendants moved to dismiss that part of the complaint that sought punitive damages, and the current appeal followed. Notice, though, the plaintiff's emphasis on the jury's decision to award her damages. She emphasizes the defendants' bad act (discriminating against her) and that she won below. A jury found in her favor, and jury decisions are difficult to overturn. By contrast, the appellants, who lost in the lower court, focus on what they believe was the trial court's error: allowing the plaintiff to seek punitive damages.

Example 12-E · Procedural facts from the plaintiff-respondent's perspective

---

Statement of the Case

On February 15, 2015, plaintiff-respondent Amy Russo filed a complaint against defendants-appellants, Williams University and Adam Lam. R. 3. The complaint alleges that Williams University and athletic director Adam Lam willfully and intentionally discriminated against the respondent on the basis of her gender by paying her unequal wages. R. 2. The complaint also alleged that, in response to Ms. Russo's stated intent to file a discrimination claim, Williams University and Adam Lam retaliated by firing her. R. 2.

On December 3, 2015, the district court judge denied the defendants' motion to dismiss Ms. Russo's claim seeking punitive damages under 29 U.S.C. § 215(a)(3). The case proceeded to jury trial. R. 85. The jury awarded Ms. Russo compensatory, liquidated, and punitive damages. R. 86. After the jury returned its verdict in favor of Ms. Russo, the defendants appealed. R. 92.

Respondent's recitation of procedural facts identifies all the important procedural steps that led to the appeal, but it also emphasizes that she won below.

Example 12-F • Procedural facts from defendants-appellants' perspective

Statement of the Case

In February 2014, plaintiff-respondent Amy Russo filed a complaint against defendants-appellants, Williams University and Adam Lam. R. 3. Before trial, the defendants sought to dismiss that part of Ms. Russo's complaint that sought punitive damages, arguing that the plain language of the Fair Labor Standards Act does not permit punitive damages. R. 80. The district court denied the motion, and after a jury verdict in favor of Ms. Russo, which included punitive damages, R. 86, the defendants filed this appeal. R. 92.

Appellant's recitation of procedural facts similarly describes all the important procedural steps leading to the appeal, but appellants focus on the decision that they believe to be in error and minimize their loss below.

E. Weed Out Irrelevant Facts

As you decide which facts to include, think carefully about which facts to exclude. Irrelevant details make it harder for the court to see which facts are important. They distract. Thus, aim to exclude any detail that is not relevant to the legal story or that do not explain the story from your client's perspective. The most common types of irrelevant material are dates, places, and names.

Specific dates can—and should—be excluded if that date is not legally significant. The date on which something occurred is not relevant if all that matters to your story is the order in which events occurred and not the precise date on which they occurred. Look at Example 12-G, an excerpt of the statement of facts for a case in which the legal issue stems from the quality of a good delivered under a contract. Since the issue in the case is not one of *when* the contract was negotiated and signed, all the dates are irrelevant and should be eliminated from, not only the legal argument, but the statement of facts as well.

Example 12-G • Irrelevant facts distract

On December 25, Defendant and Plaintiff began negotiating a contract for the sale of hops. Clark Dep. 2:16-22. They reached a tentative agreement on December 31, but on January 1, they determined that they were unsatisfied with that tentative agreement. Clark Dep. 22:1-23:2; Bruce Dep. 42:1-8. It was not until February 29 that they reinitiated negotiations. Clark Dep. 36:6-10; Bruce Dep. 55:16-56:10. The contract was finalized on April 1. Clark Dep. 41:6-10; Bruce Dep. 60:18-22.

Irrelevant dates are distracting. The judge will wonder whether these characters work only on holidays (and, by the way, was that a leap year?). Most likely, the judge is wondering, "Do I need to remember these dates?" Unless specific dates are needed, consider instead focusing on the sequence of events, as in Example 12-H.

Example 12-H · Re-write to omit irrelevant facts

The parties began negotiating the sale of hops in late 2012. Clark Dep. 2:16-22. Following on-again, off-again negotiations, they signed a contract in early April 2013. Clark Dep. 22:1-36:10, 41:6-10; Bruce Dep. 42:1-56:10, 60:18-22.

Keeping track of too many minor players' names also becomes tiresome and distracting for the judge. Thus, when introducing a minor character, it is usually best to introduce the minor character by that character's role in the story and to omit the person's proper name. For example, a minor player like "Investigating Detective Leonard Briscoe" or "Director of Operations, Erin Nalle," can be introduced as "the investigating officer" or "Director of Operations" in the facts and argument sections.

The primary parties and other significant players should be introduced by their names and their role in the story. Avoid using their status in the litigation. For example, in a civil proceeding you might introduce the parties by name and by their role in the story. Then, throughout the rest of the statement of facts, you could call that major player by name or by their role (for instance, "landlord" or "employer"). You would not, though, tend to call the parties by their litigation status of plaintiff or defendant. A person's status in the litigation will not create as strong an image in the judge's mind and is, therefore, less useful.

Despite that general advice, one time when you might designate a major player by his litigation status (as opposed to his status in the story) is if you are a prosecuting attorney. If you are a prosecutor, "the defendant" may be the best designation because it reminds the court that the person has been charged with, or perhaps has even been convicted of, a crime. On the other hand, a defense attorney would want to personalize his client and refer to the person by name.

Compare the two excerpts from a statement of facts in Examples 12-I and 12-J. The argument in that case is about whether evidence obtained from a search must be excluded because the police obtained the search warrant by relying on evidence from an involuntary confession. Accordingly, details about who executed the search warrant and where and when it was executed are irrelevant.

Example 12-I · Irrelevant facts distract

Officers Zal and Izaguirre executed the warrant at 10:34 a.m. at the defendant's residence, located at 234 Fifth Street, Canton, Ohio, 44701. Zal Aff. 1.

Example 12-J · Omitting irrelevant facts is better

Police officers executed the warrant at the defendant's trailer. Zal Aff. 1.

> **Once Upon a Time . . .**
>
> Sometimes when it comes time to write the statement of facts, you are so deep in the weeds that it is difficult to know where to begin. In that case, begin your statement of facts with "Once upon a time." Doing so will likely help you back up and provide the context your reader needs. Of course, delete the "Once upon a time" before you file your brief with the court.

To be sure, some dates, some names, and some places will be important enough to the story to warrant specificity. For example, if the issue before the court is whether an action was filed within the applicable statute of limitations, the exact dates when events occurred become extremely important. The point is to think about the details your reader will need (and which she will not need), so you can leave out those distracting details.

IV. Organize Your Statement of Facts

Once you have determined which facts to include in your statement of facts, you must decide how to organize the facts. A facts section is usually organized chronologically, topically, or perceptually, depending on the type of issues you are presenting and the complexity of the story. No matter how you choose to organize the facts section, always start the facts in a way that will grab the reader's attention and provide necessary context for your client's story.

A. Create an Opening Paragraph that Provides Context and Draws the Reader In

The first paragraph, and even the first sentence, of your facts section is a great place to attract the judge's attention and entice the judge to read more. A famous litigator once said that the opening paragraph of a statement of facts should be like a two-minute morality play for the court that establishes the characters and frames the conflict.[8] Remember, the statement of facts is your first opportunity to bring the parties and the legal issues to life.

In addition, the first paragraph or two of your statement of facts should provide context for your reader by introducing the parties, their

---

8. Conversation of one author with attorney Rudolph Aragorn, international litigator at White & Case law firm (April 2014).

status in the story, and the crux of the conflict between the parties. Giving even minimal context is more effective than jumping into the chronological details of the story without any context.

For example, in Example 12-K, look at how the lawyer uses the first two paragraphs to introduce the parties and the crux of the dispute. In explaining the crux of the dispute, the attorney stayed focused on the facts and answered the judge's basic questions: Who are the parties involved? Why is one party suing the other party? In this example, the first paragraph grabs the reader's attention, tells who the parties are, and directly presents the crux of the issue at hand.

Example 12-K · Opening paragraphs of a statement of facts[9]

Defendant's two pit bulls, running loose and without permission, spotted Plaintiff's pet cat and mauled her to death. R. 10. Plaintiff ran from her house and attempted to stop the attack, but could not. R. 10. After the dogs dropped the mauled cat and ran away, Plaintiff saw that her cat was gravely injured but still alive. R. 13. She immediately rushed her cat to the veterinarian, but the cat died en route. R. 14-15.

The trial court concluded that Defendant was negligent and awarded Plaintiffs $1,000 in compensatory damages but denied Plaintiff's claims for negligent infliction of emotional distress and loss of companionship. R. 40, 52-53. Plaintiff now appeals the trial court's denial of her claim for negligent infliction of emotional distress. R. 72.

Similarly, the opening paragraph in Example 12-L provides context and begins to generate sympathy for an employer who has fired an employee. In that case, the employer's perspective is that the employee is suing the company because she is a disgruntled employee who has been fired. Thus, the employer's statement of facts opens with the fact that the employee was dismissed after receiving a negative job review.

A statement of facts in that same case, but written from the employee's perspective, would open with different facts, as in Example 12-M. That opening introduces the employee as a successful, long-term employee, who was fired only after she became concerned that her employer was violating environmental regulations.

Example 12-L · The opening paragraph in a persuasive statement of facts (defendant's perspective)

On November 29, 2015, plaintiff Julie Stark was dismissed from her employment with defendant Michigan Power & Electric, Company (MPE). (Dep. Julie Stark, 10:21-22.) Her termination followed a negative performance review.

---

9. Based on *Lockett v. Hill*, 51 P.3d 5, 6 (Or. Ct. App. 2002).

(Dep. Julie Stark 10:1-2.) Ms. Stark now claims she is entitled to protection from being dismissed because she is a whistle-blower. (Pl.'s Compl. ¶¶ 15-22.)

Example 12-M • The opening paragraph in a persuasive statement of facts (plaintiff's perspective)

Plaintiff Julie Stark, a long-time employee of defendant Michigan Power & Electric, has also been a long-time advocate for a healthy planet. (Dep. Julie Stark, 8:2-16; 22:4-23:10.) Thus, in October 2015, when Julie Stark discovered that MPE might be ignoring environmental regulations, she spoke out. (*Id.* at 11:6-12.) MPE then fired her. (*Id.* at 12:16-22.)

The opening paragraphs of both Example 12-L and Example 12-M provide context, name the parties, and begin to provide sympathy for each client. Although they sound very different, each is an accurate presentation of the facts.

Sometimes, however, the opening paragraph will not be so exciting, particularly when the underlying issue is a procedural one. Still, you can create an opening paragraph that will introduce the parties and conflict and focus the judge's attention on the critical facts, as in Example 12-N.

Example 12-N • Opening paragraph of statement of facts in which only issue on appeal is a procedural issue

---

This case involves a dispute under the Clean Water Act, 33 U.S.C. 1251 *et seq.*, in which plaintiff Yalohosee Riverkeepers alleged that defendant Zimels Performance Fabrics illegally discharged effluent into navigable river waters. R. 2-3. Although trial took three weeks and the record is voluminous and technical, the sole issue on appeal is whether the trial court correctly denied defendant Zimels's motion for a three-week continuance under the circumstances described below. R.55. Because the sole issue on appeal is procedural, this statement of facts details only the events surrounding the trial court's ruling on the motion for a continuance.

No matter whether your underlying issues are exciting factual ones or drier procedural ones, fashion your first paragraph in a way that introduces the parties and the conflict, grabs (or at the very least focuses) the judge's attention, and begins to shape the version of the story your client wants to tell.

B. Choose a Logical Organization

After providing an opening that introduces the parties and the problem from your client's perspective, you must decide on an organizational structure for the facts that follow. You can organize chronologically (telling facts in the order in which the events occurred), topically (presenting facts by topics like issues or categories), or perceptually (presenting facts from the various participants' vantage points).

Facts are usually set forth in chronological order because readers (including judges) tend to better comprehend stories told in sequence. Accordingly, you will most often present facts in chronological order.

Although chronological order may be your default method of organization, be open to using other organizational options. A topical organization might make sense if, for example, you need to discuss both the company's corporate structure and the facts about the allegedly defective pressure cooker that the company produced. Likewise, a perceptual organization might make sense if your case involves a business transaction that occurred in three locations. You might, then, discuss how the transaction developed from the perspective of the people in those three locations.

You may even use a combination of these organizational schemes. Imagine, for example, that you have a contractual dispute that involves three very different issues under the contract with different sets of facts relevant to each issue. You could have a topical organization for each contract provision that is in dispute, but then you could tell the facts regarding the execution of that part of the contract chronologically.

One organizational approach that is rarely a good idea is to simply summarize the testimony of each witness in the order it is given, whether that be by deposition in advance of trial or on the witness stand during trial. For one thing, the testimony of every witness may not be relevant to the issues. Second, summaries can be choppy, thus interrupting the flow of a good story. Finally, summaries can be unclear, not showing how the events or characters of the story are connected. Because witnesses may be deposed or called to the stand "out of order"—usually for scheduling reasons—merely summarizing the record sequentially may simply frustrate and confuse the judge. Frustrated and confused judges are harder to persuade than happy and interested judges.[10] Your job is to figure out how the evidence connects and show those connections to the judges.

---

10. Look at how one court responded to a statement of facts presented, not as a cohesive story, but as individual witness summaries:

> We base this summary of the facts on our review of the record, assisted by plaintiff's helpful statement in her brief. In its brief, the City [the defendant] fails either to describe the facts most favorably to the jury's verdict or to do so in narrative form. Rather, it summarizes each witness' [sic] testimony seriatim, requiring the court to attempt to determine the relationship between the events that the various witnesses described. [Thus] . . . the City fails to comply with . . . basic principles of effective appellate practice.

Storm v. McClung, 4 P.3d 66, 68 n.1 (Or. Ct. App. 2000), *aff'd*, 47 P.3d 476 (Or. 2002).

When in doubt, you should organize your facts chronologically. You should not, however, be wedded to that approach. When deciding on an organization, think about how you could most easily explain the story to a friend over a dinner conversation. Using that organizational order allows you to tell the story clearly and succinctly.

C. Use Point Headings to Guide Your Reader

Point headings in your statement of facts operate much as they do in your argument. Point headings help the reader understand your organization, and they alert the reader to the main points the section will address.

The most significant difference between point headings in your argument and point headings in a statement of facts is that, in your statement of facts, the point headings do not assert a legal conclusion. Rather, they describe the kinds of facts that will be addressed in that section of your statement of facts. In other words, your point headings will be descriptive, rather than assertive.

Another difference is that, in your statement of facts, the point headings may not be complete sentences. When arguing, you want to assert a complete idea; thus, a full sentence that clearly asserts your point is both appropriate and necessary. By contrast, when your goal is to describe, rather than assert, a descriptive label may be sufficient, as in Example 12-O.

Example 12-O • A descriptive point heading

C. The night of June 21.

Of course, you are not prohibited from using a full sentence; however, if you do, be certain that you are asserting an indisputable fact and not making an argument. Compare Examples 12-P and 12-Q. Example 12-P states a fact. Example 12-Q, in contrast, likely asserts an argument.

Example 12-P • A full sentence as a descriptive point heading

---

C. Julie McGee died on the night of June 21.

Example 12-Q • A full sentence that may assert an argument

C. Defendant killed Julie McGee on the night of June 21.

One last point with respect to point headings: If you choose to include point headings, be consistent. If you use a full sentence for one point heading, use full sentences throughout. If you choose not to use full sentences, do that throughout.

D. Close Your Statement of Facts

Once you have crafted a strong opening paragraph and organized your facts logically, spend some time on your last paragraph or at least the last sentence of the statement of facts. The final paragraph or sentence should provide closure to the statement of facts, leaving the judge ready to read your arguments. Importantly, though, your statement of facts should end with a fact, and not a legal argument. For example, your final sentence in a statement of facts might be written as in Examples 12-R or 12-S. You would not want a final sentence as in Example 12-T.

Example 12-R · A final sentence that states a fact

Defendant now appeals. R. 72.

Example 12-S · A final sentence that states a fact

Plaintiff then filed a complaint alleging that she was fired in retaliation for exercising her protected First Amendment rights. Pl's. Compl. 4-5.

Example 12-T · A final sentence that (inappropriately) argues

As explained next, Plaintiff was fired in retaliation for exercising her protected First Amendment rights.

V. Create a Persuasive Statement of Facts

Because the statement of facts is the court's first introduction to your client and the controversy before the court, you will want to take advantage of every opportunity to persuade. The tone of the section, the placement of information, and even word choice can have an impact on the judge reading your motion or brief. Remember, your goal is to make the judge want to rule for your client. The way in which you write your statement of facts can influence how much the judge wants to rule for your client. The following strategies will help you draft a more persuasive statement of facts.

A. State Facts Accurately

Of all the techniques for creating a persuasive statement of facts, the most important technique is to state facts accurately and precisely. An accurate description of the facts means that any fact you describe in your statement of facts is consistent with the record in the case. An accurate statement of facts is one that includes *all* facts that will be relevant to the court's decision, whether those facts are helpful to your client or not.

Zealous advocacy should never trump your duty to be accurate. Although you want to present the facts from your client's perspective, never overstate or misrepresent a fact. Overstating or misrepresenting facts not only triggers ethical questions about your practice, but doing so can alienate your reader, especially if the reader is a judge. The facts will not always be good for your client. Some facts may be quite detrimental. Nevertheless, never avoid the detrimental facts. As discussed above, the statement of facts is your place to put them in perspective. It can, of course, be tempting to stretch the facts to serve your client, particularly when you know your client has been wronged. However, you will best serve your client by becoming an advocate that the court trusts. You will build that reputation for trustworthiness and, thereby, serve your clients best by always telling the truth, and never exaggerating, misstating, or lying. Writing a scrupulously accurate statement of facts builds credibility from the beginning.

> **Reminder!**
>
> To preserve your credibility with the court, never overstate, misrepresent, or omit a relevant fact, even if that fact is detrimental to your case. Instead, put that fact in context and explain it from your client's perspective.

B. Maintain a Reasonable Tone

Strive for a tone that suggests objectivity even while presenting the facts from your client's perspective. You may feel passionate about your client's claims, particularly after spending months (or years) on the case. Even so, judges are usually put off by highly emotional briefs; judges become wary or skeptical if the passion in the brief suggests that you are too close to the case to present your side objectively. Although your facts can be written to subtly evoke empathy for your client, keep an eye (or ear) on the tone of the section. Keep the tone objective and credible.

C. Use Strong Thesis Sentences When Appropriate

As explained in Chapter 9, *Refining Persuasive Arguments,* a "thesis" is a proposition put forward for consideration. In a legal argument, the proposition put forward for consideration is a legal conclusion. Thesis sentences can, however, also be used to great effect in a statement of facts. In a statement of facts, a thesis sentence proposes a factual conclusion. Beginning a paragraph with a thesis sentence can focus the judge on the fact you want the judge to learn after reading the paragraph.

Compare Examples 12-U and 12-V.[11] In Example 12-U, the prosecuting lawyer does not use a thesis sentence when presenting facts about a defendant who was convicted of a mass shooting. By contrast, in Example 12-V the prosecutor uses a thesis sentence to help the judge see the point that the facts support. In Example 12-V, the facts show that a pattern of violence had begun years before. By asserting that idea up front, the judge is primed to see the point the prosecutor wants to make.

Example 12-U • **A paragraph without a thesis sentence leaves the judge to reach her own conclusion about the facts**

Although the paragraph does a good job of presenting the facts chronologically, without a topic sentence, the judge will not know exactly what the paragraph is about. The paragraph is about much more than what happened when the defendant was four.

Defendant's interest in guns and knives began as early as age four. (Ex. 301, p. 860.) Defendant got "in trouble" in the second grade for bringing a knife to school. (Ex. 301, p. 972.) According to Defendant's fourth-grade teacher, Defendant had an "anger management problem." (Tr. 513.) Defendant would be aggressive if things did not go his way on the playground. (Tr. 513.) His fourth-grade teacher remembered Defendant throwing punches, placing other children in headlocks, and wrestling students to the ground. (Tr. 512.) He testified: "I think we were working on a behavioral management plan with our school counselor." (Tr. 510.) During that year, Defendant's disruptive behavior in the classroom sometimes would require his removal. In about the sixth grade, his interest expanded to bombs and explosives. (Ex. 301, p. 982.)

Example 12-V • **A strong thesis sentence can state the factual conclusion you want the court to reach**

With a strong thesis sentence, the judge will know what point the paragraph is making. By immediately understanding the context of the paragraph, the judge can focus on the detailed information.

Defendant's behavior problems and violent tendencies manifested themselves at an early age. Defendant's interest in guns and knives began as early as age four; in about the sixth grade, his interest expanded to bombs and explosives. (Ex. 301, p. 860.) Defendant got "in trouble" in the second grade for bringing a knife to school. (Ct.'s Ex. 301, p. 972.) According to Defendant's fourth-grade teacher, Defendant had an "anger management problem." (Tr. 513.) Defendant would be aggressive if things did not go his way on the playground. (Tr. 513.) His fourth-grade teacher remembered Defendant throwing punches, placing other children in headlocks, and wrestling students to the ground. (Tr. 512.) He testified: "I think we were working on a behavioral management plan with our school counselor." (Tr. 510.) During that year, Defendant's disruptive behavior in the classroom sometimes would require his removal. (Tr. 512.)

Although using thesis sentences within your statement of facts can be very effective, it can also be a little tricky. In a statement of facts, a the-

---

11. Examples 12-U, 12-V, and 12-W are based on Respondent's Brief at 3, *State v. Kinkel*, 56 P.3d 463 (2002) (CA A108593).

sis sentence must assert a factual conclusion that you want the judge to reach, and not a legal conclusion or an argument. Moreover, the facts that follow must, of course, support the assertion in the thesis sentence. Example 12-W shows an inappropriate thesis sentence when it appears in a statement of facts. The sentence is inappropriate because it asserts a legal conclusion rather than a fact.

Example 12-W · An inappropriate thesis sentence asserts a legal conclusion

---

Defendant began cultivating a mindset to commit murder during childhood. Defendant's interest in guns and knives began as early as age four. (Ex. 301, p. 860.) Defendant got "in trouble" in the second grade for bringing a knife to school. (Ex. 301, p. 972.) According to Defendant's fourth-grade teacher, Defendant had an "anger management problem." (Tr. 513.) Defendant would be aggressive if things did not go his way on the playground. (Tr. 513.) His fourth-grade teacher remembered Defendant throwing punches, placing other children in headlocks, and wrestling students to the ground. (Tr. 512.) He testified: "I think we were working on a behavioral management plan with our school counselor." (Tr. 510.) During that year, Defendant's disruptive behavior in the classroom sometimes would require his removal. In about the sixth grade, his interest expanded to bombs and explosives. (Ex. 301, p. 982.)

This thesis sentence is inappropriate because it assumes intent, an element in the underlying murder case. Because the writer asserts a legal conclusion rather than letting the facts speak for themselves, a judge is likely to become wary of whether the statement of facts is accurately presenting the facts or inappropriately slanting them in the party's favor.

Using thesis sentences in a statement of facts can be a very effective way of focusing the judge's attention on the point that you want to make. You must, however, craft your thesis sentences with care. You must avoid stating a legal conclusion, and you must be certain that the facts that follow clearly establish the proposition stated in the thesis sentence. Overstating what the facts will show will undermine your credibility.

D. Highlight Good Facts and Minimize Unfavorable Facts

Rarely, if ever, will you have a perfect set of facts. As discussed above, you are ethically required to include negative facts that are legally relevant to the court's analysis. Your job now is to highlight how the good facts support your legal arguments and minimize the impact of the inconvenient or undesirable facts, while ensuring that your statement of facts is accurate.

1. Use location to your advantage

One way to highlight favorable facts is to put them in "positions of emphasis"[12] within the section. We have previously discussed positions of emphasis in Chapter 9, *Refining Persuasive Arguments*. As explained there,

---

12. Mary Beth Beazley, *A Practical Guide to Appellate Advocacy* 122 (3d ed. 2010).

one of the best ways to emphasize your main points is to put them where a judge is most likely to see and process them. The eyes of most readers tend to rest on point headings, the first sentence of each paragraph, and the last sentence of each paragraph.[13] Thus, put the facts you want to emphasize in those positions. By contrast, disclose unhelpful information in the middle of a paragraph and in the middle of sentences, where that information is likely to receive less emphasis.

Consider Table 12-X. That table shows two different versions of the same statement of facts. The statement of facts comes from a case in which an employee alleged that her employer fired her because she was "about to report" a violation of the law to the authorities. The lawyer who wrote the statement of facts represents the employer. He will later be arguing that the employee was not "about to report," as required by statute.

Now, compare the two versions of the statement of facts provided in Table 12-X. First, read each statement of fact from start to finish. Which is better? Then, for each statement of fact, read the first and last sentence of each paragraph. Which statement of fact uses positions of emphasis more effectively? In particular, notice how the topic sentences in version one sets the stage for the employer's argument: the plaintiff is merely a disgruntled employee; she filed a report against the company because she was upset about being dismissed; she was not "about to report" a violation of law at the time of her dismissal; nor was she fired for that reason.

Table 12-X · Using positions of emphasis in a statement of facts

Version 1	Version 2
STATEMENT OF FACTS	**STATEMENT OF FACTS**
Plaintiff Julie Stark was an MPE employee who, on October 6, 2015, received a negative employment review. (Dep. Julie Stark 10:1-2.) Soon thereafter, on November 29, she was dismissed from MPE. (*Id.* at 10:21-22.) Four days after she was dismissed, Ms. Stark filed a complaint with the state attorney general alleging that defendant MPE had violated the federal Clean Air Act. (*Id.* at 11:1-4.) Ms. Stark contends that she should be protected from dismissal because she was about to report her allegations when she was dismissed. (Pl.'s Compl. ¶ 15.)	On November 29, 2015, Plaintiff Julie Stark was dismissed from her employment with defendant MPE. (Dep. Julie Stark, 10:21-22.) A month and a half before she was fired, Ms. Stark received a negative employment review. (*Id.* at 10:1-2.) After she was dismissed, Ms. Stark filed a complaint with the state attorney general alleging that MPE had violated the federal Clean Air Act. (*Id.* at 11:1-4.) Ms. Stark contends that she should be protected from dismissal because she is a whistleblower. (Pl.'s Compl. ¶ 15.)
In fact, Ms. Stark had let her concerns languish for months. (Dep. Julie Stark 11:22-12:1.) Sometime during the first few days of October, Ms. Stark	Sometime during the first few days of October, Ms. Stark downloaded a complaint form from the state attorney general's office, filled it out with allegations against MPE, and saved it to her

---

13. *Id.* at 122-23.

downloaded a complaint form from the state attorney general's office, filled it out with allegations against MPE, and saved it to her computer. (Dep. Julie Stark 11:6-11:18; *id.* at Ex. 1.) She never submitted the complaint—not that month, nor the following month. (*Id.* at 11:22-12:1.)

During that time, what she did do was express her anger at receiving a negative job review. (Dep. Eric Stark 22:3-23:12.) On October 6, Ms. Stark and her supervisor, Eric Block, reviewed her job performance. (*Id.* at 18:6-8.) Her evaluation stated, among other things, that she "fails to follow directions" and that she "lacks the degree of teamwork and cooperation that MPE seeks in its employees." (*Id.* at Ex. 1.) Ms. Stark responded by yelling at her supervisor that MPE was a bunch of "mega-polluters" and "criminals," that they would "live to regret it," and that she would "tell everyone." (*Id.* at 24:2-25:15.) It was not clear to her supervisor, Eric Block, what Ms. Stark was referring to. *Id.* at 26:4-8.

Two months followed after Ms. Stark's exchange with her supervisor. Still, she did not submit any complaint to the state Attorney General's office or to any other public official. (Dep. Julie Stark 11:22-12:15.) In fact, it was not until Monday, December 3, 2015, four days after she was dismissed from MPE, that Ms. Stark submitted her complaint. (*Id.* at 10:21-11:4, 11:19-12:2.) Thus, until she was discharged, Ms. Stark allowed her complaint to languish for months.

computer. (Dep. Julie Stark 11:6-11:18; *id.* at Ex. 1.) Ms. Stark did not, however, submit the complaint until after she had been dismissed. (Dep. Julie Stark 11:22-12:1.)

On October 6, Ms. Stark and her supervisor, Eric Block, reviewed her job performance. (*Id.* at 18:6-8.) Her evaluation stated, among other things, that she "fails to follow directions" and that she "lacks the degree of teamwork and cooperation that MPE seeks in its employees." (*Id.* at Ex. 1.) Ms. Stark responded by yelling at her supervisor that MPE was a bunch of "mega-polluters" and "criminals," that they would "live to regret it," and that she would "tell everyone." (*Id.* at 24:2-25:15.) It was not clear to her supervisor, Eric Block, what Ms. Stark was referring to. *Id.* at 26:4-8.

Two months followed after Ms. Stark's exchange with her supervisor. On Monday, December 3, 2015, four days after she was dismissed from MPE, Ms. Stark submitted her complaint. (*Id.* at 10:21-11:4, 11:19-12:2.) This litigation followed.

2. Give more airtime to favorable facts

Another way to highlight favorable facts is to describe favorable facts in more detail and to give those facts more "airtime." By contrast, address unfavorable facts more quickly and in less detail. By giving favorable facts more airtime and unfavorable facts less, you keep the judge's attention on the facts that strengthen your client's case and away from the facts that do not.

Consider version one from Table 12-X. Notice the "airtime" given to the idea that Ms. Stark was not taking any action with respect to her complaint. Lack of action helps prove that Ms. Stark was not "about to report" at the time she was fired, an important point for the employer. Thus, the employer's statement of facts repeats the idea that the employee had taken no action: She "had let her concerns languish for months"; "[s]he never submitted the complaint—not that month, nor the following month"; and "[t]wo months followed . . . [but s]till, she did not submit any complaint." By repeating that important fact, the employer emphasizes the employee's lack of action.

3. Pair unfavorable facts with favorable facts

You can also minimize the impact of an unfavorable fact by pairing that unfavorable fact with a more positive fact, either in the same sentence or the same paragraph. A good fact will provide a bad fact with context and, thereby, allows the reader to absorb the bad fact in context. Take Example 12-Y. In Example 12-Y, the employer has to acknowledge that its former employee, Ms. Stark, downloaded a complaint form and threatened to tell people about the employer's alleged environmental misdeeds. Those facts are bad for the employer because they help the employee establish that she was "about to report" the employer's environmental violations. Because those facts are bad facts, the employer places those facts in context. The employer's statement of facts notes that, although the employee downloaded the form, she did not submit it for months. Although she did say that she would report her employer, the employee made her threat when she was angry about a negative job review. The paragraphs suggest that the employee's threat was made in the heat of the moment, and the employee never actually intended to act on it. By pairing the bad facts with good facts, the lawyer minimizes the impact of the bad facts while still providing the judge with an accurate and complete view of the story.

Example 12-Y · Pair a bad fact with a good fact

The highlighted facts are "bad facts" for the employer. They are paired with "good facts," which are underlined. The good facts help mitigate or put the bad facts in context.

In fact, Ms. Stark had let her concerns languish for months. Sometime during the first few days of October, Ms. Stark downloaded a complaint form from the state attorney general's office, filled it out with allegations against MPE and saved it to her computer. (Dep. Julie Stark 11:6-11:18; *id.* at Ex. 1.) Although Ms. Stark downloaded the form, she never submitted the complaint — not that month, nor the following month. (*Id.* at 11:22-12:1.)

During that time, what she did do was express her anger at receiving a negative job review. (Dep. Eric Stark 22:3-23:12.) On October 6, Ms. Stark and her supervisor, Eric Block, reviewed her job performance. (*Id.* at 18:6-8.) Her evaluation stated, among other things, that she "fails to follow directions" and that she "lacks the degree of teamwork and cooperation that MPE seeks in its employees." (*Id.* at Ex. 1.) Ms. Stark responded by yelling at her supervisor that MPE was a bunch of "mega-polluters" and "criminals," that they would "live to regret it," and that she would "tell everyone." (*Id.* at 24:2-25:15.) It was not clear to her supervisor, Eric Block, what Ms. Stark was referring to. (*Id.* at 26:4-8.)

One way to pair an unfavorable fact with a favorable fact is to place the unfavorable fact in a dependent clause. A dependent clause provides additional information in a sentence, but it cannot stand alone as its own sentence. Because information in a dependent clause is implicitly understood by readers to be "additional" rather than "the main" information of a sentence, information in a dependent clause receives less attention. In Example 12-Z, negative information is put in a dependent clause (where it gets less attention), and the positive information is placed in the main clause.

Example 12-Z · A dependent clause minimizes a negative fact

Although neighbors harvested and kept some of the vegetables, the Neros told them they could do so. (Nero. Dep. 42:2-10; Walker Dep. 55:6-18.)

In an argument about whether a client had "exclusive possession" of land, the fact that others were allowed to harvest vegetables is a negative fact. Thus, that negative fact is paired with a more positive fact that shows "exclusive possession."

You can see the effect of the dependent clause by comparing version one and version two in Example 12-aa. Each time, the information in the dependent clause is minimized and placed in context by information in the main clause.

Example 12-aa · Information in the dependent clause receives less emphasis

Version 1: Although Moore's blood alcohol level was .13, she did not demonstrate any outward signs of intoxication. Officer Hanley Rpt. 1.

Version 2: Although she did not demonstrate any outward signs of intoxication, Moore's blood alcohol level was .13. Officer Hanley Rpt. 1.

Although dependent clauses are a great way to minimize undesirable facts, do not overuse this technique. Having too many dependent clauses in a row can be distracting to the reader. For maximum impact, use dependent clauses sparingly.

E. Choose Your Words Carefully

Subtle choices in language can make your statement of facts more compelling. Judges, like all of us, would rather read a dynamic, well-written story than a boring, uninspiring description of the record. To create a commanding narrative, choose your words carefully.

1. Choose vivid detail

One way to tell a more compelling story is to draw out graphic details that allow the judge to actually *visualize* what happened. In Example 12-bb, compare the two versions of the same event.

Example 12-bb · Neutral vs. vivid facts

Version 1: The defendant went through the red light before colliding with the plaintiff's automobile. Tr. 31-33.

Version 2: The defendant, driving his 3/4-ton pickup truck at a speed that police later determined to be twice the speed limit, sped through the red light and slammed into the plaintiff's compact car. Tr. 30-33.

Which facts more dynamically convey the story? Version one truthfully describes what happened, and it satisfies the cardinal rule that factual statements must be accurate. But does that sentence tell the story in a dynamic way? By contrast, version two includes vivid details that make one believe that the defendant is guilty of driving recklessly.

Concrete, vivid detail can help a judge see your client's story as you do; however, you must add such detail carefully. First, make sure the details are relevant to your client's story and to the legal issues being presented. Vivid, but irrelevant, detail will annoy the judge. Second, make sure the record supports your description. Vivid, but unsupported, detail will also annoy the judge. Finally, make sure the vivid detail will support your client's position. You do not want an unfavorable fact to be highlighted in vivid detail.

2. Choose strong verbs

Another way to use word choice to emphasize a fact is to choose your verbs carefully. Compare the two different verbs in Example 12-cc. Version one uses the verbs "applied" and "placed." By contrast, version two uses "choke" and "wrap." If you represent the police officer, you might want to use the wording in version one to downplay the physicality of the act and to implicitly suggest that the police officer was following proper restraint procedure. If you represent the defendant, however, you would want to emphasize, not downplay, the physicality of the restraint procedure.

Example 12-cc · The effect of verb choice

Version 1: The police officer applied a chokehold to the suspect by placing his arm against the suspect's neck. Tr. 62.

Version 2: The officer choked the suspect by wrapping his forearm around the suspect's throat. Tr. 62.

Likewise, look again at what was Example 12-bb above, and what is now Example 12-dd. Compare the effect of the verbs "went" and "colliding" with "sped" and "slammed."

Example 12-dd • The effect of verb choice

Version 1: The defendant went through the red light before colliding with the plaintiff's automobile. Tr. 31-33.

Version 2: The defendant, driving his 3/4-ton pickup truck at a speed that police later determined to be twice the speed limit, sped through the red light and slammed into the plaintiff's compact car. Tr. 30-33.

Again, you want to choose your verbs with care. Your verb choice must be appropriate, supported by the record, and favorable to your client's position.

F. Provide Clear, Accurate Citations to the Record

An effective statement of facts will always provide accurate citations to show the court where those facts can be found in the record. Citing the record shows that your description of the events is grounded in reality. If the court wants to check the facts or needs more detail than you have provided, citations to the source of your facts will help the judges get that information.

Because citations make it easier for the judges to find the facts you are describing, you should cite nearly every sentence in your statement of facts. The only kinds of sentences that you might not cite are those that summarize other facts. The underlying facts, the ones that support the summary statement, should be cited.

Courts provide different rules about how to cite the record, so make sure to consult the court rules, local rules, and your jurisdiction's citation manual to ensure that your citations are appropriate. Anything in your brief that is different from the court's usual practice distracts the judge, slows down the judge's reading, and lessens the persuasiveness of your brief.[14]

If the form of the citation is not governed by rules or custom, balance the usefulness of the citation against how much it distracts from your narrative. Judges and lawyer-staff should be able to easily find the cited item in the record, but putting too much citation detail in the text of the statement of facts will make it harder to read and will water down your story. So, for example, if you were to file a brief in the United States Supreme

---

14. Follow the citation rules for your jurisdiction. In the absence of local rules governing the form of your citation, both the *ALWD Guide to Legal Citation* and *The Bluebook* describe how to cite to court documents, transcripts, and the record. *See* ALWD & Coleen M. Barger, *ALWD Guide to Legal Citation* 252-56 (5th ed. 2014) (R. 25); *The Bluebook: A Uniform System of Citation* 19-22 (Columbia L. Rev. Ass'n et al. eds., 20th ed. 2015) (R. B17).

Court and you wanted to reference a statement on page 12 of the appendix to the petition for certiorari, choose Example 12-ee rather than 12-ff.

Example 12-ee · Effective citation to the record

See Pet. App. 12a.

Example 12-ff · Overly long, distracting citation to the record

See Appendix to the petition for certiorari of the Petitioner Xylorg Corporation, LLC, at page 12, line 22 (quoting finding of fact by the Honorable Judge Ralph Simone, entered in the record on October 26, 2012, afternoon session, United States Courthouse, White Plains, New York).

G. Let the Facts Determine the Length

Statements of fact vary enormously in their length. For example, if the issue involves whether a police officer "seized" a citizen for purposes of the Fourth Amendment, the statement of facts may include a detailed discussion of exactly where the contact took place; the time of day; who else was present; what the defendant was wearing; and the exact words the officer used when he addressed the defendant. By contrast, if the underlying legal issue is one of statutory construction, your statement of facts may be very short because the legal question will focus on the statute and its history.

Think carefully about which facts the court needs to know to resolve the issues and which facts are interesting, but extraneous. Judges want shorter briefs. They do not enjoy slogging through irrelevant detail or expending their intellectual energy figuring out which detail is important.

Accordingly, choose your facts deliberately. Every fact should serve a purpose in telling your client's story. Every fact should support your legal analysis or inform the judge about an important background or emotional fact. If a fact does not serve one of those purposes, take it out.

H. Draft and Re-Draft

Attorneys draft their statement of facts at different times—some draft before they draft their argument, some draft after their argument is finished, and some alternate between the two.

One good piece of advice is this: No matter when you initially draft your statement of facts, revisit the statement of facts after you complete your argument. Sometimes, as the argument develops, facts that once seemed helpful or important turn out to be extraneous. In rare cases, you might actually realize that you omitted a fact that turned out to be important. Moreover, the statement of facts can almost always be pared down or tightened up after your argument is done. Thus, give the statement of facts section a fresh read after your motion or brief is finished to ensure that the section is accurate, complete, and succinct, and that it effectively supports the analysis.

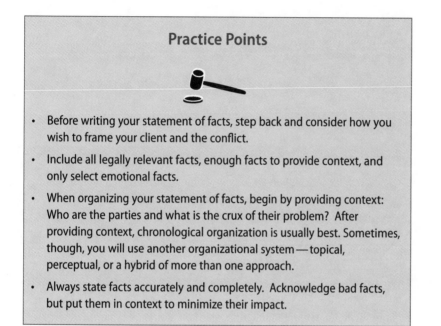

Practice Points

- Before writing your statement of facts, step back and consider how you wish to frame your client and the conflict.

- Include all legally relevant facts, enough facts to provide context, and only select emotional facts.

- When organizing your statement of facts, begin by providing context: Who are the parties and what is the crux of their problem? After providing context, chronological organization is usually best. Sometimes, though, you will use another organizational system—topical, perceptual, or a hybrid of more than one approach.

- Always state facts accurately and completely. Acknowledge bad facts, but put them in context to minimize their impact.

Chapter 13

Editing and Polishing for Persuasion

I.   Check Your Procedural and Local Rules
II. Your Argument
     A. Edit for Focus
         1. Review your thesis sentences
         2. Review your point headings
         3. Integrate your theme
     B. Edit for Emphasis
         1. Review your explanations of the law
         2. Compare your explanation of the law to your application
         3. Address your weaknesses
     C. Edit for Flow
         1. Provide roadmaps
         2. Smooth transitions
     D. Polish for Clarity
         1. Bring subject and verb close together and toward the front of the sentence
         2. Minimize passive voice
         3. Minimize nominalizations
         4. Look for and revise unwieldy sentences
     E. Polish for Credibility
         1. Check your procedural and local rules (again)
         2. Proofread
         3. Check citations
         4. Check the format
III. Statements of Fact (or of the Case)
IV. If You Are Drafting a Motion and Supporting Memorandum of Law
     A. Edit Your Introduction
     B. Edit All Remaining Sections
     C. Polish Your Introduction and All Remaining Sections
V.   If You Are Drafting an Appellate Brief
     A. Edit Your Issue Presented
     B. Edit the Summary of Your Argument
     C. Edit All Remaining Sections
     D. Polish the Question Presented, Summary of the Argument, and All Remaining Sections
VI. Customize Your Editing Checklist

If you wish to produce a persuasive legal argument, you must edit and polish your work before submitting it to the court. At the outset of this book, Chapter 1, *The Nature of Persuasion*, discussed three considerations that influence whether your message will be persuasive: the source of the message, the content of the message, and the audience receiving the message. Editing and polishing your arguments allows you to adjust the content of your message so that you are communicating a consistent and coherent message, making your message easy for your audience to absorb, and presenting yourself as a source who should be believed. In other words, effective editing and polishing can distinguish the persuasive from the unpersuasive.

Editing and polishing are two distinct tasks. Editing requires you to critically examine the structure and content of your work. When editing, you check whether each argument is complete, whether your arguments are arranged logically, and whether you have presented the facts in a way that clearly support your client's position. When polishing, you look for any snags or mistakes that might distract your reader from your message. Polishing is the final step in the writing process. Polishing takes a document that is structurally sound and makes it shine. Effective polishing ensures that your writing is clear and error-free.

Not surprisingly, these processes require time: Effective writers spend more than half their time editing and polishing.[1] These processes take time because they happen in rounds. You cannot reread your argument once and call it quits. Rather, you must check your argument from a variety of different angles to ensure that all the parts are working together so that you are putting forward the strongest argument possible.

This chapter reviews those editing and polishing techniques that will do the most to focus and polish your argument. This chapter does, however, skip one important aspect of persuasion: A persuasive argument must be logically ordered. As explained in Chapter 7, *Organizing Persuasive Arguments*, lawyers—and thus judges—have particular expectations about the way arguments are ordered. This chapter assumes that you have already ordered your arguments in a logical way, and that your goal now is to bring out the persuasive effect of those arguments.

To that end, this chapter first reviews how to edit and polish the two most substantive sections of the document you plan to submit to the court: the argument and the statement of facts (or of the case). It then addresses how to edit and polish the remaining sections of your brief. Some of those remaining sections serve a more obviously persuasive function. Others are more functional and less obviously persuasive. But, no matter their role, all sections of your brief must be edited and polished

---

1. Anne M. Enquist, *Unlocking the Secrets of Highly Successful Law Students* (2007) (available at http://works.bepress.com/anne_enquist/).

Still Struggling with Organization?

If you are still struggling with how to organize or order your arguments, return to that part of Chapter 7 that addresses the kind of argument you are developing:

§ 7.1   addresses how to order your claims and arguments within claims;

§ 7.2   addresses how to order analogical arguments;

§ 7.3   addresses how to structure rule-based arguments, such as statutory construction and policy arguments;

§ 7.4   addresses how to use rule-based and analogical arguments together; and,

§ 7.5   addresses how to structure factor analyses.

---

so that, together, they project an image of being drafted by a professional advocate. To project that image, your review should begin with the procedural and local rules that will govern your document.

I. Check Your Procedural and Local Rules

As both Chapter 4, *Motion Practice*, and Chapter 5, *Appellate Practice*, emphasize, you should review all procedural and local rules that govern the document you will be submitting *before* you begin drafting. Although you have read those rules at least once, you should now read them again. At this point, make sure that your document includes all the content that the rules require. For example, if one of the rules requires a "concise statement of the case setting out the facts relevant to the issues submitted for review, describing the relevant procedural history, and identifying the rulings presented for review, with appropriate references to the record,"[2] make sure that your statement of the case does that. Moreover, if the rules call this section a "Statement of the Case," make sure that you refer to the section in the same way rather than, for example, calling it a "Statement of Facts."

Once you have all the content in place, you are ready to edit and polish that content. Lawyers have different methods for editing and polishing their documents. Over time, you should develop a method that is most effective for you.[3] If, however, you are still developing a method

---

2. Fed. R. App. 28(a)(6).

3. This chapter ends with a discussion of editing and polishing checklists. You should adapt those checklists to fit your particular strengths and weaknesses. For example, if you never write overlong sentences, you might omit that item from your checklist. Similarly, if you struggle with overuse of commas, you might make sure to include that item.

for editing and polishing your court documents, begin with the heart of your document: the argument section.

II. Your Argument

The argument section is the primary place where you communicate your message to the court. Other sections of your document will need to be coordinated with your argument; thus, begin with your argument section and, after that section is finalized, move on to other sections of your brief.

A. Edit for Focus

When editing your argument, your primary goal should be to ensure that your argument is focused. The last thing a judge wants to read is an argument that drifts from its point or takes too long to get to its point. Such an argument is difficult to follow and, therefore, unhelpful to the judge. Moreover, as an advocate you do not want to lose the judge midway through your argument. Therefore, after you have the substance of your argument in place, you must ensure that your argument is focused—and remains focused—on the key points you want to make and that supporting themes or points of law are appropriately emphasized. At the same time, you want to look for any excess that can be discarded so that the judge can move more quickly through your argument. The techniques that follow will help you check that your argument is focused and that key supporting ideas are emphasized.

1. Review your thesis sentences

One of the best things you can do to improve the focus and persuasive effect of your document is to review the thesis sentences of your argument and the paragraphs to which they are attached. As you will recall, the first sentence of each paragraph is where your reader's eye naturally rests. The information in that sentence is therefore the information that the judge is most likely to absorb. In addition, the first sentence of each paragraph indicates the content of the paragraph that follows. The thesis sentence, therefore, also directs the judge through the content of your argument. For those reasons, your thesis sentences should, taken together, form an outline of your argument.

To check your thesis sentences, go through the argument section and read only your thesis sentences. You may highlight your thesis sentences or pull them out of the document so that you can focus your attention on just your thesis sentences, as in Example 13-A.

As you are reading your thesis sentences, ask yourself whether they provide logical outline of your argument. In particular, you should de-

Example 13-A · Checking thesis sentences for focus

- The indictment against Mr. Hidalgo must be dismissed because Arizona's anti-human smuggling statute was never meant to be used to prosecute individuals who were smuggled.

- To answer that question, this Court must construe the word "person."

- In this case, the text in context, its legislative history, and the historical context surrounding enactment of the statute all establish that the legislature never intended the prosecution of the human cargo.

- The plain text of § 13-2319(a) limits application of the statute to the smuggler, and not his human cargo.

- The most natural and obvious meaning of a "person . . . smuggling . . . for profit or commercial purpose" limits this statute to the prosecution of smugglers, not the smuggler's human cargo.

- First, the ordinary meaning of the phrase "for profit" limits the person who can be prosecuted to those in the business of smuggling.

- Next, the ordinary meaning of the phrase "for . . . commercial purpose" similarly limits the person who can be prosecuted.

- To read the statute as imposing criminal liability on individual migrants would, effectively, render the phrases "for profit" and for "commercial purpose" void and inert.

- Thus, the plain meaning of the statutory section demonstrates that human cargo falls outside the intended scope of § 13-2319(a).

termine whether each thesis sentence asserts an argument you want the court to adopt or whether it merely states a fact that is true. In a persuasive argument, your thesis sentences should reflect the argument you want the court to adopt by the time it reaches the end of the paragraph. If you find a thesis sentence that merely asserts something that is true, then revise that thesis sentence so that it asserts a point in your argument.

Compare the sentences in the two columns in Table 13-B. The statements in the left-hand column of Table 13-B assert arguments that the lawyer wants the court to adopt. By contrast, the statements in the right-hand column assert statements that are true, but do not reflect an argument that the lawyer wants the court to adopt. Notice that the statements in the right-hand column are often followed by a citation. A citation is a telltale sign that you are asserting something that is true about the law. Look also at the last row. Can you see that the sentences in the right-hand column assert a fact that is true about the world and not an argument?

Table 13-B · Thesis sentences should assert an argument

Thesis sentences assert an argument	Thesis sentences assert a truth
• The plain text of § 13-2319(a) limits application of the statute to the smuggler, and not his human cargo.	• When analyzing the plain text of a statute, Arizona courts must give "each word, phrase, clause and sentence . . . its natural, obvious, and ordinary meaning." *Arpaio v. Steinle III*, 35 P.3d 114, 116 (Ariz. Ct. App. 2001).
• First, the ordinary meaning of the phrase "for profit" limits the person who can be prosecuted to those in the business of smuggling.	• "Profit" is widely understood as "net income . . . from the conduct of business." *Webster's Third New International Dictionary* 1811 (2002).
• Next, the ordinary meaning of the phrase "for . . . commercial purpose" similarly limits the person who can be prosecuted.	• Next, "commercial" means "of or relating to 'commerce.'" *Webster's Third New International Dictionary* at 594.
• To read the statute as imposing criminal liability on individual migrants would, effectively, render the phrases "for profit" and for "commercial purpose" void and inert.	• The individual migrant is not seeking to profit or engage in the activity commercially.

In addition to checking that your thesis sentences outline your argument, you should also check that your thesis sentences match the content of the paragraph to which the thesis sentence is attached. As mentioned above, the thesis sentence tells the judge what to expect in that paragraph. If the material in the paragraph does not match the thesis sentence, the judge will be confused. If the material in the paragraph does not match the thesis sentence, you will need to adjust either the thesis sentence or the content until they match.

> **Paragraph cohesion**
>
> In comparing the thesis sentence to the content of its paragraph, you are essentially checking for paragraph cohesion. Paragraph cohesion is explained in more detail in Chapter 9, *Refining Persuasive Arguments.*

These two steps—checking that the thesis sentences outline your argument and checking that the thesis sentence and the content of the paragraph match—are intertwined steps. If you adjust a thesis sentence so that it better outlines your argument, you may then have to adjust the content of the paragraph so that it supports the thesis sentence. Likewise, if you adjust a thesis sentence so that it better reflects the content of the paragraph, you may then have to go back to check to make sure your thesis sentences are working together to outline your argument. As a result, you may move back and forth between these two steps before you are satisfied with the result.

Before leaving this discussion about thesis sentences and the content that follows, be aware of one thing: A paragraph that starts a section may function a little differently. The thesis sentence of the first paragraph of a section likely asserts the point of the section and not the point of that paragraph, as in Example 13-C. If that paragraph acts as a roadmap paragraph or provides some necessary background, the content of that first paragraph will only loosely support the thesis sentence.

Example 13-C · A thesis sentence at the start of a section

A. The plaintiff's subjective belief that he was expected to play paddleball with his supervisor was objectively reasonable.

Mark Floyd reasonably believed that he was expected to participate in the paddleball game with his supervisor. To determine whether an employee's subjective belief is objectively reasonable, California courts usually weigh three factors: (1) whether the employer was involved in the activity, (2) whether the employer benefited from the activity, and (3) whether the employer pressured the employee to participate. *Id.* at 76. In this case, Fitness Functions was involved with the paddleball game; Fitness Functions benefited from the game; and, given the circumstances, Mr. Floyd felt pressured to join the game.

> This thesis sentence asserts a proposition for section A. The rest of the paragraph provides an introductory roadmap for the section. The paragraph, by itself, does not establish the thesis.

    1. <u>Fitness Functions was involved in the paddleball game.</u>
Fitness Functions was involved in the paddleball game because it provided all the resources necessary for employees to play the game.

Although you may see some slight variations in the first paragraph, overall the thesis sentences of your arguments should outline your argument and, to avoid confusion, the content of each paragraph must support that thesis.

2. Review your point headings

Next, review your point headings. Your point headings, like your thesis sentences, should outline your argument. Each Roman numeral point heading should address the relief you seek for that claim. Sub-headings should support that main point.

Although there is no set frequency with which you should insert a point heading, the point headings should divide your argument into readable chunks. Remember that most point headings are a full sentence. Therefore, include final punctuation.

> **Thinking about point headings?**
>
> Chapter 9, *Refining Persuasive Arguments*, provides detailed advice about constructing persuasive point headings.

3. Integrate your theme

As you are reviewing your thesis sentences, keep your theme in mind. As Chapter 6, *Themes for Persuasive Arguments*, explains, a theme can

Thinking about themes?

If you need help thinking about or developing a theme for your argument, turn back to Chapter 6, *Themes for Persuasive Arguments.*

be as simple as reminding a trial court (repeatedly) of the standard for its decision or an appellate court of the standard of review. That theme should re-appear in the places where the judge's eye is most likely to fall: the point headings and the thesis sentences. Thus, if you have not done so, return to your thesis sentences and point headings and check that they reflect the theme of your argument.

B. Edit for Emphasis

The steps above will help you organize and focus your argument. Now, you want to ensure that that same focus is supported throughout your argument.

1. Review your explanations of the law

Wondering how to frame your explanation of the law most persuasively?

Chapter 8, *Developing Persuasive Arguments,* explains a variety of techniques you can use to frame your explanation of the law in the most persuasive way.

Take a moment to re-read your explanations of the law—slowly. As you read, ask yourself whether you have expressed the rules so that they support the outcome you seek. For example, you can frame the same rule in different ways; you should choose the frame that emphasizes the outcome you seek, as in Example 13-D. Similarly, you should review any case illustrations and ask yourself whether the facts you have chosen and the way in which you have described the court's reasoning is consistent with your overall argument.

Example 13-D • The summary judgment standard framed from different perspectives

The rule as written:	"The court shall grant summary judgment if the movant shows that there is no genuine dispute as to any material fact and the movant is entitled to judgment as a matter of law." Fed. R. Civ. P. 56(a).
The moving party:	Summary judgment **must** be granted if there is no issue of material fact and the moving party is entitled to judgment as a matter of law. Fed. R. Civ. P. 56(a).
The non-moving party:	Summary judgment may **not** be granted if there is an issue of material fact. Fed. R. Civ. P. 56(a).

2. Compare your explanation of the law to your application

Often, as you work your way through an argument, you refine your ideas and you focus on ways of explaining those ideas that are best suited to your argument. Because it takes time to settle on the most effective way to express your ideas, your language often will shift as you write. Thus, take a moment to compare the language that you use in your explanation of the law with the language you use in your application.

Although some disciplines appreciate "elegant variation," lawyers do not. In fact, in legal writing repetition of key ideas is usually welcomed. Legal phrases are terms of art, and each has a very specific meaning. Thus, for legally significant ideas, use the same or very similar phrasing. If you do not, the court will likely wonder whether you are talking about the same or different ideas. And you never want a judge to get bogged down in your writing, wondering what you mean.

So, look for changes in language. If a change exists, ask yourself whether the word expresses a key legal idea. If it does, then ask yourself whether that change will make a judge think you are discussing a *new* idea. If so, exchange the elegant variation for a legally consistent term. Doing so will avoid confusion and will ensure that you are emphasizing the ideas that you want emphasized.

Compare the two columns in Example 13-E. You can see how the varied language in the left-hand column can be edited to create the more consistent language in the right-hand column.

Example 13-E • Omit elegant variation

"Elegant variation" makes the reader work harder	Consistency helps your reader
The judge initially denied the defendant's motion to dismiss, based on the prosecutor's argument. On reconsideration, however, the court granted the accused's request, rejecting the argument made by the state's attorney.	The judge initially denied the defendant's motion to dismiss, based on the prosecutor's argument. On reconsideration, however, the judge granted the defendant's motion, rejecting the argument made by the prosecutor.
A university complies with Title IX if it provides equal athletic opportunities to both sexes. 34 C.F.R. § 106.41(c) (2015). Whether a violation occurred depends on an analysis of ten factors. *Id.* at 106.41(c)(1)-(10).	A university complies with Title IX if it provides equal athletic opportunities to both sexes. 34 C.F.R. § 106.41(c) (2015). Whether equal athletic opportunities exist depends on an analysis of ten factors. *Id.* at 106.41(c)(1)-(10).

3. Address your weaknesses

Much of your editing to this point has been looking for ways to emphasize the strengths of your arguments. However, you also must consider whether you have addressed any weaknesses in your arguments. Effectively addressing weaknesses is an essential step in emphasizing the strengths of your argument.

If you represent the moving party or appellant, take a moment to think about any issues that, earlier, made your stomach tighten. Often, when we initially receive a case, we immediately see all the weaknesses.

Worried about a weakness?

Return to Chapter 8, *Developing Persuasive Arguments,* for a more detailed explanation about how to address a weakness.

As we research and write, we become more convinced by our own arguments. As we become more convinced by our own arguments, we sometimes lose sight of those issues that initially gave us pause. So, take a moment to think back to any issues that gave you pause and ask yourself whether those issues need to be addressed. If so, address those issues now.

If you are the responding party, you have an advantage. You know the arguments that the opposing party has relied on. Of course, you should draft your argument from your perspective, explaining your strongest arguments first. But, now take a moment to review opposing counsel's arguments and consider whether you have addressed all the points raised.

Whether you are the moving or responding party, remember to present your argument first and avoid explaining a weakness from the opposing party's perspective. Rather, after asserting your argument, *then* explain why a weakness does not prevent the outcome you seek. Otherwise, you are highlighting opposing counsel's argument and giving it airtime. If you find yourself explaining the argument that opposing counsel will make, stop and revise. Compare Examples 13-F and 13-G. By comparing the two, you can see how a weakness explained from opposing counsel's perspective can be changed so that the weakness is addressed from your perspective.

Example 13-F · Addressing a weakness from opposing counsel's perspective

In the first paragraph, the writer describes the opposing argument. In doing so, the writer draws attention and provides airtime to the opponent's argument. In the second paragraph, the writer addresses why the argument, described above, is less effective.

Explaining the opposing argument first is a less effective approach.

Defendants argue that the officers impermissibly relied on the defendant's looks in their reason to conduct a protective search. Defendant compares this case to *Valdez* and *Bates.* In this case, the officers relied on the t-shirt that defendant was wearing, their baggy clothes, their haircut, and their tattoos to support their reason for a protective search. Defendants argue that these facts are similar to the facts in Valdez, in which the officer pointed to a "blue leisure suit, shiny black shoes" and a "neat afro" and similar to the long hair, beard, and leather jacket in *Valdez.* In both those cases, the courts held that the facts the officers presented were not sufficient to support a protective search.

This case is, however, different from *Valdez* and Bates. Here, the "look" at issue established a reasonable suspicion of gang activity and membership in the 18th Street Gang. Both the association with gang activity generally and the association with a particular gang known to carry weapons are specific, articulable facts that raise a reasonable suspicion that the defendant might pose an immediate threat. Thus, the officers relied on far more than simply the defendant's "looks."

Example 13-G • Addressing a weakness from your perspective

Here, the officers relied on far more than simply the defendant's "looks." In *Valdez* and in *Bates*, the "look" that the officers relied on—a blue leisure suit, shiny black shoes, and a "neat Afro" in *Valdez* and long hair, a beard, and a leather jacket in *Bates*—could not be particularly associated with a weapons-related activity or with a particular group of people who regularly carry weapons. By contrast, here, the "look" at issue established a reasonable suspicion of gang activity and membership in the 18th Street Gang. Both the association with gang activity generally and the association with a particular gang known to carry weapons are specific, articulable facts that raise a reasonable suspicion that the defendant might pose an immediate threat.

> Here, the lawyer addresses the opposing argument but does so from the lawyer's perspective: He immediately explains why the opposing argument will fail.
>
> In this way, the writer addresses the opposing argument without giving undue airtime to the opposing argument.

C. Edit for Flow

"Flow" refers to the smooth transition from one idea to the next. As mentioned above, your argument will be persuasive only if the judge can follow it with little effort. As the writer, make it easy for the judge to transition from one idea to the next. If you have reviewed your point headings and thesis sentences to ensure that they line up to form a logical argument, you have already done significant work to create flow in your legal argument. You can further enhance the flow of your argument by effectively deploying roadmap sections, roadmap sentences, and transitions.

1. Provide roadmaps

Roadmap sections and roadmap sentences have similar functions. Both alert your reader to the fact that a larger analytical unit breaks down into smaller analytical units. The difference between the two is that you use a roadmap section when the smaller units of analysis share some governing law. So, any time an argument breaks down into one or more elements or factors, you will need a roadmap section. By contrast, a roadmap sentence is a helpful way to explain ideas—such as a court's reasoning—that have different parts.

Take a moment to skim through your argument. Look for governing rules that have more than one element or factor. If the governing rule has more than one element or factor, you will need to alert the judge to that divide through a roadmap section.

Next, take a moment to consider any complex explanations of law, case illustration, or analyses. To the extent that you can separate those complex explanations into parts and explain to the reader how you have organized your explanation, your explanation will be easier to understand. Use a roadmap sentence, as in Example 13-H, to explain how the ideas are grouped together.

> **Need more help with roadmap sentences or roadmap sections?**
>
> Section 7.1, *Organizing Claims and Arguments*, discusses both roadmap sentences and roadmap sections, and when to use one versus the other.

Example 13-H • A roadmap sentence explains the organization of more detailed information to come

This roadmap sentence explains how the writer has structured his explanation of the court's reasoning.

The court provided two independent reasons for affirming the trial court's decision. *Id.* at 62. First, ...

2. Smooth transitions

A "transition" is any word or phrase that tells the reader the relationship between two ideas. By explaining the relationship between two ideas, transitions create a bridge from one idea to the next. In addition, transitions can be used as "signposts" to remind the reader where she is within the structure of the analysis as a whole.

Table 13-I illustrates common transitions, each of which explain the relationship between your last idea and your next idea. You should check all existing transitions to ensure that the transition you chose accurately explains the relationship between the two ideas.

Table 13-I • Transitional words and phrases[4]

Introduce	Sequence	Exemplify	Contrast	Add
First	First, second,	For example	However	Again
Initially	Initially	For instance	Although	Moreover
To begin	Then	To illustrate	But	Additionally
The first reason	Finally	In particular	Yet	Similarly
Primarily	Before	Namely	Unlike	Also
In general	Next	Specifically	In contrast	Likewise
Alternatively	Last		Nevertheless	Further
A further reason		**Emphasize**	Nonetheless	
	Connect	Certainly	Rather	**Conclude**
Restate	Because	Above all	Despite	Finally
That is	Thus	Indeed	Instead	As a result
In other words	As a result	Especially	Still	Thus
More simply	Thereby	Accordingly	On the other	Therefore
As noted	Therefore	Since	hand	In short
	Hence	Not only . . . but also		Consequently

---

4. Excerpted from Laurel Currie Oates, Anne Enquist & Kelly Kunsch, *The Legal Writing Handbook: Analysis, Research and Writing*, 613-22 (3d ed. 2002), and supplemented by Bryan A. Garner, *Legal Writing in Plain English: A Text with Exercises* 68 (2001).

In addition, check whether you have an appropriate transition in places where transitions typically show up. For example, you will often need a transition between two legal arguments. Wherever two legal arguments abut, ask yourself how those arguments relate and which transition most effectively conveys that relationship. You are also likely to need transitions to explain the relationship among a series of rules and between the parts of a case illustration. Thus, check those parts of your argument to ensure that you have appropriate transitions as necessary.

D. Polish for Clarity

Another way to ensure that your reader—the judge—stays with your argument is to ensure that each sentence is clear and easy to absorb. A variety of techniques can help you develop such sentences.

> Many of these techniques for improving the clarity of your writing were explained in Chapter 9, *Refining Persuasive Arguments*. However, lawyers who are careful about their writing review for these issues again during the final stages of editing.

1. Bring subject and verb close together and toward the front of the sentence

The first step in creating sentences that are clear and easy to absorb is to write sentences that have a clear subject and verb, placed close together, toward the front of the sentence. When reading, people naturally look for *who* is doing *what* in every sentence they read. As a result, a reader who can quickly identify the subject (the "who") and action (the "doing what") will more easily absorb the sentence and remember its contents. Compare the sentences in the left column in Table 13-J to those in the right column. Which sentences are easier to read?

Table 13-J • Subject and verb should be placed closed together toward the front of sentences

Subject and verb are separated	Subject and verb close together
The prosecuting attorney, repeatedly and throughout his lengthy closing argument, <u>made</u> numerous improper statements that deprived the defendant of a fair trial.	The prosecuting attorney <u>made</u> numerous improper statements that deprived the defendant of a fair trial. These statements were made repeatedly and throughout the prosecuting attorney's lengthy closing argument.
The defendant, even though he was unaware of the contents of the glove compartment, <u>was arrested</u> for possessing a firearm.	The defendant <u>was arrested</u> for possessing a firearm even though he was unaware of the contents of the glove compartment.
The spousal privilege, in both criminal and civil cases, which <u>allows</u> communications made between spouses during the marriage to remain confidential, <u>applies</u> to both words and acts intended to be a private communication.	In both criminal and civil cases, the spousal privilege <u>allows</u> communications made between spouses during the marriage to remain confidential. The spousal privilege <u>applies</u> to both words and acts intended to be a private communication.

2. Minimize passive voice

In a sentence that uses the "passive voice," the actor is not identified or the reader has to wait to find out who the actor is. Since, as mentioned above, readers naturally like to know who is doing what, a sentence that uses the passive voice is often more difficult to absorb. In addition, when a sentence fails to identify the "who," the reader finds it more difficult to form a picture in his head about what is happening. Abstract legal concepts are difficult enough to absorb. Do not make those concepts more difficult to absorb by hiding the actor. Instead, use the active voice.

The sentence pairs in the Table 13-K demonstrate the difference between active and passive voice. When you read each pair, ask yourself which sentence more clearly identifies *who* did the action.

Table 13-K · Prefer the active voice

The active voice clearly identifies who is doing what.

Passive Voice	Active Voice
Reasonable suspicion to stop a defendant is found if specific, articulable facts connect the defendant to a crime.	A court will find that a police officer has reasonable suspicion to stop a defendant, if the officer can point to specific articulable facts that connect the defendant to a crime.
The anti-smuggling statute was never intended to be used to target the human cargo.	The legislature never intended that the state would use the anti-smuggling statute to target the human cargo.
Sufficient evidence was found by the jury to convict both defendants.	The jury found sufficient evidence to convict both defendants.

As you review your writing, you can identify the passive voice in one of two ways. First, you can simply look for the action in the sentence and ask, "Who is doing that?" If you can't tell, the sentence likely uses the passive voice.

You can also identify the passive voice by its verb structure. The passive voice is composed of a "be" verb and a past participle, as shown in Table 13-L. The past participle is simply the past tense form of a verb. See if you can find that verb structure in the sentences in the left-hand column in Table 13-K.

Although the passive voice should usually be avoided, occasionally the passive voice is the better choice. In particular, the passive voice is the better choice if you want to obscure who the actor is or if you don't know who the actor is. As a general rule, use the active voice unless you have a strategic reason to use the passive voice.

Table 13-L · Passive voice structure

"Be" verb		The past participle includes a word ending in
Be		-d
Am	+	-ed
Is		-n
Are		-en
Was		-t

3. Minimize nominalizations

Another way to ensure that you are writing clear sentences is to minimize your use of nominalizations. A nominalization is a noun that could be expressed as a verb. For example, the noun "supervision" is a nominalization of the verb "to supervise." Because nominalizations embed verbs within nouns, nominalizations make it difficult for your reader to find the action in a sentence. Removing these nominalizations will make your sentences more active and easier to read.

To find nominalizations, use the find function to search for words ending in "-ion," "-men," and "-al." These endings are frequently used in nominalizations. Then, convert the noun to a verb to see if the sentence can be restructured more effectively using the verb. Table 13-M demonstrates the differences between sentences using nominalized verbs as nouns and the same words in their verb form. Although not all nominalizations should be omitted, often using the verb form will make your sentence stronger.

Table 13-M · Minimize nominalizations

Sentence with a nominalization	Revised sentence
It was Congress's intention to remove uncertainty in the recusal requirements.	Congress intended to remove uncertainty in a judge's decision to recuse.
The decline in wood stork population has occurred in direct correlation to increased urban and rural development.	The decline in wood stork population correlates directly to increased urban and rural development. *Id.*
This Court's analysis begins with an examination of the plain meaning of the statutory language.	This Court first examines the plain meaning of the statutory language.

4. Look for and revise unwieldy sentences

A sentence can become unwieldy because it contains too many ideas or because it contains too many empty words. You should review your writing for each of these ailments.

Sentences that contain too many ideas are sometimes a little difficult to spot, but here are two possible options. First, you can look for a sentence that contains a series of prepositions. Prepositions are words that create a relationship between a noun and another part of the sentence.[5] Prepositions include the words "of," "after," "in," "between," "about," and, in some cases, "to." The sentence in Example 13-N contains five prepositions (which are shaded). That is too many relationships for a reader to comfortably absorb.

Second, you can look for a sentence that has a lot of commas. A sentence with a lot of commas usually has too many ideas embedded in the sentence, and the sentence should be broken apart with each embedded idea given its own sentence. Example 13-O is an example of a sentence that became too long because it had too many embedded ideas.

Example 13-N · Overly long sentence

Prepositions create new relationships. A sentence with too many prepositions often has more relationships than a reader can absorb.

In *Armstrong*, a police report broadcasted an hour after the incident provided details to officers on patrol about an armed robbery that happened earlier that night.

Example 13-O · Overly long sentence

Commas set aside parenthetical statements. As the number of parenthetical statements increases, a sentence becomes more complex and difficult to absorb. Consider breaking apart the sentence.

In both criminal and civil cases, the spousal privilege, which allows communications made between spouses during the marriage to remain confidential, applies to both words and acts intended to be a private communication.

Sentences also become unwieldy if they include too many empty words. Removing unnecessary words will make your sentences structurally simpler and easier to comprehend. To hone your sentences, you need to examine each sentence individually. Every sentence contains both working words and glue words. Working words carry meaning. Glue words connect the working words together to complete the sentence. Although every sentence must contain both working and glue words, problems arise when the proportion of glue words becomes too high.[6]

---

5. *See* Bryan A. Garner, *The Redbook: A Manual on Legal Style* 176 (2d ed. 2006).

6. Richard Wydick, in *Plain English for Lawyers* 7 (5th ed. 2005), introduces and explains the idea of omitting surplus words by looking for "working words" and "glue words" and omitting as many of the "glue words" as possible.

Table 13-P · Omit surplus words

More glue words	Fewer glue words
Addressing the "professional character as spiritual advisor" element, the element is satisfied when the congregant has the purpose of seeking spiritual guidance.	A minister acts in her "professional character as a spiritual advisor" when the congregant seeks spiritual guidance.
It is clear that the officer in Mr. Hepworth's case held a reasonable suspicion that Mr. Hepworth was connected to the Starbucks robbery.	The officer reasonably suspected that Mr. Hepworth was connected to the Starbucks robbery
This Court should hold that DataX has a legitimate interest in restricting Mr. Oliver's employment because it can be shown that Mr. Oliver has established a personal hold over DataX's customers.	DataX has a legitimate interest in restricting Mr. Oliver's employment because Mr. Oliver has a personal hold over DataX's customers.

Compare the examples in Table 13-P. The working words are shaded. All the other words are glue words. Notice how, in the revised versions, glue words are squeezed out to create a higher proportion of working words and a more powerful sentence. Review your sentences—especially the long ones—to determine whether any glue words can be squeezed out.

Finally, you can always do a quick check for unwieldy sentences by looking for any sentence that exceeds two typed lines.[7] Although a well-structured sentence can exceed two lines, any sentence longer than two lines is suspect and should be reviewed carefully.

E. Polish for Credibility

Up to this point, this chapter's discussion about editing and polishing has focused on honing the content of your message so that you communicate a consistent, coherent message that your audience will find easy to absorb. In addition, editing and polishing allows you to enhance your credibility. These next steps may have some effect on the content of your message, but will also go a long way toward establishing yourself as a careful, detail-oriented professional.

---

7. This advice—to examine any sentences that exceed two lines—assumes that your document has one-inch margins and you are using Times New Roman in 12-point font. If your margins are wider or your font is larger, you will have less text on a line. In such a case, a sentence can reasonably extend to two-and-a-half or three lines.

1. Check your procedural and local rules (again)

Above, we recommended that your editing and polishing begin by reviewing all the procedural and local rules that govern your document. That review was to ensure that you have all the necessary content in place.

Now, you need to review the rules again. The procedural and local rules will likely have rules, not just about content, but also about format. The rules may, for example, dictate the typeface, the size of the font, line spacing, and the size of the margins. Now is the time to check those details. Although it may all look the same to you, it will not look the same to a judge who reads thousands of pages each month. The judge will recognize the difference and wonder why you were unable to follow the rules. The judge may begin to wonder whether you were sloppy in other ways. Avoid raising those doubts in the judge's mind. Comply with the rules.

2. Proofread

Polishing also requires you to carefully re-read what you have written. Sometimes, though, catching your own errors is easier said than done. Our brains are the "original autocorrectors."[8] With little effort, your brain makes sense of the unintelligible. You may have seen sentences like this one:

> For emaxlpe, it deson't mttaer in waht oredr the ltteers in a wrod aepapr, the olny iprmoatnt tihng is taht the frist and lsat ltteer are in the rghit pcale. The rset can be a toatl mses and you can sitll raed it wouthit a pobelrm.[9]

Even this mad scramble of letters and words can be intelligible thanks to your auto-correcting brain. Although this "code-cracking"[10] skill has its benefits, the skill is detrimental for finding errors in your own work, particularly when you read on a screen. A couple of strategies can help you find pesky errors.

First, use spell check and grammar check frequently, but do not rely on them. Spell check and grammar check are not foolproof. For example, spell check will not catch common typographical errors such as when you have typed "trail" instead of "trial" or "statue" instead of "statute." In addition, spell check does not notice if you have omitted a crucial word, such as "not" in this example: "The information disclosed is con-

---

8. Yuka Igarashi, *Why Do We Make Mistakes? Your Brain, the Original Autocorrector,* The Guardian, http://www.theguardian.com/media/mind-your-language/2013/aug/09/mind-your-language-brain-mistakes (Aug. 9, 2013).

9. Natalie Wolchover, *Why Yuor Barin Can Raed Tihs,* LiveScience, http://www.livescience.com/18392-reading-jumbled-words.html (Feb. 9, 2012).

10. *Id.*

fidential and **may** [**not**] be used for any other purpose . . . ."[11] Thus, spell check and grammar check, while useful tools, should never replace carefully re-reading what you have written.

To carefully re-read a document, you have to override your internal autocorrector. You can do this in a variety of ways. First, print your document—reading from paper lessens our brain's tendency to fill in what ought to be on the page. Next, take a colored piece of paper and use it to cover everything but the line you are reading. Move the paper as you go, so that only the lines you are reading are uncovered. The color provides a contrast to your page, making errors stand out. The colored paper will also prevent you from skipping lines and moving ahead too quickly, thereby further lessening the tendency to skim and overlook errors.

A second effective technique is to read your document aloud. Even better, read aloud while standing. Reading aloud will cause you to read more slowly, and you will hear mistakes that your eyes may not see. You will also more easily see (or hear) convoluted phrasing, misspelled words, abrupt transitions, omissions of words, grammatical errors, and even punctuation issues like a misplaced comma. You will particularly notice those overly long sentences that bog down the reader or those too-short, choppy sentences that interrupt the flow of ideas. Standing while reading aloud seems to heighten one's ability to see errors—maybe because when your brain is focusing on maintaining its balance and posture, the brain has less inclination to be diverted by other distractions.

Finally, you can also read the document backward. Reading backwards—sentence by sentence—is a particularly useful way to catch errors in spelling and word choice because your mind does not become overwhelmed by content.

No matter what deadlines you might face in law practice, always save time to carefully proofread your document. A clean document, free from errors, will enhance both your argument and your credibility.

3. Check citations

Finally, check your citations. Citations tell the judge and his staff how to find the authorities on which you have relied. In addition, clear and accurate citations demonstrate your attention to detail. If your citations are inaccurate, you will frustrate the judge and the judge's staff. You will also convey that you are an unreliable source of information.[12] Because

---

11. Example taken from www.oregonlegislature.gov/bills_laws/.../2014R1or Law0026ss.pdf.

12. Creating consistent, professional citations depends following your local rules, the rules from *The Bluebook* or the *ALWD Citation Manual*, or some combination of the two. This section does not provide specific citation rules. Rather, it provides tips for checking your citations.

citations depend on the content of each sentence, your final citation review should occur only after your text is finalized.

To check citations, first determine whether local citation rules apply. If
so, familiarize yourself with those rules. Then, print out a clean copy of
your document and highlight each citation. Check that each citation is accurate and has a correct pinpoint cite. Remember, too, to check that the
cases are still good law. You do not want to have to send a letter of apology
to the judge for having failed to acknowledge that a case was vacated in part.

4. Check the format

The format of your document refers to the visual appearance of your
document. A document's format depends on the font size and type, the
width of your margins, the total number of pages, line spacing, headers
and footers, and any required structures you should use while writing
your brief. Some aspects of your document's format are dictated by court
rules, and your document should already conform to those rules. But, other
formatting aspects are discretionary, and your choices can either add to
or detract from the impression that you are a capable lawyer, attentive to
details. Here, we address some common formatting issues.

- **Use traditional formatting for point headings, tables of content,
  and tables of authorities.** If you are unsure what traditional formatting looks like, return to Chapter 9, *Refining Persuasive Arguments*, which addresses how to format point headings and Chapter
  11, *Constructing Appellate Briefs*, which addresses how to format
  tables in an appellate brief.

- **Do not divorce a heading from its text.** That is to say, you should
  always have at least one line of text on the same page as a heading.
  If you do not have at least one line of text after a point heading,
  insert a page break before the heading so that the heading appears
  on the next page with the text.

- **If in doubt, add white space.** White space helps chunk material and
  allows readers to see more easily where one idea ends and another
  begins. Especially if you have single spaced text, such as a bulleted
  list (like this one) or an excerpt of a statute, add white space between
  the bullet points or sections of the statute. White space makes dense
  material easier to read.

- **Keep an eye out for any inconsistencies.** Little inconsistencies pop
  out to readers trained to look for detail. So, for example, check
  that the amount of space before and after section titles and point
  headings is consistent; that all section headings use the same font;
  and that all paragraphs are indented by the same amount. Many
  judges will even notice if you have two spaces after some periods and
  only one space after others. If they notice that inconsistency, they
  are distracted from your argument.

Although formatting issues other than the ones noted above may arise, those set out above are a few common issues that you can address in your own writing.

III. Statements of Fact (or of the Case)

The next section that must be carefully edited is the statement of facts (or of the case). That section is the judge's first opportunity to meet your client and hear about the case from your client's perspective. In reviewing this section, you will have several goals. First, you will want to ensure that it effectively presents your client's story. Next, you will want to check that it includes all the relevant facts, and that those facts are stated accurately. Finally, like all other sections of your brief, it should be easy to read and absorb.

Your review should begin by ensuring that the statement of facts includes all the relevant facts. To do that, review your argument and highlight every fact that you rely on. Then, make sure that those facts are included in your statement of facts. Think carefully about negative facts and whether you have included those facts in your argument and in your statement of facts.

Next consider your opening. Do the opening sentences provide context for the facts ahead? As we explained at the beginning of Chapter 9, *Refining Persuasive Arguments*, a reader is better able to absorb details, if you first provide context for those details. In a statement of facts, you can provide that context by introducing the parties and the crux of the conflict at the outset of your statement of facts. Do not rely on a preceding preliminary statement or question presented to provide that context. The statement of facts should be a self-contained unit. Thus, when editing your statement of facts, make sure that, instead of jumping into the facts, you have begun with context.

Then consider whether any descriptions of the facts need to be adjusted so that the statement of facts is consistent with your argument. For example, sometimes as you were drafting your argument, certain facts took on more significance than you initially thought they would. Now is the time to highlight those facts in your statement of facts.

Finally and most importantly, ensure the accuracy of all the facts and citations to facts. Doing so is essential to your credibility. The judge and the judge's staff should be able to find every fact that you rely on and agree that the fact is as you say it is.

* * *

Your argument and the statement of facts are usually the two most important sections in terms of persuading the judge to adopt the outcome you seek. Thus, these sections will absorb the bulk of your editing and

> **Just beginning to draft your statement of facts or statement of the case?**
>
> Return to Chapter 12, *Statements of Fact and of the Case*. It provides a detailed discussion about statements of fact and statements of the case—which facts to include, how to organize those facts, and how to emphasize favorable facts and address unfavorable facts.

polishing time. However, the other sections of your brief must also be reviewed. Below we describe the additional steps you will need to take to edit and then polish your motion and supporting memorandum or your appellate brief before submitting it to the court.

IV. If You Are Drafting a Motion and Supporting Memorandum of Law

If you are drafting a motion and memorandum of law in support of that motion, you still have a few more sections to review. Although it will depend on the rules and customs of your jurisdiction, the remaining sections likely include the following:

- The motion itself
- The introduction to the memorandum of law
- The final conclusion to the memorandum of law

Of those sections, the introduction to your memorandum of law plays the most significant role with respect to persuading a judge. The remaining sections—the motion and the final conclusion—are more functional than persuasive, but they, too, need to be reviewed because they contribute to the overall impression that your work will convey to the judge.

A. Edit Your Introduction

As discussed in Chapter 10, *Constructing Motions and Supporting Memoranda of Law*, some introductions to a memorandum of law merely state the procedural posture of the case. Others, preview the argument to come.

If your argument focuses on the procedural posture, then you should review the content to ensure that it accurately explains the procedure. It should also be selective. Rather than explaining all the procedural points between the time litigation was initiated and the current motion, choose those procedural events most relevant to the motion at hand.

If your introduction previews the argument, then you must first review your introduction to be sure that it is still consistent with the argument in the body of the memorandum. Consider, for example, whether your introduction uses the same language for key ideas as you now use in the arguments section. Often, when you edit the argument section, you adjust your language. Now is the time to ensure that the language of the introduction is consistent with the argument section, given any changes you might have made to the argument section.

In addition, if your introduction is argumentative and more than one paragraph long, check your thesis sentences for each paragraph. Each

> **Need help constructing an introduction to a memorandum of law?**
>
> Return to Chapter 10, *Constructing Motions and Supporting Memoranda of Law*, part III.B for a discussion about the different kinds of introductions and examples of each.

thesis sentence should assert your point. The thesis sentence for the first paragraph will likely assert the overall conclusion you wish the court to reach. The thesis sentences for other paragraphs should assert major sub-points that lead to your conclusion.

Finally, because the introduction is usually short and is the first overview the court will have of your argument, check the final sentences of each paragraph. A reader's eyes tend to also rest on the final sentence of paragraphs and so those should re-assert the point made in the paragraph, albeit with different words than the thesis sentence at the outset of the argument.

B. Edit All Remaining Sections

At this point, the remaining sections you will need to review are the motion itself and the final conclusion of your brief. Neither require particular crafting, rather you must simply ensure that you have the appropriate content. To that end, we recommend that you (once again) review the rules that govern your motion and, as necessary, return to the relevant portions of this book. The role and content of a motion are discussed in Chapter 10, *Constructing Motions and Supporting Memoranda of Law*, Part II. That same chapter, in part III.B, discusses the final conclusion to a memoranda of law.

C. Polish Your Introduction and All Remaining Sections

For all of these sections, you must polish for credibility, as described in part II.D, and polish for credibility as described above in part II.E. That means, as appropriate for the section, create active, readable sentences; proofread; check all citations; and ensure that the formatting looks professional. Doing so will ensure that the judge's first impression will be that this motion was submitted by a consummate professional.

V. If You Are Drafting an Appellate Brief

If you are drafting an appellate brief, you also have several more sections to review. Although it depends on the jurisdiction, those sections likely include the following:

- The cover
- The table of contents
- The table of authorities
- The issues (or questions) presented
- The statement of jurisdiction

- The summary of argument
- The final conclusion.

Of those sections, the issues (or questions) presented and the summary of the argument play the most significant roles with respect to persuading a panel of judges. The remaining sections are more functional than persuasive, but they, too, need to be reviewed because they contribute to the overall impression of your work.

A. Edit Your Issue Presented

Need help structuring your issue presented?

Return to Chapter 11, *Constructing Appellate Briefs,* Part I.E, for a discussion about the "Under-Does-When" approach and the "Statements and a Question approach."

When editing the issue presented, you should ask yourself whether the question, as it is currently written, leaves the reader with a clear "yes" or "no" answer in mind. Your question presented should lead your reader— the judge—to the answer you want the judge to reach.

One key to leading a judge to the answer you seek is to include facts supported by the record, rather than your characterization of the facts. If your question presented is supported by record facts, rather than your interpretation of them, the judge must accept them. For example, in Example 13-Q, the facts lead the judge to conclude that the citizen has been stopped for Fourth Amendment purposes. By contrast, in Example 13-R, the judge first has to determine whether your characterization of the facts is accurate before she knows whether the answer is "yes" or "no." That diversion makes the question presented less persuasive.

Example 13-Q · An issue presented that relies on facts

When Officer Lee approached the defendant she was dressed in her official police uniform. Her badge was clearly visible, as was her gun in its holster. She approached the defendant the defendant and stated, "Sir, I strongly suggest that you tell me whether you have any controlled substances on your person." Under the Fourth Amendment to the United States Constitution, did that interaction constitute a "stop"?

Example 13-R · An issue presented that characterizes the facts

In a full show of authority, in uniform and flaunting her gun and her badge, Officer Lee advanced on the defendant and demanded to know whether he had drugs on him. Under the Fourth Amendment to the United States Constitution, did that interaction constitute a "stop"?

After ensuring that you have the content that you want, then you must ensure that the content reads well. That inquiry often focuses on how many facts you have chosen to include in your question presented.

If the custom or requirement in your jurisdiction is to write a question presented in a single sentence, then you will have to work especially hard to make your question presented readable. Your question presented should include only the determinative facts; other details should be omitted. If the court's conclusion depends on its analysis of a lot of facts, then you may not be able to include all the determinative facts. Rather, you should choose the facts that are most likely to sway the court toward the outcome you seek and rely on just that subset of facts.

B. Edit the Summary of Your Argument

An effective summary of the argument should not repeat the argument. Instead, it should focus on the analytical conclusions that lead to the outcome you seek. When you are reviewing the summary of your argument you should, first, ensure that your summary is consistent with your argument. Often, as you edit the argument section, you adjust the language you use to make your point. Now is the time to ensure that the language you use in your summary of the argument is consistent with the language you use in the argument section.

> **Confused about how to summarize your argument?**
>
> Chapter 11, *Constructing Appellate Briefs*, Part I.G, provides examples for you to review.

In addition check the first and last sentence of each paragraph. As explained in Chapter 9, *Refining Persuasive Arguments*, a reader's eyes tend to rest on the first and last sentence of a paragraph. So, check those sentences to ensure that they assert an analytical conclusion you want the court to reach.

C. Edit All Remaining Sections

At this point, the remaining sections you will need to review are the cover, the table of contents, the table of authorities, the statement of jurisdiction, and the final conclusion to your brief. Those sections do not require particular crafting; rather, you must simply ensure that you have the appropriate content. To that end, we recommend that you (once again) review the rules that govern your motion and, as necessary, return to the relevant portions of this book, as listed in Table 13-S.

Table 13-S · Find the content to edit the remaining sections of your appellate brief

Remaining sections	Discussed in
Cover	Chapter 11, Part I.A
Table of contents	Chapter 11, Part I.B
Table of authorities	Chapter 11, Part I.C
Statement of jurisdiction	Chapter 11, Part I.D
Conclusion	Chapter 11, Part I.H

D. Polish the Question Presented, Summary of the Argument, and All Remaining Sections

Now that your brief has been edited, you must polish your brief for clarity, as described above in part II.D, and for credibility, as described above in part II.E. That means, as appropriate for the section, create active, readable sentences; proofread; check all citations; and ensure that the formatting looks professional. Doing so will ensure that the judges' first impression will be that this brief is written by a consummate professional.

VI. Customize Your Editing Checklist

Editing checklists are an excellent way to ensure that you systematically and thoroughly edit and polish your work. Table 13-T, below, is a sample checklist for editing and polishing your brief. Although general checklists are helpful, as you gain more experience, you should customize your checklist to include those items with which you consistently struggle—and all writers have them. The checklist below can, however, serve as a useful starting point.

Table 13-T · An editing checklist

I. Check your procedural and local rules

1. Locate and review your jurisdiction's procedural and local rules. They are usually available on the court's website. Sometimes procedural and local rules are listed separately. Other times, they are integrated into one list of rules.

    ❑ Skim the table of contents to ensure that you have found all rules that might possibly apply to your brief.

    ❑ Check your brief against all possibly relevant rules.

    ❑ Check that your brief includes all required content.

    ❑ Check that your brief conforms to all format requirements.

2. If your case has been assigned to a judge, check whether that judge has any standing orders. If the court's website does not have a link for standing orders, check with the clerk of court. Again, ensure that your document complies with any standing orders.

II. Argument

1. Edit for focus.

    ❑ Read only your thesis sentences.

    ❑ Does each thesis sentence assert a conclusion you want the court to reach and not merely something that is true?

❑ Together, do your thesis sentences outline your argument?

❑ Does each thesis sentence match the content of the paragraph to which it is attached?

❑ Read only your point headings.

  ○ Does each point heading assert a conclusion you want the court to adopt?

  ○ Together, do your point headings outline your argument?

  ○ Does each assertive point heading have a final punctuation mark?

❑ Integrate your theme.

  ○ Does your theme consistently reappear in point headings and thesis sentences?

2. Edit for emphasis.

❑ Are your rules drafted so that they emphasize the outcome you seek?

❑ Are case illustrations drafted to emphasize facts and reasoning that support the outcome you seek?

❑ Are your explanation of the law and application of the law to the facts consistent with each other—emphasizing the same key ideas and using similar language?

❑ Have you addressed any weaknesses and explained why, despite that weakness, the outcome you seek is warranted?

3. Edit for flow.

❑ Have you used roadmap sections whenever one issue breaks down into two or more issues? Use a roadmap section when the two or more issues share governing law.

❑ Have you used roadmap sentences to alert the judge to the structure of any complex or lengthy detail ahead?

❑ Check the transitions between paragraphs. Do they accurately explain the relationship between the two paragraphs that they connect?

4. Polish for clarity.

❑ Look for any sentence that is more than two lines long. Consider whether it should be shorter.

  ○ Does it have too many embedded phrases, signified by more than one set of commas? If so, break the sentence up.

  ○ Does it have too many prepositional phrases? If so, break the sentence up or consider whether any ideas can be omitted.

   ○ Are there words that can be omitted? Look for redundancies; empty phrases such as "it is" or "there are"; and words or ideas that are not actually necessary.

  ❑ Minimize passive voice.

   ○ Look for a "to be" verb + a word ending in -d, -ed, -n, -en, or -t and consider whether the sentence would be more effective using the active voice.

  ❑ Minimize nominalizations.

   ○ Look for any words with verbs in their root. Consider whether the verb form can be used.

   ○ Look also for any words ending in -ment, -ion, or -al.

5. Polish for Credibility.

  ❑ If you have not done so already, check your procedural and local rules (as well as any standing orders) to ensure that your format conforms to those rules (and orders).

  ❑ Proofread a hard copy of your argument.

   ○ Use spell check and grammar check, carefully considering the advice given.

   ○ Re-read your brief aloud, standing up, or backwards.

  ❑ On a hard copy of your brief, highlight every citation and check it for accuracy and consistency with local and professional citation rules.

  ❑ Does your document look nice? Is the formatting in your document consistent throughout?

III. Statement of Facts (or of the Case)

1. Highlight every fact in your argument and ensure that it is included in the statement of facts.

2. Check your opening. Does it provide context by doing the following:

  ❑ Identifying the parties?

  ❑ Explaining the crux of the conflict that brought the parties to court?

3. Re-read your statement of facts considering whether positive facts are appropriately highlighted and that unfavorable facts are placed in an appropriate context. If not, adjust.

4. Check all citations in the statement of facts.

  ❑ Compare your statement about a fact to the fact in the record. Is it accurate? If not, adjust.

  ❑ Check the format of each citation to ensure that it conforms to local and professional rules.

IV. If You Are Drafting a Motion and Supporting Memorandum of Law

1. Edit the introduction.

   ❑ With respect to procedural facts, check your introduction for accuracy.

   ❑ With respect to any overview of your argument, check to ensure it is consistent with your argument as it currently stands.

   ❑ Check thesis and final sentences to ensure that they assert conclusions you want the court to adopt.

2. Edit all remaining sections.

   ❑ Compare your motion against the requirements listed in the procedural and local rules to ensure you have all the required content.

   ❑ Review your final conclusion to be sure that it is asking for the relief that you are seeking.

3. Polish your introduction and all remaining sections.

   ○ Return to part II.4, *Polish for Clarity*, and part II.5, *Polish for Credibility* in this checklist and apply as appropriate to the introduction and all other remaining sections.

V. If You Are Drafting an Appellate Brief

1. Edit the issue presented.

   ❑ Does your issue presented lead the court to the "yes" or "no" answer you want the court to reach? If not, edit.

   ❑ Does your issue presented rely on facts that both parties would accept as true? If not, revise.

   ❑ Is your issue presented readable? If not, revise.

2. Edit the summary of the argument.

   ❑ Is your summary of the argument consistent with your argument as it currently stands?

   ❑ Check thesis and final sentences to ensure that they assert conclusions you want the court to adopt.

3. Edit all remaining sections.

   ❑ Compare your cover, table of content, table of authorities, statement of jurisdiction, conclusion, and any other remaining parts against your jurisdictional and local rules to ensure that you have all the required content.

   ❑ Review your final conclusion to ensure it is asking for the appropriate remedy. *See* Chapter 11, *Constructing Appellate Briefs*, part I.I for details about the different kinds of relief an appellate court can grant.

4. Polish your introduction and all remaining sections.

   ❑ Return to part II.4, *Polish for Clarity*, and part II.5, *Polish for Credibility* in this checklist and apply as appropriate to the issue presented, summary of the argument, and all other remaining sections.

Chapter 14

Oral Argument

Oral argument before a trial judge or an appellate court is the most visible part of the persuasive process. Television shows and motion pictures focus on the drama of the courtroom rather than on the long hours spent alone with a computer drafting a memorandum in support of a motion or polishing a brief. But how does oral argument fit into the bigger picture of the persuasive process? What are the keys to a good oral argument, and how do you prepare for it? What are the pitfalls you should be aware of? This chapter addresses those issues and more.

As is true with written work, your oral argument will be most effective if you keep in mind the purpose of oral argument and the needs of your audience. Accordingly, the chapter begins with § 14.1, which addresses the purpose of oral argument and how both the advocate's and the court's needs can be met. Next, § 14.2 addresses how to prepare for oral arguments. Then § 14.3 examines how to present your argument. The advice in those first three sections holds true no matter the tribunal in which you will argue. Lawyers, however, present oral arguments to trial judges and to appellate judges (as well as to administrative law judges and administrative boards). So, the last section, § 14.4, focuses on the differences between trial courts and appellate courts.

Section 14.1

The Purpose of
Oral Argument

I. The Court's Goals
   A. Clarify Factual and Legal Points
   B. Determine the Practical Impact of a Ruling
II. The Advocate's Goals
   A. Ensure that the Court Understands Your Argument
   B. Correct Misapprehensions and Address Concerns
   C. Respond to Claims That You Did Not Address in the Briefs

---

Before oral argument, both you and your adversary will have submitted briefs to the court, but brief writing is a one-way information exchange.[1] The court has not had a chance to ask questions or otherwise interact with the advocates who wrote the briefs. In contrast, oral argument is an interaction among advocates and judges. It is the opportunity for the judges to interact and have a conversation with advocates that distinguishes oral argument from the rest of the persuasive process.

At oral argument, the judges' overriding goal is to enlist the advocates' help in understanding the arguments that have been made in the briefs and the implications of those arguments. As an advocate, you, of course, want to make sure that the court understands your argument and that the court is comfortable with the implications of ruling in your favor. Thus, properly done, oral argument satisfies both the court's goals and the advocate's goals.

As explained in more detail below, oral argument is more a question-and-answer conversation than a speech. Although the broad goal of oral argument is for the court to better understand the case by asking questions—and for the advocates to explain the case and further their positions by responding to those questions—both the court and the advocates

---

1. As noted elsewhere, a persuasive document filed in a trial court is often referred to as a memorandum. In this chapter, all persuasive documents are referred to as briefs.

have other goals that they will attempt to achieve. Understanding the court's goals in asking questions and thinking about the goals you would like to accomplish in answering the questions will add value to your brief instead of simply repeating it.

I. The Court's Goals

In asking questions, courts have a variety of goals. As you move up the judicial hierarchy from trial courts to appellate courts, the goals (and thus the nature of the questions each court asks) tend to shift. This section addresses the different kinds of questions that each court is most likely to ask in furthering its goals. However, some kinds of questions you can expect no matter which court you are appearing in.

A. Clarify Factual and Legal Points

First, courts will seek to clarify factual and legal points that have been presented in the briefs. For example, the state in a criminal case may represent in its brief that the officer "invited" the defendant to accompany him to the police station, while defense counsel may state that the police officer "ordered" the defendant to accompany the officer to the police station. Legally, whether the officer's words were an invitation or an order may make a difference. Oral argument presents an opportunity for judges to seek the advocates' help in clarifying exactly what the officer said and how it was said. In addition to clarifying factual points, the court may seek to clarify a legal point, for example, whether the holding in a binding case is broad or narrow, or whether more recent cases have overruled an older case without expressly stating so.

B. Determine the Practical Impact of a Ruling

At oral argument judges are likely to ask the advocates to help them examine the practical impact of a ruling. A court is concerned not only with the practical impact of its ruling on the parties in the case before it, but also its effect on future cases.

Consider this example. In *Oregon v. Ashcroft*, the State of Oregon was defending its recently enacted Death With Dignity Act. The Act allows doctors to prescribe lethal doses of federally controlled narcotics to certain terminally ill patients, but the United States Attorney General sought to bar doctors from prescribing those drugs for purposes of assisted suicide. At oral argument, the Justices expressed concern about how a ruling outlawing prescription of those drugs would affect patients. Example 14.1-A illustrates how the United States Supreme Court justices considered the practical effect of their ruling.

Example 14.1-A • Examining the legal effect of an argument

[SOLICITOR] GENERAL CLEMENT: [T]he interpretation of the Attorney General . . . does not purport to foreclose the issue of assisted suicide —

JUSTICE SOUTER: Well, they say . . . that, in practical terms, that is exactly what it does, because the only way they can administer their law sensibly is by using these kinds of drugs, scheduled drugs.

GENERAL CLEMENT: . . . [P]hysician-assisted suicide and the use of federally controlled substances for physician-assisted suicide are not coextensive.

JUSTICE GINSBURG: But we're told that the — those methods are less gentle to the patient, the methods that the State of Oregon has authorized its physicians to prescribe. We are told, at least in some of the briefs, that, from the patient's point of view, it's much less upsetting.

Oral argument in *Gonzales v. Oregon*, 543 U.S. 1145 (2005),
aff'g *Oregon v. Ashcroft*, 368 F.3d 1118 (9th Cir. 2004).

Similarly, courts—especially appellate courts—are concerned with the impact a decision in one case will have on other, future cases. For example, imagine a case in which a child and her parents argue that, under the common law "public trust doctrine," the state must enact legislation to regulate greenhouse gases. In the case, the child and her parents would argue that, although the "public trust doctrine" was originally focused on waterways, the doctrine equally protects the atmosphere and obligates the state to regulate emissions. At oral argument, the court would likely be concerned about the impact of its ruling. If the court were to accept the argument that the public trust doctrine requires the government to regulate emissions, what else might the public trust doctrine require the state to do? Might the state need to regulate tree cutting and bee breeding? The court may similarly be concerned about its ability to determine under that doctrine when the state had sufficiently performed its duty to regulate the environment.

When they are concentrating on their client's legal arguments, advocates can easily lose sight of the real-world effect of a court's ruling. But courts need to know the practical effect of their rulings, and judges often use oral argument as a tool for getting at those practical effects.

II. The Advocate's Goals

Just as the court has its goals in hearing oral argument, the advocate also has goals in presenting oral argument. Generally, those two sets of goals are compatible. A good oral argument satisfies both the court's goals and the advocate's goals.

A. Ensure that the Court Understands Your Argument

As an advocate, your first goal is to make sure that the court understands your argument. For example, in rereading your brief, you may realize that you did not present a portion of your argument as coherently as you might have hoped. Oral argument is the chance to "fix" that defect. Or it may be that your opponent's briefing has pointed out some ambiguity in your argument as you briefed it. Oral argument provides an opportunity to clarify your argument in an interactive manner. Assuming that the argument you made in your brief is a good one, ensuring that the court understands it will make it more persuasive.

B. Correct Misapprehensions and Address Concerns

Oral argument is also an opportunity to demonstrate the soundness of your position in light of any concerns the court may have. As explained above, judges are concerned about the practical impact of their rulings. A judge's concerns will come to light from the questions that judge asks. Judges may be concerned that, if they adopt the position espoused in the brief, it will have negative side effects or that it will cut too broadly, or not broadly enough. At oral argument, you can address any concerns and provide the judge with a degree of comfort that ruling in your favor will not lead to untoward consequences, as in Example 14.1-B.

Example 14.1-B · Reassuring the court that ruling in your favor will not cause unanticipated results

---

COUNSEL: Thus, your honor, section 12.73 of the Penal Code is unconstitutional and should be struck down.

THE COURT: Counsel, if I rule in your favor, won't that effectively mean that roughly thirty percent of the inmates in our state prisons will have to be released immediately?

COUNSEL: No, Your Honor, such a ruling would affect only a small fraction of state inmates, for several reasons. First, …

C. Respond to Claims That You Did Not Address in the Briefs

Finally, you may need to respond to a claim that you did not have an opportunity to address in your brief. For example, suppose that you, as a respondent, argue that appellant's claim on appeal was not preserved in the trial court. The appellant, in the reply brief, has argued that the claim is, in fact, preserved. As the respondent, you do not have the opportunity to submit a written response to the new argument presented in appellant's reply brief. Thus, oral argument will be the first—and only—opportunity you will have to respond to the argument that the claim really was not preserved, so one of your goals at oral argument should be to respond to that argument. Similarly, suppose that the United States Supreme Court issues a decision in a case similar to yours the day before your oral argument. Oral argument may be the only opportunity you have to address the effect of that case on your case.

By keeping in mind what the court and advocates seek to achieve in oral argument—and how those goals fit into the context of the persuasive process—you are more likely to persuade the court that your position is correct and thus to have the court rule in your favor.

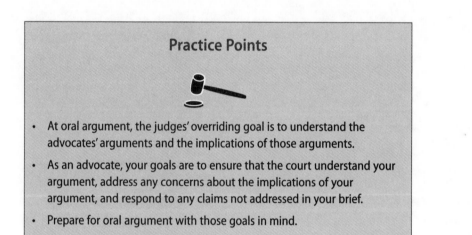

Practice Points

- At oral argument, the judges' overriding goal is to understand the advocates' arguments and the implications of those arguments.

- As an advocate, your goals are to ensure that the court understand your argument, address any concerns about the implications of your argument, and respond to any claims not addressed in your brief.

- Prepare for oral argument with those goals in mind.

Preparing for Oral Argument

I. Create a Strong Foundation
   A. Review the Briefs
   B. Know the Record
   C. Know the Law
   D. Review the Court's Rules

II. Prepare Your Argument
   A. Determine "Where the Game Will Be Played"
   B. Determine the Strengths and Weaknesses of Your Position and Your Opponent's Position
   C. Know the Boundaries of Your Position
   D. Anticipate Every Question the Court Will Ask and Prepare Responses
   E. Involve Others

III. Prepare Written Materials
   A. Script Your Opening
      1. Movant's or appellant's opening
      2. Respondent's opening
   B. Create Lectern Materials

IV. "Where Do I Park?" and Other Practical Matters
   A. Visit the Courtroom
   B. Investigate Court Protocol
   C. Choose Your Attire

When should you start preparing for oral argument? The answer is simple: Start preparing for oral argument as soon as you begin drafting your brief.

The first question you must ask is whether you will be allowed to present oral argument. Many courts do not allow oral argument in support of a motion or on appeal as a matter of course.[1] Thus, first make sure that you are entitled to present oral argument.

---

1. For example, parties do not have an automatic right to a hearing on a summary judgment motion. *E.g., Villanueva v. CNA Ins. Companies*, 868 F.2d 684, 688 (5th Cir.

Assuming you are permitted to argue, then you should be thinking about oral arguments as you draft your brief. As you draft each section of your brief and each argument, ask yourself, "When the judge reads this, what questions might she have?" If you can anticipate questions that a judge might ask at oral argument and address those questions in the brief, your brief will be more persuasive. It is never too early to begin preparing for oral argument, at least by having it in mind as you draft your brief.

Once all the briefs have been filed and a date for oral argument is set, your preparation begins in earnest. As you prepare, your overarching goal will be to plan for the questions that a judge is most likely to ask. But you also must be familiar with both sides' arguments, the facts in the case, and all relevant legal authority. This section explains how you can prepare for the court's questions and achieve the necessary familiarity with the facts and the law.

As you read, keep in mind that your level of preparation will vary depending on the importance and complexity of the issues and the court that you are appearing before. For example, an argument about a dispositive trial court motion may entail more preparation if it involves complex or novel legal issues, if the decision is likely to create an important precedent, or if the record is unusually lengthy. In contrast, your preparation may be minimal and your argument may be brief and straightforward for a simple, one-issue argument on a motion or on appeal. In addition, preparation tends to increase as you move up the judicial hierarchy. As you move from trial to appellate courts, oral arguments become more formal and frequently are longer.

Consider Saving Hypotheticals and Examples for Oral Argument

Some material is more effectively presented at oral argument. Certainly, all essential components of your argument must be presented in writing, and failure to do so may waive your right to present those issues. Some supporting material, however, may be best presented at oral argument. For example, as you prepare your brief you may think of a hypothetical that brilliantly illustrates your point. That hypothetical may not fit into the argument as you are drafting it. Make a note of that hypothetical and plan to use it at oral argument. The same approach applies to examples you think of that flesh out your argument. Make a note of those examples so that you will have them at hand for oral argument.

1989). Similarly, the federal circuit court panel to whom an appellate case is assigned may choose to have it submitted without oral argument. Fed. R. App. P. 34(a).

This section is directed at preparing for arguments on significant trial court motions and appellate arguments. Whittle down or expand the suggestions set out below as appropriate to the particulars of your case.

Finally, keep in mind that different advocates prepare for oral argument differently; if you know that a certain method of study helps you remember and synthesize material, use it. Despite those individual differences, experienced oral advocates have learned a number of common approaches to preparing for oral argument, which are discussed below.

I. Create a Strong Foundation

At oral argument, the court will expect you to be the expert on your case. Among other things, the court will look to you to explain or clarify the relevant law and facts. Because the court will expect you to be the expert about your client's case, your first step is to ensure that you can fulfill that role by knowing the facts of the case and the applicable law. In addition, the court will expect you to be familiar with courtroom procedure. So along with knowing the law and facts of your case, you will need to review the court's rules governing the presentation of oral arguments.

A. Review the Briefs

Because some time—and in appellate courts, often a long time—has passed since you filed your brief, your first step should be to review all briefs that have been filed in the case. As you review, "put your judge hat on." Read the briefs in the order that the judge will, and to the extent possible, try to view the briefs from a neutral judge's perspective.

As you read each brief, ask yourself these questions:

- Which arguments are "must win" arguments?
- Which points can be conceded if necessary?
- What are the strengths and weaknesses in each argument?
- Which arguments would benefit from additional explanation or clarification at oral argument?

Highlight important passages in the briefs, take notes, or outline the arguments, if those methods help you remember and understand the briefs. As you review, begin to develop a list of questions the judges may ask—because the facts are not clear, because an argument is not clear, or because the impact of an argument is not clear.

As you review the briefs, remember that courts tend not to look kindly on arguments raised for the first time at oral argument. Rather, at oral argument, courts expect you to clarify arguments already presented. If, as you prepare your argument, you think of new arguments that you

---

Don't Raise an Argument for the First Time at Oral Argument

JUSTICE: . . . Well, what I'm saying is, I'm confused. I've read the briefs. . . . And so we're hearing new theories here for the first time. . . .

[COUNSEL]: I am — I, I, I appreciate that. . . .

JUSTICE: I mean, we're here to discuss the issues that were briefed on appeal. You, you don't get multiple briefings. . . . It's not okay to come and make your arguments that have been ne — never made to any court. . . . I don't — the arguments you're making here, and I've read those briefs pretty carefully, and I wouldn't claim to remember everything I read, but some of these seem to me — to be new to me. Am I, am I incorrect on that?

Oral argument in *Henry v. J.P. Morgan Chase Bank*,
B249535, 2014 WL 1481139
(Cal. Ct. App. Apr. 16, 2014).

---

wish you had made in your brief, try to present them as extensions of or variations on arguments that you have already made in writing.

B. Know the Record

In light of the number of cases they hear, judges cannot be expected to know your case as well as you do. You are the expert on your case, and a judge must be able to rely on your expertise. Accordingly, you must be familiar with the record, either the relevant evidence in a trial court argument or the record on appeal in an appellate argument.

Make sure you know where in the record the court will find important documents or testimony. For example, if the case turns on a provision in a complex contract, and the contract was introduced as an exhibit at trial or attached to a motion, you should be able to tell the judge where to look in the file or appellate record for that provision. In a similar vein, if certain testimony is a crucial part of the argument, make sure that you know what the testimony says and where it can be found. Again, highlighting and taking notes on the record are useful ways of processing it in a way that will keep it in your memory.

C. Know the Law

You should reread the cases and other legal authorities that were cited in the briefs and make sure you are familiar with them. Although you need not memorize every authority, you should be familiar with every legal authority that you or your opponent has cited in the briefs. The more central an authority is to an argument, the more familiar you should be with that authority. Again, processing the authorities in a way that will ingrain them in your memory (for example, highlighting, outlining, or summarizing them) will benefit you at oral argument.

You must also update all authorities to ensure that they are still good law, using Shepherd's®, KeyCite®, Bcite℠, or another citator. It would be embarrassing if, at oral argument on a summary judgment motion, a judge asked, "Counsel, didn't the governor sign a bill last week that takes effect immediately and that repeals the statute at issue in this case?" and you were unaware of the bill. Similarly, no advocate should be caught having to answer "I don't know" to the following question from an appellate court bench: "Counsel, didn't we issue an opinion in a different case yesterday that rejected your position?" Be prepared and up-to-date.

D. Review the Court's Rules

The last step in creating a strong foundation is to review the court's rules that govern oral argument. As stated throughout this book, knowing and following the court's procedural rules is a fundamental prerequisite to persuading a judge of anything. You should check the court's website for the rules of trial or appellate procedure for that jurisdiction, as well as the court's local rules.

In reviewing the court's rules, be sure to determine how much time you will have in which to present your argument. Preparing for a thirty-minute argument (the time allotted each side in the U.S. Supreme Court) is different from preparing for a ten-minute argument (as each side is allotted in some cases in the federal courts of appeals and other courts). Knowing how long you have for your argument will prevent you from trying to shoehorn seven major points into a ten-minute argument on a simple motion. Similarly, knowing that you have a half-hour will allow you to prepare to spend your time convincing the court of the four points you need to prevail, rather than having to choose only one.

II. Prepare Your Argument

As explained above, as you review the briefs, the record, and the law, you should begin to ask yourself certain questions:

- Which arguments are "must win" arguments?
- Which points can be conceded if necessary?
- What are the strengths and weaknesses in each argument?
- Which arguments would benefit from additional explanation or clarification at oral argument?

Those questions will allow you to determine "where the game will be played" at oral argument, that is, what points the court will focus on. As you prepare, you will need to dig deeper into your arguments by examining the limits of your argument and imagining questions that the court will have. The text below guides you through those thought processes.

A. Determine "Where the Game Will Be Played"

Begin your preparation by considering "where the game will be played." Often, one point in your argument is a "pivot point" (as one judge calls it).[2] If you lose that point, you lose the argument. For example, in an appeal in which the parties dispute whether a claim of error was preserved for review, that argument about preservation is a "pivot point": If the appellant does not convince the court that the error was preserved for appellate review, the court will not consider the merits, and the appellant will lose. It might be, in such a case, that the merits of the claim are not in serious dispute. In such a case, each side's preparation should focus on convincing the judges that the claim of error was (the appellant) or was not (the respondent) preserved. That is, the "game" at oral argument will be "played" around the pivot point of preservation.

Similarly, the primary legal issue in your motion for summary judgment may be well-briefed and fairly straightforward, but whether the trial court has jurisdiction may be a much thornier proposition. Although the merits of the case may be much "sexier," you should prepare to use your time at oral argument addressing the threshold technical issue of jurisdiction. That is where the game will be played.

Always consider where the game will be played as you prepare, and make sure that you plan to spend the bulk of your time at oral argument addressing those issues.

B. Determine the Strengths and Weaknesses of Your Position and Your Opponent's Position

Next, consider which parts of your argument are strongest and which are weakest. If you have presented a strong argument in your brief on a certain point and your opponent has not refuted it, you will waste precious oral argument time if you choose to discuss that point. Instead, in preparing, think about weaker or more difficult aspects of your argument and how you can build on what is in the brief to persuade the court that your position is correct.

Of course, even if you believe that your brief adequately addresses an issue that is central to resolution of the case—that is, the game will be played around that issue—you should consider devoting some time to it. In short, when preparing, take into account both those points that you believe need bolstering and those points that are central to your case.

---

2. Chief Judge Rick Haselton of the Oregon Court of Appeals.

C. Know the Boundaries of Your Position

Having taken the steps set out above, you must now begin to rigorously question your position. In particular, you must determine the limits of your position. To determine the limits of your position, you must clarify what rule you are asking the court to adopt and then consider how that rule will apply under different scenarios that the court might, one day, be confronted with.

Imagine, for example, that you are defending a criminal defendant who has been charged with burglary, a crime that requires that the perpetrator enter a "building or occupied structure" with the intent to commit a crime therein. Your client entered a recreational vehicle (RV) and took

---

Know Your Position: An Example

The *Oregon v. Ashcroft* case, introduced in § 14.2, provides an example of the importance of knowing your position. That case focused on the legality of a state law permitting physicians to prescribe lethal doses of controlled substances to terminally ill patients. The state took the hard position that the U.S. Attorney General had no authority to determine whether a medical practice allowed by state law was or was not "legitimate." Thus, the state argued, the Attorney General could not revoke a physician's license to prescribe controlled substances if the doctor had prescribed a controlled substance in accordance with the state's Death with Dignity law.

Clearly, the judges hearing the case would be concerned about the limits of the state's argument. Was the state arguing that, no matter what a state allows a physician to do, the U.S. Attorney General has no authority revoke the physician's license under the federal Controlled Substances Act? That was, in fact, the state's position. Although it might make the advocate nervous to take such an extreme position, that logically had to be the state's position.

At oral argument, this exchange occurred:

Q: Counsel, under your analysis, if Oregon passed a law allowing physicians to prescribe morphine (a controlled substance) for the sole purpose of increasing a patient's psychological well-being, could the U.S. Attorney General determine that such a use was not "legitimate" and revoke a physician's license to prescribe controlled substances?"

A: No, Your Honor, that would be outside of the U.S. Attorney General's authority . . . .

Without thinking in advance about the logical end of the state's position, the advocate might be worried that answering the question "no" would seem unpalatable to the judges. But, given the state's theory, the answer had to be "no" and recognizing that point before oral argument made the advocate's response more confident and persuasive.

fifty dollars in cash. You move to have the indictment dismissed, arguing that an RV is not a building or occupied structure.

At oral argument, the judge may ask, "If the RV has not been moved for one year and has a family living in it, would it qualify as a building or occupied structure?" If you have not thought carefully about the limits of your position, you might struggle with your response. But if you have thought carefully about the rule you are proposing, the answer will be straightforward. If you are advocating for a rule that says that any vehicle *capable* of being moved cannot be a building or occupied structure, you will confidently respond, "No, Your Honor, and let me explain why...." If, however, your preferred rule is more narrow, you might respond, "Yes, Your Honor, that might be a building or occupied structure, but that was not the case here."

In short, think carefully about what rule you want the court to apply to your case. Test the rule under different factual scenarios to see how it works. If you know the boundaries of that rule, you will be able to confidently respond to the hypothetical fact scenarios that the court throws out at oral argument.

D. Anticipate Every Question the Court Will Ask and Prepare Responses

As you think about where the game will be played, the strengths and weaknesses of your argument, and the limits of your position, begin to develop a list of questions that the court is likely to ask. As stated above, what makes oral argument unique in the persuasive process is its interactive nature: Judges ask questions and advocates respond. It follows that perhaps the most important part of preparing for oral argument is to anticipate the questions that the judge or judges will ask and to have prepared responses to those questions. Although you may sometimes be forced to answer an unanticipated question on the fly, you will be more articulate, and your answers will be more persuasive, if you have predicted which questions the judge or judges will ask and have prepared for them. As suggested above, you should begin anticipating the judges' questions from the moment you start drafting the brief. You can also anticipate questions later in your preparation by reviewing the briefs and asking yourself about the weaknesses in your case or anything that might, on rereading your brief, be less clear than you had hoped.

In addition, you should consider the court and its role. If you are arguing before a trial court, the judge is likely to be concerned about the controlling law and which facts are in dispute. By contrast, if you are arguing before an appellate court, that court is likely to be more concerned about how a decision in this case will affect future, similar cases. Therefore, you should try to imagine what rule your case will stand for in the future and whether that rule is one that a court will feel comfortable adopting.

The way in which you prepare for the court's questions will vary depending on the complexity and importance of the case. In a relatively simple case, you might simply keep a list of likely questions as you brief the case and prepare for argument, thinking about what your response will be. In more complex or important cases, you might write out answers to each potential question as a way of bringing your thoughts together and ensuring that you have a good answer. In the biggest cases, you might actually host one or more moot courts in which experienced attorneys act as judges, posing questions while you practice responding.[3] In sum, the bulk of your preparation energy should be devoted to planning carefully for the court's questions.

E. Involve Others

Finally, you should consider seeking help from others. Because you are so close to your case and because you are wedded to one position, having others listen to your argument can be invaluable. Explaining your argument to another person—even, or perhaps especially, a person who is not law-trained—will help you recognize rough patches in your presentation, will allow you to identify difficult aspects of your argument, and will generate additional questions for which you can prepare responses should those questions arise at oral argument. As suggested above, when a case is particularly important or complex, you may want to arrange for a formal moot court with attorneys who have read the briefs and will act as judges. In fact, conducting such moot courts— sometimes a number of them before different attorneys—is the standard practice in United States Supreme Court cases.

III. Prepare Written Materials

Although, as explained above, oral argument is more of a conversation than a presentation, some materials should be prepared in advance. In particular, you should script and memorize your opening. In addition, you should create materials that you will bring with you to the lectern.

A. Script Your Opening

To ensure a smooth start to their arguments, most advocates write out their opening statement and memorize it. In trial courts you are

---

3. The "moot courts" that are used by experienced attorneys to prepare for oral arguments should be distinguished from the moot court competitions in law school, which are discussed in Appendix A.

likely to introduce yourself as in Example 14.2-A, and in appellate courts, you are likely to introduce yourself as in Example 14.2-B.

Example 14.2-A • The standard trial court salutation

Your Honor. My name is _____. I represent defendant [or plaintiff] XYZ Corporation.

Example 14.2-B • The standard appellate court salutation

May it please the court. My name is _____. I represent appellant [or respondent] XYZ Corporation.

After uttering those stock phrases, your opening will vary depending on whether you represent the party that is arguing first (the moving party or the appellant) or the responding party.

1. Movant's or appellant's opening

Let's assume that you are first to the lectern as the moving party (at trial) or the party who lost below, the appellant (on appeal). In that case, you should memorize the first twenty to thirty seconds of your argument. That opening will set the tone for the argument, and especially in an appellate court, it may be the last time during the argument that you have control over what is being discussed. Take advantage of that opportunity. Preparing and memorizing—not reading—the opening also will give you a chance to launch into your argument on "autopilot" so that you can hit your stride without worrying about what you're going to say.

After introducing yourself with one of the stock phrases mentioned above, your opening should introduce your theme and then give an overview of what you plan to address. Example 14.2-C provides a typical opening that the moving party might make on a motion for summary judgment. Example 14.2-D provides a typical opening that an appellant might make.

Example 14.2-C • A moving party's opening

Notice how the lawyer begins with a conclusion.

The lawyer then provides a roadmap of the argument.

Your Honor. My name is Sol Cohen, and I represent J&B Corporation. In this case, there is no genuine issue of material fact, and my client is entitled to judgment as a matter of law. I will begin by explaining why the exhibits that plaintiff introduced—although they suggest a possible issue of fact—do not demonstrate that there is an issue of *material* fact. I will then explain why the material facts are undisputed, and why, given those facts, the law clearly dictates that we are entitled to judgment. This court should grant J&B's motion for summary judgment.

Example 14.2-D • An appellant's opening

May it please the Court. My name is Andreas Rojas, and I represent the State. Although this case takes place in the context of important issues surrounding the end of life, the issue before this court — and the issue I will address today — is much more mundane: What is the authority of the Attorney General to override state law governing medical practice? Unless the Court has questions, I do not intend to address the jurisdictional issue, which is adequately addressed by the briefs. Rather, I will explain why the Attorney General exceeded his authority in this case.

> Here, the lawyer introduces the theme of his argument.
>
> The lawyer then provides a roadmap of his argument.

Local customs may vary with respect to whether you should ask the court for a recitation of the facts. However, when arguing before a trial court, lawyers commonly begin with an overview of the facts. In appellate courts, normally you do not ask the court if it would like a recitation of the facts; you should assume that an appellate court is familiar with the facts of your case unless you have reason to suspect otherwise. You should, in any event, be prepared to provide a summary of the facts in the event a judge asks for it.

Example of a Short U.S. Supreme Court Opening

MR. GARTLAN: Mr. Chief Justice, and may it please the Court: This case presents three questions. The first is, "Does article 36 of the Vienna Convention on Consular Relations confer rights to individuals such as Mr. Sanchez-Llamas?" The second is, "Can Mr. Sanchez-Llamas enforce the right in a State criminal prosecution?" And the third is, "Can the right be enforced by suppression?"

Oral argument in *Sanchez-Llamas v. Oregon*, 548 U.S. 331 (2006).

Example of a More Complex U.S. Supreme Court Opening

MS. KAPLAN: Mr. Chief Justice, and may it please the Court:
I'd like to focus on why [the Defense of Marriage Act (DOMA)] fails even under rationality review. Because of DOMA, many thousands of people who are legally married under the laws of nine sovereign States and the District of Columbia are being treated as unmarried by the federal government solely because they are gay.

These couples are being treated as unmarried with respect to programs that affect family stability, such as the Family Leave Act, referred to by

Continued on next page

Justice Ginsburg. These couples are being treated as unmarried for purposes of federal conflict of interest rules, election laws, and anti-nepotism and judicial recusal statutes.

And my client was treated as unmarried when her spouse passed away, so that she had to pay $363,000 in estate taxes on the property that they had accumulated during their 44 years together.

Oral argument in *United States v. Windsor*, 133 S. Ct. 2675 (2013).

2. Respondent's opening

If you are representing the responding party (either the non-moving party in a trial court or the respondent in an appellate court), a prepared opening is less important. A responding party must be more flexible in her argument, adapting it in light of the opposing party's argument, the court's questions during that argument, and the responses to the questions. Thus, a previously prepared opening for a responding party may be completely inappropriate in light of the direction that the argument already has taken. Nonetheless, it can be comforting and useful to prepare an opening in the event that nothing unanticipated takes place during the opposing party's argument.

One very effective way to begin if you are responding is to introduce yourself and then build on some part of the argument that has preceded you. For example, you can begin by focusing on a point that appeared to be important to the court during opposing counsel's argument, as in Examples 14.2-E and 14.2-F.

Example 14.2-E · Respondent's opening on appeal

May it please the court: My name is Matan Bar-Lev, and I represent BustaMove, LLC. I would like to turn first to the question that Judge Ruiz asked about appellant's third argument. Judge Ruiz is right to be skeptical of appellant's position for two reasons.

Example 14.2-F · Respondent's opening in a trial court

Your Honor, my name is Dan Olson, and I represent the County. Before turning to the main focus of my argument, I'd like to note that the testimony that Your Honor asked about can be found in the Arnold Deposition, pages 12 to 14. And Your Honor can see that there simply is no mention of waiver in that passage.

**Example of U.S. Supreme Court Respondent's Opening
That Builds on the Previous Argument**

MR. FEIGIN: Thank you, Mr. Chief Justice, and may it please the Court: I'd like to begin, if I could, by addressing Justice Kagan's question, which Justice Sotomayor then followed up on. We think that the probable cause finding and the fact that they want to repeat essentially the speech that was made earlier are the two critical factors in this case and without that, none of their claims would be justiciable. As it is, we think that their purely legal First Amendment challenges are ripe for those particular case-specific reasons.

Oral argument in *Susan B. Anthony List v. Driehaus*,
134 S. Ct. 2334 (2014).

**Example of U.S. Supreme Court Respondent's Opening That Builds on
the Previous Argument Without Any Introduction**

[SOLICITOR] GENERAL VERRILLI: Mr. Chief Justice, and may it please the Court:

The line drawn in *Abood* is sound. It has the force of stare decisis behind it, it is completely consistent with this Court's First Amendment jurisprudence, and it requires affirmance. If I could, I'd like to turn to the questions that Justice Kennedy has raised because I do think it gets to the key issue in the case.

Oral argument in *Harris v. Quinn*, 134 S. Ct. 2618 (2014).

Although as counsel for the responding party you have the opportunity to begin by picking up on a point the court had previously been discussing, it may be that nothing unanticipated or that requires a response happened before you stand up. In that case, your prepared opening may be both comforting and an appropriate place to begin.

B. Create Lectern Materials

Although some advocates may present oral argument with no notes at all, that is a good idea only in the simplest of cases. Even experienced advocates have notes with them to which they can refer. Having those materials accessible during oral argument is important, but it is the preparation of the notes that is the key to a successful and low-stress argument. Many experienced oral advocates carefully prepare an outline of their argument, but find that they never consult it during the argument. But that is a good sign: In preparing the outline, the advocate has internalized the argument.

Experienced advocates also work hard to condense their lectern materials. Minimizing the number of items you bring with you to the lectern will prevent you from fumbling through the pages as you search for information. In addition, and perhaps more importantly, condensing your case into a small enough bundle to take to a lectern forces you to understand your case and be prepared to present and discuss the pivotal aspects of the case.

Accordingly, most advocates use either a manila folder or a thin (perhaps one inch thick) three-ring binder to organize their lectern materials. Everything should be prepared in a way that makes it easy to find and easy to read when you are nervous. Many experienced advocates recommend using at least fourteen-point type and double-spacing your materials.

What goes onto an advocate's manila folder or into a binder varies, but at a minimum you should include an easily accessible list of "must-make" points. As explained below, sometimes the court's questions can take you away from your planned argument. Thus, create a short (no more than three to five items) list of the major points you must make during argument. This list can be placed on the inside front cover of a binder or stapled to the front of a manila folder. In either case, the list should be in big, bold print. With that list easily accessible, you will find it easier to return to your argument and to ensure that you have made all critical points before the argument is over.

The next document to include is an outline of your argument. The outline can be as short as one page and should never be more than a few pages long (in fourteen-point type). Although some advocates write out the entire argument *as part of their preparation*, your binder should not include a full-text version of your argument. The temptation to read your argument will be too great, and if you succumb to that temptation, your

---

Lectern vs. Podium

Strictly speaking, a podium is a raised platform on which a speaker stands to deliver a speech. A lectern is a raised stand, often with a slanted top, that the speaker can use to hold her notes. Courtrooms have lecterns, not podiums. Nonetheless, most discussions of oral argument refer to the "podium" rather than the "lectern." We use the term "lectern."

argument will suffer. Outline your argument using phrases in your notes instead of full sentences to avoid that temptation to read. Practice your argument from the outline.

After your outline, include materials that you might need to access during argument. For example, if the case involves the interpretation of a statute, you should include the text of the statute in your binder. If there are two pages of key testimony that will be important in the argument, include those pages of transcript in the binder. If your argument will depend heavily on a discussion of the concurring and plurality opinions in a U.S. Supreme Court case, include those opinions in the binder. Likewise, if the case turns on the interpretation of paragraph 34.1.2.55(j) of a contract, you should include the exact wording of that paragraph in your materials.

When preparing those supplemental materials, some advocates simply photocopy or print them from their original sources. Another approach—and probably the better one—is to import or type them into a word processor and format them for easy reading at the lectern. If a judge has a question about a statutory provision, or if you want to quote it, your argument will be smoother if you have the provision in your lectern materials, tabbed for easy access, and printed in fourteen-point type. Rather than squinting at a photocopy of a Westlaw® or Lexis® printout, you will be able to pay attention to what you are saying and maintain eye contact with the court. Moreover, the additional "processing" of the material will help you understand and remember it better.

Finally, at the very top of your materials include any personal reminders that might be helpful. For example, if you have a tendency to talk too fast, make a note to yourself: "Slow down!" If you are nervous about how you are going to begin your argument and you think you will stumble, write, "May it please the court…." Put that personal reminder on the first page of your binder or, better, on the inside left cover in big, bold print. Many advocates find those highly personal reminders comforting during what can be a tense experience.

Preparing lectern materials is a vital part of preparing for oral argument. Yet you may find, as do many advocates, that after spending hours preparing a gorgeous lectern binder, you hardly ever look at it during oral argument. Rather than viewing all that preparation as a waste of time, recognize that in preparing the binder you mentally processed the material and winnowed it down sufficiently to produce a focused oral argument. The more time you spend preparing those materials, the less likely you are to need them at the lectern.

An example of what your lectern materials might look like is presented in Figure 14.2-G.

Figure 14.2-G · Lectern materials

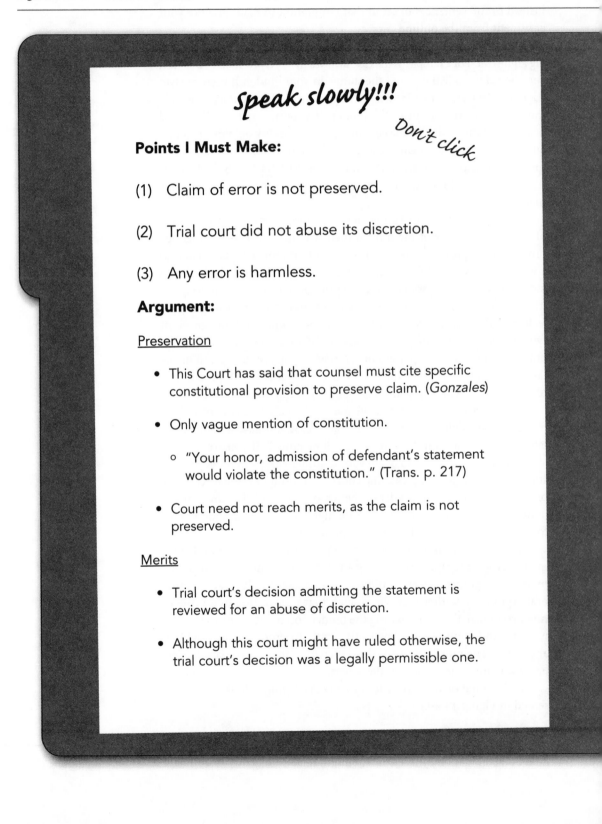

- To make later statement to police inadmissible, defendant must unequivocally invoke right to counsel. (*Davis*)

- Defendant's statement: "I have nothing to say." (Trans. p. 112)

- "I have nothing to say" is not unequivocal invocation.

  o See *Davis* ("if a suspect makes a reference to an attorney that is ambiguous or equivocal in that a reasonable officer in light of the circumstances would have understood only that the suspect might be invoking the right to counsel, our precedents do not require the cessation of questioning").

Harmless Error

- If the disputed testimony is merely cumulative of other evidence that already established the same fact, then the error is harmless. (*Holcomb*)

- Defendant's statement that the trial court admitted was identical to the statements of three other witnesses. (*Izaguirre*, *Bigelow*, and *Sparks*)

- Even if the trial court should have excluded the statement, any error was harmless.

Unless the court has further questions, I have nothing to add. Thank you. (sit down!)

IV. "Where Do I Park?" and Other Practical Matters

On the day of your argument, you will want to be focused on your argument and not on such questions as "Where do I park?" To that end, take care of practical details—such as determining where you park, where the courtroom is located, and what to wear—before the day you are to argue.

A. Visit the Courtroom

Before oral argument, you should visit the courtroom and, if possible, observe an argument. By actually going to the courtroom, you will ensure that you know how to get there, where to park, how much travel time you will need to arrive on time, where the restrooms are, whether water will be provided at counsel table, where the clerk or bailiff sits, and other aspects of the setting. Learning the lay of the land beforehand will make you more comfortable and allow you to focus on your argument when you give it.

As you watch others' oral arguments, note the timing, pace, and style of attorneys' arguments, and what seems effective. Note the concerns of the judge or panel of judges, how they present their questions, and how counsel most effectively answers their questions. If you can, try to observe the judge or judges who will be hearing your case. You will learn about the particular preferences of the judges, the degree of formality expected, and the dynamics of that particular courtroom.

B. Investigate Court Protocol

In addition to visiting the courtroom, you may also want to search the Internet to find useful guides to oral argument specific to the court in which you are to argue. For example, the North Carolina Bar Association produces a useful guide entitled, "Guide for Counsel for Oral Arguments Before the North Carolina Court of Appeals" that covers everything from where to park, to the table at which appellant's counsel sits, to how to address the court. Similarly, the U.S. Supreme Court provides a "Guide for Counsel in Cases to Be Argued Before This Court," which "is designed to assist attorneys preparing cases for argument before [the] Court, especially those who have not previously argued" there. Look for such guides and follow them.

Finally, ask around. The particular courtroom customs in one county, district, or level of court often are not written down. Attorneys who have gone before you are great resources for those unwritten rules.

C. Choose Your Attire

The overriding goal in choosing your attire is to wear clothing that will not distract the court from your message. Just as failing to follow court rules will distract a judge from your written message, anything unusual or unexpected about your dress will distract the court from your oral message. In courtrooms, business attire is always appropriate. You want the judges focused on what you are saying, not squinting at you trying to figure out what the symbol on your tie is or what that strange-shaped pin on your blouse is supposed to be. Your attire for oral argument cannot be too boring or conservative. As the U.S. Supreme Court guide says, "Appropriate attire for counsel is conservative business dress in traditional dark colors (e.g., navy blue or charcoal gray)."

Preparing for your first oral argument can be nerve-wracking. Table 14.2-H can help ensure that you are prepared. In sum, remember what the court's goals are and what your goals are. Process the material until you are comfortable with it, remembering that the judges expect you to be the expert on your case. Know your position and try to anticipate and prepare a response to every possible question. Prepare for a conversation, not a speech. Prepare user-friendly lectern materials. When you have done all that, you will sleep soundly the night before the argument.

Table 14.2-H • Oral Argument Preparation Checklist

A. General preparation
- ❑ Determine whether oral argument will be held in your case. (You should make this determination before submitting your brief.)
- ❑ Review court rules regarding oral argument; conduct any other research, such as consulting a guide on the court's website or talking to other lawyers who have argued in that court.

B. Big-picture preparation
- ❑ Review all briefs.
- ❑ Review the lower court opinion(s), if any.
- ❑ Review key documents or the appellate record.
- ❑ Review the authorities cited in the briefs.
- ❑ Draft a list of questions that might be asked.
- ❑ Prepare (orally or in writing) responses to questions.
- ❑ Think about and know the weaknesses and strengths in your position and in your opponent's position.
- ❑ Make sure that you can articulate your position precisely.

C. Short-term preparation

- ❑ Shepherdize™, KeyCite™, BCite℠, or otherwise update all authorities.
- ❑ Conduct moot courts or discuss the case with others.
- ❑ Prepare an opening and memorize it.
- ❑ Prepare your oral argument notes, including your outline, important documents, "must-make" points, and personal reminders.

D. Final preparation

- ❑ Select your attire, make sure you know how to get to the courthouse, where to park, etc.
- ❑ Review your oral argument notes materials.
- ❑ Get a good night's sleep.

Section 14.3

Presenting Oral Argument

I.   Your Frame of Mind
II.   Inhabit Your Space Confidently
III. Leave Your Baggage Behind
IV.   Make Eye Contact
V.   Speak Slowly and Simply
VI.   Have a Conversation
VII. Use Humor with Care
VIII. Assert Conclusions, Not Your Beliefs
IX.   Deliver Your Opening
X.   Respond to Questions from the Bench
    A. Stop Talking and Listen
    B. Pause
    C. Ask for Clarification, If Necessary
    D. Respond With "Yes" or "No"; Then Explain Your Answer
    E. Never Praise a Judge's Question
    F. Always Answer a Question When It Is Asked
    G. Embrace Hypotheticals
    H. Recognize Friendly Questions
    I. Admit When You Do Not Know the Answer
    J Do Not Ask Any Other Questions
    K. Recognize the Logical End of an Answer
    L. After Answering the Court's Question, Return to Your Planned Argument or Adjust as Necessary
XI.   Conclude
XII. Listen When the Court Questions Opposing Counsel
XIII. Rebuttal

When the day of argument finally arrives, get to court early, and get settled in the courtroom as you wait for your case to be called. Remember that, even though you may not be at counsel table or the lectern yet, you are still in the formal setting of the courtroom. It will not advance your case if, by the time you approach to argue your case, the judges have already seen you texting, whispering, or rolling your eyes at others' arguments.[1] Act professionally at all times.

This section addresses how to present your argument from the moment you stand to speak to when you return to your chair. As explained above, the core of oral argument is answering questions. Moreover, that is the part of oral argument that many new advocates find the most daunting, so this section spends the most time on that subject.

I. Your Frame of Mind

Your frame of mind throughout the argument should be that you are an intelligent person with special knowledge of your case trying to help other intelligent people reach the right result. You should think of yourself as a helpful expert, there to guide the court to your preferred outcome. If you maintain that frame of mind—the perspective that you are there to be helpful to the court—your argument and responses to questions will be more persuasive. By contrast, if your tone is combative or suggests that your agenda is more important than the court's questions, you will be less persuasive and you will not endear yourself to the people who ultimately will decide the fate of your case.

Remember, too, that there is no "best" argument style. Some advocates are like pit bulls, forcefully (though respectfully) presenting their arguments. Others are effective by calmly showing the court how reasonable their approach to the problem is. Think about what style comes naturally to you and use it, remembering to be respectful and professional within that style. Advocates tend to run into trouble when they attempt to adopt a style that does not feel natural to them. Unless you are particularly obnoxious or overbearing, the best advice is this: Be yourself.

II. Inhabit Your Space Confidently

When your turn arrives, stand, and if the custom in the court is to speak at a lectern, approach the lectern confidently and with your materials in hand.

Once you are standing, either at counsel table or at the lectern, get comfortable and stand up straight. Your hands should not be in your pockets or clasped behind you. If you are at a lectern, a good default position is to *rest* your hands on the sides of the lectern; do not grip the sides, holding on for dear life. Do not sway or rock back and forth. Plant

---

1. *See, e.g.,* Ga. R. App. P. 28(g)(2) ("Talking, reading newspapers or other material, and audibly studying briefs and arranging papers are prohibited in the courtroom.").

your feet, take a deep breath, and begin. Speak clearly and confidently, making eye contact with the judge or each member of the panel of judges.

III. Leave Your Baggage Behind

As discussed in § 14.2, *Preparing for Oral Argument*, you should prepare a thin notebook or folder of essential materials. Do not have additional materials in front of you, other than the relevant briefs, especially if you are addressing the court from a lectern. We have seen attorneys with loose notes, extra books, piles of briefs and files, and several notebooks arrayed before them. If you have prepared properly, you do not need all of those materials at the lectern or directly in front of you at counsel table. They can only cause problems. You do not want to be leafing through reams of materials as you search for the answer to a judge's question or have books fall to the floor because you have put too much material on the limited space provided to you. Your binder and perhaps the briefs are all you should need.

Should you have a pen or pencil in hand? Most attorneys do, but jettisoning the pen may be a wiser decision. Attorneys seem uncomfortable without a writing implement. But what will you do with that pen? What do you need to write? More likely, you will play with the pen in your nervousness. The pen is just one more item that can cause you—or worse, the judges—to be distracted from your message.[2] Place your pen on counsel table before you stand. If you really feel that a pen or pencil is necessary, take care not to continually click it or flip it around during your argument.[3]

IV. Make Eye Contact

Take care to make eye contact with the judge or judges who are hearing your argument. Making eye contact is important for two reasons. First, it engages the judge or judges in your message; listeners are more captivated by a speaker who looks them in the eye. Making eye contact helps you engage with each judge and allows you to have a conversation. Second, if you are making eye contact with a judge, you will be able to see when the judge has a question, so that you can pause or prepare for

---

2. One of the authors of this book described to the other authors her own experience with bringing a pen to the lectern: "I would click the cap incessantly, and once, in a passionate hand gesture, I flung my pen across the lectern toward the panel of judges. After that day, if I took a pen, I let it rest on the table."

3. Be especially vigilant if you have brought water to the lectern. One author watched an advocate squeeze a water bottle so tightly, the water shot out of the water bottle like a fountain. Another author watched as a colleague poured a glass of water over his notes.

the question. And, as previously explained, the advocate should welcome questions from the bench.

V. Speak Slowly and Simply

Next, remember that you are attempting to persuade *orally*. Speakers communicate differently to listeners than writers do to readers. When communicating orally, you should speak in short sentences, using simpler language with fewer syllables than you might if you were writing a brief. In short, speak the spoken word.

In addition, speak slowly. Unlike the written word, spoken language takes longer for the listener to process. It is exceedingly rare to hear an advocate speak too slowly. Rather, given the excitement of the argument and the often too-short time allotted, most oral advocates tend to speak too fast. If in doubt, slow down.

A slow delivery has another advantage. Some attorneys speak so fast that they never pause, making it more difficult for a judge to pose a question. As emphasized throughout this chapter, however, you should welcome questions and make sure that judges are able to pose them easily. Thus, your delivery should be slow enough that the judges can interject with questions.

VI. Have a Conversation

In presenting your argument, be conversational but not too familiar. Having a conversation means that you do not read from notes and (except for your opening) you do not recite from memory. As the Federal Rules of Appellate Procedure caution, "Counsel must not read at length from briefs, records, or authorities."[4] Explain. Listen. Respond. Make eye contact. In other words, have a conversation.

VII. Use Humor with Care

Although oral argument is a kind of conversation, use humor with care. When using humor, you always run the risk of offending someone—for example, a judge or a crime victim in the courtroom—or distracting from your argument. Generally, if the subject matter of your argument is not too delicate and you are familiar with the judges, humor may be a helpful way to make a point. But when in doubt, avoid it. Only if you are confident that your humor will not offend, and if you have

---

4. Fed. R. App. P. 34(c).

Oral Argument Humor

At the oral argument before the U.S. Supreme Court in the *Ashcroft* case, the following exchange took place between the Court and the attorney arguing for the State of Oregon:

JUSTICE O'CONNOR: Would you speak up just a little, please?

MR. ATKINSON: I'm sorry, Your Honor, I will.

JUSTICE SCALIA: Maybe elevate your — the microphone.

JUSTICE O'CONNOR: Maybe you could raise the podium.

JUSTICE SCALIA: You're too tall.

[Laughter.]

MR. ATKINSON: I'll work on that, Your Honor.

Oral argument in *Gonzales v. Oregon*, 546 U.S. 243 (2006),
aff'g Oregon v. Ashcroft, 368 F.3d 1118 (9th Cir. 2004).

---

appeared a number of times before that court, should you consider using humor during oral argument.

VIII. Assert Conclusions, Not Your Beliefs

Many lawyers will begin a statement to the court with "I believe" or "it is our contention that." Lawyers do that either because they are not confident in their assertions or because they are stalling for time. Whatever the reasons, those empty words will dilute your argument. Present your argument as truth, not your opinion. Thus, rather than stating, "It is our position that the contract is unenforceable," simply say, "The contract is unenforceable." Don't say, "A review of the record shows that the officer did not turn on his overhead lights until after he had stopped defendant." Rather, omit the empty words: "The officer did not turn on his overhead lights until after he had stopped defendant."

IX. Deliver Your Opening

As mentioned in § 14.2, *Preparing for Oral Argument*, you should have a prepared opening, and it should be memorized. That opening will set the tone for the argument, and depending on the court, it may be the last time during the argument that you have control over what is being discussed. Take advantage of that opportunity. Preparing and memorizing—not reading—the opening may also give you a chance to slide gently into your argument so that you can hit your stride after having warmed up.

Of course, in some courts, especially in appellate courts, you may be interrupted by questions after you utter your first word, and you will never get to your prepared opening. Nevertheless, have your opening down pat in case you are not.

X. Respond to Questions from the Bench

As we have suggested throughout this chapter, oral argument is primarily about the judges' questions. Sometimes, the advocate can manage to get out only a sentence or two before the court interrupts with questions, as in Example 14.3-A.

Example 14.3-A • The Court interrupts almost immediately with questions

---

MR. BOIES: Mr. Chief Justice, may it please the Court:

The district court below found, and it is not disputed here, that the plaintiff fulfilled all of the requirements of Rule 23(a) for class certification. The district court also found, and the court of appeals affirmed, that the plaintiffs demonstrated all of the requirements for class certification under 23(b)(3) except for the Fifth Circuit's loss causation requirement. The court below recognized that whether or not there was an efficient market was not disputed. It was conceded that we have an efficient market here. There were no challenges—

CHIEF JUSTICE ROBERTS: Mr. Boies, if could I just stop you there.

MR. BOIES: Certainly.

Oral Argument in *Erica P. John Fund, Inc. v. Halliburton,*
131 S. Ct. 2179 (2011).

Although the inexperienced advocate might be put off by immediately being interrupted and redirected, the veteran advocate appreciates the interruption so that she can address the topic in which the court is interested. That information is invaluable because it gives the advocate the opportunity to address the court's concerns, rather than wasting time on matters that may be less important to the court.

As you know, the court's questions and the advocates' responses really form the core of oral argument. Some advice about how to handle those questions follows, but recognize that putting the advice into practice requires, well, some practice.

A. Stop Talking and Listen

When a judge asks a question at oral argument, counsel must immediately do two things: stop talking and listen carefully. As soon as you see a judge's mouth open, stop talking, even if you are mid-word. It is a serious breach of oral argument etiquette to "talk over" a judge.

Moreover, you must stop talking so that you can listen carefully. Hearing the question correctly and responding to the question asked is harder than one might imagine. Advocates are sometimes so nervous that they simply have difficulty listening carefully. As a result, they will answer the question that they hoped was asked, or the question that they had prepared to answer, rather than the question that actually was asked. Thus, as soon as a judge starts talking, focus on the judge's question and make sure that you respond to the question actually asked.

B. Pause

After you have listened, you can take another moment or two to think through your answer. Although you may feel panicked inside, pausing for a moment will actually suggest to the judge who asked the question that it is an important question and that you are carefully considering your response. You project the image of a thoughtful, careful advocate.

Rather than pausing, many attorneys confronted with an unanticipated question start talking, often wandering around orally, as they search for an answer. Judges find that approach frustrating, and it wastes some of the precious time you have at the lectern.

Of course, if you have prepared properly, you will have anticipated the question, and you may not need to pause long to think. But if the question takes you by surprise, pause for a moment (it may seem like an hour to you, but it really is just a moment), think about what the answer should be, and then, as explained below, respond "yes" or "no."

C. Ask for Clarification, If Necessary

If you are not sure what the judge is asking, ask for clarification. For example, you might ask the judge to repeat the question. At the very least, the repetition will give you more time to process the question. Or, rather than simply asking the judge to repeat the question, you might state your understanding of the question: "If I understand correctly, Your Honor, you are asking whether we agree that dismissal is an appropriate remedy in this case?" Such a question will allow the judge to tell you whether you have understood her question. (But, as discussed below, asking a clarifying question is the only instance in which you should ask a question of a judge.)

D. Respond with "Yes" or "No"; Then Explain Your Answer

If possible—and it almost always is—respond to questions with a "yes" or "no" and then explain your answer. Judges want to know your bottom line up front. So, concisely state your bottom line, then explain your answer. For example, "No, Your Honor, that is not the case here. Our

---

Answer "Yes" or "No," and then Explain

JUSTICE ALITO: Let me be clear about exactly what your argument is. Your argument is that there is nothing that a State can do to limit minors' access to the most violent, sadistic, graphic video game that can be developed. That's your argument?

MR. SMITH: My position is—

JUSTICE ALITO: Is it or isn't it?

MR. SMITH: My position is that strict scrutiny applies, and that given the facts in the record, given the fact that the—the problem is already well controlled, the parents are already empowered, and there are greatly less alternatives out there—

JUSTICE SOTOMAYOR: So, when you—

MR. SMITH: —there isn't any basis to say scrutiny is satisfied.

JUSTICE SOTOMAYOR: So, when you say that—

CHIEF JUSTICE ROBERTS: So, just to be clear, your answer to Justice Alito is, at this point, there is nothing the State can do?

MR. SMITH: Because there's no problem it needs to solve that would justify—

CHIEF JUSTICE ROBERTS: Could I—could I just have a simple answer?

MR. SMITH: The answer is yes, Your Honor.

Oral argument in *Brown v. Entm't Merch. Ass'n,*
131 S. Ct. 2729 (2011).

---

case differs in two important ways. First . . . ." Answering "yes" or "no" and then explaining your response projects confidence in your response and lets the judge know that you are not being evasive.

E. Never Praise a Judge's Question

Judges like to assume that all their questions are good, and they do not take kindly to attorneys telling them so. Although oral argument is a conversation, the parties are not on equal footing. Thus, even though sometimes you might be tempted, do not say, "That's a good question, Your Honor," even if it really *is* a good question. Doing so may sound obsequious. Simply answer the question. Do not comment on the quality of the question.

F. Always Answer a Question When It Is Asked

Never put off a question. You may, for example, think that the dispositive issue in the case has to do with the proper interpretation of a

> **Answer the Question When It Is Asked:**
> **Go Where the Court Wants to Go**
>
> MR. COOPER: Thank you, Mr. Chief Justice, and may it please the Court: New York's highest court, in a case similar to this one, remarked that until quite recently, it was an accepted truth for almost everyone who ever lived in any society in which marriage existed . . .
>
> CHIEF JUSTICE ROBERTS: Mr. Cooper, we have jurisdictional and merits issues here. Maybe it'd be best if you could begin with the standing issue.
>
> MR. COOPER: I'd be happy to, Mr. Chief Justice.
>
> Oral argument in *Hollingsworth v. Perry*, 133 S. Ct. 2652 (2013).

constitutional provision, and you have prepared your argument accordingly. But when the judge asks instead about a technical procedural issue, you should not put the question off or, by your demeanor or response, suggest that the question is not important. Or you may think that the question relates to your fourth point and you want to discuss your first three points before that. Nonetheless, recognize that the judge asking the question may see things differently, and your task is to address the judge's concern. Thus, never postpone responding to a judge's question.

G. Embrace Hypotheticals

Embrace hypotheticals that judges propose. Remember the tough job that judges have: They have to issue a decision that resolves the case before them and (in the case of most appellate courts and some trial courts) write an opinion that persuades the reader why their decision is correct. They also have to make sure that their decision fits within existing, binding case law and, to the extent that their decision will act as precedent in future cases, that it will yield correct results in other cases.

Appellate courts are particularly concerned about the rule of law that one case will establish for future cases. Thus, appellate judges in particular tend to use hypotheticals at oral argument to test the limits of your position, determine if there would be any untoward consequences if they adopt your position, and ensure that the rule they announce "works." By carefully listening to any hypothetical and explaining to the court how your position would play out under those facts, you help the court achieve its goals.

As you prepare for oral argument, you should be thinking about hypothetical situations that test the limits of your position, and you should consider what the result would be under your proposed rule. If, as explained in § 14.2, *Preparing for Oral Argument*, you have carefully determined the precise limits of your position, you will be prepared for hypotheticals. If you are confronted with a hypothetical that you had not considered, your response will be obvious if you know your position precisely. Take a deep breath, think for a moment, and explain to the judge the result of his hypothetical under your position. And if, under that hypothetical, your client would lose, say so. But end on a strong point, such as, "But, Your Honor, this case differs from your hypothetical in three ways. First, ... Second, ...Third, ... Thus, in this case, my client should prevail."

H. Recognize Friendly Questions

Recognize and respond appropriately to so-called "friendly questions." Sometimes advocates are so bent on being adversarial that they do not recognize a friendly question. Judges, however, sometimes ask questions that are helpful to your position. When you hear such a question, you should accept it at face value, answer "yes" or "no," and use it as a launch pad for your argument: "Yes, that's correct, Your Honor, for two reasons. First, ..." It is frustrating indeed to watch an oral argument in which the advocate is unwilling to take "yes" for an answer.

I. Admit When You Do Not Know the Answer

Do not be afraid to say these three words: "I don't know." Judges understand that advocates do not always know the answers to their questions. Although attorneys hate to say that we do not know something, doing so is better than the alternatives of bluffing or being flat-out wrong, both of which damage your credibility with the court. In some courts, advocates may offer to file a post-oral argument memorandum in response to a judge's question. If that is the practice in the court in which you are appearing, and if it seems appropriate to do so, offer to file such a memorandum—and then remember to do it.

Do Not Be Afraid to Say, "I Don't Know."

JUSTICE GINSBURG: Mr. Dreeben, something that you said about the encryption. What—what is the experience of the police? Isn't it so that most cell phones when they're found on a person are not open, that—that they are locked?

MR. DREEBEN: Justice Ginsburg, I would not be able to answer a question about what condition most cell phones are found in. The fact that this issue has arisen repeatedly in cases across the country indicates that at least in a significant number of cases, the phones are not locked and the officers are able to obtain access to the information.

Oral argument in *Riley v. California*, 134 S. Ct. 2473 (2014).

Some questions are factual. When responding to a factual question, you must note whether your answer is based on facts in the record or if it has a different source. Sometimes you can respond to a question by first making it clear that the answer to the judge's factual inquiry is not in the record, but then offering information that the judge might find useful.

J. Do Not Ask Any Other Questions

Other than when you ask a judge to clarify a question posed or ask a procedural question, do not ask questions of the judges. In particular, do not ask, "Does that answer your question, Your Honor?" Most judges believe that their role is to ask questions, and your role is to respond to them. They may be offended or at least surprised if you ask them questions. The first exception is, as mentioned above, when you ask a judge to clarify her question. The second exception is when you are asking a procedural question, such as, "I see that my time is up. May I respond to Your Honor's question?" As long as you speak slowly and make eye contact, judges will be able to ask the questions they have.

K. Recognize the Logical End of an Answer

If, at the outset, you took a moment to think through your answer, you will also recognize the end of your answer when you get there. As you think about a question, consider whether the question requires a single sentence to answer or several paragraphs. For example, if the court asks you, "Was anyone else present during the interrogation?" you can assess whether a simple "No, Your Honor," is sufficient or whether that question needs to be addressed in detail. When you unnecessarily tack on several paragraphs to what could have been a simple "No, Your Honor," you waste your time and the court's time.

L. After Answering the Court's Question, Return to Your Planned Argument or Adjust as Necessary

After answering a question, you should try to return to the points that you want to make. Returning smoothly to your plan after minutes of wide-ranging argument on other points is one of the hardest skills to master; it takes practice. Remember, however, that it will be easier to return to your argument and keep track of your "must-make" points if you have listed them at the beginning of your lectern materials.

When you return to your argument, you will need to make a choice: "Do I return to where I was in my argument before the questions? Or, do I pick up at the place in my argument where the questioning left off?"

That depends. Sometimes you can give a quick answer to a judge's question and return to exactly where you left off before the question.

Other times the questions will persist, and then you will need to make a decision. If, after the questioning on an issue is over, you have more or less provided all the information you planned to provide on the issue about which you were questioned, you can now leave that issue and return to an unfinished issue or move on to another issue. If, however, the questions did not bring out all you wanted to say on that issue, address it completely before moving on. If judges spend time asking questions about a particular issue, they consider that issue important.

As you proceed through your argument, be aware of the remaining time and manage your time appropriately. You can, of course, pause for a moment, take stock of where you are and what points remain, and then decide how to continue. Remember this: The court does not expect a polished speech, but a helpful, enlightening conversation.

XI. Conclude

You should conclude your argument when you have said everything that you have to say, and you are satisfied that the court has no further questions. You are not required to use all the time allotted. One of the common mistakes that novice advocates make is to continue talking simply because they have more time. The court will appreciate your not wasting its time by going back over matters that have been thoroughly addressed or by addressing matters that are not in contention. In addition to annoying the judges, spending unnecessary time arguing might open you up to questions that take away from the points you wanted to leave the court with. When you have nothing useful left to say, conclude confidently and sit down, always making sure that the court has no further questions first.

Ideally, when you are done with your argument, you will provide a very brief summary of your argument or a simple conclusion. How brief that summary is depends on whether you have a time limit and how close you are to that time limit.

If you have no time limit or if you have one or more remaining minutes, you might provide a conclusion that reiterates or emphasizes important points and then state the relief that you are seeking, as in Example 14.3-B. If the court's questions throughout your argument repeatedly returned to one point, you might choose to emphasize your position on that point in concluding, as in Example 14.3-C.

Example14.3-B · A closing when you have the time for a closing

In conclusion, this court should deny the motion for two independent reasons. First, as we explained in our trial memo and as we've discussed here today, trial counsel's conduct did not fall below an objective standard of reasonableness. Failing to object to the victim impact evidence was a reasonable tactical choice. Second, even if that choice not to object was objectively unreasonable, it had no tendency to affect the outcome of the trial. That is, petitioner has not demonstrated prejudice. If the court agrees with us on either point, it should deny the motion. Unless the court has additional questions, I have nothing further to add. Thank you.

Example14.3-C · A closing that emphasizes a point on which the court focused

---

In closing, I would like to draw the court's attention to the discussion it had with opposing counsel regarding preservation of error. As the court's questions suggested, the vague reference to the Constitution at trial below was not sufficient to preserve a claim of constitutional error. For that reason, as well as the reasons discussed in our brief, this court should affirm the trial court's judgment. Unless the court has other questions, I have nothing further to add. Thank you.

If you have only a few seconds left, your closing may have to be shorter. You might say a simple, "Thank you," and then sit down. Or, you might say, "Unless the court has further questions [pause to ensure that the judges have no further questions], I have nothing else to add. Thank you." You should make eye contact to determine whether the court has any remaining questions. Assuming the court does not, say, "Thank you." Then, gather your materials and return to your seat.

XII. Listen When the Court Questions Opposing Counsel

Counsel for a responding party has a distinct advantage at oral argument: the opportunity to listen to the questions posed during opposing counsel's argument and thereby gain insight into the court's concerns.[5] That is, by the time counsel for the responding party begins her argument, she may have a much better idea about "where the game is being played." Thus, if you are representing the responding party, listen carefully to opposing counsel's argument and the questions the court asks; that information is invaluable.

Then, shape your argument in light of what you have heard. In other words, counsel for the responding party has to be flexible enough to con-

---

5. This advantage is somewhat offset by the appellant's opportunity to present rebuttal (the appellant's or moving party's opportunity to respond to the respondent's or nonmoving party's argument), thus getting the last word in.

struct aspects of an argument while opposing counsel is arguing. To be sure, if you are counsel for a responding party, you may make a number of planned arguments regardless of what opposing counsel argued. But, if you represent the responding party, take advantage of having listened to the court, and tweak your argument in light of what you have heard. For example, if during opposing counsel's argument, the court has indicated that it is not persuaded by one of the arguments, you may choose to spend less time on that argument than you had initially planned.

Responding counsel who fails to take into consideration what has taken place and simply presents a canned argument loses an opportunity to address the court's concerns and may annoy the judge or judges. Instead, use your position as responding party to get to the heart of what the court cares about.

XIII. Rebuttal

Similarly, if you have an opportunity to rebut, listen carefully while responding counsel is arguing to determine how you can best use your rebuttal time.

In a trial court, counsel who opens the argument will usually be given time to respond to opposing counsel's argument. At the end of the responding party's argument, the judge will ordinarily turn to counsel who opened the argument and ask, "Counselor, do you have anything further?"

Rebuttal time in appellate courts is more formal. Appellate court rules often govern how much time an appellant may reserve for rebuttal, and rebuttal time typically comes out of the appellant's total allotment. Thus, if the appellant has thirty minutes total, reserving five minutes for rebuttal leaves twenty-five minutes for the principal argument. Most courts allow the appellant to use part of her rebuttal time as principal argument if she desires, reserving the remaining time for rebuttal. Thus, an exchange like that in Example 14.3-D might take place for an appellant who has reserved five minutes of rebuttal.

Example14.3-D · Using some of your rebuttal time

THE COURT: Counsel, your red light is on. You are welcome to continue, but you are into your rebuttal time.

COUNSEL: Thank you, Your Honor. I'd like to just finish the point I was making. [Counsel continues for one minute and concludes.]

THE COURT: Thank you, counsel. You will have four minutes remaining for rebuttal.

In general, in an appellate court, reserve no more than five minutes for rebuttal and, in many cases, one to three minutes is appropriate, especially for shorter arguments. Because they normally can go into rebuttal time during the principal argument if circumstances call for it, appellants should always reserve rebuttal time.

How should you use rebuttal time? During the responding party's argument, listen carefully to the questions and counsel's responses and take notes, perhaps on a single sheet of paper in your binder. You will have the opportunity to get the last word in, and keeping track of the court's concerns during your opponent's argument will allow you to use that time to your benefit.

When it is your turn for rebuttal, you should quickly choose the one to three most important points that came up during the respondent's argument to address. If you have less time for rebuttal, you may choose to address only one point; even with more time, it is rarely appropriate to address more than three points in rebuttal.

Rebuttal is not a time to repeat what you said during your principal argument or a time to make additional arguments, but a time to rebut statements made by the respondent or to address questions that came up during the respondent's argument. Just as judges do not appreciate a reply brief that does nothing but repeat the opening brief, they are unlikely to be persuaded by a rebuttal that tells them what they have already heard. Novice advocates often try to do too much with rebuttal, attempting to address every little quibble they have with what the respondent said. But that approach is rarely useful. Instead, choose up to three major points, address them quickly and clearly, chose a strong ending, and then sit down.

The discussion above provides general advice about preparing for and presenting oral arguments. As noted at the beginning of this chapter, oral arguments differ—both in their preparation and presentation—depending on whether you are arguing before a trial court or an appellate court. In the next section, you will learn how to adjust your argument to suit the court in which you are arguing.

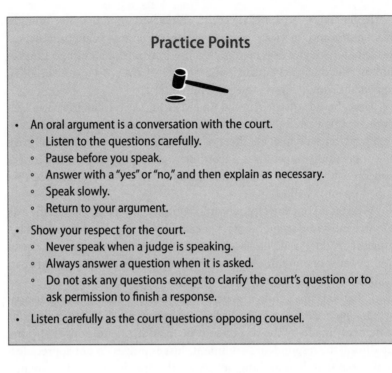

Practice Points

- An oral argument is a conversation with the court.
  - Listen to the questions carefully.
  - Pause before you speak.
  - Answer with a "yes" or "no," and then explain as necessary.
  - Speak slowly.
  - Return to your argument.

- Show your respect for the court.
  - Never speak when a judge is speaking.
  - Always answer a question when it is asked.
  - Do not ask any questions except to clarify the court's question or to ask permission to finish a response.

- Listen carefully as the court questions opposing counsel.

Trial Courts vs. Appellate Courts

I. Arguing Before Trial Courts
   A. Jurisdictional Variation
   B. Your Audience: One Judge
   C. Busy Dockets
   D. Shorter Timelines to Oral Arguments
   E. Addressing the Court
   F. Typical Questions from the Trial Court's Perspective
   G. Time Allotted for Oral Argument
II. Arguing Before Appellate Courts
   A. Jurisdictional Variation
   B. Your Audience: A Panel of Judges
   C. Appellate Courts Have More Time to Prepare
   D. Longer Timelines to Oral Arguments
   E. Addressing the Court
   F. Typical Questions from the Appellate Court's Perspective
   G. Time Allotted for Oral Argument

The preceding sections provide guidance about preparing for and delivering argument in trial and appellate courts. The guidance in those sections applies generally to both types of courts—as well as to other tribunals, such as administrative agencies. This section delves deeper into the differences between oral arguments in trial courts and in appellate courts. As you read, remember that the differences addressed below tend to be matters of degree.

I. Arguing Before Trial Courts

The following discussion about arguing before a trial court refers particularly to presenting an argument to a court after one party has submitted a motion and both parties have had an opportunity to brief the court on the motion. An argument on a motion is usually called a "hearing."

Other arguments do occur during a trial—many of which you have seen on TV, in a movie, or perhaps in real life. For example, at trial, an attorney may present an opening statement or closing argument to a jury. In addition, while a witness is on the stand, one attorney may object to opposing counsel's question and may need to quickly explain the basis for that objection. All of those activities are "arguments" in the broadest sense.

The advice that follows is largely focused on the more formal arguments that are presented after a motion has been filed and briefs have been submitted. Those arguments, for the most part, occur before or after trial and much less frequently during a trial.

A. Jurisdictional Variation

The most important thing to know about arguing at the trial level is that practice varies greatly—from federal district to federal district, from state to state, from county to county, and even from judge to judge in the same courthouse. For that reason, research the procedure in the particular courtroom in which you will be arguing before you arrive. Many courts have information about practicing in that court on their websites. Some bar associations publish information, and especially in larger states and in the federal courts, practice guides and treatises may be available. However, some courts and judges adhere to unwritten rules, and the best resource is often your colleagues. Thus, the suggestion earlier in this chapter to talk to others is especially important in trial courts.

B. Your Audience: One Judge

One obvious characteristic of oral argument at the trial level is that you will be arguing to only one person.[1] Because argument on a motion in a trial court is before a single adjudicator, it is worth knowing the particular preferences of that judge. Does the judge you are appearing before typically like a recitation of the facts? Does the judge generally ask a lot of questions or few? Has the judge ordinarily read the briefs beforehand, or does the judge need a summary of the brief?

Usually, the best way to find out about the idiosyncrasies of a particular judge is to ask others who have appeared before the judge and visit that judge's courtroom when the judge is hearing motions. As sug-

---

1. Rare exceptions exist. For example, 28 U.S.C. § 2284(a) (2012) requires a district court to convene a three-judge panel for a limited number of issues:

> A district court of three judges shall be convened when otherwise required by Act of Congress, or when an action is filed challenging the constitutionality of the apportionment of congressional districts or the apportionment of any statewide legislative body.

gested earlier, the Internet is also an invaluable resource. For example, the website for the Federal District Court for the Central District of California lists each judge with a link to that particular judge's procedures.[2]

C. Busy Dockets

Trial judges—especially state court trial judges—have very busy dockets. Thus, trial judges may not have the luxury of preparing thoroughly for your argument. They may not have had time to read the brief you submitted the day before argument or may not have been able to review the 500 pages of deposition testimony that your motion for summary judgment depends on. Thus, when arguing before a trial judge, you are more likely to recite the facts or recap the argument you gave in your brief. Although you should be prepared to provide such overviews, each judge is different. You can determine the likelihood that you will need to provide such an overview by talking to colleagues who have practiced before that particular judge.

D. Shorter Timelines to Oral Arguments

Trial courts move quickly. Thus, after submitting your brief, oral arguments might be scheduled within a few weeks or, in some cases, the within the next few days. The accelerated timeline means that you will compress your preparation. Fortunately, the law, the record, and your arguments will be significantly fresher in your mind, making the compressed timeframe more manageable.

E. Addressing the Court

Depending on a number of factors, such as whether you are in state or federal court, which particular judge you have drawn, and local custom, a trial courtroom is likely to be less formal than an appellate courtroom. For example, some trial judges allow counsel to address the court while standing at counsel table or even while seated; appellate courts rarely, if ever, do. Accordingly, find out before argument what the custom is.

As stated in § 14.2 *Preparing for Oral Argument*, even though a trial courtroom may be less formal, when you first stand to address the court, you should say, "Your Honor, my name is _____, and I represent [name the party you represent]." Thereafter, address the judge as

---

2. *See FAQs About Judges' Procedures and Schedules*, U.S. Dist. Court, Cent. Dist. of Cal., http://court.cacd.uscourts.gov/CACD/JudgeReq.nsf/FAQs+about+Judges%27+Procedures+and+Schedules?OpenView (last visited Mar. 22, 2015).

"Your Honor." Although in some courts it is common to address the judge as "Judge _____" or just plain "Judge," practice varies, and you cannot go wrong with "Your Honor" as a default.

F. Typical Questions from the Trial Court's Perspective

Trial courts decide cases; they are less concerned with setting precedent and setting out rules of law than are appellate courts. Thus, trial judges are more likely to be concerned about what law governs the outcome of the case and about the facts of your case than about the rule of law that the case will stand for. It follows that trial judges will more likely have questions about the facts of the case—and especially about what facts are in dispute. Trial judges are also more likely to be concerned about—and thus ask questions about—what the law requires them to do, with less attention to the effect of their rulings on future parties.

G. Time Allotted for Oral Argument

In trial courts, oral argument—if it is permitted at all—may be much more of a free-ranging discussion among counsel and the judge than it might be in an appellate court. The judge may not have a strict limit on the time each lawyer may speak; rather, the judge may allow the lawyers to argue for as long as they wish. Or, the judge may allow only a very short time to argue a simple motion. Similarly, a trial court judge may permit more back-and-forth between the lawyers than would be permitted in an appellate court. Thus, for example, the nonmoving party may have another chance to argue after the moving party does rebuttal. In short, as with other aspects of trial court oral argument, expect more variation in the amount of time and conduct.

Practice in trial courts varies more than it does in appellate courts; trial practice is often less formal, and the trial judge often has not had an abundance of time to prepare for an argument on a motion. Because of the greater variation among trial courts, it is essential to familiarize yourself with the practice in the particular court in which you will be arguing.

II. Arguing Before Appellate Courts

By the time oral argument rolls around, the appellate judges most likely will have read your brief, your opponent's brief, any reply brief or amicus briefs, and the opinion or other disposition below. They may have read a bench memorandum, prepared by a law clerk or staff attorney, summarizing the issues in the case and the record. They may have already engaged in a pre-argument conference and discussed their initial impressions of the case; in some courts, a draft opinion may have been prepared. In most appellate courts, the judges are quite prepared to address your case at oral argument.

In preparing for argument in appellate courts, in addition to other resources, you also may be able to read transcripts of arguments or listen to recordings of them. For example, both audio recordings and written transcripts of U.S. Supreme Court arguments are readily accessible from the Court's website. Westlaw® and Lexis® also provide access to some other oral argument transcripts. Be careful, however, not to assume that the nature of argument in your court (for example, in a state intermediate appellate court) is the same as that in the U.S. Supreme Court.

A. Jurisdictional Variation

As suggested previously, appellate courts are more like one another than trial courts are. Accordingly, the relevant portion of the Federal Rules of Appellate Procedure (as supplemented by any additional circuit rules) will give you a pretty good idea of what to do at oral argument in any appellate court in a given federal circuit. The same goes for state courts: An argument in the Fourth District of the California Court of Appeal is likely to resemble an argument in the First District, despite their distance from one another. Thus, although it still is important to research the court you will be arguing in, you generally can expect less variation in the oral argument practices in appellate courts than you will find in trial courts.

B. Your Audience: A Panel of Judges

When arguing an appeal, you will argue before a panel of judges. The panel of judges will range in size from the usual three-judge panel in an intermediate appellate court to a panel of five, seven, or nine judges in courts of last resort, including the United States Supreme Court. In fact, some advocates will argue before as many as fifteen judges for an en banc argument in the United States Court of Appeals.

Arguing before a panel of judges, rather than a single judge, has at least three implications. First, a single judge's idiosyncrasies are less important because at least two other judges are involved in the process. Second, you need to persuade at least two (and maybe as many as six or more) judges that your position is correct. Thus, in preparing for an appellate court argument, think about the different arguments that might appeal to different judges. For example, one judge might be persuaded that you should prevail because the trial court did not err; a second judge of the three-judge panel might be persuaded that the trial court erred, but that the error was harmless. In such a case, by presenting both an argument on the merits and a harmless error argument, you are more likely to prevail.

Third, maintaining eye contact, especially while answering questions, differs in the context of an appellate argument. Maintaining eye contact with three or more judges sitting in a semicircle in front of you is more difficult than maintaining eye contact with a single judge. Thus, when responding to questions—especially a series of questions from the same judge—focus primarily on the judge who asked the question, but be careful not to exclude the other judges. Sometimes, a judge and an advocate can engage in a back-and-forth that lasts several minutes. If you don't make eye contact with the other judges, they will feel excluded, and you will lose a chance to persuade them.

C. Appellate Courts Have More Time to Prepare

As compared to trial courts, appellate courts have significantly more time to prepare for oral argument. In most appellate courts today, the judges have read your brief (or a bench memorandum summarizing it), have thought about it, and may have already discussed it with the other judges. Thus, repeating the brief is a poor use of your time at an appellate oral argument. Rather, oral argument should complement the brief, emphasizing important points, expanding on arguments made in the brief, and explaining difficult points.

Most importantly, you should use your limited time to listen to the court's questions, assess the concerns that the court has, and respond to those concerns. Appellate judges have had more time to prepare for oral argument than their colleagues on the trial bench, and they expect that you will have, too.

D. Longer Timelines to Oral Arguments

At the appellate level, months may pass between when an appellate brief is filed and oral argument is heard. Thus, you will need to engage in significantly more review to remind yourself of the law and facts of the case. In addition, you must update the law to ensure that the cases you cited are still good law, that no other relevant cases have been decided, and that no relevant legislative changes have occurred.

E. Addressing the Court

In virtually all appellate courts, you will address the court only when standing at a lectern.

Once at the lectern, begin with, "May it please the court." (An exception is the U.S. Supreme Court, where advocates begin with, "Mr. Chief Justice, and may it please the Court.") Following that stock greeting, you should introduce yourself by saying, "My name is_____. I represent _____." If you are the appellant, and if it is the practice in that court, you should then reserve rebuttal time.

When responding to a judge's question, you may use the judge's name, or you may refer to the judge as "Your Honor." Given how embarrassing it is to address a judge by the wrong name, when in doubt, stick with "Your Honor."

Calling a Judge by the Wrong Name

During oral argument in *United States v. Comstock*, 560 U.S. 126 (2010), then-Solicitor General Elena Kagan mistakenly referred to Justice Scalia as the Chief Justice in responding to Justice Scalia's question:

[SOLICITOR] GENERAL KAGAN: Mr. Chief—excuse me, Justice Scalia—I didn't mean to promote you quite so quickly.

(Laughter.)

CHIEF JUSTICE ROBERTS: Thanks for thinking it was a promotion.

(Laughter.)

JUSTICE SCALIA (looking at CHIEF JUSTICE ROBERTS): And I'm sure you didn't.

(Laughter.)

GENERAL KAGAN: Justice Scalia, ...

That gaffe did not, of course, prevent Elena Kagan from later being appointed to the Supreme Court.

F. Typical Questions from the Appellate Court's Perspective

Appellate courts have a somewhat different task than do trial courts. As stated above, trial courts resolve cases. Appellate courts—although they must dispose of the case before them—decide the law. It follows that the questions posed by appellate judges during argument tend to have a different flavor. Because the opinions issued by appellate courts create binding precedent, appellate judges are more concerned than trial judges about the effect of their ruling on other cases. They use oral argument to examine the implications of the rule that the case will stand for; to clarify which issues are properly before them and which are not; to assess the practical effect of their decision in the case, both for parties and nonparties; to determine the reach of their ruling; and to consider other, more jurisprudential, aspects of the case.

Thus, appellate judges are more likely to pose hypothetical situations and ask the advocates what the result would be in those situations under the advocate's proposed rule. They are more likely to poke and prod the advocate's positions, looking for unintended consequences or other problems. Finally, as explained in Chapter 5, *Appellate Practice*, the appellate judge's universe is only that which is in the record on appeal. Accordingly, appellate judges are likely to have questions about the record.

One goal of the court at oral argument on appeal often is to identify the scope of the parties' claims. For example, in the *Ashcroft* case, discussed earlier, a judge might wonder whether the state is taking the position that the U.S. Attorney General never has authority to issue a directive that purports to interpret a statutory provision, or whether only a directive that conflicts with a state law is impermissible. Oral argument allows the judges to determine the scope of the rule of law that each party is advocating, either through direct questions or through the use of hypotheticals. That is why, as discussed in § 14.2, *Preparing for Oral Argument*, advocates must be confident that they know the scope of the rule they advance.

When the Red Light Goes On, Stop!

MS. JACKSON: Your Honor, I don't think that *Chadha* is identical, with respect. In—for two main reasons. In *Chadha*, the Court was, I think, quite careful to avoid deciding whether the United States had Article III standing. It intensively analyzed a statute, since repealed, 1252, which gave this Court mandatory jurisdiction in cases in which a federal statute was held unconstitutional and the U.S. was a party. And it framed its analysis of whether the statute permitted the appeal.

[Counsel's red light goes on.]

What I think was—oh, may I reserve my time for rebuttal?

CHIEF JUSTICE ROBERTS: You can finish your sentence.

MS. JACKSON: Thank you.

What was—what was going on there was the Court said, well, the statute wanted to reach very broadly, perhaps implicit, not stated, perhaps more broadly than Article III. Congress said whenever you have this configuration, you go up to the Supreme Court. Then the Supreme Court in *Chadha* says, of course, in addition to the statute, there must be Article III case or controversy, the presence of the congressional intervenors here provides it. And that—

CHIEF JUSTICE ROBERTS: Thank you, counsel. That was more than a sentence.

MS. JACKSON: Oh, I'm sorry. I'm sorry, Your Honor. Thank you.

Oral argument in *United States v. Windsor*,
133 S. Ct. 2675 (2013).

G. Time Allotted for Oral Argument

Be aware of time limits. Appellate courts set strict time limits for the argument, and those limits usually are found in the relevant rules of appellate procedure. In some appellate courts, counsel is expected to keep track of the time. Most appellate courts, however, provide a system of lights and, in some courts a countdown timer, to inform counsel of the time remaining. In those courts with a system of lights, a white or yellow light usually illuminate when counsel has two minutes remaining, and a red light illuminates when counsel's time is up.

Appellate courts usually strictly enforce the time limits. When the red light illuminates, counsel is expected to utter no more than a couple of words before leaving the lectern. Some courts expect counsel to stop mid-syllable if the red light goes on. If you are answering a question when your red light goes on, you should ask the presiding judge or justice (the one at the center of the bench) if you may finish your response, even if another judge asked the question. But even if permission is granted to do so, you should not add more than a few more sentences at the most.

In an oft-quoted statement, U.S. Supreme Court Justice Robert H. Jackson, who argued numerous appellate cases before going on the bench, accurately summarized the experience of oral argument:

> I used to say that, as Solicitor General, I made three arguments of every case. First came the one that I had planned—as I thought, logical, coherent, complete. Second was the one I actually presented—interrupted, incoherent, disjointed, disappointing. The third was the utterly devastating argument that I thought of after going to bed that night.[3]

The goal of the oral advocate is to thoroughly plan the first argument, to recognize that the second argument will inevitably occur, and to try as much as possible to incorporate that golden third argument into the first and second arguments. Although speaking style, good posture, engagement with the court, and all the other techniques discussed above are necessary elements of a successful oral argument, the true key to ensuring that oral argument is persuasive to the court and satisfying to the advocate is thorough preparation. If you prepare properly, you will represent your client well, you will be helpful to the court, you will reduce the inherent stress of an oral presentation, and you may really enjoy the experience.

---

3. Robert H. Jackson, *Advocacy Before the Supreme Court: Suggestions for Effective Case Presentations*, 37 A.B.A. J. 801, 803 (1951).

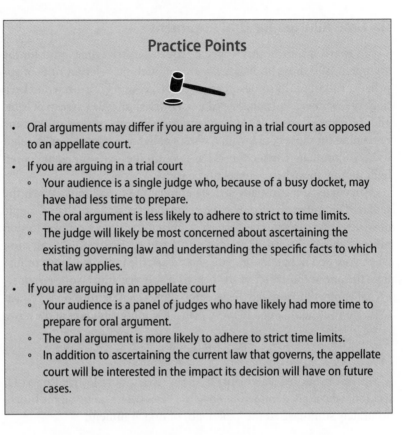

Practice Points

- Oral arguments may differ if you are arguing in a trial court as opposed to an appellate court.

- If you are arguing in a trial court
  - Your audience is a single judge who, because of a busy docket, may have had less time to prepare.
  - The oral argument is less likely to adhere to strict to time limits.
  - The judge will likely be most concerned about ascertaining the existing governing law and understanding the specific facts to which that law applies.

- If you are arguing in an appellate court
  - Your audience is a panel of judges who have likely had more time to prepare for oral argument.
  - The oral argument is more likely to adhere to strict time limits.
  - In addition to ascertaining the current law that governs, the appellate court will be interested in the impact its decision will have on future cases.

Appendix A

Moot Court Arguments

Many students have the opportunity to participate in moot court competitions during law school. A moot court competition is a simulated oral argument. Usually, students have prepared a brief for a hypothetical appellate case. Then, local attorneys and judges participate by acting as appellate judges, asking the students about the case.

Some schools require a moot court experience, while others do not. In addition, many schools have intramural competitions, and various organizations sponsor regional, national, or even international competitions. Competing in moot court allows you an opportunity to practice important skills, including how to really get to know your case, how to stand up in front of attorneys and judges and present your case, and how to answer questions when you are on the "hot seat."

Although moot court competitions simulate the appellate oral argument experience and allow you to practice many of the skills you will need if you become a trial or appellate attorney, the competitions differ in important ways from oral arguments in the "real world." This appendix addresses those differences and how they affect your argument in moot court.

The first major difference between appellate court oral arguments and moot court oral arguments is the audience. Although you may have real appellate judges as the "judges" in your moot court competition, more likely than not, at least some of the judges will be non-judge attorneys or even law students. Usually those attorneys, and certainly the law students, are not appellate specialists, so they may not be familiar with oral arguments in real appellate courts. Accordingly, you should not expect the judges to be experts in appellate practice.

A second difference is that the judges, in most cases, are not as well-prepared for argument and are not as familiar with your case. The judges may not have read your brief but, rather, may have been presented with a bench memorandum or bench brief that summarizes your case and the arguments on either side. And, because they are volunteering their time on a weekend or after a busy day at the office, many lawyers and judges will not have had time to carefully review the provided materials.

Accordingly, you will prepare for a moot court competition differently than you would for an actual oral argument. For example, because the judges will not, in most cases, have read your brief, you will not seek to complement the brief you have written. Instead, you should prepare a self-contained oral presentation on the assumption that the judges are not as familiar with your case as real judges would be. Thus, although the discussion in § 14.2, *Preparing for Oral Argument*, generally applies in the moot court context, the judges will likely need more background to understand your arguments.

A third difference is that the judges and competitors in a moot court competition have different goals than do the advocates and decision makers in a real case. In a real case, the judges seek to reach the "right" result in a real dispute, and each advocate seeks to persuade the judges to rule in her favor. In a moot court competition, the judges seek to test the competitors' knowledge of the record and the law, the ability to present orally, and the ability to answer questions. In short, the judges are looking for the best performance, not trying to resolve the legal question before them.

Accordingly, performance may become more important than substance, and you should practice presenting the material in as smooth a manner as possible. For example, students who win moot court competitions sometimes bring no notes with them to the lectern. We have seen law students prevail in a moot court round despite a weaker grasp of the law and record simply because they presented like professional actors playing attorneys. Thus, polish counts.

A fourth difference is that, in most moot court competitions, competitors argue both "on-brief" and "off-brief." That is, although they have briefed only one side of the case, they argue both sides in different rounds. While it is always helpful to prepare by carefully considering your opponent's arguments, in real life of course, the attorneys do not actually argue their opponents' side of the case.

Finally, be aware of two moot court conventions. First, in moot court competitions, the convention is to ask the judges, "Would you like a recitation of the facts?" As mentioned in § 14.4, *Trial Courts vs. Appellate Courts*, in most appellate courts, the judges have read the briefs and are familiar with the facts. They will ask you if they have questions. Nonetheless, in moot court, participants traditionally ask that question. Check to see whether, in your moot court setting, you should ask the court if it would like such a recitation.

The second convention is that moot court judges often expect you to use all the time allotted and are surprised if you do not. Given the differences between the purpose of a moot court competition and a real appellate argument, that difference may make sense. Because the judges in a moot court competition seek to rate you on your performance, they expect you to use every last second to show them what a good performer you are. Ending early would be like a competitive figure skater ending her routine early because she believed that she had covered all the moves that were necessary. So, in preparing for a moot court competition, plan to use all your time.

In conclusion, although moot courts differ from appellate arguments in the real world, competing in moot court allows you an opportunity to develop and practice important lawyering skills. Consider competing in moot court during your law school career.

Appendix B

Prakash v. Starr Publishing Corp.

Appendix A provides examples of the central documents in a motion for summary judgment: the motion, the memorandum of law in support of the motion, and the responding memorandum of law in opposition to the motion for summary judgment. Before you jump into the examples, it may help to have some background. This overview begins with a brief summary of the arguments. The summary should make it easier to absorb the legal arguments. Once you have absorbed the legal arguments, then you will be able to look beyond the arguments and examine the skills that the lawyers used to build their arguments. To that end, this overview also lists some of the skills that you should look for as you review these examples.

I. Summary of the Arguments

In this case, two law professors have sued a publishing company for defamation *per se*. The professors argue that they were defamed when the publishing company wrote "by Amit Prakash and Helen Vinocur ... and the Publisher's Staff" on a pocket part update, even though Professors Prakash and Vinocur did not participate in the production of that edition of the pocket part.

The publisher now seeks summary judgment on several grounds: (1) the plaintiffs cannot establish that the attribution was defamatory; (2)

369

the plaintiffs cannot prove they were harmed; (3) the contract permitted the publisher to use the professors' names in connection with the pocket part, even if they did not participate in producing it; (4) truth is a defense to defamation, and the attribution to the professors was true or substantially true. The professors argue to the contrary on each of these points.

II. Skills and Techniques

In reviewing these examples, you can see many of the techniques discussed in this book. You may want to adopt some of the techniques you see and use them in your own writing. If you do decide to adopt a technique from one of these samples, please keep in mind that no two documents are ever the same. Each client's legal problem is different. Therefore, these samples will be most useful if you go beyond the words on the page. Ask yourself *why* the writer drafted the argument as the writer did. What point was the writer trying to make? How did the writer shape the text to make that particular point? Then, ask yourself whether you can use that same technique in your document. If you think you can use the same technique in your own document, then ask yourself one final question: How will you adjust that technique to suit your client's particular problem?

Please remember, though, that the format for motions and their supporting memoranda vary from jurisdiction to jurisdiction. Thus, be particularly careful about adopting the format of these documents. With respect to the format of your documents, check your local rules and follow those rules. If you are still unsure about how your document should look, ask a trusted colleague for an example of a motion or memorandum of law that has been submitted to the same court.

Fortunately, the skills for writing an effective memorandum of law are the same no matter the jurisdiction. Thus, in the argument section, you might look for these skills and techniques:

- Assertive **point headings** that outline the argument.

- Arguments that are **structured in a traditional way**—with a conclusion, an explanation of the law, an application of the law to the facts, and a final conclusion.

- **Thesis sentences** that clearly and accurately assert the point that will be established in each paragraph.

- Arguments that use **rule-based reasoning**.

  ○ Notice how the lawyers take key language from the rule and integrate that language into the application. The re-integration of key ideas from the rule into the application emphasizes how the lawyer's analysis is consistent with the law.

- Arguments that use **analogical reasoning**.
  - Notice how counsel uses parallel structure to draw out the factual similarities between the current case and a prior case.
  - Notice also how counsel always explains the legal conclusion that results from the factual similarity.
- Arguments that **address weaknesses**, without giving undue airtime to that weakness.
- **Polished writing**, which includes
  - Sentences that have a clear subject and verb and use the active voice.
  - Words that are simple and easy-to-understand.
  - No grammatical, punctuation, or citation errors.

More substantively, you might look at the different approaches each party takes to the summary judgment standard and the defamation claim. Ask these questions:

- **Summary judgment standard**
  - How does each party describe the standard for summary judgment?
  - Throughout the argument, how does each party emphasize those aspects of the standard that are favorable to that party?
- **Defamation** *per se*
  - Compare the arguments side by side. For each issue that the party addresses, does one seem more compelling? Why?
  - How does each party deal with weaknesses in its own argument?

Outside of the argument section, you might look for these skills:

- A **preliminary statement** that gives a concise and persuasive overview of each party's arguments.
- A **statement of facts** that
  - Provides context before jumping into the details.
  - Includes all legally relevant facts.
  - Presents the party in a favorable light.
  - Places unfavorable facts in perspective.
  - States legally relevant facts in precise detail.

III. The Documents

The documents that follow include the publisher's motion for summary judgment and the memorandum of law in support of the publisher's motion.[1] In reply, the professors submit a memorandum of law in opposition to the motion for summary judgment.

---

1. The sample documents were drawn from the arguments presented in *Rudovsky v. West Publishing Corp.*, 2010 WL 2804844 (E.d. Pa. 2010) (No. 09-cv-00727-JF). These documents were chosen for the excellent advocacy demonstrated on both sides.

A. Defendant's Motion for Summary Judgment

IN THE UNITED STATES DISTRICT COURT
FOR THE EASTERN DISTRICT OF PENNSYLVANIA

Amit Prakash and Helen Vinocur,	: CIVIL ACTION
Plaintiffs,	: NO. 15-CV-727
v.	:
Starr Publishing Corporation, Defendant.	: **DEFENDANT'S MOTION FOR SUMMARY JUDGMENT**

Pursuant to Federal Rule of Civil Procedure 56, defendant Starr Publishing Corporation moves to enter judgment in favor of defendant and to dismiss plaintiff's amended complaint in its entirety with prejudice.

As explained in the accompanying memorandum of law in support of defendant's motion for summary judgment, the undisputed facts show that plaintiffs Prakash and Vinocur cannot, as a matter of law, establish their claim for defamation.

This motion, like most motions, states the rule on which the motion is based and cross-references the memorandum of law where the court will find the arguments in support of the motion.

Dated: April 21, 2015   Respectfully submitted,

/s/ _____
James F. Collier, Esq.
Aaron M. Goldstein, Esq.
Donahue Hartgrove LLP
1750 Market Street, 48th Floor
Philadelphia, PA 19103-7599
(215) 617-9200
jcollier@donhart.com
agoldstein@donhart.com

B. Memorandum of Law in Support of Defendant's Motion for Summary Judgment

**IN THE UNITED STATES DISTRICT COURT
FOR THE EASTERN DISTRICT OF PENNSYLVANIA**

Amit Prakash and Helen Vinocur, Plaintiffs,	:	CIVIL ACTION
	:	
	:	NO. 15-CV-727
v.	:	
	:	
Starr Publishing Corporation, Defendant.	:	**MEMORANDUM OF LAW IN SUPPORT OF DEFENDANT'S MOTION FOR SUMMARY JUDGMENT**

Defendant Starr Publishing Corporation submits this memorandum of law in support of its motion seeking summary judgment on the claims of plaintiffs Amit Prakash and Helen Vinocur as set forth in the March 24, 2015 amended complaint.

Preliminary Statement

Discovery has now confirmed that Starr Publishing Corporation should be granted judgment in its favor. Plaintiffs allege that they were defamed when Starr published a pocket part to update "Starr's Pennsylvania Criminal Practice & Procedure" and listed the plaintiffs as authors; however, plaintiffs' claim fails as a matter of law and undisputed fact.

First, plaintiffs cannot establish the essential elements of a defamation claim. Plaintiffs cannot, for example, establish that attributing the authorship to the plaintiffs is a defamatory statement. In addition, plaintiffs cannot establish that they suffered damages. The record includes no evidence that plaintiffs suffered economic damage or that their reputations were harmed.

Plaintiffs' defamation claim also fails because they consented to the use of their names in connection with the 2014-2015 pocket part even if they did not participate in its production. Finally, plaintiffs' defamation claim must fail because the statement that the 2014-2015 pocket part was "by Amit Prakash and Helen Vinocur" and "The Publisher's Staff" is true or substantially true.

For all of these reasons, plaintiffs' claim for defamation fails as a matter of law, and summary judgment in Starr Publishing's favor should be granted.

Statement of Facts

Starr Publishing is engaged in the business of publishing legal casebooks, treatises, and practice guides. Am. Compl. ¶ 6; Carter Decl., ¶ 1. Plaintiffs Amit Prakash and Helen Vinocur are law professors who have had distinguished careers in law. Am. Compl. ¶¶ 1-2. Plaintiffs assert that Starr Publishing made a

The preliminary statement (or introduction) provides an overview of the publisher's argument. This section is the publisher's first opportunity to persuade. Notice how the section asserts the publisher's arguments as indisputable conclusions. By doing so, the section outlines the publisher's arguments and does so persuasively.

The statement of facts opens by providing context. The first paragraph explains who the parties are and the crux of the dispute.

1

Here, to provide the court with context and explain why the parties are in court, the publisher explains that the professors were dissatisfied. To minimize the impact of that admission, the publisher couples that fact with a fact that's good for the publisher — that the professors produced most of the content.

false statement of fact that defamed them when Starr published the cover page to a 2014-2015 pocket part. Am. Compl. ¶ 37. The cover page of the 2014-2015 pocket part provides that it was "by Amit Prakash and Helen Vinocur" and "The Publisher's Staff." Am. Compl. ¶ 37. Although plaintiffs had themselves written "the overwhelming majority" of the 2014-15 pocket part, they were unsatisfied with the updates made by the publisher's staff. Am. Compl. ¶¶ 24-29; Vinocur Tr. 212:4-11.

Starr Publishing's relationship with the plaintiffs began in 2006. In that year, plaintiffs executed an agreement that allowed Starr Publishing to use the plaintiffs' name on the pocket parts to the treatise *Starr's Pennsylvania Criminal Practice & Procedure*, even if plaintiffs did not participate in the production of the pocket part. Prelim. Inj. Hr'g Tr. 38:14–39:3, 39:22–40:16. The 2006 Agreement defines "Work" as *Starr's Pennsylvania Criminal Practice & Procedure*. 2006 Agmt. §§ 1, 2(b). The 2006 Agreement also provides that references to the "Work" "also apply to such upkeep as well as to the original work." The

Notice that the publisher starts with the facts that the publisher believes are most powerful for it: that the professors signed a contract allowing the publisher to use the professors' names, even if the professors did not participate in producing the work.

agreement provides Starr Publishing with the right to use the plaintiffs' names in connection with the Work and upkeep of the Work, and in advertising and promotion, even if plaintiffs did not participate in its upkeep. 2006 Agmt. §§ 3(A)(2), 7(4). Section 3(A)(2) of the agreement states

> **Use of Authors' Names.** Publisher will have the right to use Authors' names in connection with the Work and upkeep of the work. If the Work or upkeep is prepared by a person other than Authors, Publisher may identify that person on the new material and any related advertising and give him or her authorship credit in addition to or in lieu of credit given to Authors.

When specific words are important to your argument, you should quote those words. Here, the publisher quotes the contract language and the professors' admissions. In both of those cases, the exact words are important to the publisher.

Under the 2006 Agreement, plaintiffs were required to deliver the first update of the Work to Starr Publishing in 11 months, and plaintiffs agreed that "subsequent upkeep will be due annually thereafter." 2006 Agmt. § 2(B)(1).

Plaintiffs prepared annual pocket parts to update the material each year, until they declined to do so for the 2014-2015 pocket part. Carter Decl. ¶¶ 6-8; Am. Compl. ¶¶ 11, 18. Nevertheless, the pocket part was ultimately published. Am. Compl. ¶ 19. Plaintiffs acknowledge that the plaintiffs authored the "overwhelming majority of the content" of the 2014-2015 pocket part. Vinocur Tr. 212:4-11; *see also* Am Compl. ¶ 24.

Plaintiffs cannot identify anyone whose opinion of them has changed based on the publication of the pocket part. Ms. Vinocur testified that she could not identify anyone who thought less of her as a result of the 2014-2015 pocket part, and Mr. Prakash testified that he had "received no such complaints." Vinocur Tr. 6:12-18, 7:16-22; Prelim Inj. Hr'g Tr. 49:15-22. Starr Publishing has searched its records and has found no complaints from any customer concerning the sufficiency and quality of the 2014-2015 pocket part. Carter Decl. ¶¶ 3, 6.

Plaintiffs also have not identified any injury. Plaintiffs testified that they suffered no emotional distress or similar damages. Vinocur Tr. 6:12-15, 7:16-19; Prelim. Inj. Hr'g Tr. at 24:16-20. Even the Court questioned Mr. Prakash about his potential emotional distress, and Mr. Prakash could find no such damages:

THE COURT: Would you agree then that you suffered emotional distress as a result of this whole thing?

THE WITNESS: I—distress, I—I would say—I—I won't characterize it as emotional distress, Judge, at—at this point.

Prelim. Inj. Hr'g Tr. 24:16-20.

Nevertheless, plaintiffs assert that they have suffered $75,000 each in reputational damages, but they point to no evidence to show how this sum was determined. Vinocur Tr. 196:12-15. Plaintiffs' counsel stipulated that "there will be no specific claim made with respect to any lost opportunity, revenue as a result of lost opportunity, lost jobs, lost teaching assignments, anything like that. There will be no specific evidence offered in that regard. However, [plaintiffs] will be making a claim for presumed injury to reputation . . . ." Vinocur Tr. 123:5-21. Plaintiffs' counsel has similarly agreed that no witnesses will be called to testify as to plaintiffs' loss of reputation—only that plaintiffs enjoy good reputations. Vinocur Tr. 182:20-186:15.

Starr Publishing replaced the allegedly offensive pocket part with a new pocket part in April 2015. Carter Decl. ¶ 5. Nonetheless, a complaint and this lawsuit followed.

> Read the topic sentences of each paragraph of the statement of facts. Notice how facts are organized both chronologically and topically. The topic sentences both identify the topic of the paragraph and, importantly, state something that casts the publisher in a positive light or the professors in a negative light.

Summary Judgment Standard

Summary judgment is appropriate if "there is no genuine issue as to any material fact and that the moving party is entitled to judgment as a matter of law." Fed. R. Civ. P. 56(a). Although the party seeking summary judgment initially bears responsibility for informing the court of the basis for its motion and identifying those portions of the record that it believes demonstrates the absence of a genuine issue of material fact, it is not required to support the motion with affidavits or other materials that negate the opponent's claim. *See Celotex Corp. v. Catrett*, 477 U.S. 317, 322-23 (1986).

Once the moving party has satisfied its initial burden, Rule 56(e) requires the nonmoving party to "go beyond the pleadings and by her own affidavits, or by the 'depositions, answers to interrogatories, and admissions on file,' designate 'specific facts showing that there is a genuine issue for trial.' " *Id.* at 324 (quoting Fed. R. Civ. P. 56(e)); *see also Lujan v. Nat'l Wildlife Fed'n*, 497 U.S. 871, 888 (1990) (holding that the non-moving party must bring forth "specific facts" to support its Complaint and cannot rely on conclusory allegations at the summary judgment stage).

Here, the submitted declarations, deposition testimony, and stipulations establish that there is no genuine issue of material fact for trial and that summary judgment should be granted in favor of Starr Publishing.

> For some lawyers and in some jurisdictions the custom is to set out civil procedure standards separately from other legal rules, as the summary judgment standard is here. Others include the civil procedure standards within the argument section. Follow the custom or rules of your jurisdiction.

> Compare the publisher's description of the standard for summary judgment with plaintiffs' description. Here, the publisher emphasizes what the professors must do to withstand a motion for summary judgment.

Argument

I. Plaintiffs' claim for defamation should be dismissed based on any of the four reasons explained below.

Discovery now confirms that plaintiffs cannot prove their claim of defamation *per se*, and therefore, summary judgment should be granted in Starr

> The publisher's argument begins with a roadmap section. Like all roadmap sections, it begins with a conclusion and states the governing rule. The explanation of the governing rule spans two paragraphs.

Publishing's favor. To succeed in a claim for defamation, plaintiffs must establish seven elements: (1) the defamatory character of the communication, (2) its publication by the defendant, (3) its application to the plaintiff, (4) the understanding by the recipient of its defamatory meaning, (5) the recipient's understanding that the communication is intended to be applied to the plaintiff, (6) special harm resulting to the plaintiff from its publication, and (7) abuse of a conditionally privileged occasion. 42 Pa. Cons. Statutes § 8343(a).

A claim of defamation *per se* requires the plaintiffs to establish all the elements of defamation except the sixth element, special harm. Instead of establishing special harm, plaintiffs must show that the words impute "(1) a criminal offense, (2) a loathsome disease, (3) business misconduct, or (4) serious sexual misconduct." *Synygy, Inc. v. Scott-Levin, Inc.,* 51 F. Supp. 2d 570, 580 (E.D. Pa. 1999). Plaintiffs have the burden of proving each of the seven elements. *Id.*

In this case, plaintiffs allege defamation *per se* on the ground that the words imputed business misconduct. As explained below, the undisputed facts establish that plaintiffs cannot establish their claim of defamation *per se*, and summary judgment should be granted based on any one of the four reasons explained below.

A. Plaintiffs cannot establish the first element of a defamation claim — that the statement was defamatory.

Plaintiffs cannot establish the first element of their defamation claim — the defamatory nature of the communication. Whether the statement at issue is capable of a defamatory meaning is a question for the court, not the jury, to resolve. *Cornell Cos. v. Borough of New Morgan,* 512 F. Supp. 2d 238, 271 (E.D. Pa. 2007). For the court to conclude that a statement imputes business misconduct, "the statement must be more than mere *general disparagement*." *Synygy,* 51 F. Supp. 2d at 580 (emphasis added). The statement must be of the type that would be "particularly harmful to an individual engaged in the plaintiff's business or profession." *Id.* Moreover, the defamatory meaning must be apparent on its face. *See* Robert D. Sack, *Sack on Defamation: Libel, Slander and Related Problems* § 2.8.3 (4th ed. 2010). If extrinsic facts are required to understand the defamatory statement, the statement is not *per se* defamatory. *Id.*

Here, plaintiffs' defamation claim should fail as defamation *per se* because the allegedly defamatory communication does not on its face impute any business misconduct to plaintiffs. The statement at issue is the phrase "by Amit Prakash and Helen Vinocur" and "The Publisher's Staff." On its face, those words impute no business misconduct and make no statement that would be particularly harmful to a lawyer or a law professor. Because plaintiffs cannot prove that the statement at issue has a defamatory character, plaintiffs' claim for defamation must be dismissed.

B. Plaintiffs have suffered no general damages.

Plaintiffs also cannot prove that they suffered any damages. In cases of defamation *per se*, a plaintiff cannot rely on presumed damages but must prove

---

The last paragraph focuses the judge's attention on the particular defamation claim that is at issue and the outcome the publisher seeks.

Notice how the publisher emphasizes that the trial court has four separate grounds on which to grant the motion for summary judgment. That statement lets the trial court know that it does not have to agree with every assertion to grant the motion.

An effective persuasive argument will provide an outline of the argument in both the point headings and the thesis sentences. After you have read through this argument once, try reading just the point headings or just the thesis sentences to see whether they achieve that goal.

Part A presents a short rule-based argument. Notice how the publisher re-uses key language in the application. (The key language is shaded in both the explanation and the application.) Re-using key language in the application helps the judge see how your argument is consistent with the law.

"general damage, *i.e.,* proof of reputational harm." *Synygy*, 51 F. Supp. 2d at 581; *see also Walker v. Grand Cent. Sanitation, Inc.,* 430 Pa. Super. Ct. 236, 634 A.2d 237, 242 (1993). Reputational damages must be "judged by the reaction of other persons in the community, and not by the party's self-estimation." *Pyle v. Meritor Sav. Bank*, No. Civ. A. 92-7361, 1996 WL 115048 at *3 (E.D. Pa. Mar. 13, 1996).

Part B uses both a rule-based and an analogical argument to make its point.

For example, in *McNulty v. Citadel Broad. Co.,* a radio broadcaster's claim for defamation *per se* was dismissed because the broadcaster could not prove that his reputation was actually damaged in anyone's eyes. 58 Fed. Appx. 556, 567 (3d Cir. 2003) (unpublished). Witnesses testified that the defendant's statements about the plaintiff's age and inability to attract a younger audience were the "kiss of death" in the plaintiff's industry. *Id.* After the district court granted summary judgment in the defendant's favor, the Third Circuit affirmed, concluding that plaintiff had not proved "that his reputation was actually damaged in anyone's eyes." *Id.*

Discovery has established that plaintiffs can offer no proof of reputational harm. At deposition, Ms. Vinocur testified that she could not identify anyone in the legal community who reacted negatively to the attribution or who thought less of her as a result of the 2014-2015 pocket part. Similarly, Mr. Prakash testified that he had received "no such complaints." Moreover, although plaintiffs were apparently angry about the publication of the 2014-2015 pocket part, the record demonstrates that plaintiffs suffered no emotional distress or similar damages. Plaintiffs simply assert that they have suffered $75,000 each in reputational damages, without providing any evidence substantiating how that sum was determined. Plaintiffs' self-estimation of their harm is an insufficient basis for a claim of defamation *per se.*

Here, in the rule-based argument, notice again how key language from the rule (shaded) is reused in the application.

Thus, this case is like the *McNulty* case in which the Third Circuit affirmed the district court's grant of summary judgment. Just as the plaintiff in *McNulty* failed to produce any evidence of actual damages, so too have the plaintiffs here failed to produce any evidence of any actual damages. Therefore, based on the undisputed facts, summary judgment should be granted in favor of Starr Publishing, and plaintiffs' claim for defamation should be dismissed.

The rule-based argument is supported by an analogical argument, comparing this case to *McNulty*. Notice how the publisher uses parallel language (underlined) to emphasize the similarity between the prior case and this case.

C. Plaintiffs consented to the use of their names in connection with the 2014-2015 pocket part.

Plaintiffs' claim for defamation should also be dismissed because plaintiffs consented to have their names used in connection with the pocket part whether or not plaintiffs participated in its production. Courts applying Pennsylvania law have long held that a plaintiff's consent to a defendant's communication precludes any liability for defamation. *See Sharman v. C. Schmidt & Sons, Inc.,* 216 F. Supp. 401, 405 (E.D. Pa. 1963) (stating that release signed by plaintiff precluded any liability on behalf of defendant with respect to the communications at issue); *Baker v. Lafayette Coll.,* 504 A.2d 247, 249 (Pa. Super. Ct. 1986) (concluding that professor's consent to publication of performance evaluations gave college absolute privilege against defamation claim with respect to those evaluations).

In this rule-based argument, the publisher uses parenthetical explanations to emphasize the rule. Here, parenthetical explanations of the case help strengthen the rule. However, if the publisher had wanted to create an analogical argument, the publisher would have described the cases in a case illustration.

Here, plaintiffs consented to the use of their names on the pocket part. In the 2006 agreement, which both Starr Publishing and plaintiffs signed, plaintiffs agreed that Starr Publishing would have the right to use plaintiffs' names in connection with the treatise and its upkeep even if plaintiffs did not participate in its upkeep:

> Publisher will have the right to use Authors' names in connection with the Work and upkeep of the Work. *If the Work or upkeep is prepared by a person other than Authors, Publisher may identify that person on the new material and any related advertising and give him authorship credit <u>in addition to or in lieu of credit given to Authors</u>.*

2006 Agmt. § 3(A)(2) (emphasis added). Notably, plaintiffs agreed if "the Work or upkeep is prepared by a person other than Authors," Starr Publishing could identify that new person "in addition to . . . [the] Authors." Thus, plaintiffs gave Starr Publishing the authority to do exactly what it did. Plaintiffs cannot now complain of an act that they previously agreed to.

Plaintiffs have previously argued that the 2006 Agreement does not apply. That argument is still without merit. The applicability of the parties' 2006 Agreement to plaintiffs' action is a question of law for this court to decide. *Great Am. Ins. Co. v. Norwin Sch. Dist.*, 544 F.3d 229, 243 (3d Cir. 2008). Plaintiffs' argument is predicated on the idea that the 2006 Agreement is superseded by a 2013 Agreement.

That argument misreads the 2013 Agreement. The 2013 agreement includes this integration clause:

> This is the entire agreement of the parties. All prior negotiations and representations are merged into this Agreement. This Agreement supersedes all previous agreements concerning the Work.

The integration clause is limited to the "Work" as defined in the 2013 Agreement. The 2013 Agreement defines the "Work" as *Starr's Pennsylvania Criminal Practice & Procedure 2013 Supplement* and "negotiations, representations, or agreements concerning the 2013 supplement." Thus, the integration clause in the 2013 Agreement is an integration clause as to the 2013 supplement. It does not affect any agreements about any work other than the 2013 supplement.

Accordingly, this Court should reject any argument that the 2006 Agreement is superseded by the 2013 Agreement. Under that 2006 Agreement plaintiffs consented to the use of their names in connection with the upkeep of the Work, including all pocket parts. Their consent is a bar to any defamation claim based on the use of their names in connection with the upkeep of the Work. Plaintiffs' defamation claim must therefore be dismissed.

D. The statement that the 2014-2015 pocket part was "by Amit Prakash and Helen Vinocur" and "The Publisher's Staff" was true or substantially true.

Plaintiffs' claim should also be dismissed because the statements, as a matter of law, are true or substantially true. Under Pennsylvania law, "truth . . .

Margin notes:

Because the contract language is critical to publisher's argument, the publisher provides the contract's exact language.

Here, the publisher addresses the professors' arguments head-on. Because of earlier exchanges — a motion for a preliminary injunction and a motion to dismiss — the publisher has an idea of the arguments the professors will make. The publisher takes this opportunity to explain why summary judgment is still appropriate.

Notice that the publisher emphasizes that this issue is a question for the court to decide. The defendant does not want the case to go to the jury.

Notice, too, that the publisher does not provide a detailed explanation of plaintiffs' argument. The publisher acknowledges that plaintiffs have an argument based on the integration clause, but the publisher focuses on how it believes the integration clause should be understood.

is a defense to a defamation claim." *Pierce v. Capital Cities Comm., Inc.,* 576 F.2d 495, 507 n.46 (3d Cir. 1978); *Bobb v.* Kraybill, 511 A.2d 1379, 1380 (Pa. Super. 1986). Moreover, a defendant "need only show substantial rather than complete truth" to establish such a defense. *Pierce v. Capital Cities Comm., Inc.,* 576 F.2d 495, 507 n.46 (3d Cir. 1978); *Bobb v.* Kraybill, 511 A.2d 1379, 1380 (Pa. Super. 1986).

This argument is also a rule-based argument that integrates the key language of the rule into the application.

Here, the statement that the pocket part was by "The Publisher's Staff" and plaintiffs is substantially, if not completely, true because both plaintiffs and staff members contributed to the pocket part. A pocket part, by its nature, is a cumulative work, and plaintiffs have consistently asserted that virtually all of the content in the 2014-2015 pocket part was work they authored. Indeed, Ms. Vinocur admitted at deposition that plaintiffs were *the* authors of "the overwhelming majority of the content" contained in the 2014-2015 pocket part. Vinocur Tr. 212:4-11. Thus, the complained-of statements about the pocket part—that it was "by Amit Prakash and Helen Vinocur" and "The Publisher's Staff"—are true or substantially true, and Starr Publishing should be granted summary judgment.

CONCLUSION

Pursuant to Federal Rule of Civil Procedure 56, defendant respectfully requests that the Court grant its motion for summary judgment and dismiss the amended complaint in its entirety.

As with most supporting memoranda of law, the final conclusion is formulaic.

Dated: April 21, 2015

Respectfully submitted,

/s/ _____

James F. Collier, Esq.
Aaron M. Goldstein, Esq.
Donahue Hartgrove LLP
1750 Market Street, 48th Floor
Philadelphia, PA 19103-7599
(215) 617-9200
jcollier@donhart.com
agoldstein@donhart.com

CERTIFICATE OF SERVICE

I, Aaron Goldstein, hereby certify that the foregoing memorandum of Law in Support of Defendant's Motion for Summary Judgment has been filed electronically and is available for viewing and downloading from the Court's ECF system. I further certify that on this date I served the foregoing upon counsel listed below by hand delivery as follows:

Richard L. Handelman
Handelman Moore & Fields, P.C.
1500 Market Street, Suite 700
Philadelphia, PA 19102-1907
(215) 865-1155
rhandelman@handelman.com

April 21, 2015

/s/ _____
James F. Collier, Esq.
Aaron M. Goldstein, Esq.
Donahue Hartgrove LLP
1750 Market Street, 48th Floor
Philadelphia, PA 19103-7599
(215) 617-9200
jcollier@donhart.com
agoldstein@donhart.com

C. Memorandum of Law in Opposition to Defendant's Motion for Summary Judgment

**IN THE UNITED STATES DISTRICT COURT
FOR THE EASTERN DISTRICT OF PENNSYLVANIA**

Amit Prakash and Helen Vinocur,	: : :	CIVIL ACTION
Plaintiffs,	:	NO. 15-CV-727
	: :	
v.	: :	
	:	
Starr Publishing Corporation,	:	**MEMORANDUM OF LAW IN**
Defendant.	:	**OPPOSITION TO DEFENDANT'S**
	:	**MOTION FOR SUMMARY**
	:	**JUDGMENT**
	:	
	:	

Preliminary Statement

Summary judgment is inappropriate. Despite defendant's assertion to the contrary, discovery has confirmed both the strength of plaintiffs' claims and the egregiousness of defendant's misconduct. That misconduct provides sufficient evidence for a jury to conclude that Starr Publishing Corporation has defamed the plaintiffs.

In 2015, defendant sold a 2014-2015 pocket part that allegedly updated "Starr's Criminal Practice & Procedure." The pocket part's cover stated that it was "by AMIT PRAKASH and HELEN VINOCUR" even though Mr. Prakash and Ms. Vinocur made absolutely no contributions to the pocket part. Defendant now argues that plaintiffs' defamation claims must be dismissed. None of defendant's arguments have any merit.

First, the record includes sufficient evidence that ascribing the names of plaintiffs to an incomplete and misleading pocket part is defamatory.

Second, the record also has sufficient evidence for a jury to conclude that plaintiffs were damaged. Both plaintiffs have testified that they were angry and outraged by the defamatory statements, and that evidence is more than sufficient to support an award of general damages.

Third, nothing in the 2006 agreement between defendant and plaintiffs gave defendant the right to defame plaintiffs. Moreover, the 2006 agreement was superseded by a 2013 agreement between plaintiffs and defendant and, thus, does not apply to the 2014-2015 pocket part at issue in this case. If the conflict between the 2006 and 2013 agreements creates any ambiguity, such ambiguity is a question for the jury, and cannot be resolved on a motion for summary judgment.

Finally, the defendant's only other argument on defamation—that the statements at issue were "true or substantially true"—is frivolous because, as everyone agrees, plaintiffs had nothing to do with the 2014-2015 pocket part.

Just like the publisher's preliminary statement (or introduction), the professors provide an overview of their arguments.

Notice how the professors emphasize that "sufficient evidence" exists for the "jury" to find in plaintiffs' favor. At summary judgment, the professors must establish that the evidence is sufficient for a jury to find in their favor.

Statement of Facts

The first two paragraphs of the statement of facts provide context. Those paragraphs introduce the parties and the conflict. Notice how the professors take some time to establish their eminent reputations even though, strictly speaking, such facts are not legally relevant.

Plaintiffs in this case, Amit Prakash and Helen Vinocur, are distinguished and long-standing members of the Bar of the Commonwealth of Pennsylvania, each residing in the Eastern District of Pennsylvania. Am. Compl. ¶¶ 1-2. During their careers, they have each practiced law, served as faculty members at law schools, and authored legal books and articles. Am. Compl. ¶¶ 1-2. In each of these roles, their work has focused on criminal, constitutional, and civil rights law. Am. Compl. ¶ 1-2. Mr. Prakash and Ms. Vinocur both enjoy excellent reputations in the legal and academic communities. Am. Compl. ¶ 1-2.

Defendant is a well-known regional publisher of legal casebooks, treatises, practice guides, and other materials. Am. Compl. ¶ 6; Carter Decl. ¶ 1. This litigation results from Starr's statement that the 2014-2015 pocket part was "by Amit Prakash and Helen Vinocur" when the plaintiffs took no part in its production.

A. The most recent agreement between Starr Publishing and the plaintiffs

The most recent agreement between Starr Publishing and the plaintiffs was signed in 2013. 2013 Agmt. (Ex. D.) Another agreement had been in place between 2006 and 2013. Under that earlier agreement, plaintiffs agreed to produce a second edition of the treatise, "Starr's Pennsylvania Criminal Practice & Procedure." 2006 Agmt. §§ 1-2 (Ex. C.) Plaintiffs also agreed to produce supplements and pocket parts, which they did until 2013. *Id.* In 2013, plaintiffs and Starr Publishing signed another agreement, which governed the publication of the 2012-2013 pocket part. That agreement includes a merger clause. 2013 Agmt. § 25. The merger clause states that the 2013 agreement "is the entire agreement of the parties." *Id.*

> This is the entire agreement of the parties. All prior negotiations and representations are merged into this Agreement. This Agreement supersedes all previous agreements concerning the Work.

Id.

This statement of facts uses point headings to help organize the information. As is appropriate for point headings in a statement of facts, the point headings are descriptive rather than assertive.

B. Starr's decision to assign an inexperienced editor to produce the 2014-2015 pocket part

In early 2014, Starr staff members, including Ms. Melanie Vargas, who was Starr's Attorney Editor for the treatise, and Ms. Roberta Jones, who was the Team Coordinator for Starr's State Practice Group, recommended terminating publication of the treatise. Jones Dep. 31:13-32:2. Rather than terminate the publication, however, Starr offered to pay plaintiffs half of their prior compensation (i.e., to cut their payment from $5,000 each to $2,500 each) to prepare a pocket part for 2014-2015. Vargas Dep. 58:19-59:9. Plaintiffs declined this offer. Vinocur Dep. 45:7-9.

After plaintiffs declined an offer that cut their compensation in half for doing the same amount of work, Starr took no action with respect to the treatise until early November 2014, when a number of Starr employees met to discuss the future of the treatise. Jones Dep. 20:2—20:16. Although all in attendance had agreed that Starr should stop publishing the treatise, the decision was not executed during 2014 because "it was close to the end of the year," and Starr did not have enough time to obtain all the necessary formal approvals to terminate the publication. Jones Dep. 21:17-22:18; 25:6-17. Accordingly, Starr's decision to terminate the treatise would not be implemented until 2015. Jones Dep. 25:24-26:3.

That decision put Ms. Jones between a rock and a hard place: Because the treatise would not be terminated during 2014, their business unit was expected to produce a supplement to the treatise for 2015; however, because the supplement was part of their unit's "Publishing Plan" for 2014-2015, they had made an internal "commitment" to Starr to publish one by year's end. Jones Dep. 26:8-16. Ms. Jones believed that it was necessary to publish a supplement, even though Starr had decided to terminate the treatise, because the revenue from the sale of the treatise to the paying subscribers was included within her unit's revenue projections for 2014. Jones Dep. 47:1-48:24. Accordingly, if Ms. Jones failed to produce a "2015 Supplement" to be sent to paying subscribers, Ms. Jones's State Practice Unit would not meet its revenue target. Jones Dep. 49:15-22.

Responsibility for producing the supplement was assigned to Ms. Francesca Quinn, a newly hired Attorney Editor trainee. Vargas Dep. 60:20-61:7. Ms. Quinn had graduated from law school in May 2013 and had been employed as an Attorney Editor at Starr for a little more than a year. Quinn Dep. 8:12-14. She testified that she was trained for that position by "shadowing" Melanie Vargas. Quinn Dep.16:10-17:6. Ms. Vargas, however, testified that Ms. Quinn did not shadow her. Vargas Dep. 37:11-22. Ms. Vargas believed that a woman named Caroline Abbott had trained Ms. Quinn. Vargas Dep. 37:16-22. Ms. Quinn, however, could not remember being trained by Ms. Abbott. Quinn Dep. 20:10-21:4. Given the contradictory testimony of the two Starr witnesses, the record does not elucidate whether anyone at Starr actually trained Ms. Quinn to be an Attorney Editor.

Although Ms. Quinn had not authored any manuscript on her own at that point and had virtually no background in or knowledge of criminal law (much less Pennsylvania criminal law or procedure), Quinn Dep. 66:19-67:13, no one at Starr provided her with any input on how to update a supplement on her own. Quinn Dep. 66:1-18; Jones Dep. 43:2-44:15. Even more incredibly, once Ms. Quinn completed her manuscript, no one at Starr ever reviewed it to determine whether it was worthy of publication. Jones Dep. 49:16-51:4.

Instead, Quinn's manuscript went directly to Starr's production department, where it was packaged as the 2014-2015 supplement to the treatise, and was sent to each of approximately 400 subscribers to the treatise, each of whom was charged $46.50 for it. Quinn Dep.74:1-8.

C. Deficiencies in the 2014-2015 pocket part

Starr's 2014-2015 supplement to the treatise had serious deficiencies. For example, while the prior pocket parts that Prakash and Vinocur had prepared typically included citations to between 100 and 150 cases decided since the

[margin note:] All of part B of the statement of facts is legally irrelevant. Do you think the professors benefit from including these facts? Or will the judge be frustrated at the time spent on irrelevant facts?

Because a reader's eyes rest on the first sentence of a paragraph, the professors carefully selected the first sentence of each paragraph to emphasize facts that were important to the professors. Read the first sentence of each paragraph to see the key facts that plaintiffs chose to emphasize.

prior version was published, the "2014-2015 Pocket Part" contained only three new cases that had not been cited in the 2013-2014 pocket part. Hr'g Tr. (Prakash) 10:3-12:5.

Moreover, the 2014-2015 pocket part failed to include a number of cases in which the Pennsylvania Supreme Court reversed or vacated lower courts, including at least the following:

- *Commonwealth v. Mallory*, 888 A.2d 854 (Pa. Super. Ct. 2011), vacated by 941 A.2d 686 (Pa. 2012), cert. denied, 129 S. Ct. 257 (2013);
- *Commonwealth v. Brown*, 853 A.2d 1029 (Pa. Super. Ct. 2012), rev'd by 925 A.2d 147 (Pa. 2013);
- *Commonwealth v. West*, 868 A.2d 1267 (Pa. Super. Ct. 2005), rev'd by 938 A.2d 1034 (Pa. 2013);
- *Commonwealth v. Wilson*, 866 A.2d 1131 (Pa. Super. Ct. 2010), rev'd by 934 A.2d 1191 (Pa. 2013);
- *Commonwealth v. Bennett*, 842 A.2d 953 (Pa. Super. Ct. 2010), vacated by 930 A.2d 1264 (Pa. 2013);
- *Commonwealth v. Gravely*, 918 A.2d 761 (Pa. Super. Ct. 2013), allowance of appeal granted, ___ A.2d ___, 2012 WL 878654 (Pa. Apr 02, 2013); and
- *Commonwealth v. Lee*, 935 A.2d 865 (Pa. 2013).

Hr'g Tr. (Prakash) 10:3-12:5.

Finally, the 2014-2015 pocket part also failed to reflect relevant changes to pertinent rules. For example, the 2014-2015 pocket part failed to include any reference to the amendment to Pennsylvania Rule of Appellate Procedure 2111, which added new section (a)(7), providing that an appellant's brief must include a "[s]tatement of the reasons to allow an appeal to challenge the discretionary aspects of a sentence, if applicable." Hr'g Tr. (Prakash) 12:10-15.

D. Starr Publishing's attribution of the deficient 2014-2015 pocket part to Mr. Prakash and Ms. Vinocur

Even though Prakash and Vinocur did not in any way prepare the 2014-2015 pocket part, its cover page identified it as being "by AMIT PRAKASH [and] HELEN VINOCUR," modified only by the innocuous qualifier and, in smaller type, "THE PUBLISHER'S STAFF." *See* Ex. E. Nothing on the supplement, or mailed with the supplement, informed subscribers or readers that Prakash and Vinocur had not prepared the supplement.

E. Prakash and Vinocur shocked by the attribution

Both Prakash and Vinocur testified to the harm they suffered from the publication. When Prakash received the 2014-2015 supplement in the mail sometime after the New Year in January 2015, he was "stunned" that it was a virtual copy of the prior version, and he found it "very upsetting." Hr'g Tr. (Prakash) 12:5, 23:19-21; Vinocur, for her part, "was really, angry . . . very, very angry" and "pretty upset." Vinocur Dep. 40:16-20, 53:24-54:12. As Mr. Prakash explained,

> My understanding . . . if someone found that we did not include—or you did not include—a case that was highly relevant, I wouldn't expect them

to call me and complain. I would expect them to think, Prakash and Vinocur aren't up to snuff.

Hr'g Tr. (Prakash) 24:1-3. Likewise, Ms. Vinocur testified that,

> Besides the fact that it is an incompetent effort, there is still a harm to Mr. Prakash and me because many users are not going to know that this wasn't prepared by us when they use this volume and, therefore, we can be associated with this incompetent effort of a pocket part.

Vinocur Dep. 17:12-14.

Plaintiffs filed the complaint in this case on February 19, 2015, along with a motion for preliminary injunction on March 24, 2015. Only after this action was filed did Starr finally agree to send a letter to subscribers informing them that the 2014-2015 supplement was deficient. Exhibit I.

Here, the professors quote their statements under oath. The quotations are more effective than a description of what they said. The quotations are evidence of the professors' reactions. If their reactions were not quoted, the judge would be left wondering what the professors actually felt and actually said.

Summary Judgment Standard

Rule 56(a) of the Federal Rules of Civil Procedure provides that summary judgment is appropriate only if "the movant shows that there is no genuine dispute as to any material fact and the movant is entitled to judgment as a matter of law." The party moving for summary judgment bears the burden of demonstrating the basis for its motion and identifying "particular parts of materials in the record" that demonstrate the absence of a genuine issue of material fact. Fed. R. Civ. P. 56(c); *Celotex Corp. v. Catrett*, 477 U.S. 317, 322 (1986).

Compare the professors' explanation of the summary judgment standard with the defendant's explanation of the same standard.

In determining whether a dispute is genuine, the Court's function is not to weigh the evidence or determine the truth of the matter, but only to determine whether the evidence of record "is such that a reasonable jury could return a verdict for the nonmoving party." *Anderson v. Liberty Lobby Inc.*, 477 U.S. 242, 248-49 (1986). "The evidence of the non-movant is to be believed." *Id.* at 255.

All inferences must be drawn in the light most favorable to the non-moving party. *Am. Eagle Outfitters v. Lyle & Scott Ltd.*, 584 F.3d 575, 581 (3d Cir. 2009). "[W]hen there is a disagreement about the facts or the proper inferences to be drawn from them, a trial is required to resolve the conflicting versions of the parties." *Id.* "Summary judgment may not be granted . . . if there is a disagreement over what inferences can be reasonably drawn from the facts even if the facts are undisputed." *Ideal Dairy Farms, Inc. v. John Labatt, Ltd.*, 90 F.3d 737, 744 (3d Cir. 1996).

Here, the professors emphasize those aspects of the summary judgment standard that are beneficial to the them: the limited role of the court, the inferences that are to be drawn in the non-moving party's favor, and when summary judgment may not be granted.

Argument

I. Summary judgment is inappropriate because the record establishes sufficient evidence for a jury to find defamation per se.

This Court should deny defendant's motion for summary judgment because discovery has produced sufficient evidence for a jury to conclude that defendant defamed plaintiffs per se. Defendant correctly explains the seven elements necessary to establish defamation and that the sixth element, special harm, need not be proved in a claim of defamation per se. Def.'s Mem. of Law in Support of Def.'s Mot. Summ. J. 4. Rather, a plaintiff can establish that the

These first two paragraphs are a roadmap section. The professors accept the publisher's statement of the law of defamation, probably because it is not in dispute and to re-state it would create not just repetition but a lengthy repetition.

defamatory words imputed "business misconduct." *Id*. In that case, the plaintiff need not establish special harm. *Id*.

As explained below, the evidence is sufficient for a jury to conclude that defendant defamed plaintiffs per se. First, the evidence is sufficient for a jury to conclude that the statement was defamatory. Second, the evidence is sufficient for a jury to conclude that the plaintiffs suffered damages. Finally, plaintiffs never consented to the defamation, and the alleged truth of the statements is not a bar to proceeding to trial. For all of these reasons, defendant's motion for summary judgment should be dismissed and a trial date set.

A. The statements were defamatory.

First, the evidence is sufficient for a jury to conclude that the statement was defamatory. As a general rule, a statement alleges business misconduct when "the particular quality disparaged . . . is peculiarly valuable in the plaintiff's business and profession." *Id*. (quoting Restatement (Second) of Torts § 573, cmt. e (1977)).

With respect to lawyers, a statement imputes business misconduct when the statement suggests "a total disregard of professional ethics." *Clemente v. Espinosa*, 749 F. Supp. 672, 678 (E.D. Pa. 1990). Professional ethics require lawyers to make a reasonable inquiry into the law before submitting briefs to the court. Part of that reasonable inquiry is "Shepardizing, or otherwise checking the validity of the legal authority for an argument." Georgene M. Vairo, *Rule 11 Sanctions: Case Law, Perspectives, and Preventive Measures* § 6.05[d][6] (3d ed. 2004). In fact, lawyers have been sanctioned for failure to update their legal authority. *Id*. The purpose of a pocket part is to update the law so that lawyers can perform their professional duties. *See Black's Law Dictionary* 1343 (Bryan A. Garner 10th ed. 2014) (defining a pocket part as a "supplemental pamphlet inserted usu. into the back inside cover of a lawbook . . . to update the material in the main text"). For these reasons, a legal scholar who asserts that a legal authority is up-to-date when, in fact, the legal authority is not up-to-date would be acting with "total disregard for professional ethics."

Based on the evidence in the record, a jury could find that the statement "by Amit Prakash and Helen Vinocur" and "The Publisher's Staff" was defamatory because it imputes a total disregard for professional ethics. A lawyer would expect that a pocket part labeled "2014-2015" would be up-to-date through 2015. This pocket part was not.

The deficiencies of the pocket part include the following:

- It failed to identify relevant rule changes, such as amendments to Pennsylvania Rule of Appellate Procedure 2111, which created a new briefing requirement for criminal appellants.
- It failed to include at least seven cases in which the Pennsylvania Supreme Court had reversed or vacated the lower court.
- It included only three new cases while prior pocket parts authored by plaintiffs have included between 100 and 150 new cases.

Margin annotations:

The professors take this opportunity to focus the court's attention on the arguments it will make below.

Part A is a rule-based argument. The first sentence is the conclusion. The rest of the first paragraph and the second paragraph explain the law. Key ideas from the explanation of the law (shaded) are repeated in the application to emphasize how the professors' analysis is consistent with the law.

The professors have done a very good job of creating rules that will be helpful to them. No case in Pennsylvania has addressed whether an assertion that a professor produced a deficient pocket part attributes business misconduct to that professor. So, the professors marshal authorities that will lead the judge to conclude that such an assertion would be attributing business misconduct to a professor.

Part A is responsive to the publisher's argument that the professors cannot prove that the statements were defamatory. In responding to the publisher's assertion, the professors never outline defendant's argument. Rather, the professors simply assert their own argument as to why the attribution was defamatory.

A jury could find that the use of the plaintiffs' names on a deficient work product imputed business misconduct to the plaintiffs. As Professor Prakash explained

> My understanding . . . if someone found that we did not include — or you did not include — a case that was highly relevant, I wouldn't expect them to call me and complain. I would expect them to think, Prakash and Vinocur aren't up to snuff.

Likewise, Ms. Vinocur testified that

> Besides the fact that it is an incompetent effort, there is still a harm to Mr. Prakash and me because many users are not going to know that this wasn't prepared by us when they use this volume and, therefore, we can be associated with this incompetent effort of a pocket part.

Vinocur Dep. 17 (Ex. G). Starr's assertion that the plaintiffs authored the deficient pocket part went to the core of plaintiffs' professional reputations as lawyers, law professors, legal writers, and authorities on Pennsylvania criminal law and procedure. A jury could thus find that the statement "by Amit Prakash and Helen Vinocur" and "The Publisher's Staff" was defamatory, and summary judgment is not appropriate.

B. The evidence in the record allows a jury to find that the plaintiffs suffered harm to their reputations.

Part B uses analogical arguments.

The evidence is also sufficient for a jury to conclude that plaintiffs suffered harm to their reputations. When the issue is defamation *per se*, plaintiffs can show harm by establishing harm to their reputation and standing in the community, personal humiliation, or mental pain and suffering. *Clemente*, 749 F. Supp. at 680. "Such harm may be temporary in nature." *Id.*

Throughout, the professors integrate the summary judgment standard into their argument. Here the professors emphasize that "the evidence is sufficient for a jury to conclude" in their favor.

The suffering need not be great. For example, in *Marcone v. Penthouse Int'l Magazine for Men*, the plaintiff testified that he was "frustrated, distraught, upset, and distressed." 754 F.2d 1072, 1080 (3d Cir. 1985.) The Third Circuit held that the plaintiff's testimony constituted sufficient evidence of harm and entitled the plaintiff to recover for injury to his reputation. *Id.* Similarly, in *Brinich v. Jencka*, a general contractor brought a defamation claim against a homeowner. 757 A.2d 388, 392 (Pa. Super. Ct. 2000). The jury returned a $33,000 verdict in favor of the contractor. *Id.* at 395. The superior court affirmed the verdict, holding that the damages award was supported by the contractor's testimony that he became "so angry" that he confronted the defendant was sufficient evidence to prove damages. *Id.* at 398. Likewise, in *Clemente*, the court awarded general damages after a bench trial on the basis of the plaintiff's testimony that he suffered anxiety, embarrassment, humiliation, and a sense of being shunned. 749 F. Supp. at 680-81.

The hook, "[t]he suffering need not be great," states an implicit rule that counsel found in the *Marcone, Brinich*, and *Clemente* cases.

In both this paragraph and the paragraph below, the hooks for the case illustrations do double-duty as thesis sentences, pointing out concepts the plaintiffs want to emphasize.

To establish damages plaintiffs need not show that other peoples' opinions have changed. *Sprague v. American Bar Ass'n*, 276 F. Supp. 2d 365, 370 (E.D. Pa. 2003). In *Sprague*, the defendant moved for summary judgment on the ground that "all of the numerous witnesses presented by plaintiff concede that their estimations of plaintiff did not falter as a result of" the defamatory statements. *Id.* The court rejected the defendant's argument, stating that although the witnesses said that their opinion did not change, the witnesses said their opinion did not change because they knew the plaintiff. *Id.* The witnesses did say they were "outraged," which suggests an inference that without personal knowledge of plaintiff, the alleged defamation would result in a reputational loss to the plaintiff. *Id.*

Here, the professors compare the facts in their case to the facts in the prior case to prove that their reactions to the allegedly defamatory publication is sufficient to establish damages.

Defendant's assertion that plaintiffs suffered no general damages is unsupported by the evidence. Both plaintiffs testified about the adverse emotional reactions that they suffered as a result of Starr's defamatory statements. Mr. Prakash testified that it was "unsettling" and "very upsetting," that he was "stunned" and "concerned," and that he "couldn't believe it." Likewise, Ms. Vinocur testified at her deposition that she was "angry," "upset," and "outraged." Ms. Vinocur also confirmed that Mr. Prakash was "very upset." Thus, Mr. Prakash's and Ms. Vinocur's reactions were similar to the reactions of the plaintiff in *Marcone*, who was "frustrated, distraught, upset, and distressed"; similar to the plaintiff in *Brinich*, who was "so angry"; and similar to the plaintiff in *Clemente*, who suffered "anxiety, embarrassment, humiliation, and a sense of being shunned." Accordingly, and just as in those prior cases, the evidence is sufficient for a jury to conclude that the plaintiffs suffered damages.

After comparing the facts, the professors explain the legal consequence of the factual similarity.

Here, the professors introduce new law in the application. Usually, all law is explained in the explanation of the law before the application begins. Here, however, the professors' point is that these cases are inapplicable, and so the choice to delay explaining them is a reasonable one. Some lawyers might, however, introduce these cases in their explanation of the law. As a reader, what is your reaction to new law presented in the application section?

In fact, even in those cases in which the plaintiffs could not prove injury, the court has explained that the result would have been different if, as in this case, the evidence showed that the plaintiffs suffered adverse emotional reactions to the defamation. *See Walker v. Grand Cent. Sanitation, Inc.*, 634 A.2d 237, 245 (Pa. Super. Ct. 1993) (stressing that "Walker did not testify that she suffered any adverse emotional reaction" to the defamation); *Synygy, Inc. v. Scott-Levin, Inc.*, 51 F. Supp. 2d 570, 582 (E.D. Pa. 1999) (stressing that there was "no evidence that plaintiff suffered humiliation").[1] Because the evidence in the record supports a finding that plaintiffs suffered adverse emotional reactions, summary judgment is not appropriate.

For all of these reasons, the evidence of general damages is sufficient to support an award of general damages for defamation.

C. Plaintiffs did not "consent" to defamation.

Plaintiffs never consented to being defamed. Defendant's argument to the contrary rests on the assertion that the 2006 agreement still binds the parties. However, as explained below, the 2006 agreement has been superseded. Moreover, even if the 2006 agreement has not been superseded, the evidence is not sufficient to conclude as a matter of law that plaintiffs consented to being defamed.

---

1. Defendant also cites *McNulty v. Citadel Broadcasting Co.*, 58 Fed. Appx. 556 (3d Cir. 2003). The *McNulty* court, however, designated that its opinion is "Not for Publication." Under the Third Circuit's Internal Operating Procedures, such opinions have no precedential value. United States Court of Appeals for the Third Circuit, Local Appellate Rules, Appendix I, Internal Operating Procedure 5.7.

First, the 2006 agreement no longer binds the parties; it has been superseded by the 2013 agreement. The 2013 agreement has an integration clause that states the 2013 agreement is the entire agreement between the parties:

> This is the entire agreement of the parties. All prior negotiations and representations are merged into this Agreement. This Agreement supersedes all previous agreements concerning the Work.

The first sentence of this integration clause states that the 2013 agreement is now controlling for all purposes, *i.e.,* that it is the entire agreement of the parties. The second sentence encompasses *all* prior negotiations and representations, regardless of whether those negotiations and representations led to the 2013 agreement or to the 2006 agreement. Finally, "the Work," as defined in the 2013 agreement is the "*Pennsylvania Criminal Practice & Procedure 2013 Supplement.*" The 2006 agreement applied to "supplements" and upkeep. Because the 2013 agreement also addresses a supplement, it—by virtue of the integration clause—supplants the 2006 agreement.

Moreover, if the court concludes that the language of the integration clause is ambiguous, resolving that ambiguity is a question for the jury because the interpretation of an ambiguous contract is a question of fact. The question, therefore, cannot be resolved on a motion for summary judgment. When the jury resolves the question, any ambiguity should be resolved against defendant because defendant authored both the 2006 agreement and the 2013 agreement. *See, e.g., Am. Eagle Outfitters,* 584 F.3d at 587; *Dardovitch v. Haltzman,* 190 F.3d 125, 141 (3d Cir. 1999).

Even if the 2006 agreement did apply here, plaintiffs did not consent to the defamation. In defamation actions, Pennsylvania adheres to the Restatement (Second) of Torts. *See Walker,* 634 A.2d at 244. Under the Restatement's definition, a plaintiff "consents" to the publication of a defamatory statement only if the plaintiff "knows the exact language" that the defendant will use in those statements or "has reason to know that" such language "may be defamatory." Restatement (Second) of Torts § 583 (1977).

In this case, not a shred of evidence indicates that plaintiffs knew "the exact language" of the 2014-2015 pocket part before it was published or that plaintiffs had any reason to know that they would be defamed. Accordingly, Starr's consent argument has no basis in fact or law.

D. Defendant is not entitled to summary judgment on the supposed "truth" of the defamatory statements.

Defendant's next argument that, absent a contract, the truth is a defense to its defamation is similarly without merit. Although "truth" can be a defense to a claim of defamation, in this case, the statement was not true. The test for determining the truth or falsity of a defamatory statement is whether the statement "as published would have a different effect on the mind of the reader from that which the pleaded truth would have produced." Whether an alleged defamatory statement is true, substantially true, or false is a question for the jury. *McDowell v. Paiewonsky,* 769 F.2d 942, 947 (3d Cir. 1985); *see also Krochalis*

In part C the professors make two distinct arguments: (1) the 2006 agreement does not apply, and (2) even if the agreement does apply, the jury resolves conflicting contractual interpretations. Either way, summary judgment in favor of the publisher is not appropriate.

The professors are using the summary judgment standard to their advantage.

The arguments in part C are responsive to the publisher's argument that 2006 contract bars the professors' claims. The professors effectively respond to the publisher's arguments without detailing the publisher's arguments for the court.

Another rule-based argument that effectively integrates key language from the rule into the application.

The professors again emphasize the role of the jury. They want this case to go to the jury. Again, the professors are reminding the court of the role of the jury and the court's limited role in deciding a motion for summary judgment.

v. Ins. Co. of N. Am., 629 F. Supp. 1360, 1366 (E.D. Pa. 1985) (denying defendant's motion for summary judgment in defamation action because "[t]ruth is typically an issue resolved by the jury in a defamation action").

In this case, the statement was not true because Starr represented that plaintiffs authored the 2014-2015 pocket part when, in fact, plaintiffs had nothing to do with the preparation of that publication. The publishers took work that the plaintiffs had done and incorporated it into the 2014-2015 pocket part, but the 2014-2015 pocket part was entirely the work of the defendant. The plaintiffs had nothing to do with it. For most readers, the statement as published would have told them that the plaintiffs had been involved in the production of the 2014-2015 pocket part. The pleaded truth demonstrates that the plaintiffs were not involved. Thus, the statements were not true. Instead, the statements were indisputably false.

Even if a question exists regarding the truth or falsity of the statement, that question is reserved for the jury and is not an appropriate ground on which to grant summary judgment. Accordingly, the Court should deny defendant's motion for summary judgment.

CONCLUSION

A typical perfunctory conclusion

For all the foregoing reasons, defendant's motion for summary judgment should be denied.

Respectfully submitted,

/s/ *Zev Marinoff*
Richard L. Handelman, Esq.
Zev Marinoff, Esq.
Cynthia Maldonado, Esq.
Handelman Moore & Fields, P.C.
1500 Market Street, Suite 700
Philadelphia, OA 19102-1907
(215) 865-1155
zmarinoff@handelman.com

Attorneys for plaintiffs,
Amit Prakash and
Helen Vinocur

Dated: May 12, 2015

Certificate of Service

I hereby certify that on this 12th day of May, 2015, I served a true and correct copy of the foregoing Plaintiffs' Memorandum of Law in Opposition to Defendant's Motion for Summary Judgment upon the following counsel for defendant, as follows:

via the Court's Electronic Case Filing System:
    James F. Collier, Esq.
    Aaron M. Goldstein, Esq.
    Donahue Hartgrove LLP
    1750 Market Street, 48th Floor
    Philadelphia, PA 19103-7599
    (215) 617-9200
    jcollier@donhart.com
    agoldstein@donhart.com

            /s/ *Zev Marinoff*
            Zev Marinoff, Esq.
            (I.D. No. 89012)

Appendix C

State v. Lynwood
Appellate Briefs

Appendix C provides examples of an appellant's and a respondent's appellate brief. As with the examples in Appendix B, you will likely find it helpful if you have some background about the case before you jump into this set of examples. To that end, this overview begins with a brief summary of the arguments. Then, it lists some of the skills that counsel used when drafting each brief. As you write an appellate brief on behalf of a client, consider how these skills can be adapted to your client's context.

I. Summary of the Arguments

In this case, defendant Jeffrey Lynwood was convicted on two counts of endangering the welfare of a minor. On appeal, the issue is whether the evidence was sufficient to support Mr. Lynwood's convictions. The argument breaks down into two sub-arguments.

The first argument is a statutory construction argument. In that argument, the parties focus on the statutory word "permit." Oregon Revised Statutes § 163.575(1)(d) creates criminal liability for anyone who "permits" a minor to enter or remain in a place where unlawful activities involving drugs are maintained or conducted.

Mr. Lynwood argues for a narrow definition of the verb "permit." He argues that a person can be guilty of permitting something only if that person has authority to deny permission. Mr. Lynwood argues that the defendant must engage in some affirmative conduct to "permit."

By contrast, the state argues that "permit" has a broader definition and that broader definition is more consistent with the legislature's in-

---

Need examples of analogical arguments?

If your brief requires you to construct analogical arguments, please look at the trial memoranda in Appendix B.

Analogical arguments are constructed in the same way whether those analogical arguments appear in a trial memorandum or an appellate brief. Thus, you can use these appellate briefs to see how an appellate brief is formatted and how rule-based arguments are structured, but look to the trial memoranda in Appendix B for examples of analogical arguments.

You may also want to return to § 7.2, *Structuring Analogical Arguments*, and § 7.4, *Using Rule-Based and Analogical Arguments Together*, for additional examples of analogical arguments.

---

tent. Under that definition, simply "allowing" or "making it possible" for a child to enter or remain in a place where there is unlawful drug activity is sufficient to "permit." That definition would make a defendant guilty of endangering the welfare of a child if that defendant passively permits a child to be present in a place of illegal drug activity.

After arguing for a broader or narrower definition, the parties address whether, given that definition, the evidence was sufficient to convict Mr. Lynwood of endangering the welfare of a minor. Mr. Lynwood was convicted of endangering the welfare of two minors because he maintained an illegal marijuana-grow operation in the children's home and provided them with marijuana. The father and owner of the house knew of and allowed the marijuana-grow operation and permitted Mr. Lynwood to give the children marijuana.

Mr. Lynwood argues that he did not have sufficient authority to exclude the children from the place with the illegal drug activity and therefore he was incapable of "permitting" them to enter or remain. For that reason, Mr. Lynwood argues, the evidence was insufficient to support his conviction.

The state, by contrast, argues that the evidence was sufficient to support the convictions. First, the defendant participated in the illegal grow, knowing that children were present, and he gave them marijuana when

---

Addressing an issue of statutory construction, but in a memorandum of law?

If your client's legal problem involves a question of statutory construction, you can use these examples even if you are drafting a memorandum of law. A statutory construction argument is developed in the same way whether that argument appears in a memorandum of law or in an appellate brief.

---

they asked. By agreeing to care for the children, he made it possible for the children to remain in the home. Finally, the state points out that even if Mr. Lynwood's authority was limited in his role as babysitter and house-guest, he had sufficient authority to refrain from his own conduct that permitted the children to be in the presence of illegal drug activity.

II. Skills and Techniques

This book provides examples so that you can see how the various techniques discussed in the book are actually put to work. Examples must, however, be used carefully. Although the introduction to Appendix B provided this warning, it bears repeating here: After reading these examples, you may want to adopt some of the techniques you see and use them in your own writing. When you do that, please keep in mind that no two documents are ever the same. Each client's legal problem is different. Therefore, these samples will be most useful if you go beyond the words on the page. Ask yourself *why* the writer drafted the argument as the writer did. What point was the writer trying to make? How did the writer shape the text to make that particular point? Then, ask yourself whether you can use that same technique in your document. If you think you can use the same technique in your own document, then ask yourself one final question: How will you adjust that technique to suit your client's particular problem?

With that in mind, look for these skills and techniques in the argument section:

- Assertive **point headings** that outline the argument.
- **Thesis sentences** that clearly and accurately assert the point that will be established in each paragraph.
  - ○ Read just the thesis sentences to see how they outline the argument.
  - ○ Note how every sentence in the paragraph supports that point.
  - ○ Note how the paragraphs reassert the thesis at the end of the paragraph.
- Arguments that **address weaknesses** without giving undue airtime to that weakness.
  - ○ When addressing an opposing argument, each party explains how that party wants the court to understand the issue. The party does not flesh out the opposing party's argument.
- **Polished writing**, which includes
  - ○ Sentences that have a clear subject and verb and use the active voice.

Need more help with a statutory construction argument?

If you need more help with a statutory construction argument or you would like to see an additional example, return to § 7.3, *Structuring Rule-Based Arguments*.

- ° Words that are simple and easy to understand.
- ° No grammatical, punctuation, or citation errors.

Because the bulk of the argument addresses an issue of statutory construction, the argument section relies heavily on rule-based arguments. Thus, you can use this example to more closely analyze how to construct complex rule-based arguments. Look for two important skills.

First, in a successful rule-based argument, the application will track the stated rule. The arguments in the examples track the rules in two ways.

- The application **repeats or echoes key language** from the rule in the application.
- The application **does what the rule says to do**.
  - ° For example, if the rule says that "words of a statute are best understood in the context of surrounding statutes," the application examines the surrounding statutes as the rule suggests.

Second, a successful rule-based argument emphasizes the point of each argument. Therefore, the arguments

- State a **conclusion** at the outset of the argument and at the end of the argument.
  - ° The conclusion is the point that counsel wants the court to walk away with after the court reads that argument.
  - ° Sometimes a rule-based argument is one paragraph long; sometimes it spans several paragraphs. Each rule-based argument is one building block within the larger argument.

When reading the other sections of the brief, you might look for these skills and techniques:

- **Tables** that are carefully formatted and easy to read.
- A **question presented** that selects facts to suggest the outcome each party seeks.
- A **summary of the argument** that gives a concise and persuasive overview of each party's arguments.
  - ° Notice how each summary simply asserts the conclusions that each party wants the court to reach.
- A **statement of the case** that
  - ° Provides context before jumping into the facts.
  - ° Includes all of the legally relevant facts.
  - ° States legally relevant facts in precise detail.
  - ° Places unfavorable facts in perspective.
  - ° Includes selected facts that are not legally relevant for the impact that those facts will have on the court.

III. The Briefs

Appellant's and respondent's brief follow.[1] For clarity, we refer to the appellant as "defendant" or "Mr. Lynwood," and we refer to the respondent as the state or the State of Oregon.

---

1. The sample briefs were drawn from arguments presented in *State v. McBride*, 256 P.3d 174 (Or. App. 2011), *rev'd*, 281 P.3d 605 (Or. 2012).

A. Appellant's Opening Brief

IN THE COURT OF APPEALS OF THE STATE OF OREGON

—————————

STATE OF OREGON,	)	Mercer County Circuit Court
Plaintiff-Respondent,	)	No. 15C50799
	)	
v.	)	CA A139020
	)	
JEFFREY SCOTT LYNWOOD,	)	
Defendant-Appellant.	)	
	)	
	)	

—————————

APPELLANT'S OPENING BRIEF

—————————

Appeal from the Judgment of the Circuit Court
For Mercer County
Honorable Charity A. Beckah Judge

An appellate brief cover provides basic information about the litigation: the names of the parties, the appellate court in which the case is being heard, the court from which the appeal is taken, and the names and contact information for counsel.

Traditionally, the appellant's cover is blue, and the brief is colloquially referred to as the "blue brief."

KEN NAKANO #842314
  Chief Defender
VIJAY GREWAL #952421
  Deputy Public Defender

VIVIAN L. KEARA #707902
  Attorney General
ANIYA P. LINDSIE #761699
  Solicitor General
JENNIFER SCHWARZ #500187
  Assistant Attorney General

Office of Public Defense Services
18 Polo Street NE, Suite 412
Salem, Oregon 97231
(513) 341-6439

Oregon Department of Justice
129 Gavel Ave. NE
Salem, Oregon 92123-9301
(514) 321-5938

Attorneys for Defendant-Appellant

Attorneys for Plaintiff-Respondent

Table of Contents

The table of contents provides the first overview of the argument.

Read through the point headings listed in the table of contents. Can you understand the gist of the defendant's argument?

Notice also the formatting. All point headings are evenly spaced, and they line up in a consistent format. A crisp table of contents projects the impression that the brief was written by a professional who cares about the details.

Table of Authorities

Cases

The table of authorities is a resource to the court. It explains where in the brief the court can find counsel's discussion of different authorities.

As with the table of contents, a crisp, accurate, consistently-formatted table of authorities will reinforce the impression that the brief was written by a professional who cares about the details.

Statutes

<u>Other Authorities</u>

Question Presented

Under Oregon Revised Statute § 163.575(1)(b) (2015), which prohibits a person from "permitting" a child to enter or remain in a home in which illegal drug activity is occurring, does a person "permit" a child to enter or remain when that person is a babysitter with no authority to exclude that child from the home?

Statement of the Case

Defendant Jeffrey Lynwood was a houseguest in the home of Wesley Brenton when police executed a search warrant at Mr. Brenton's home. (R. at 119.) When the police executed the search warrant, Mr. Lynwood, Mr. Brenton's daughter Q., and her friend H., were all inside Mr. Brenton's home. (R. at 119.) Mr. Lynwood was subsequently charged with two counts of endangering the welfare of a minor. (R. at 190.) Both after the state rested its case and after the close of all evidence, Mr. Lynwood moved for a judgment of acquittal on the two counts of endangering the welfare of a child, arguing that the state had failed to prove its case. (R. at 190.) The trial court denied both motions. (R. at 191-93.) Mr. Lynwood now appeals those decisions.

Mr. Lynwood became a houseguest in Mr. Brenton's home in 2015. (R. at 37.) Mr. Brenton was a medical-marijuana cardholder, who started growing marijuana in his home in 2014. (R. at 38-40, 42-46.) Mr. Brenton later decided to move the operation outdoors into a greenhouse, and he asked Mr. Lynwood to build a greenhouse for him, which Mr. Lynwood did. (R. at 41.) In June 2015, Mr. Lynwood planted marijuana in the greenhouse. (R. at 38-40, 42-46.) Three months later, in September 2015, they harvested the marijuana and brought the cuttings inside the house to dry. (R. at 52-54, 86, 119-20.) Mr. Lynwood did not have a medical-marijuana card. (R. at 55-56, 82-83.)

Throughout the time of the foregoing events, Mr. Brenton's 15-year-old daughter, Q., lived in the house with him. Around July 2015, Mr. Brenton allowed Q.'s 16-year-old friend, H., to move into the house. (R. at 52, 70.)

In early October 2015, Mr. Brenton asked Mr. Lynwood to move into the house in order to "keep an eye on the house and help [him] with the kids and the marijuana," which he did. (R. at 37.) Mr. Brenton explained that he had asked Mr. Lynwood to keep an eye on the house because he wanted additional adults in the home to help prevent people from stealing the marijuana. (R. at 74, 77.)

Furthermore, Mr. Brenton was concerned about Q.'s use of methamphetamines. (R. at 73-74.) On one occasion, Mr. Lynwood confiscated a substance he believed was methamphetamine from the girls' belongings. (R. at 75.) Mr. Lynwood gave the substance to Mr. Brenton to destroy. (R. at 75.) Consequently, Mr. Brenton worried that some of Q.'s friends would try to bring more methamphetamines into his home.

At trial, defense counsel questioned Mr. Brenton further about "the purpose of [having Mr. Lynwood] at the house with regards to [his daughter]," which produced the following colloquy:

The question presented both identifies the issue before the court and tries to persuade. Read the question presented. Does it suggest the outcome that the defendant seeks?

This question presented is written as a single sentence, whereas state's question presented is written using multiple sentences. Is one easier to read than the other?

The statement of facts provides all the facts that the court will need to reach its decision.

The opening paragraph provides context by introducing the main players—the defendant, the children who he was accused of endangering, and the decision from which the defendant is appealing.

Here, counsel acknowledges a negative fact: that his client did not have a medical marijuana card. That fact is not relevant to the legal issue, but helps explain one aspect of his prosecution. Notice that counsel does not avoid the negative fact but acknowledges it forthrightly.

This statement of facts is organized both chronologically and topically. At the outset, when it explains how the defendant came to live with the minor children, the statement of facts is chronological.

Beginning with the fourth paragraph of the statement of facts, the organizational structure changes. Counsel wants to emphasize the degree of authority that the defendant had. Thus, in the paragraphs that follow, counsel addresses that issue topic-by-topic.

[Mr. Brenton]:   [Mr. Lynwood] was helping me with my daughter—keep[ing] an eye on her. I was, again, at work most of the day and I was concerned for her activities that she may have been involved in while I was gone.

[Defense Counsel]:   . . . And what was the purpose of [Mr. Lynwood] being in the house with regards to those children?

[Mr. Brenton]:   To help, again, make sure that there wasn't anybody coming to the house that we didn't want there or didn't trust there.

[Defense Counsel]:   Were there other people coming by the house—your ex-wife or her friends—that you were asking [Mr. Lynwood] to protect your children from?

[Mr. Brenton]:   Yes. There were a couple of—I don't know who they were specifically. They were driving by the house a couple of times. My daughter noticed them and she told me they were some people that she had met, through her mom, in Salem.

[Defense Counsel]:   Now, hadn't [Mr. Lynwood] actually found what he was fearful of was methamphetamine in some of the girls' stuff, and hadn't he presented that to you to destroy?

[Mr. Brenton]:   Yes.

[Defense Counsel]:   So he was trying to protect your daughter?

[Mr. Brenton]:   Yes. I believe that.

(R. at 76-77.)

Counsel acknowledges additional negative facts—that the defendant had given marijuana to the girls and smoked it in their presence. Those facts are coupled with a fact that is positive for the defendant—that the father had given him permission to do just that.

The final paragraph of the statement of facts returns to the chronology.

In addition, Mr. Brenton testified he had given Mr. Lynwood permission to give Q. and H. marijuana if they asked. (R. at 93.) Mr. Brenton also testified that, subsequently, Mr. Lynwood reported to Mr. Brenton that Mr. Lynwood had given the girls marijuana on a few occasions and that Mr. Lynwood had smoked marijuana while Q. and H. were present. (R. at 93-94.)

In late October 2015, police officers executed a search warrant at Mr. Brenton's home and arrested Mr. Lynwood. At the time, Q. and H. were in the house. (R. at 119.) Mr. Lynwood was subsequently tried and convicted of several crimes, including two counts of endangering the welfare of a minor. (R. at 190, 223-24, 226.) The trial court denied Mr. Lynwood's motions for a judgment of acquittal on the two counts of endangering the welfare of a minor, which Mr. Lynwood contends constitutes reversible error. (R. at 191-93.)

Summary of the Argument

This summary of the argument provides an overview of the main points that the brief will establish. The summary of the argument is another way to provide context for the court before it begins reading the detailed argument.

In this case, the evidence was insufficient to convict Jeffrey Lynwood of endangering the welfare of a minor. The endangering statute imposes criminal liability on a person who knowingly "[p]ermits a person under 18 years of age to enter or remain in a place where unlawful activity involving a controlled substance is maintained or conducted." Or. Rev. Stat. § 163.575(1)(b) (2015). This case poses the following question: When the legislature enacted the child endangerment statute, upon whom did the legislature intend to impose liability? To answer that question, this Court must construe the phrase "permits a person under 18 years of age to enter or remain."

The text, its context, and the legislative history all point to the conclusion that to "permit" something, one must have authority to forbid it. By hinging liability on the affirmative act of "permitting," the legislature indicated its intent to impose liability on persons in positions of authority vis-à-vis a minor's presence in a drug location. A person who lacks the authority to forbid the minor's entry or remaining is not in a position to permit it.

The authority to "permit" a minor to be in a drug location logically flows from two sources: (1) legal authority over the premises, or (2) authority or control over the minor. Thus, homeowners and parents typically have sufficient authority over their homes or children, respectively, to be liable for "permitting" under the statute. Whether others have the requisite authority depends on the authority or control they possess.

Here, the evidence that Mr. Lynwood was a houseguest or babysitter for the children was insufficient to establish that he "permitted" the homeowner's child and her roommate to enter or remain in the homeowner's home. The homeowner gave Mr. Lynwood the authority to exclude third parties from entering the home during his absence. However, the record contains no evidence that the homeowner gave Mr. Lynwood the authority to prohibit the daughter or roommate from entering into the home. For those reasons, the evidence was insufficient to convict the Mr. Lynwood of violating Oregon Revised Statute § 163.575(1)(b), Oregon's child endangerment statute. Accordingly, Mr. Lynwood's convictions for endangering the welfare of a minor should be reversed.

Argument

I. The evidence at trial was insufficient to convict Mr. Lynwood of endangering the welfare of a child.

Defendant Jeffrey Lynwood's motions for judgment of acquittal should have been granted because the evidence at trial was insufficient to establish that Mr. Lynwood violated Oregon's child endangerment statute. Oregon's child endangerment statute provides that

> a person commits the crime of endangering the welfare of a minor if the person knowingly permits a person under 18 years of age to enter or remain in a place where unlawful activity involving controlled substances is maintained or conducted.

Or. Rev. Stat. § 163.575(1)(b) (2015). As explained below, a person can "permit" something only if that person has authority to deny permission. Because Mr. Lynwood did not have the authority to deny the minors the right to enter or remain in their own home, the evidence was insufficient to convict Mr. Lynwood of child endangerment.

This appellate brief addresses a single issue: whether the evidence was sufficient for the jury to convict the defendant. Accordingly, the appellate brief starts with a Roman numeral I, but has no Roman numeral II.

That one issue will be broken down into two sub-issues: (1) how to construe the statutory language, and (2) the application of that construction to this case.

This first paragraph of the argument is a roadmap section. It begins with a conclusion (the first sentence), states the governing rule (block quote), and then provides a roadmap to the argument to follow.

A. The child endangerment statute applies only to those who have authority over the minor or the premises.

The first sub-issue (part A) addresses an issue of statutory construction. A statutory construction argument is a series of nested, rule-based arguments.

The first issue in this case is the meaning of the word "permit." This issue of statutory construction is subject to this Court's plenary review. *See, e.g., State v. Gaines*, 206 P.3d 1042, 1050-51 (Or. 2009) (interpreting Oregon Revised Statute § 174.020 anew). Using Oregon's traditional methodology, this Court first considers the plain meaning of the word "permit." *Portland Gen. Elec. Co. v. Bureau of Labor & Indus.*, 859 P.2d 1143, 1146 (Or. 1993). Because the meaning of a word is best understood in context, this Court also considers the word in its context. *Id.* at 1146; *Lane Cnty. v. Land Conservation & Dev. Comm'n*, 942 P.2d 278, 283 (Or. 1997). "Context" includes other provisions of the statute and other related statutes. *Portland Gen. Elec. Co.*, 859 P.2d at 1146. Finally, this Court considers the statute's legislative history. Or. Rev. Stat. § 174.020 (2009); *Gaines*, 206 P.3d at 1050-51. As explained below, the statutory phrase "permits a [minor] to enter or remain in a place" makes culpable only one who (1) has legal authority over the place or sufficient authority over a minor to exclude the minor from a place, and (2) consents to, gives leave for, or authorizes the child's entry or remaining in the place.

The paragraph provides a roadmap section for the statutory construction argument. The roadmap section, among other things, explains the governing rule, which is the jurisdiction's methodology for construing a statute. Those rules are then applied in sections 1, 2, and 3, below.

1. The plain meaning of the statute creates liability only for people who have authority over the place or the minor.

A rule-based argument begins with a conclusion. Here, counsel asserts how the court should interpret the verb "permit." ────→

The plain meaning of the verb "to permit" presupposes the authority to permit or to deny permission. When construing statutory text, this Court "presumes that the legislature intended terms to have their plain, natural, and ordinary meaning." *Portland Gen. Elec. Co.*, 859 P.2d at 1146. To determine the plain, natural, and ordinary meaning of a word, this Court turns to the dictionary. *Dowell v. Or. Mut. Ins. Co.*, 343 P.3d 283, 286 (Or. Ct. App. 2015). The dictionary supplies several relevant definitions for "permit":

Next, a rule-based argument explains the relevant rule. Here, the rules explain how this jurisdiction construes the plain meaning of the text.

> 1: to consent to expressly or formally: grant leave for or the privilege of: ALLOW, TOLERATE . . . 2: to give (a person) leave: AUTHORIZE . . . 4: to make possible.

Counsel also includes a rule derived from the dictionary: the definition of the verb "permit."

Webster's Third New International Dictionary of the English Language 1683 (unabridged ed. 2002).

Each of these definitions contemplates a transfer of a "privilege." To "permit," according to the definitions, requires a person to "consent," "grant" or "give." In other words, the person who permits must first possess the right to "consent," "grant," or "give" a privilege to another. Accordingly, the plain and ordinary meaning of "permit" requires the guilty person to first have the authority over the minor or the premises such that the person is capable of consenting to, granting or giving a prohibited privilege.

The application begins here. The shaded text identifies key ideas from the rules that are integrated into the application. That integration of key ideas from the rule into the application is the hallmark of an effective rule-based argument.

In fact, this Court has previously construed the verb "permit" to require a pre-existing authority to forbid. In *State v. Pyritz*, this Court analyzed the dictionary definition of "permit" and prior definitions from case law. 752 P.2d 1310, 1312-13 (Or. Ct. App. 1988). This Court then concluded, "Before one can be said to 'permit' something, one must have authority to forbid it." *Id.* at 1313 (discussing *Lemery v. Leonard*, 196 P. 376 (Or. 1921)).

The discussion of the *Pyritz* and *Lemery* cases is a second rule-based argument.

The first paragraph discussing the *Pyritz* & *Lemery* cases states a conclusion and extracts a rule from those cases.

Thus, the plain meaning of "permit" requires a pre-existing authority to deny permission. When this definition is applied to the child endangerment statute, a person can be guilty of endangering a child only if that person has authority to deny the child the ability to enter or remain on the premises. Such authority exists only if the person has authority over the child or the premises.

(a) Babysitters do not have the authority to deny children access to their own home.

A babysitter has limited authority over a minor. Authority or control over a minor begins with the parents or legal custodians of a child. *Troxel v. Granville*, 530 U.S. 57, 65-66 (2000). Parents and the legal guardians of children have the primary right to make decisions regarding care, custody, and control of their children. *Id.* Parents may delegate authority and control over their children to others. For example, parents may transfer temporary control over their children to babysitters. A babysitter is typically tasked with watching over and keeping children from harm during a parent's absence from the home. Consequently, babysitters have sufficient control of the children to be liable for criminal neglect. *See State v. Mills*, 629 P.2d 861, 862 n.1 (Or. Ct. App. 1981) (quoting legislative commentary to child neglect statute, which notes that babysitters may be liable under the statute because they can have sufficient "custody or control" to be responsible for neglect).

The authority of the babysitter, however, is derived from the parent and is, therefore, limited. That limitation is evident in Oregon's statutory code. For example, a babysitter who removes children from their home without parental permission may be guilty of kidnapping. Under Oregon law, a kidnapping occurs when a person takes another person "from one place to another" without consent or legal authority. Or. Rev. Stat. § 163.225 (2015). In the case of a minor child, "without consent" is "without the consent of the lawful custodian." Or. Rev. Stat. § 163.215 (2015). Thus, Oregon law assumes that the authority of other adults, such as a babysitter, is inferior to the authority of a parent.

Because Oregon law assumes that the authority of other adults is inferior to the authority of a parent, it follows that an adult such as a babysitter has no authority to either permit or deny a child's entry into a home when the parent has explicitly authorized that entry.

(b) Houseguests do not have the authority to limit access of residents.

Similarly, a houseguest's control over a house is also limited. A co-inhabitant typically has the authority to permit or deny access to third parties when the owner is not present. *See, e.g., United States v. Matlock*, 415 U.S. 164, 171 n.7 (1974) (holding that co-inhabitants presumably have right to permit entry by police into common areas of home; other co-inhabitants assume the risk that they will do so); *State v. Carsey*, 664 P.2d 1085, 1093 (Or. 1983) (holding that joint occupier presumed to have authority to permit search of common areas). Thus, courts presume that owners transfer to those living in their homes the authority to grant or deny entry to third parties, like police officers. When the owner

The next paragraph applies that rule to the statute at hand.

In this section of the brief, counsel wants to establish that a babysitter's authority is limited by the authority that a parent gives to that babysitter. Oregon case law has never addressed the relationship between a parent's authority and a babysitter's authority. Therefore, counsel proposes a rule that is implicit in existing Oregon law: A babysitter's authority is derived from and limited by the authority that a parent gives to the babysitter.

leaves a guest in the home alone, the owner assumes the risk that the guest may permit officers to enter into the common areas of the home. *Id.*

However, Oregon courts have never held that a houseguest has the authority to exclude residents from a home. If a non-owner's authority over property is based on what he has been given by its owner, the authority is necessarily limited by the terms of the grant. Therefore, when an owner permits two different people to enter and remain in his home, neither person gains the authority to exclude the other. Rather, the guest's authority is subordinate to the owner's and, therefore, cannot override the permission given by the owner to the other guest. In such situations, only the owner can be said to have "permitted" the entry.

Conclusion to the plain language argument

Accordingly, the words of the statute require a person to first have authority to deny access to a location before that person can be liable for permitting minors into the location. Neither a babysitter nor a houseguest has the authority to deny children access to their home.

2. Context corroborates Mr. Lynwood's interpretation.

Counsel's context argument is composed of two rule-based arguments.

Conclusion

Rules

The context of the statute corroborates the above reading. Context includes other provisions of the statute and related statutes. *Portland Gen. Elec. Co.*, 859 P.2d at 1146. When the legislature uses different terms within a statute, those terms are assumed to have different meaning. *State ex rel. Dep't of Transp. v. Stallcup*, 138 P.3d 9, 14 (Or. 2006).

The application begins here.

In this case, the context shows that the legislature intended to criminalize the affirmative act of "permitting" and did not intend to criminalize a passive failure to act. The endangering statute includes five other provisions, each of which proscribes a different type of conduct that creates risks for children. It targets a person who

> (a) induces, causes or permits a child to witness sexual acts;
> (b) permits a child to enter or remain in a drug environment;
> (c) induces, causes or permits a child to gamble;
> (d) distributes, sells or allows to be sold tobacco to a child; or
> (e) sells drug paraphernalia to a child.

Or. Rev. Stat. § 163.575(1). Subsection (b) creates culpability if a person merely "permits." Paragraphs (a) and (c) create culpability if a person "induces, causes or permits" certain conduct. The verb "to induce" may include "to move and lead" as well as "to bring on or bring about." *Webster's Third New International Dictionary of the English Language, supra,* at 1154. "Cause" is defined as "to serve as cause or occasion of: bring into existence: MAKE." *Id.* at 356. The verb "permit"

Again, in the shaded text, you can see how key ideas from the rules are integrated into the application.

cannot be defined as "to make possible" because such an interpretation fails to give the word "permit" a meaning that is different from the meaning of "induce" or "cause." If the verb "permit" is defined as "to make possible," the word "permit" begins to invade the space occupied by "induce," which is defined as "to bring about," and "cause," which is defined as "to bring into existence." Under such an interpretation, the prohibitory language in paragraph (b) has the same scope as the prohibitory language in paragraph (a) and paragraph (c), despite the legislature's choice to use different terms. Such an interpretation would undermine the legislature's choice to use a different term. Thus, the context also suggests that the legislature did not intend "permit" to have its broadest meaning.

Other statutes that protect children demonstrate that when the legislature intends to create liability for failing to act, it says so. The Oregon Supreme Court has previously relied on statutes that share a common purpose to construe a statute currently at issue. *See State v. Bailey*, 213 P.3d 1240, 1245 n.4 (Or. 2009). Here, the endangering statute is one of eight "offenses against family" and was enacted during the 1971 criminal code revision. *See* 1971 Or. Laws ch. 743. The other offenses against family include bigamy, incest, abandonment of a child, buying or selling a child, child neglect (first and second degree), criminal nonsupport, and failing to supervise. Or. Rev. Stat. §§ 163.515, 163.525, 163.535, 163.537, 163.545, 163.547, 163.555, 163.577 (2015). To be guilty of any of the other crimes requires an affirmative act: marrying (to be guilty of bigamy), engaging in sexual activity (incest), deserting (abandonment), buying or selling, and leaving (neglect). By contrast, criminal nonsupport and failing to supervise criminalize the failure to act, and they do so explicitly by including the phrases "fails to provide support" and "failing to supervise." Or. Rev. Stat. §§ 163.555, 163.577. Thus, when the legislature imposes liability for failing to act to protect children, it expressly says so. Here, the legislature did not expressly create liability for the failure to act. Because the legislature chose not to include liability for the failure to act, such liability should not be read into the statute.

Accordingly, the statute's context also supports the conclusion that the legislature was criminalizing affirmative conduct and not the passive failure to act.

3. The legislative history supports Mr. Lynwood's construction.

The legislative history also supports the above construction. In its commentary to § 163.575, the Criminal Law Revision Commission emphasized that the statute was intended to criminalize particularized conduct:

> Throughout the criminal code revision, the Commission has sought to articulate clear and concise statements of the substantive offenses, prohibiting *particularized conduct* and applying defined elements of culpability. Many of the provisions relate to conduct detrimental to the welfare of minors.

Oregon Criminal Law Revision Commission, *Proposed Oregon Criminal Code*, Final Draft and Rep., § 177, at 178 (1970) (emphasis added) (hereinafter Commentary). The commission further explained that § 163.575 was "designed to provide coverage for *specific acts* injurious to the welfare of minors." *Id.* (emphasis added). In other words, the legislature intended to criminalize affirmative actions and not a passive failure to act.

This same conclusion results when considering the statute that preceded the child endangerment statute. The child endangerment statute was intended

---

Margin annotations:

Conclusion

Conclusion to the next rule-based argument

Rule

The application begins. Here, the application does not integrate key words from the rule. Rather, the application does what the rule says is permissible: It looks at related statutes and makes an argument based on a distinction in those statutes. In that way, the application applies the rule.

Conclusion to this rule-based argument

Conclusion to the context argument

Counsel's legislative history argument is composed of 3 rule-based arguments.

Conclusion to the first legislative history rule-based argument

The explanation of the legislative history acts as the rules to this rule-based argument.

This final sentence is both an application of and a conclusion to this rule-based argument. Although the last sentence does not re-use the identical language from the legislative history, can you see that counsel chose echoing language?

Conclusion to the second legislative history argument

The rule is, again, an excerpt from the legislative history.

to cover the same conduct as the former delinquency of a minor statute. Oregon Criminal Law Revision Commission, *Subcommittee No. 2 Minutes, Mar. 6, 1970*, at 10 (1970) (explaining that the endangering statute was an attempt "to cover everything the statute on contributing to the delinquency of a minor encompassed that has not been provided for elsewhere in the proposed code"). The contributing to the delinquency of a minor statute, *former* Oregon Revised Statute §167.210, also required affirmative conduct before it imposed criminal liability. That statute makes criminally liable

> any person responsible for the act of encouraging, causing, or contributing to the delinquency of such child, or any person who . . . endeavors to induce any child to perform any act or follow any course of conduct which would cause it to become a delinquent child . . . .

Key language from the rule is integrated into the application.

The last half of this sentence acts as the conclusion to this second rule-based argument.

Former Or. Rev. Stat. § 167.210 (repealed 1971). Thus, the prior act required affirmative conduct — encouraging, causing, contributing, or inducing. It did not criminalize merely permitting something to take place by failing to act. Because the current act was intended to cover the same conduct as the contributing to the delinquency of a minor statute, it should be construed to also require affirmative conduct before liability is imposed.

This paragraph is the last rule-based argument. Again, excerpts from the legislative history are used as a foundation on which counsel builds an argument about the legislature's intent.

        Finally, at the same time that the legislature passed the child endangerment statute, it explicitly recognized that criminal liability requires affirmative conduct. During the 1971 revision, the legislature also passed Oregon Revised Statute §§ 161.085 and 161.095 (1971). Oregon Revised Statute § 161.095 establishes that the "minimal requirement for criminal liability is the performance by a person of conduct which includes a voluntary act or the omission to perform an act which he is capable of performing." Oregon Revised Statute § 161.085 defines "omission" as a "failure to perform an act the performance of which is required by law." Those provisions reflect an awareness by the legislature of the prevailing view of Anglo-American law preferring criminal liability for affirmative acts, and generally permitting liability based on omission only when there is a pre-existing legal duty to act. *See, e.g.,* Wayne R. LaFave, *Handbook on Criminal Law* § 26, 182-84 (1970). Thus, part of the context of the legislature's enactment of the endangering statute in 1971 was its understanding of those basic principles of criminal law.

This last paragraph provides a final conclusion to the legislative history argument and to the statutory construction argument.

        Thus, the legislative history, like the text in context, establishes that the legislature intended to require an affirmative act before imposing criminal liability. It did not intend to criminalize the mere failure to prevent a child's presence in her own home by a person with no pre-existing legal duty to the particular child.

In Part B, counsel argues that, based on the statute as construed above, the evidence was insufficient to convict the defendant.

B. The evidence was insufficient to establish that Mr. Lynwood knowingly permitted the children to enter or remain in a place in which drug activity was conducted.

        Because Mr. Lynwood was not authorized to exclude the children from their own home, the evidence was insufficient to establish that Mr. Lynwood permitted the children to enter or remain in a place where drug activity was conducted. Whether the evidence is sufficient to convict a defendant is a question of law subject to this Court's plenary review. *See, e.g., State v. Cunningham*, 880 P.2d 431, 440 (Or. 1994) (exercising plenary review). When exercising plenary review, this Court applies the same standard as the trial court applied. *Id.* Accordingly, this Court must determine whether the evidence, viewed in the light most favorable to the state, was sufficient for a rational fact-finder to find the essential elements of the crime beyond a reasonable doubt. *Id.; Jackson v. Virginia*, 443 U.S 307, 318-19 (1979).

This sentence states the standard of review. "Plenary review" is the same standard as "de novo" review. Under either term, no deference is given to the trial court's decision.

As explained above, "permits," as used in Oregon Revised Statute § 163.575(1)(b), refers to the act of consenting to or granting leave for a child to enter or remain in the prohibited location, and necessarily requires a person to have authority such that they could forbid the child's entry.

Compare how the standard of decision is explained here and in the state's brief. In this argument, counsel provides the rules but does not emphasize them because these rules—which are deferential to the jury's decision—do not help the defendant.

The evidence in this case never established that Mr. Lynwood had authority to exclude the girls from their home. The evidence established the following:

Here, counsel provides the statutory rule as construed above.

(1) the parent of a teenage girl permitted the teenage girl and her friend to live in his home with his marijuana grow operation;

(2) after those circumstances had existed for a time, Mr. Lynwood was asked to assist in building a greenhouse and otherwise to assist with the grow operation;

(3) Mr. Lynwood had no familial relationship to the teenage girls and no ownership interest in the home;

(4) the parent asked Mr. Lynwood to stay in the home while the marijuana was harvested; and

(5) Mr. Lynwood was also asked to keep an eye on the house and girls because the father was concerned that the girls' methamphetamine connections would seek them out.

Thus, Mr. Brenton, the homeowner and father, never gave Mr. Lynwood the authority to exclude the teenagers from their home. While a houseguest may have the authority to exclude strangers who knock on the door of a home while the homeowner is not present, nothing permits a houseguest to prevent a resident from entering her own home. In fact, had Mr. Lynwood locked the teenage girls out of their home he might have faced criminal liability for criminal mischief. Had he tried to remove them, he could have faced additional criminal liability for kidnapping.

Because Mr. Lynwood could not lawfully have excluded the teenagers from their own home, the evidence was insufficient to find that he "permitted" them to enter or remain there.

CONCLUSION

This Court should reverse Mr. Lynwood's convictions for endangering the welfare of a minor.

Respectfully submitted,
KEN NAKANO
CHIEF DEFENDER

OFFICE OF PUBLIC DEFENSE SERVICES

ESigned
By Vijay Grewal at 2:43 pm, Dec 01 2016

VIJAY GREWAL OSB #974573 DEPUTY PUBLIC
DEFENDER
Vijay.Grewal @opds.state.or.us
Attorneys for Defendant-Appellant
Jeffrey Scott Mr. Lynwood

CERTIFICATE OF COMPLIANCE WITH ORAP 5.05(2)(d)

Brief length

I certify that (1) this brief complies with the word-count limitation in ORAP 5.05(2)(b) and (2) the word-count of this brief is 4,428 words.

Type size

I certify that the size of the type in this brief is not smaller than 14 point for both the text of the brief and footnotes as required by ORAP 5.05(4)(f).

NOTICE OF FILING AND PROOF OF SERVICE

I certify that I directed the original Appellant's Opening Brief to be filed with the Appellate Court Administrator, Appellate Courts Records Section, 1543 Maple Street, Salem, Oregon 97231, on November 4, 2015.

I further certify that, upon receipt of the confirmation email stating that the document has been accepted by the eFiling system, this Appellant's Opening Brief will be eServed pursuant to ORAP 16.45 (regarding electronic service on registered eFilers) on Jennifer Schwarz, #761699, Solicitor General, attorney for Plaintiff- Respondent.

Respectfully submitted,
KEN NAKANO
CHIEF DEFENDER
OFFICE OF PUBLIC DEFENSE SERVICES

ESigned

VIJAY GREWAL OSB #974573
DEPUTY PUBLIC DEFENDER
Vijay.Grewal@opds.state.or.us
Attorneys for Defendant-Appellant
Jeffrey Scott Lynwood

B. Respondent's Answering Brief

IN THE COURT OF APPEALS OF THE STATE OF OREGON

———————

STATE OF OREGON,	)	Mercer County Circuit Court
Plaintiff-Respondent,	)	No. 15C50799
	)	
v.	)	CA A139020
	)	
JEFFREY SCOTT LYNWOOD,	)	
Defendant-Appellant.	)	
	)	
	)	

———————

RESPONDENT'S ANSWERING BRIEF

———————

Appeal from the Judgment of the Circuit Court
For Mercer County
Honorable Charity A. Beckah Judge

KEN NAKANO #842314
Chief Defender

VIJAY GREWAL #952421
Deputy Public Defender

VIVIAN L. KEARA #707902
Attorney General

ANIYA P. LINDSIE #761699
Solicitor General

JENNIFER SCHWARZ #500187
Assistant Attorney General

Office of Public Defense Services
18 Polo Street NE, Suite 412
Salem, Oregon 97231
(513) 341-6439

Oregon Department of Justice
129 Gavel Ave. NE
Salem, Oregon 92123-9301
(514) 321-5938

Attorneys for Defendant-Appellant

Attorneys for Plaintiff-Respondent

The state's brief cover provides the same basic information as the defendant's brief cover: the names of the parties, the appellate court in which the case is being heard, the court from which the appeal is taken, and the names and contact information for counsel.

Traditionally, the respondent's cover is red, and the brief is colloquially referred to as the "red brief."

The table of contents provides the first overview of the state's argument.

Read through the point headings listed in the table of contents. Can you understand the gist of the state's argument?

Notice also the formatting. All the point headings are evenly spaced and line up consistently. A crisp table of contents projects the impression that the brief was written by a professional who cares about the details.

Table of Contents

Table of Authorities

Cases

Page

Statutes

The table of authorities is a resource to the court. It explains where in the brief the court can find counsel's discussion of different authorities.

Again, a crisp, accurate, consistently formatted table of authorities reinforces the impression that the brief was written by a professional who cares about the details.

Other Authorities

Questions Presented

1. Oregon's child endangerment statute provides that a person is guilty of endangering the welfare of a minor if he or she "permits" a child to enter or remain in a place where unlawful activities involving drugs are maintained or conducted. For purposes of that statute, what does the term "permit" encompass?

2. Did defendant permit the children to enter or remain in a place of unlawful activity involving controlled substances when the defendant provided the children with marijuana, smoked marijuana with the children, and sold marijuana from the children's home?

Statement of the Case

Defendant appeals his convictions for endangering the welfare of a minor. In the summer and fall of 2014, defendant was entrusted with the care of two minor children. (R. at 38.) While the children were entrusted in defendant's care, defendant ran his own marijuana selling business from the children's home, gave marijuana to the children several times, and smoked it with them regularly. (R. at 90-92, 121-22, 148-65.) The jury convicted defendant of endangering the welfare of the children. (R. at 223-24.)

Defendant came to be the children's caretaker after his friend Wesley Brenton asked defendant to move into Brenton's house. Brenton, who had a medical marijuana card and another card allowing him to grow marijuana for another person, grew marijuana in his house. (R. at 38-40, 42-46.) Also in the house were Brenton's 15-year-old daughter, Q., and Q.'s 16-year-old friend, H. (R. at 52, 70.) Both Q. and H. lived in the house "full time." (R. at 52, 70.) Brenton worked a full-time job, "wasn't home a lot during the day," and sometimes did not get home until 9:00 or 10:00 p.m. (R. at 35-36, 62.)

Therefore, Brenton asked and defendant agreed to move into the house to help grow and harvest the marijuana, and to "keep an eye on the house and help with the kids and the marijuana." (R. at 37.)

With respect to the grow operation, Brenton agreed to share the marijuana with defendant, and there was an "option" for defendant to sell some of it. (R. at 42-46, 83-84.) Later that fall, defendant helped harvest the marijuana and store it in Brenton's house. (R. at 52-54, 86, 119-20.) Brenton received half of the marijuana, with defendant getting the other half. (R. at 56-57, 84, 89.) Defendant did not have a medical marijuana card. (R. at 55-56, 82-83.)

With respect to the children, Brenton was "concerned for the activities that Q. may have been involved in" while Brenton was at work. (R. at 72, 83.) Brenton wanted defendant to be in the house to "make sure that there wasn't anybody coming to the house that we didn't want there or didn't trust there." (R. at 74.) Brenton did not want some of Q.'s friends coming to the house because he "didn't trust them" and because he believed that one of them had broken into the house and stolen marijuana. (R. at 74, 77.) Brenton also wanted defendant to protect the children from "other people" coming by the house, including Q.'s mother (Brenton's ex-wife) or her friends. (R. at 75.)

The state's question presented addresses the two sub-issues of the argument: how to construe the statute and whether, based on that construction, the evidence was sufficient to convict the defendant. By contrast, the defendant created one question presented, which addressed both issues.

The state's first question presented is a fairly "straight" question presented. It does not suggest a particular outcome. The second question presented, however, uses facts more aggressively to suggest the legal conclusion the state is seeking.

The opening paragraph of the statement of facts provides context by introducing the main players—the defendant, the children whom he was accused of endangering, and the decision from which the defendant is appealing.

What differences do you see when you compare defendant's opening and the state's?

The state acknowledges facts that are helpful to the defendant, namely, that the homeowner and father had given specific instructions to the defendant about his responsibilities with respect to the children.

Brenton gave his daughter marijuana on a regular basis — "maybe every other day" — and he assumed that Q. was sharing it with H. (R. at 57.) Brenton instructed defendant to provide Q. and H. with marijuana "if they asked." (R. at 93.) On "[m]aybe three to five" occasions the girls asked defendant for marijuana, and he gave it to them. (R. at 93-94.) Brenton observed defendant smoking marijuana with Q. and H. (R. at 78.) Brenton was mostly concerned about Q.'s other drug use, particularly her methamphetamine use. (R. at 73-74.) To "protect" the girls, on one occasion defendant examined some of their "stuff" and confiscated a substance he believed to be methamphetamine, giving it to Brenton to destroy. (R. at 75.)

Initially, defendant stayed at Brenton's home only during the daytime when Brenton was at work. Beginning in October 2014, defendant slept there at night, had his own room, and had keys to that room. (R. at 95, 103, 106.) While living in the home, defendant ran his own marijuana business out of the house. (R. at 90.) He sold his portion of the harvest to a number of people and stored the marijuana he was selling in the bedroom he used. (R. at 90-92, 121-22, 148-65.)

In late October 2014, police executed a search warrant at Brenton's home and arrested defendant. Q. and H. were present in the house during the execution of the warrant. Defendant told police that he had been staying there and "was caring for [Q. and] the house." (R. at 119.)

> These facts are not legally relevant because the only issue on appeal is about the two counts of child endangerment. The state may have included these facts to paint a negative picture of the defendant. Notice how the state provides facts without characterization and allows the court to reach a conclusion about the defendant's character.

The state charged defendant with two counts of delivery of a controlled substance to a minor, Oregon Revised Statute § 475.906 (2015); one count of manufacturing marijuana, Oregon Revised Statute § 475.856 (2015); one count of felon in possession of a firearm, Oregon Revised Statute § 166.270 (2015); and two counts of endangering the welfare of a minor, Oregon Revised Statute § 163.575 (2015). At trial, after the state rested its case and, again, after the close of all evidence, defendant moved for a judgment of acquittal on all counts. (R. at 190, 223-24.) The court denied both motions. (R. at 191-93, 226.) The jury then considered the evidence presented against defendant and convicted defendant on all counts except felon in possession of a firearm. (R. at 223-24, 226.) Defendant now appeals his convictions for endangering the welfare of a minor.

Summary of the Argument

> This summary of the argument provides an overview of the main points that the brief will establish. The summary of the argument is another way to provide context for the court before it begins reading the detailed argument.

The evidence was sufficient for a jury to reasonably find that defendant endangered the welfare of two children. A person endangers the welfare of a minor if he or she knowingly "[p]ermits a person under 18 years of age to enter or remain in a place where unlawful activity involving controlled substances is maintained or conducted[.]" Or. Rev. Stat. § 163.575(1)(b) (2015). The text, context, and legislative history demonstrate that the legislature intended the statute to reach conduct whereby a person allows or makes it possible for a child to remain in the presence of unlawful drug activity.

In this case, defendant's actions easily fall within the ambit of Oregon Revised Statute § 163.575(1)(b). At the same time that defendant chose to act as a caretaker for two children, defendant also chose to actively participate in a marijuana growing operation in the children's house, run a drug-dealing business from the children's house, give the children marijuana, and smoke marijuana with them. By actively engaging in that conduct, defendant violated Oregon Revised Statute § 163.575(1)(b).

Defendant's argument to the contrary is without merit. According to defendant, to violate Oregon Revised Statute § 163.575(1)(b) an adult must have been given explicit, specific authority to prevent a child from entering or remaining on the premises and must choose not to exercise that authority. But defendant's narrow reading of Oregon Revised Statute § 163.575(1)(b) is inconsistent with the statute's text, context, and legislative history. Moreover, incorporating such a requirement into the statute flies in the face of the legislature's intended goal of protecting children from deliberate exposure to harmful activities.

Assuming that defendant's reading of Oregon Revised Statute § 163.575(1)(b) is correct, the trial court nonetheless correctly denied his motions for judgment of acquittal. Contrary to defendant's claim, the state's evidence did establish that defendant had sufficient authority to prevent the children from remaining in the house and that he failed to exercise that authority. The evidence showed that defendant chose repeatedly to engage in unlawful drug activity in the children's presence and in their home. Whatever authority he had over the children or the house is irrelevant because he possessed the ability to decline to engage in that conduct.

> This argument is an "even if" argument: Even if the court does not accept the state's construction of the statute, the evidence was still sufficient for the jury to convict the defendant.
>
> Lawyers often make "even if" arguments to provide a way for the court to find in their client's favor even if the court does not adopt every argument in the client's favor.

In addition, the evidence established that defendant was acting in the role of the children's babysitter. As such, defendant was authorized, and in fact obligated, to remove them from danger. Finally, even assuming defendant lacked the authority to physically expel or exclude the children, he was certainly authorized to take some step—including, for example, calling the police to prevent the children from remaining in the house. Because he chose not to do so, defendant permitted the children to remain in a place where unlawful drug activity was occurring. Thus, defendant violated Oregon Revised Statute § 163.575(1)(b), and the jury appropriately found that he had endangered the welfare of two children.

> Here, the respondent (the State of Oregon) would like a broad construction for the word "permit" because such a construction would be helpful in future prosecutions. Even if the state does not get its preferred broad construction, it still seeks to have the conviction of this defendant upheld.

Argument

I. The jury's conclusion that defendant endangered the welfare of two children was supported by the evidence.

The evidence was sufficient for the jury to conclude that defendant was guilty of two counts of endangering the welfare of a minor. A person commits the crime of endangering the welfare of a minor if he knowingly

> permits a person under 18 years of age to enter or remain in a place where unlawful activity involving controlled substances is maintained or conducted.

Or. Rev. Stat. § 163.575(1)(b) (2015). Whether the jury had sufficient evidence to convict defendant requires a two-step analysis. This Court must first determine the scope of the verb "permit." Then, in light of that understanding, this Court must determine whether the evidence was sufficient to support the jury's

> The argument begins with a roadmap section that asserts the state's conclusion (in the first sentence), provides the governing rule (in the second sentence), and a map of the arguments to come (in the final three sentences). Compare the map of the arguments in this roadmap section to defendant's map. Here, by explaining that the analysis is a "two-step analysis," the state provides a more explicit map. One is not necessarily better than the other, but you should be aware of the different ways lawyers might map the arguments to come.

finding that defendant did in fact "permit" two minors to enter or remain in a place where marijuana was being unlawfully grown.

A. A person violates Oregon's child endangerment statute if that person allows or makes it possible for a child to enter or remain in a place where unlawful drug activity occurs.

The text, the text in context, and the legislative history all show that the legislature intended the word "permit" to have a broad reach so that children would be shielded from unlawful drug activity. To ascertain the meaning of a statutory text, this Court first examines the text of the statute. *Portland Gen. Elec. Co. v. Bureau of Labor & Indus.*, 859 P.2d 1143, 1146 (Or. 1993). When construing the text of a statute, this Court gives the words of the text their plain and ordinary meaning. *Id.*; *State v. Gaines*, 206 P.3d 1042, 1050 (Or. 2009). If the legislature has not defined the meaning of a word, this Court may look to a dictionary for the word's plain and ordinary meaning. *Dowell v. Or. Mut. Ins. Co.*, 343 P.3d 283, 286 (Or. Ct. App. 2015). This Court does not, however, look at the words of a statute in isolation; rather, it construes each part together with the other parts to produce a harmonious whole. *Portland Gen. Elec. Co.*, 859 P.2d at 1146; *Lane Cnty. v. Land Conservation & Dev. Comm'n*, 942 P.2d 278, 283 (Or. 1997). To that end, this Court determines the meaning of text by considering that text in the context of the statute and related statutes. *See Portland Gen. Elec. Co.*, 859 P.2d at 1146. Finally, a party may proffer legislative history, and after examining the text and context of the statute, the Court will examine the legislative history "where that legislative history appears useful to the court's analysis." *Gaines*, 206 P.3d at 1050-51.

Applying those steps to the child endangerment statute shows that the legislature intended the word "permit" to encompass any conduct that allows or makes it possible for a child to remain in a place where illegal drug activity occurs.

1. By its definition alone, the word "permit" can have a broad or narrow meaning.

Like many words, the verb "permit" does not have just one meaning. Rather, its definition includes a broader and a more narrow construction. "Permit" is defined as

1: to consent to expressly or formally: grant leave for or the privilege of: ALLOW, TOLERATE . . . .

2: to give (a person) leave: AUTHORIZE

. . .

4. to make possible.

Webster's Third New International Dictionary of the English Language 1683 (unabridged ed. 2002).

The narrower meaning of the verb "permit" contemplates a formal consent or grant that authorizes a person to do something. If the legislature intended "permit" in its narrower sense, the child endangerment statute prohibits a

---

Part A addresses the question of how to construe the word "permit." Like the defendant, the state outlines the methodology for construing the statute. Below, the state applies those steps to the statute at issue.

These first two paragraphs constitute the roadmap section for part A of the state's brief.

The state's plain language argument is less aggressive than the defendant's. Rather than assert that the verb "permit" has just one meaning, the state asserts that "permit" can have a broader or narrower meaning— one meaning that supports the defendant's argument and one meaning that supports the state's argument.

The benefit to a less aggressive approach is that it may seem more reasonable to the court and, therefore, make the state seem more reasonable. In addition, the less aggressive argument allows the state to more easily address a reality— that the definition of "permit" does include a narrower definition.

On the other hand, the less aggressive approach requires the state to rely on only the "context" and "legislative history" to make its argument.

person in a position of authority from specifically consenting or authorizing a child to enter or remain in a place where drug activity is ongoing.

But the verb "permit" also has a broader meaning, which includes to "allow," "tolerate," or "make possible." If the legislature intended "permit" in the broader sense, then the child endangerment statute prohibits conduct that allows, tolerates, or makes it possible for a child to enter or remain in a place where drug activity is ongoing.

In this rule-based argument, the state uses a dictionary definition as part of its rule. It then integrates the language of that rule into the application, here.

In asserting that the verb "permit" has only one meaning, defendant misreads both the dictionary definition and prior case law. As explained above, the plain and ordinary meaning of the verb "permit" allows for a narrower or a broader definition. Similarly, prior case law also contemplates a broader and narrower definition. In *Lemery v. Leonard*, the Oregon Supreme Court interpreted the verb "permit." 196 P. 376, 378 (Or. 1921). The statute at issue made it unlawful for any owner to permit sheep "to run at large or go on the lands of another without the permission of such owner[.]" *Id.* at 376-77. The Oregon Supreme Court held that "[t]o 'permit' means to allow by tacit consent by not hindering, taking no steps to prevent, or to grant leave by express consent or authorization." *Id.* at 378. Although defendant focuses on the phrase "by express consent or authorization," the Oregon Supreme Court noted that "to permit" also means "not hindering" and "taking no steps to prevent." In other words, the Oregon Supreme Court defined "permit" as containing definitions both narrow and broad. Nothing in *Lemery* stands for the proposition that the legislature intended "permit" to be interpreted as narrowly as defendant claims.

Here, the state addresses defendant's argument. Notice that the state does not address defendant's argument until after presenting its own argument.

Although the state acknowledges that it is responding to the defendant's argument, notice that the state avoids giving additional airtime to the defendant's argument. The state simply explains why, from its perspective, the defendant's argument is wrong.

In sum, the plain meaning of the verb "permit" allows for both a broad and narrow construction. The context and legislative history show that the legislature intended the broader construction.

Final conclusion to the plain language argument and a transition to the next argument

2. **The statute's context establishes that the legislature intended the verb "permit" to broadly encompass any action that allows a child to be in the presence of controlled substances.**

Although the verb "permit" can be understood narrowly or broadly, an examination of the text in context shows that the legislature intended the verb to be understood more broadly. The context establishes that the legislature intended to protect children, and the broader interpretation fulfills that intent. "Context" includes both the provisions that immediately surround the statute in question and statutes that share a common purpose. *Portland Gen. Elec. Co.*, 859 P.2d at 1146; *State v. Bailey*, 213 P.3d 1240, 1245 n.4 (Or. 2009). Oregon's child endangerment statute includes five subsections. A person "endangers the welfare of a minor" if that person does any of the following:

The first sentence is a conclusion to the rule-based argument. The second sentence is a more focused conclusion that asserts what the context will show.

This is the rule that is then applied.

The application begins here. The first part of the application examines the surrounding subsections and argues what those subsections show.

(a) Induces, causes or permits an unmarried person under 18 years of age to witness an act of sexual conduct as defined by Oregon Revised Statute § 167.060;

(b) Permits a person under 18 years of age to enter or remain in a place where unlawful activity involving controlled substances is maintained or conducted;

5

(c) Induces, causes or permits a person under 18 years of age to participate in gambling as defined by Oregon Revised Statute § 167.117;

(d) Distributes, sells, or causes to be sold, tobacco in any form to a person under 18 years of age; or

(e) Sells to a person under 18 years of age any device in which tobacco, marijuana, cocaine, or any controlled substances as defined in Oregon Revised Statutes § 475.005 is burned and the principal design and use of which is directly or indirectly to deliver . . . into the human body.

Or. Rev. Stat. § 163.575(1).

The common thread that underlies all of the subsections is the protection of the children. More specifically, each subsection protects children from an adult's actions that harm the child. Thus, at a minimum, the context demonstrates that the legislature intended to protect children. Consistent with that intent, "permits" should be construed broadly so that the statute protects children from unlawful drug activities and the actions of adults who expose them to or involve them in those activities.

The second part of the application compares the stated purpose of the criminal laws and uses that stated purpose to argue that the word "permit" should be understood more broadly.

This broader construction of the word "permit" is also consistent with the legislature's stated purpose in revising § 167.060 and other parts of Oregon's criminal code. At the outset of chapter 743, the same chapter in which § 163.575(1)(b) is located, the legislature explained its "purposes" and "principles of construction." Simply put, the legislature intended to protect individuals from harm:

(1) The general purposes of Chapter 743, Oregon Laws 1971, are: . . .

(b) To forbid and prevent conduct that unjustifiably and inexcusably inflicts or threatens substantial harm to individual or public interests.

Or. Rev. Stat. § 161.025 (2015). That broad goal applies to § 163.575(1)(b). The intent to "forbid or prevent conduct" that "inflicts or threatens substantial harm" on or to an individual supports a broad reading of the word "permit"—one that encompasses any conduct that allows or enables a child to be in the presence of controlled substances.

The final part of the application examines related provisions and argues that a broader definition of the word "permit" would be consistent with the related provisions.

Examining other statutes on the same subject also supports the conclusion that "permits" should be read broadly and that formal authority over a child or premises is not necessary to "permit." When language is present in one statute, but absent from another, this Court will assume the absence of that language was intentional. *See, e.g., State v. Rodriguez*, 175 P.3d 471, 478 (Or. Ct. App. 2007) ("The legislature knows how to say that when it so intends."); *Karson v. Or. Liquor Control Comm'n*, 74 P.3d 1163, 1167 (Or. Ct. App. 2003) ("When the legislature wants to impose such a duty, it knows how to say so."); *State v. Walker*, 86 P.3d 690, 697 (Or. Ct. App. 2004) ("Numerous statutes demonstrate that the legislature knows how to say 'the Department of Human Services' when that is the agency it intends.").

The Oregon legislature knows how to limit liability to those with formal authority over children; here, it chose not to. Oregon's child endangerment statute is one of eight statutes categorized as "offenses against family." At the same time that the legislature passed the child endangerment statute in 1971, it also passed statutes that prohibited abandoning a child, Or. Rev. Stat. § 163.535 (2015); second-degree child neglect, Or. Rev. Stat. § 163.545 (2015); and criminal nonsupport, Or. Rev. Stat. § 163.555 (2015). *See* 1971 Or. Laws ch. 743 §§ 173, 174, 175. To be guilty under any of those three statutes, a defendant must have "custody or control" of the child. In contrast, the child endangerment statute does not require custody or control of the child to endanger that child's welfare. The legislature's decision to not use the word "custody or control" at the very time that it used that language elsewhere points to the conclusion that the legislature intended the child endangerment statute to encompass the actions of people who do not have such authority over a child. Thus, in the context of similar statutes, "permits," as used in § 163.575(1)(b), should be construed broadly such that it does not require "authority" over children.

Despite defendant's argument to the contrary, the broader definition of "permit" does not invade the space of "induce" or "cause." "Induce" means to "influence" or "persuade." *Webster's Third New International Dictionary of the English Language, supra*, at 1154. "Cause" means "to bring into existence." *Id.*, at 356. "Permit" means "to allow" or "make possible." The person who allows or makes an outcome possible acts differently from the person who influences, persuades, or brings into existence. Thus, the definition of "permit" does not overlap with the definitions of "induce" and "cause," even when read broadly. The context of § 163.575(1)(b) does not support a narrow reading of the word "permit."

3. The legislative history confirms that the word "permit" should be given a broad interpretation.

The legislative history further supports the conclusion that the legislature intended the statute to extend to situations in which adults allow or make possible a child's presence among illegal substances. Section 163.575(1)(b) was intended to shield children from unlawful drug activities and the actions of persons who expose them to such activities. In 1971, the legislature enacted § 163.575(1)(b) as part of its revisions to the Oregon Criminal Code. *See* 1971 Or. Laws ch. 743 § 177. The commentary to those revisions reflects that the child endangerment statute was a catchall provision designed to "provide coverage for specific acts injurious to the welfare of minors not specifically prohibited elsewhere in the proposed Code[,]" and that the proposed revisions related to "conduct detrimental to the welfare of minors[.]" Oregon Criminal Law Revision Commission, *Proposed Oregon Criminal Code, Final Draft and Rep.*, § 177 (1970) ("hereinafter Commentary"); *see also*, Statement of Roger Wallingford, Research Counsel for the Commission (April 3, 1970) (the endangering the welfare of a minor statute attempted to encompass crimes that had not been provided for elsewhere in the proposed code).

A broader interpretation of the word "permit" allows the statute to reach conduct that the legislature intended it to reach. Conducting an illegal marijuana grow in front of children, providing children with marijuana, smoking marijuana in front of children, and taking no steps to halt such activities are all

Here, the state responds to an argument in the defendant's brief. Again, notice that the state focuses its attention on its view of how the words of the statute should be read. The argument does not give airtime to defendant's argument.

Conclusion to the legislative history argument

Rules derived from the legislative history argument, which are then applied in the remainder of the paragraph

A statutory construction argument should not refer to facts from the client's case; a statutory construction argument should instead focus on what

continued on next page

the statute means. Here, the state narrowly skirts that issue by discussing general conduct and unspecified children. The text does not mention the defendant or the specific children at issue in this case.

This paragraph and the next respond to arguments raised by the defendant.

"conduct detrimental to the welfare of children." Thus, the legislature intended to reach such conduct, and giving the word "permit" its dictionary definition of "to allow" or "make possible" is consistent with that intent.

Defendant's interpretation of the legislative history either misunderstands the phrase "particularized conduct" or ignores the background of that phrase. The Criminal Law Revision Commission explained that the 1971 revisions to the criminal code were intended to prohibit "particularized conduct":

> Throughout the criminal code revision, the Commission has sought to articulate clear and concise statements of the substantive offenses, prohibiting particularized conduct and applying defined elements of culpability.

Commentary, at 178. In criminalizing "particularized conduct," the legislature was attempting to rectify the vagueness problem in former Oregon Revised Statute § 167.210 (1969) (contributing to the delinquency of a minor) that caused this Court to declare that statute unconstitutional in *Hodges*. See Oregon Criminal Law Revision Commission, *Minutes, Apr. 3, 1970*, at 26 (1970). The legislature's efforts to "articulate clear and concise statements of the substantive offenses, prohibiting particularized conduct" were intended to preclude vagueness problems, not straitjacket the child endangerment statute.

Appellate courts are concerned about the effect that a ruling in one case will have on future cases. Here, the state is pointing out the negative consequences of ruling in defendant's favor.

Moreover, adopting defendant's proposed narrow reading of "permit" and, concurrently, his conclusion that "permit" must include a transfer of authority over the children or the property, will lead to absurd results. When a statute is still susceptible to two or more plausible meanings, a court will not adopt the meaning "that would lead to an absurd result that is inconsistent with the apparent policy of the legislation as a whole." *See State v. Vasquez-Rubio*, 917 P.2d 494, 497 (Or. 1996). For example, if the defendant began selling marijuana in a public playground, under defendant's proposed reading, he would not be guilty of endangering the welfare of a child, because he did not "permit" the children to enter or remain in the playground. That is so because no one "transferred" to the defendant the "authority" over the playground or over the children who frequent it, and the defendant therefore would have no right to "exclude" the children from the playground. Yet, by conducting the unlawful drug sales there in the first place, the defendant's actions allowed or made possible the children's presence at the illegal activity. In other words, but for defendant's actions, the children would not be entering or remaining where drug dealing was occurring. It would be absurd in such a case to conclude that the defendant did not "permit" the children to enter or remain in the park because he had no legal right to "exclude" them from that location. The defendant would unquestionably be guilty of endangering the welfare of a minor.

Final conclusion to the statutory construction argument

In sum, nothing in the text, context, or history of § 163.575(1)(b) supports defendant's narrow reading of the statute. On the contrary, as explained above, the text, context, and legislative history demonstrate that the legislature intended the statute to be understood broadly, and that it would apply to persons who engage in conduct that allows or makes it possible for children to remain in a place where illegal drug activity is occurring. Thus, in enacting the child endangerment statute, the legislature intended to shield children from unlawful drug activities, and the actions of persons who expose them to such activities. "Permits" should be interpreted broadly to accomplish that aim.

B. Defendant violated Oregon Revised Statute § 163.575(1)(b) because he made it possible for the children for whom he was caring to remain in a place where unlawful drug activity was occurring.

The jury had sufficient evidence to convict defendant of endangering the welfare of both minor children. After a jury has found a defendant guilty of a crime, a court reviews the conviction to determine whether the evidence was sufficient for a rational fact-finder to find the essential elements of the crime beyond a reasonable doubt. *State v. Cunningham*, 880 P.2d 431, 440 (Or. 1994); *see also Jackson v. Virginia*, 443 U.S. 307, 316 (1979). The evidence is viewed in the light most favorable to the state. *Cunningham*, 880 P.2d at 440. In reviewing the evidence, this Court does not determine whether it believes that the defendant was guilty beyond a reasonable doubt; rather, this Court simply considers whether the evidence was sufficient for the jury to so find. *Id.* Given that the legislature intended the term "permit" to encompass activity whereby an individual allows or makes it possible for a child to remain in the presence of unlawful drug activity, defendant's actions easily fall within the statute's prohibitions. As explained below, that is so for either of two independently sufficient reasons.

Compare the state's explanation of the standard or review with the defendant's. Notice how the state emphasizes the deference the court gives to the jury's decision. Since the state wants the jury decision to stand, it makes sense that the state and not the defendant would emphasize the limited role of the court.

1. Defendant permitted the children to be in the presence of unlawful drug activity by repeatedly engaging in such activity in the children's presence.

First, a jury could reasonably find that defendant "permitted" children to "enter or remain in a place where unlawful activity involving controlled substances" was conducted because defendant engaged in illegal drug activity in the presence of the children. He actively participated in growing, harvesting, and selling marijuana in the house, knowing that the children were living there. He gave the children marijuana to smoke when they asked for it. He even admitted to smoking marijuana with the children on several occasions. By engaging in that conduct, defendant allowed and made possible — and thus "permitted" — the children to remain in a place where they were continuously exposed to defendant's own illegal activity. As a result, he endangered the welfare of the two children living in the home.

The state wants to emphasize all the evidence that supports the convictions. Notice how the point headings help make that point.

The point headings expand the space allocated to the supporting evidence.

The point headings allow the initial conclusion to be repeated.

The point headings also suggest that the text that follows is substantial enough to be designated by its own point heading. Thus, the point headings add heft to each point made.

2. Defendant permitted the children to be in the presence of unlawful drug activity by agreeing to perform the role of their caretaker amid a drug operation.

Even if defendant had not participated in the illegal activity, his decision to act as a babysitter in a house in which he knew marijuana was being illegally grown was sufficient for a jury to find him guilty of endangering a child. By agreeing to take on the role of a "babysitter" amid an ongoing drug operation, defendant allowed and made it possible for the children to remain in the house and be exposed to illegal activity. The reason Brenton asked defendant to "babysit" the children was because he did not want them to remain there unattended. By knowingly enabling the children's presence, defendant thus "permitted" the children to remain in a place where they would be continuously exposed to illegal drug activity. Defendant's behavior was well within the scope of conduct prohibited by § 163.575(1)(b).

C. Even under defendant's reading of the statute, he "permitted" the children to enter or remain in the house with the illegal drug activity.

Even if this Court adopts a narrow reading of the statute, defendant's argument still fails. Regardless of defendant's authority over the house or the children, defendant violated § 163.575(1)(b) because he actively enabled their presence in a place where they were exposed to illegal drug activity. Contrary to defendant's claim, the state's evidence did establish that defendant had sufficient authority to prevent the children from remaining in the house and that defendant failed to exercise that authority. As explained below, that is true for any of three reasons.

First, defendant chose to act as a "babysitter" knowing full well that the marijuana was being illegally grown in the house. Once defendant agreed to be the children's "babysitter," he accepted responsibility to keep them safe. Just as defendant's "babysitter" status provided him with the authority to remove the children from any other dangerous situation such as a house fire or a burglary—it provided him with the necessary minimum authority to remove them from the dangerous illegal drug operation.

Second, even assuming he was not authorized to physically remove the children from the home himself, he certainly had the authority—and given his role has the children's caretaker, the obligation—to take steps to protect the children and prevent their continued presence there. For example, he could have called the police to put a stop to the situation. Instead, he gave the children marijuana to smoke when they asked for it and even joined them in smoking the illegal substance. He had the authority and responsibility to end the situation, and by failing to do so, defendant "permitted" the children to remain amidst the drug activity.

Third, defendant deliberately and repeatedly engaged in illegal drug activity in the children's presence in their home. Defendant grew, harvested, and sold marijuana in a home where the children lived. It is beside the point whether defendant could "exclude" the children. He had the authority to stop his own illegal conduct—the conduct that exposed the children to illicit drugs. Defendant's contention that he lacked the requisite authority to stop his own illegal activities is nonsensical.

In sum, the evidence in this case was sufficient to establish that defendant had the authority to stop the children from remaining in the house and that he failed to exercise that authority. Accordingly, even under defendant's reading of the statute, the evidence was sufficient to establish that defendant violated

The arguments in section C are all rule-based arguments. The state wants to show that even if the court adopts defendant's proposed construction of the statute, the evidence was still sufficient to convict the defendant.

Under defendant's proposed construction of the statute, a person must have authority to deny permission before being guilty of permitting something. The state takes that rule and applies it to the facts of this case. Notice how the state connects the word "authority" to the facts in this case to make its point.

§ 163.575(1)(b). The trial court therefore correctly denied defendant's judgment of acquittal.

CONCLUSION

This Court should affirm the trial court's judgment.

Respectfully submitted,
VIVIAN L. KEARA
Attorney General
ANIYA P. LINDSIE
Solicitor General

/s/ Jennifer Schwarz

_____

JENNIFER SCHWARZ #500187
Assistant Attorney General
Jen.schwarz@doj.state.or.us

Attorneys for Plaintiff-Respondent
State of Oregon

NOTICE OF FILING AND PROOF OF SERVICE

I certify that on December 1, 2015, I directed the original Respondent's Answering Brief to be electronically filed with the Appellate Court Administrator, Appellate Records Section, by using the court's electronic filing system.

I further certify that on December 1, 2015, I directed the Respondent's Answering Brief to be served upon Ken Nakano and Vijay Grewal attorneys for appellant, by having the document personally delivered to:

Ken Nakano #870467
Chief Defender
Office of Public Defense Services

Vijay Grewal #974573
Deputy Public Defender
1320 Capitol Street NE, Suite 200
Salem, Oregon 97301

/s/ JENNIFER SCHWARZ
_____

Jennifer Schwarz #500187
Assistant Attorney General
Jen.schwarz@doj.state.or.us

Attorney for Plaintiff-Respondent
State of Oregon

Certificate of Compliance with ORAP 5.05(2)(d)

I certify that (1) this brief complies with the word-count limitation in ORAP 5.05(2)(b) and (2) the word-count of this brief (as described in ORAP 5.05(2)(a)) is 4,899 words. I further certify that the size of the type in this brief is not smaller than 14 point for both the text of the brief and footnotes as required by ORAP 5.05(4)(f).

/s/ Jennifer Schwarz

_____
JENNIFER SCHWARZ #500187
Assistant Attorney General
Jen.schwarz @doj.state.or.us

Attorney for Plaintiff-Respondent
State of Oregon

Index